Imbeciles

Imbeciles

The Supreme Court,

American Eugenics,

and the Sterilization

of Carrie Buck

Adam Cohen

PENGUIN PRESS

NEW YORK

2016

PENGUIN PRESS
An imprint of Penguin Random House LLC
375 Hudson Street
New York, New York 10014
penguin.com

Photograph credits
Library of Congress: insert pages 1 (top, bottom), 2; courtesy of Harry H. Laughlin
Papers, Special Collections Department, Pickler Memorial Library, Truman
State University: 3, 5 (bottom), 8 (bottom); Arthur Estabrook Papers,
University at Albany, State University of New York: 4, 5 (top);
Library of Virginia: 6 (top, bottom), 7, 8 (top)

LIBRARY OF CONGRESS CATALOGING-IN-PUBLICATION DATA
Names: Cohen, Adam (Adam Seth), author.
Title: Imbeciles : the Supreme Court, American eugenics,
and the sterilization of Carrie Buck / Adam Cohen.
Description: New York : Penguin Press, 2016.
Identifiers: LCCN 2015044207 | ISBN 9781594204180 (hardback)
Subjects: LCSH: Buck, Carrie, 1906–1983—Trials, litigation, etc. |
Involuntary sterilization—Law and legislation—United States. | Eugenics—
Law and legislation—United States. | Involuntary sterilization—Law and
legislation—Virginia. | BISAC: HISTORY / United States / 20th Century. |
LAW / Legal History. | LAW / Civil Rights.
Classification: LCC KF224.B83 C64 2016 | DDC 344.7304/8—dc23
LC record available at http://lccn.loc.gov/2015044207

Printed in the United States of America
3   5   7   9   10   8   6   4   2

BOOK DESIGN BY AMANDA DEWEY

For Beverly Sher Cohen

Professing to be wise, they became fools . . .

Contents

Imbeciles

Introduction

O
n May 2, 2002, the governor of Virginia offered a "sincere apology" for his state's "participation in eugenics." In an effort to improve the genetic quality of its population, Virginia forcibly sterilized at least 7,450 "unfit" people between 1927 and 1979, more than any other state but California. "The eugenics movement was a shameful effort in which state government never should have been involved," the governor declared. "We must remember the commonwealth's past mistakes in order to prevent them from recurring."

Virginia's apology came on the seventy-fifth anniversary of the United States Supreme Court's ruling in *Buck v. Bell*. In that dark legal landmark, the court upheld eugenic sterilization and allowed the state to sterilize Carrie Buck, a young woman wrongly labeled "feebleminded." The court that decided *Buck v. Bell* included some of the most distinguished men in the annals of American law. The chief justice was William Howard Taft, who had served as president before ascending to the bench. Louis Brandeis, the towering progressive who had made his name as "the people's attorney," signed on to the majority opinion, as did Oliver Wendell Holmes Jr., widely considered to be one of the greatest legal minds—if not *the* greatest—in American history.

It was the legendary Oliver Wendell Holmes who wrote the 1927 ruling, and he included in it one of the most brutal aphorisms in American jurisprudence. Holmes, the Harvard-educated scion of several of Boston's most distinguished families, was scornful of the poorly educated Carrie and her working-class mother. Based on scant information about the two Buck women—and about Carrie's daughter, who was a small child at the time—he famously declared: "Three generations of imbeciles are enough."

Holmes's opinion for an 8–1 majority did not merely uphold Virginia's sterilization law: it delivered a clarion call to Americans to identify those among them who should not be allowed to reproduce—and to sterilize them in large numbers. The nation must sterilize those who "sap the strength of the State," Holmes insisted, to "prevent our being swamped with incompetence." In words that could have been torn from the pages of a eugenics tract, he declared: "It is better for all the world, if instead of waiting to execute degenerate offspring for crime, or to let them starve for their imbecility, society can prevent those who are manifestly unfit from continuing their kind."

The United States in the 1920s was caught up in a mania: the drive to use newly discovered scientific laws of heredity to perfect humanity. Modern eugenics, which had emerged in England among followers of Charles Darwin, had crossed the Atlantic and become a full-fledged intellectual craze. The United States suddenly had a new enemy: bad "germplasm," and those who carried it. The "unfit," the eugenicists warned, threatened to bring down not only the nation but the whole human race.

America's leading citizens led the charge to save humanity. John D. Rockefeller Jr., the world's wealthiest man, funded scientific research into how what he called the "defective human" could be bred out of the population. Alexander Graham Bell became chairman of the Board of Scientific Directors of the Eugenics Record Office in Cold Spring Harbor, New York, the leading organization advocating eugenic sterilization. And former president Theodore Roosevelt took to the pages of a national magazine to insist that the unfit must be "forbidden to leave offspring behind them."

Prominent scientists formed organizations to research and promote eugenics, with names like the Committee to Study and to Report on the Best Practical Means of Cutting Off the Defective Germ-Plasm in the American Population. Social reformers embraced biology as the fastest route to their goal of a better world. Some spoke gently of the need for laws to prevent the unfit from passing on their defects. Others were more severe, like the upper-class New York advocate for the mentally ill who warned her fellow philanthropists that they put society at risk when their well-meaning charity helped "men and women who are diseased and vicious to reproduce their kind."

In big cities and small towns, hereditary improvement was the intellectual issue of the day. Albert Edward Wiggam, a popular lecturer, traveled the country promoting the "New Decalogue of Science," an updated version of the Ten Commandments based on eugenic principles. Women's clubs filled their agendas with lectures on identifying the hereditarily defective and arranging eugenic marriages. Clergymen competed in national eugenic sermon contests organized on topics like "Religion and Eugenics—Does the Church Have Any Responsibility for Improving the Human Stock?"

Eugenics permeated the popular culture. Bestselling books explained the concept of "race betterment" to an eager public, and mass-market magazines urged their readers to do their part to breed superior human beings. The "inspiring, the wonderful, message of the new heredity," *Cosmopolitan* explained, was that it offered the promise of preventing once and for all the birth of the "diseased or crippled or depraved." Hollywood released a feature-length horror movie, which filled theaters from coast to coast, showing the frightening consequences of allowing "defective" babies to live.

Conferences and public events were held to promote eugenics research and education. New York's American Museum of Natural History hosted the Second International Eugenics Congress—and the U.S. State Department sent out the invitations. The congress opened with a plea from the museum's president about the need to "enlighten government in the prevention of the spread and multiplication of worthless members of society." At the Sesquicentennial Exposition in Philadelphia, celebrating the Declaration of Independence's 150th anniversary, the American Eugenics Society mounted an exhibit that explained the terrible threat with flashing lights. Every forty-eight seconds, the lights indicated, a mentally deficient person was born in the United States, while only every seven and a half minutes was a "high grade person" born, who would "have [the] ability to do creative work and be fit for leadership."

Universities were quick to embrace eugenics and give it their intellectual imprimatur. Eugenics was taught at 376 universities and colleges, including Harvard, Columbia, Berkeley, and Cornell. Prominent professors were outspoken in support, including Earnest Hooton, the chairman of Harvard's anthropology department, who warned that educated Americans were selling their "biological birthright for a mess of morons," and called for a "biological purge." Eugenics was so popular on campus that F. Scott Fitzgerald, as a Princeton undergraduate, wrote a song for the college's Triangle Show called "Love or Eugenics," which asked the musical question: "Men, which would you like to come and pour your tea. / Kisses that set your heart aflame, / Or love from a prophylactic dame?"

The driving force behind the eugenics movement of the 1920s was, historians suggest, the collective fears of the Anglo-Saxon upper and middle classes about a changing America. Record levels of immigration were transforming the nation's ethnic and religious makeup. And with increased industrialization and urbanization, community and family ties were fraying. These anxieties were being redirected and expressed in the form of fears about the unfit.

The eugenics movement offered two solutions: one for the threat from without and one for the danger from within. Its answer to the foreign threat was new immigration laws to limit the number of Italians, eastern European Jews, and other non–northern Europeans admitted to the country. The eugenicists claimed the groups they wanted to exclude had inordinately high levels of physical and mental hereditary defects that were degrading America's gene pool. They offered what purported to be scientific evidence, including intelligence tests claiming that between 40 and 50 percent of Jewish immigrants arriving at Ellis Island were mentally defective.

Congress held hearings at which eugenicists explained the biological deficiencies of various nationalities. Their arguments were well received by senators and representatives who overwhelmingly shared the eugenicists' prejudices. "Thank God we have in America perhaps the largest percentage of any country in the world of the pure, unadulterated Anglo-Saxon stock," Senator Ellison DuRant Smith of South Carolina declared, in support of new immigration policies. Acting on these eugenic arguments, Congress adopted the Immigration Act of 1924, which opened the door to more immigrants from northern Europe and shut it on southern and eastern Europeans.

The eugenicists' answer to the internal threat was a set of laws designed to prevent the "unfit" from reproducing. They began in 1895 with a law prohibiting various kinds of people deemed to be hereditarily unworthy from marrying in Connecticut and got other states to pass such laws. Next, they promoted "segregation": placing "defective" people in state institutions during their reproductive years to prevent them from passing their flaws on to a new generation.

Finally, the eugenicists turned to sterilization, their favored solution. Marriage laws were weak: eugenicists feared defective people would simply reproduce out of wedlock. Segregation was expensive: states could not build enough institutions to house all the people the eugenicists wanted to stop from having children. Sterilization, however, was completely effective, and it could be carried out on a mass scale.

Starting with Indiana in 1907, states adopted legislation authorizing forced sterilization of people judged to have hereditary defects. Within six years, twelve states had such laws. They called for sterilizing anyone with "defective" traits, such as epilepsy, criminality, alcoholism, or "dependency"—another word for poverty. Their greatest target was the "feebleminded," a loose designation that included people who were mentally challenged, women considered to be excessively interested in sex, and various other categories of individuals who offended the middle-class sensibilities of judges and social workers.

Fears of "the rising tide of feeblemindedness" rose to panic levels. Experts studied the problem intensively and issued reports on subjects like the "menace of feeble-mindedness" among California public school children. A leading psychologist published an influential study arguing that feeblemindedness "underlies all our social problems," including crime, poverty, and prostitution.

The eugenicists insisted society's response had to be commensurate with the enormity of the threat. It was not enough for a few states to sterilize the inmates of their mental hospitals. A nationwide program was required, with each state doing its part. Every American had to be eugenically investigated—and evaluated for possible sterilization. The eugenic sterilization movement's most prominent leader insisted that to remove the "lowest one-tenth" of the nation, fifteen million people would have to go under the knife.

Virginia was not in the forefront of the eugenic sterilization movement—quite the opposite. What set it apart was its relative cautiousness. Virginia did not enact its sterilization law until 1924, seventeen years after Indiana's. Then, on the advice of counsel, the state's mental hospitals decided they would not sterilize anyone until Virginia's law was tested in the courts—all the way up to the United States Supreme Court. To accomplish this, the hospitals decided to create a test legal case.

It was Carrie Buck's misfortune to be at the wrong place at the wrong time. She had been sent to Virginia's Colony for Epileptics and Feeble-Minded just when the superintendent was trying to find an inmate to put at the center of the test case. Carrie had precisely the personal attributes the eugenicists were looking for: she had been designated feebleminded, and as a woman who had given birth out of wedlock at seventeen, she embodied the eugenic nightmare of the feebleminded reproducing rapidly and flooding the nation with "defectives." Carrie also came from the sort of family the eugenicists wanted to put in the spotlight. Her mother was also a colony inmate who had been designated feebleminded, and she had other relatives in the institution, which could help the state establish a hereditary pattern.

There was more to Carrie's story, but no one was interested in hearing it. She was not, in fact, feebleminded, despite what the state's unreliable intelligence testing reported. Her school records, which the colony ignored, revealed her to be of perfectly normal intelligence. And the real facts about how Carrie had ended up at the colony—and how she had come to be pregnant—showed that she was not a threat to society, but its victim.

Nations rely on civil society—private institutions devoted to higher values—to promote truth and justice and to keep them on the right path. To maintain freedom of speech and religion, a just legal system, and equal rights for all requires not only good government officials but also enlightened and fair-minded professional classes, nonprofit organizations, and educational institutions.

Four of the nation's most respected professions were involved in Carrie Buck's case—medicine, academia, law, and the judiciary—in the form of four powerful men. They were the kind of influential individuals who were in a position to put a check on the popular mania over eugenics, and to protect the people who were wrongly being branded a threat. In each case, however, these men sided forcefully with the eugenic cause, and used their power and prestige to see that Carrie was sterilized.

Albert Priddy was the physician who selected Carrie to be the first person operated on under Virginia's law. Dr. Priddy served as superintendent of the Colony for Epileptics and Feeble-Minded, where Carrie was an inmate. Before he chose Carrie, he had lobbied the legislature to pass the eugenic sterilization law, and he was a key part of the defense team that worked to get it upheld in court.

In his campaign for eugenic sterilization, Dr. Priddy had much of the medical profession behind him. Across the country, doctors took a leading role in promoting eugenics and eugenic sterilization, lending their expertise and authority to the cause. Medical journals were full of polemical articles advocating sterilization, with titles like "Race Suicide for Social Parasites." In the critical years, not every prominent doctor supported eugenic sterilization, but very few spoke out against it.

Harry Laughlin, the head of the Eugenics Record Office, was the scientist who gave his expert opinion that the Virginia law should be upheld and that Carrie should be sterilized. Laughlin had been a key supporter of the Immigration Act of 1924, arguing that national quotas were needed to keep out genetically inferior Italians and eastern European Jews. He was the most prominent advocate for eugenic sterilization, and the author of a 502-page treatise on the subject. It was Laughlin who proposed sterilizing fifteen million people—and he was doing more than anyone else to make that vision a reality.

Laughlin, a college professor who had a doctorate in biology from Princeton, was also, to a great extent, representative of his professional peers. Many of the nation's leading academic scientists publicly supported eugenics and eugenic sterilization, and for decades those who opposed it largely remained silent. *Scientific American* editorialized repeatedly in support of eugenics, insisting society must tell its "unfit" members, "You may live, but you must not propagate."

Aubrey Strode was the lawyer who drafted the Virginia sterilization law, and he went on to defend it all the way to the United States Supreme Court. Unlike Dr. Priddy and Laughlin, Strode was not a pro-eugenics ideologue. He was, rather, a lawyer whose job it was to represent people who believed deeply in eugenic sterilization—and he was more than willing to advocate for his clients' position.

The legal profession provided critical support to the eugenics movement. Some of the nation's leading lawyers endorsed the cause, including, early on, the president of the American Bar Association, who declared eugenic marriage laws necessary to protect "future generations from the evil operation of the laws of heredity." The Municipal Court of Chicago, a national leader in law reform, conducted eugenics research and underwrote Laughlin's sterilization treatise. The eugenic sterilization movement was fundamentally a legal undertaking, and lawyers like Strode were an integral part of it.

Finally, it was the great Oliver Wendell Holmes who had the last word on Carrie's fate, and who—with his broadside against society's "imbeciles"—lent his enormous intellectual prestige to the sterilization cause. Holmes had long been a supporter of eugenics, and he had suggested years earlier that the best route to societal reform lay in "taking in hand life and trying to build a race." Holmes was not a man who easily found enjoyment, but he would later say that upholding Virginia's eugenic sterilization law and Carrie's sterilization had given him real pleasure.

Of all of the professions, the judiciary played the most disappointing role. Not all of the judges of that era were pro-eugenics. Indeed, over the years, courts around the country had struck down state eugenic sterilization laws. But America's courts are hierarchically ordered, and when the issue reached the nation's highest court, the legal analysis was shoddy, and the vote was not close. The institution established by the Founders to protect the American people from injustice became injustice's loudest cheerleader.

When legal scholars rank the Supreme Court's worst decisions, the competition is considerable. Throughout its history, the court has often—critics would say predictably—been on the wrong side of justice. Before the Civil War, when Dred Scott, an enslaved man transported to parts of the country where slavery was illegal, sued for his freedom, the court ruled that as a "negro whose ancestors were imported into this country and sold as slaves," he had no right to sue in federal court. In the Jim Crow era, when Homer Plessy, a man of mixed race, challenged a Louisiana law under which he had been forcibly removed from a "whites only" railway car, the court rejected his complaint and upheld legally enforced racial segregation.

During World War II, when Fred Korematsu contested an order that all Japanese Americans report to internment camps, the court ruled that the nation's need to protect itself outweighed the civil liberties of Americans of Japanese descent. And midway through the modern gay rights era, when Michael Hardwick challenged a Georgia law that made it illegal for him to have sex with a man in his own home, the court upheld the law and insisted that one of Hardwick's most important constitutional claims was "at best, facetious."

Of course, the Supreme Court does not always side with injustice or with society's most powerful sectors. It ordered the South to end racial segregation and recognized the right of same-sex couples to marry. And it has corrected some of its worst mistakes: it reversed the ruling against Plessy after fifty-eight years, and against Hardwick after seventeen. Overall, however, its record is so deficient that a prominent law school dean recently concluded, "The Court has frequently failed, throughout American history, at its most important tasks, at its most important moments." He made the observation after more than thirty years of teaching constitutional law in a book he called *The Case Against the Supreme Court*.

There will always be differences of opinion over which rulings should be on a list of worst decisions, and how they should be ranked. But there can be no doubt that *Buck v. Bell* must have a prominent place. In its aftermath, not only was Carrie Buck sterilized against her will, but states across the country sterilized another sixty to seventy thousand Americans. Many of the victims were, like Carrie, perfectly normal both mentally and physically—and they desperately wanted to have children.

The reach of *Buck v. Bell* extended beyond the United States. The Nazi Party, which was on the rise in Germany, used America as a model for its own eugenic sterilization program. The Supreme Court's ruling influenced the *Erbgesundheitsgerichte,* the Hereditary Health

Courts that decided who should be forcibly sterilized. And at the Nuremberg trials that followed World War II, Nazis who had carried out 375,000 forced eugenic sterilizations cited *Buck v. Bell* in defense of their actions.

While many of the court's worst decisions are now central parts of American history, *Buck v. Bell* is little remembered today. Even in constitutional law courses, it is rarely discussed or is mentioned only in passing. The second edition of *American Constitutional Law,* by the Harvard law professor Laurence Tribe, which weighed in at 1,778 pages, devoted just half a sentence and a footnote to the case. A recent 953-page biography of Brandeis, written by another respected law professor and hailed by some critics as "definitive," did not try to explain why the legendary progressive joined the *Buck v. Bell* majority; it relegated the case to a single sentence in a footnote.

Many of those who would airbrush *Buck v. Bell* from history offer a simple explanation: it is an anomaly. The Supreme Court, they argue, was briefly caught up in eugenics, but it was a short-lived, onetime mistake. Today there are rights that did not exist in 1927—including rights of liberty and privacy—that would produce a different outcome. The ruling can be dismissed in half a sentence, the argument goes, because it is outside the sweep of American constitutional law, and the issues it raises are ones the nation long ago put behind it.

This rationale for consigning *Buck v. Bell* to the dustbin of history has serious flaws. The first is that there is nothing outdated about the case's subject matter. Oregon ordered its last forced sterilization in 1981, and up until 1983 its Board of Eugenics was still functioning, though it had been renamed the Board of Social Protection. In 2013 investigative reporters discovered that nearly 150 female prisoners in California had been sterilized between 2006 and 2010, not always with the women's consent.

More broadly, the twenty-first century is being hailed as "the Century of Biology," an era that experts say will be defined by "the new biology of genome research," with a vastly deeper understanding of the genetic blueprint for individual humans. Questions at the intersection of genetics and law—including to what degree the state and private actors should be able to use people's genetic markers against them—will become more common and more complex.

Another reason *Buck v. Bell* cannot be left in the past is that unlike so many of the Supreme Court's worst rulings it has never been overturned. In a later case, the court struck down an Oklahoma law providing for sterilization of certain criminals, but it did so because of its objection to the definition of which crimes would lead to sterilization. The court did not overturn or even limit *Buck v. Bell,* and after the ruling, states continued to sterilize thousands of people. In the twenty-first century, federal courts are still ruling that the government has the right to forcibly sterilize—and citing *Buck v. Bell.*

Finally, *Buck v. Bell* remains critically important because its deepest subject is a timeless one: power, and how those who have it use it against those who do not. Carrie was at the bottom of the nation's economic and social hierarchies. In her plea to the court, she was asking for protection from powerful people and institutions that threatened to do her harm. Throughout the history of American law, that position has not been a good one to be in.

The Code of Hammurabi is one of the world's great legal artifacts. When French archaeologists discovered it in 1901, they learned that ancient Babylonia had a strikingly sophisticated legal system. The code, which was carved onto a black stone slab, included 282 distinct laws covering such modern-seeming doctrines as liability for negligent acts and the presumption of innocence. As significant as these individual rules was the code's eloquent statement of its own purpose, contained in the preface: "to bring about the rule of righteousness in the land . . . so that the strong should not harm the weak."

That simple ideal remains, more than 3,500 years later, the law's highest calling. It is a vision that the American legal system has failed to live up to all too often. Dred Scott, Homer Plessy, Fred Korematsu, and Michael Hardwick were all weaker parties unjustly harmed by stronger ones, who came to the Supreme Court seeking justice. In each case, the court sided with the strong.

In fact, a tendency to favor the powerful could be said to be one of American law's defining features. Legal historians note that American courts have had this predisposition since the nation's earliest days— and even before. In the Massachusetts Bay Colony, judges were willing to try people for witchcraft, but their enthusiasm waned when accusations began to be made against prominent members of society, including the president of Harvard College. In modern times, there has been no shortage of cases in which the rich and well connected wrongly escaped unscathed, or in which the poor and weak were crushed.

Legal sociologists explain that the justice system systematically favors the strong over the weak. The rich and powerful are less likely, all other things being equal, to be arrested, convicted, or imprisoned. The poor are, holding everything else constant, more likely to be incarcerated, institutionalized, and sterilized. The legal theorist Donald Black explains that American law is a great respecter of hierarchy— and that it operates most harshly on those at the bottom. "Law of every kind," he says, "is more likely to have a downward direction than an upward direction."

There is a great deal about *Buck v. Bell* that is troubling. The Supreme Court got the most basic facts about Carrie Buck and her family wrong, and relying on those errors it allowed a terrible injury to be done to her. The court exhibited a shockingly narrow conception of individual rights. It gave its unqualified endorsement to a cruel procedure. And when a young woman came seeking to be protected from an immense wrong, the court showered her with insults and allowed her to be harmed.

In the end, however, what is most disturbing is the worldview the court revealed. *Buck v. Bell* presented the court with a stark choice between Hammurabi's ideal and its precise opposite. The ancient principle of justice teaches that the purpose of law is to ensure that the strong do not harm the weak. The state of Virginia, and the eugeni-cists who were in league with it, insisted that the strong must harm the weak—and that it was the law's duty to help.

Faced with this choice, the Supreme Court did not merely side with the strong: it enthusiastically urged them on by insisting it would be "better for all the world" if society's strongest members simply fin-ished off people like Carrie once and for all. Even the ancient Babylo-nians understood that helping the strong to obliterate the weak is antithetical to the purpose of law—and no way to bring about the rule of righteousness in the land.

One

Carrie Buck

In early 1924 Carrie Buck, a dark-haired seventeen-year-old girl with a tomboy spirit, was living with a foster family in downtown Charlottesville, Virginia. John Dobbs, an officer of the peace, and his wife, Alice, had taken Carrie in as a toddler, from a single mother who had fallen on hard times. The situation seemed to offer Carrie the chance to grow up in a well-off, loving family, but that was not to be. In her years of living in the Dobbses' tidy home on Grove Street, Carrie had been less a daughter than a housemaid. She would later recall the "endless work" and "servants' chores"—and a wistful feeling of "never being a family member."

John and Alice Dobbs liked to tell people they had taken Carrie in as an "act of kindness." If that had been their initial motivation, the wellspring of goodwill had long since been depleted. Carrie had always fit in well with the household, and had been working harder than ever since her foster parents decided to take her out of school. Recently, however, there had been trouble. The Dobbses said they could no longer care for their young charge, and they had decided it was time for her to leave.

John Dobbs made an appointment with Mary Duke, the secretary of public welfare, whose job involved helping Charlottesville's less fortunate—and helping the city's better-off residents deal with the problems they posed. At their meeting, Dobbs confided the real problem in his household: Carrie had become pregnant out of wedlock. The Dobbses wanted help in sending her away to an institution. When Duke learned who the young woman was, she was predisposed to believe the worst. She had never met Carrie, but she had encountered her mother, Emma, while doing charitable work around town. Emma Buck, Duke had decided, was "of bad character."

Duke went to talk with Alice Dobbs to learn more. Mrs. Dobbs said she and her husband had done everything in their power to help Carrie. They sent her to church and Sunday school, but despite the instruction she had received, she could not be trusted to lead a moral life. Mrs. Dobbs told Duke she had left Carrie home alone a few days the previous summer, but Carrie had not behaved herself—and the result was her pregnancy.

Under Duke's guidance, the Dobbses began the formal process of having Carrie sent away. They did not try to place her in a home for unwed mothers. Instead, they petitioned Charlottesville's Juvenile and Domestic Relations Court to have Carrie, "a white female child of the age of seventeen years," declared feebleminded and epileptic. They told the court they could no longer have her in their home, and asked that she be committed to the Virginia Colony for Epileptics and Feeble-Minded.

The term "feebleminded" was widely used at the time but only vaguely defined. There was no precise medical description. A catchall term that covered a wide range of purported deficiencies, it might mean that a person was of low intelligence, or that he or she behaved in ways that offended the middle-class sensibilities of doctors, judges, or social workers. In the case of young women, it often meant exhibiting what was regarded as an excessive or inappropriate interest in sex.

In most cases, it did not take much evidence to have someone declared feebleminded and locked up—and so it was with the charges against Carrie. The Dobbses had no proof she was mentally deficient, and her grades from school, for as long as she had been allowed to attend, showed no lack of intelligence. Nor were there any medical records to support the claim that Carrie was epileptic—because she was not. The Dobbses' petition was set down for an inquisition on January 23 before a Commission of Feeblemindedness. The commission, made up of a judge and two physicians, would take evidence and then decide Carrie's fate.

With her foster parents and the Charlottesville Department of Public Welfare aligned against her, Carrie would be on her own. Even though she was just seventeen and had limited education, there were no provisions for assigning her a lawyer or a guardian to look out for her interests. As a result, there would be no one at the hearing to argue that she was neither feebleminded nor epileptic. Nor would there be anyone to bring up the hidden facts the Dobbses did not want mentioned— such as just how it was that Carrie had come to be pregnant.

Carrie Elizabeth Buck was born in Charlottesville on July 2, 1906. Charlottesville was the seat of Albemarle County, a rural county in west-central Virginia that had some of the state's best farmland, nourished by the Rivanna and James Rivers. Lying some 125 miles northwest of Jamestown, the first permanent English outpost in America, Albemarle County was settled early on by explorers who saw a bright future in its lush landscape.

The English who arrived in the 1600s found that the region's rich soil was particularly well suited to growing tobacco, which soon became the staple crop for exporting back to England. Other crops were no less successful: hemp, also for export; wheat, barley, and rye to sell locally; and the Albemarle pippin, which would become Queen Victoria's favorite apple. In a letter back home, one gratified settler described land "so rich and so fertile that when a man has fifty acres of ground, two men-servants, a maid and some cattle, neither he nor his wife do anything but visit among their neighbors."

Plantations soon arose on the region's lucrative soil, carved out of the land of the Saponi Indians and other tribes, and built on the backs of enslaved Africans and their descendants. The plantations, in turn, gave rise to an affluent and well-educated agricultural elite. The Virginia planters in the region around Charlottesville were in the forefront of agricultural science, military affairs, and, above all, politics, forming a significant part of the intellectual leadership of the emerging American Republic.

The land produced great statesmen as readily as it did fine tobacco. Thomas Jefferson, the principal drafter of the Declaration of Independence, was born in the area and lived on Monticello, a five-thousand-acre plantation outside of Charlottesville. James Madison, the primary architect of the U.S. Constitution, was the master of Montpelier plantation, twenty-five miles north of Charlottesville. They and James Monroe—who lived on Highland plantation, near Monticello—would become three of the new nation's first five presidents.

The Virginia planters created something else that endured: the University of Virginia, known as "Mr. Jefferson's University." Jefferson founded the school in 1819, after retiring from public life. He designed its legendary campus, which a poll of leading architects and critics would one day call "the proudest achievement in American architecture." When Jefferson was a student at the College of William & Mary, he had chafed at the role of religion and the clergy. Jefferson resolved to infuse his new university with the spirit of the European Enlightenment—one not "afraid to follow truth wherever it may lead."

The University of Virginia soon became one of the South's leading institutions of higher learning. Its lecture halls, libraries, and student residences filled up with young minds pursuing Jefferson's forward-looking ideals. By the early twentieth century, the University of Virginia had grown so large that Charlottesville was hardly recognizable as the agricultural and transportation center it had once been. It was now primarily a university town whose leafy neighborhoods were, as one guidebook observed, "undisturbed by the bustle of commerce."

Carrie had grown up in the shadow of this rarefied intellectual world, but her family had never been a part of it. She belonged to what one scholar of the region has called the "southern poor white caste." Carrie's people were a step up in the social hierarchy from blacks, who were relegated to the bottom as a matter of law. In the post–Civil War South, one study observed, class lines were sharply drawn and "the status of the white poor" was in most cases "fixed and rigid." Carrie's family, however, was an exception to the general rigidity of class lines in the South at the time. It had moved—downward.

Before the Civil War, Carrie's paternal grandfather, Fleming Buck, had been a property owner and slaveholder. His fortunes shifted after the Confederacy fell and slavery ended. When Fleming Buck died in 1868, he left his widow and two young sons with land but no free labor to work it. Carrie's father, Frank Buck—who was one of these two sons—left the hardscrabble farming life behind to become a tinner. As it turned out, however, the prospects for tinners in the impoverished post–Civil War South were not much better than for hardscrabble farmers. With low-cost metal flooding in from the North, tin prices were low, and Frank had difficulty making a living.

Carrie Buck's mother, who was born Emma Adeline Harlowe, belonged to another family with a downward economic and social trajectory. Her father, Richard Harlowe, was a farmer who worked his own land. Emma's mother, Adeline Dudley Harlowe, died in childbirth. While Emma's father was alive, he eked out a modest living, but when he died after injuring his spine, Emma was left with little. She dropped out of school after the fifth grade, though she could read and write and had good penmanship.

When Emma was turning twenty-four, in 1896, she married Frank Buck. They were still married ten years later, when Carrie was born, but the marriage ended soon afterward. There were rumors about what became of Frank, including reports that he had abandoned the family. Records at the Colony for Epileptics and Feeble-Minded would later say Frank had been "accidentally killed." Whatever the reason, Emma was left to raise Carrie on her own.

Emma's opportunities for earning a living were limited. Times were hard in Virginia, as they were across the South, which still had not recovered from the Civil War. The job prospects for a single woman like Emma ranged, as one historical account put it, from "bleak" to "desperate." Emma had the added burdens of a modest education and a small child to care for. The people who would later lock Emma away said she turned to prostitution, a line of work that would have been available to her in Charlottesville's thriving red-light district, though the record is unclear. Emma did receive help from the city's charitable organizations. Anne Harris, a nurse involved in outreach to the poor, recalled that Emma "was on the charity list for a number of years, off and on—mostly on."

Emma and her baby drifted through some of Charlottesville's poorest neighborhoods. In the absence of a husband, she took up with other men, eventually giving birth to two more children, Carrie's half sister, Doris, and half brother, Ray. Emma's men no doubt provided her with financial help, though likely not enough. Harris recalled that during this period Emma and her young children struggled to survive and "they were on the streets more or less."

Emma's life on the margins put her relationship with Carrie at risk. The Progressive Era, which began in the 1890s, had reshaped the nation's social and economic relations—and, among other things, ushered in a new concern about the children of the poor. There was growing sentiment among child welfare advocates, who had taken to calling themselves "child-savers," that children of the poor were best off not in their own families, or in state facilities, but in middle-class homes. Reformers had pushed for new laws to facilitate foster care and adoption and encourage better-off families to take in children from deprived backgrounds.

Given this popular sentiment, it was not difficult for the Dobbses to take Carrie from her mother, with the offer of a better life. As an officer of the peace, John Dobbs had come across the Buck family in his travels around town and concluded that Emma was not caring for her children well enough. He and Alice decided to take Carrie home for themselves. When the municipal court gave its approval, Carrie joined a family that included John and Alice Dobbs and their daughter, who was slightly older than Carrie.

Carrie's life in the Dobbs household bore little relation to the idealized vision of adoptive families that the "child-savers" promoted. "I had good days and I had bad days," Carrie would later say. The Dobbses treated Carrie much differently than their own daughter, offering her little in the way of parental love or support. Carrie called her foster parents by their last names, as a servant girl would—never "Mother" and "Father."

Carrie attended grade school, but her education was cut short, as her mother's had been. The reason was not a lack of intelligence, contrary to the claims that would later be made. Carrie's school records show that she performed well and was promoted at the end of each year. Though she occasionally got into trouble for writing notes to boys, Carrie was far from a delinquent. She had proceeded from grade to grade without incident, and had left school only when the Dobbses removed her, likely so she could do more housework. Her last teacher marked her down as "very good—deportment and lessons."

It was not unusual in the early 1900s for poor children to be put to work, particularly in the South. In some southern states, nearly 30 percent of textile workers were between ten and fifteen years old. Reformers had begun to mobilize against child labor. In 1906, the year of Carrie's birth, the left-wing writer John Spargo had written a muckraking book, *The Bitter Cry of the Children*, which decried "the enslavement of children" and lamented that "this great nation in its commercial madness devours its babes." But even as progressives fought child labor, the business and political establishments, especially in the South, defended it. Parents "should be left alone," one southern governor insisted, "and allowed to manage their own children [and] . . . their own affairs."

With her education complete—or as complete as the Dobbses would allow—Carrie was freed up to do domestic work full-time. She had more time to help Alice Dobbs with chores around the house. She was also now available for the Dobbses to hire out during the day to do paid housework for the neighbors. With Carrie performing "servants' chores" for paying customers, as well as for her own foster family, the arrangement that the Dobbses insisted had begun as an "act of kindness" was looking increasingly like a shrewd financial move.

Carrie's day-to-day existence was not entirely joyless. She found time for hikes on the hills around Charlottesville, and went fishing with boys from the neighborhood. It was a life with a great deal of responsibility and drudgery, but her basic needs were being met. From time to time, Carrie ran into her mother and half siblings on the street, and she could see that her family could not always say the same.

In 1920, just as Carrie was about to turn fourteen, her mother's life changed dramatically. Emma was taken in and deposited at the municipal court. It was not clear what she would be charged with. Emma could have been accused of vagrancy or prostitution, but on April 1 Judge Charles D. Shackelford convened a Commission of Feeblemindedness to consider claims that she had a "mental peculiarity" that caused her to exhibit "a lack of moral sense and responsibility."

Judge Shackelford probed Emma's life history. Emma said she had been born in Albemarle County forty-seven years earlier and currently lived in Charlottesville. She was a widow with three children—none of them, she insisted, mentally defective. Asked her profession, she offered none, though she said she had inherited money from her father. Emma said she had been convicted of prostitution, though women in that era were charged as prostitutes for a wide range of activities, including vagrancy.

After hearing all the evidence, Judge Shackelford ruled that Emma was "feeble-minded"—though she had not been given a formal intelligence test—and "without means of support." The court directed that Emma be committed without delay to the Colony for Epileptics and Feeble-Minded. Five days after the hearing, a social worker traveled with Emma by train to Lynchburg, the nearest city to the colony. A hospital orderly was waiting to take her from the Lynchburg station to her new, court-ordered home.

On her arrival at the colony, Emma was given a vigorous cleaning and a medical examination. The institution's records described her as "well-nourished" and "fat" but "pale, nervous and restless." She was found to be suffering from rheumatism, pneumonia, and syphilis. The examiner observed what appeared to be track marks on Emma's arms, suggesting she might have used intravenous drugs. The records included a list of the belongings she brought with her: "$4.80, waist shirt, overshoes, 1 pr. shoes, 1 pr. hose, 1 coat, hat, undershirt 2, skirt." The clothing, it was noted, was "in very bad condition."

In keeping with the colony's standard practice, Emma was given an intelligence test. The colony used a version of the Binet-Simon, the leading test at the time and one that was highly unreliable. On the basis of her performance, Emma was judged to have an IQ of 50 and designated, in her intake records, as "Mental Deficiency, Familial: Moron." As a result of the diagnosis, she would be locked up for the rest of her life.

Four years had passed since Emma's arrival at the colony, and Carrie was now facing her own inquisition. The Dobbses' petition was assigned to Judge Shackelford, the same judge who had sent Emma away. The Commission of Feeblemindedness that heard Carrie's case was made up of Judge Shackelford and two Charlottesville medical doctors whom he had appointed: Dr. J. F. Williams and Dr. J. C. Coulter, who was the Dobbses' family physician.

In their petition, John and Alice Dobbs said they had taken care of Carrie since she was "three or four," and she had not developed symptoms of being feebleminded or epileptic until she was "ten or eleven years of age." Carrie's symptoms grew progressively worse and she became "so affected" that they could "no longer control or care for her." Though it should not have been relevant to the commission, the Dobbses said their only income was Mr. Dobbs's salary, and they were "no longer able to care for" Carrie "financially."

The Dobbses submitted interrogatories with more information about Carrie's condition. Taken together, the petition and interrogatories presented a picture that bore little relation to the truth. The Dobbses said Carrie was "feebleminded," but that was contradicted by her academic records, which showed that she had reached the sixth grade, with generally good grades and comportment, before the Dobbses pulled her out of school.

As to her medical condition, when asked "At what age was any mental peculiarity first noticed?" the Dobbses wrote "since birth," even though they had only known Carrie from the age of four. Their answer to the question "At what age did epilepsy first appear?" was "since childhood." But they answered no when asked "Is she now or has she ever been subject to epilepsy, headaches, nervousness, fits or convulsions of any kind ?" The Dobbses offered no medical or school records to support their claim that Carrie suffered from epilepsy. Years later, when Carrie was released from the colony, the superintendent, a doctor who had observed her closely for years, would flatly state, "She is not an epileptic."

There was more to the story than the Dobbses were telling the commission. In their petition, they did not mention that Carrie was pregnant—or how her condition had come about. Alice's nephew, a young man named Clarence Garland, had come to visit the previous summer. During the visit, Carrie later said, Clarence, "forced himself on me." According to Carrie, the pregnancy that Alice Dobbs had blamed on Carrie's not being trustworthy had actually been the result of rape.

Carrie was a sexually inexperienced young woman at the time of the attack. She played with neighborhood boys, she later recalled, but did not date any of them. "I didn't run around," she said, "I wasn't allowed to." She was, she insisted, a "good girl." Carrie said that after Clarence forced himself on her he promised he would marry her, but he instead left Charlottesville.

Carrie's condition put the Dobbses in a difficult position. Pregnancy outside of marriage carried a considerable stigma, and having Carrie remain in the household would be an embarrassment for the Dobbs family. The situation was made far worse by Carrie's account of being attacked. If she went public with her story, Clarence could be charged with rape. These problems might be solved, however, if Carrie were quickly and permanently sent away.

In the 1920s it was not difficult to have someone like Carrie institutionalized as feebleminded. The nation was in the midst of a panic over feeblemindedness. The feebleminded, however the term was defined, were regarded as a burden on government and private charity, a menace to public safety, and a threat to the national gene pool. *The Survey*, an influential social workers' journal, editorialized that of all of the matters facing state governments "none is more pressing than the care of the feeble-minded" who "involve every social problem." The Georgia Department of Public Welfare was more blunt in warning about the feebleminded. "What shall it profit Georgia," the department asked in a report, "if we stop the loss from the boll weevil and fail to stamp out the germs of dependency and delinquency that eat the heart out of the human family itself?"

States had been building institutions at a rapid rate, and sending the feebleminded away in record numbers. In 1904, 17.3 feebleminded people were institutionalized for every 100,000 people in the population. By 1921 the number had nearly tripled, to 46.7. The main purpose of this drive to institutionalize—in state hospitals and specialized schools for the feebleminded—was not better care or training. It was to remove a group deemed to be a threat and to "segregate" them: lock them up in secure facilities where they could not reproduce. "The ultimate aim of the school," said the head of the newly established North Carolina School for the Feeble-Minded, "is the elimination of feeblemindedness from the race by segregation."

Many factors were working against Carrie at her Commission of Feeblemindedness inquisition, starting with the fact that she was a woman. The campaign against feeblemindedness was focused on young women, who were deemed both a moral and a demographic threat. The medical establishment had long been sounding the alarm: Dr. Walter E. Fernald of Massachusetts, a leading authority, cautioned that "feeble-minded women are almost invariably immoral and if at large usually become carriers of venereal disease or give birth to children who are as defective as themselves." Hastings Hart, the director of the Russell Sage Foundation's child-helping division, warned states that feebleminded girls were "vastly more dangerous to the community" than feebleminded boys, and recommended that "every feebleminded woman should be faithfully segregated for twenty years."

Feebleminded women were believed to have unusually strong sex drives and loose morals and, as a result, it was said that they bore more children than other women, a problem known as "differential fecundity." Henry Goddard, the research director of the Vineland Training School for Feeble-minded Girls and Boys in Vineland, New Jersey, and a pioneer in the field, warned that everything possible must be done to "not allow native morons to breed." Because of these concerns many states, including Virginia, gave women of childbearing age priority in admission to institutions for the feebleminded.

Given the national panic at the thought of feebleminded women reproducing, Carrie's greatest disadvantage at the inquisition was a simple one: she was pregnant. She was in her seventh month, which would have been noticeable to the commission's doctors, who conducted a "personal examination." Dr. J. C. Coulter, the Dobbses' family physician who was one of the commission's three members, would presumably already have been aware. As an unmarried, pregnant, feebleminded minor, Carrie embodied the worst fears of those warning against the rising tide of feeblemindedness.

A final factor working against Carrie was the nature of the proceeding itself. Even though she could be locked away for life, she had no right to a lawyer or even an adult guardian to represent her. The Dobbses knew a great deal about the legal issues from the advice of Mary Duke, the secretary of public welfare, and Mr. Dobbs's experience as an officer of the peace, but Carrie had no one to help her to understand or challenge the claims being made against her, or to introduce witnesses or academic or medical records to defend herself.

The Commission of Feeblemindedness met, as scheduled, on January 23, 1924. The court had deputized Mr. Dobbs as a "Special Constable," and directed him to serve notice on his wife; Carrie; Carrie's parents, Frank and Emma Buck; and the two medical doctors on the commission. He completed most of his assignment, but he told the court that Frank and Emma Buck "were not found in my county or city." Emma, who was by now living at the colony, was apparently not told about her daughter's hearing or allowed to attend.

Judge Shackelford explained to Carrie what the hearing was about. After considering the evidence, including the doctors' personal examination of Carrie, the commission formally pronounced her "feebleminded or epileptic," a notably vague designation. In brief written findings, the commission said nothing about how it had evaluated her mental abilities or what, if any, evidence it had identified of epilepsy. Judge Shackelford then ordered Carrie to be delivered to the superintendent of the Colony for Epileptics and Feeble-Minded.

Once Carrie was declared feebleminded, the Dobbses wanted her gone quickly. She was not only a source of embarrassment and possible legal troubles for the family, but a distraction. The Dobbses' daughter was also pregnant, and would end up giving birth three days before Carrie. Mrs. Dobbs wanted to be able to leave home to be with her daughter without having to worry about Carrie.

There were, however, delays in carrying out the court's order. Mary Duke forwarded the court papers to the colony, but they were sent back for technical deficiencies. New papers were sent, and a lawyer representing Duke wrote to the colony urging it to speed up Carrie's admission. It was long past time, the lawyer said, for "the girl" to be "placed upon the waiting list and taken into your institution, where she so badly needs to be as soon as possible."

Caroline Wilhelm, a Red Cross social worker assigned to supervise Carrie's transfer, also asked the colony to move quickly. Wilhelm wrote her own letter to the colony's superintendent about the "long delayed" commitment, explaining the urgency in more detail. Carrie was due to give birth in mid-April, Wilhelm said, and it was "very important" that she "be admitted to the Colony before that time if it can be arranged."

The colony, however, would not be rushed. The superintendent, Dr. Albert Priddy, informed Wilhelm that his institution made it a rule "to positively refuse admission of any expectant mothers." He told her she would have to "make some provision to keep" Carrie "until the child is born and disposed of." Only after Carrie had given birth and her baby was "disposed of," as Dr. Priddy put it, would the colony be prepared to admit her.

In the final month of her pregnancy, Carrie was in limbo. The Dobbses had secured a legal order to remove her from their home, and they were insisting she leave immediately. But her future home, the colony, would not take her in. Her own family was not available: her father was likely dead, and her mother was locked up at the colony. Wilhelm found Carrie a temporary home not far from the Dobbses' where she could stay until she gave birth. On March 28, earlier than expected, Carrie's baby was born—a girl, who was given the name Vivian.

Wilhelm did not know what to do with Carrie's newborn. She wrote Dr. Priddy to tell him that finding a home was proving "very difficult" because she and her colleagues believed "a baby whose mother and grandmother are feeble-minded ought not to be placed out in a home for adoption." Wilhelm said there had been one offer to take Vivian in—from John and Alice Dobbs. They emphasized, however, that if the baby turned out to be feebleminded they would insist on institutionalizing her.

Dr. Priddy did not care where the baby ended up or if she was feebleminded. He told Wilhelm that Vivian could not come to the colony, because the law did not allow state hospitals for the feebleminded to admit anyone under the age of eight. The only advice Dr. Priddy offered about Carrie's baby was that Wilhelm could "place it in the City Almshouse." In the end, she placed Vivian with the Dobbses.

On June 4, Carrie set off on the same trip her mother had taken four years earlier. Wilhelm escorted Carrie and a man named Walter Allen, who had also been committed to the colony. The Red

Cross social worker and her two charges traveled by train from Charlottesville to Lynchburg, which was then a bustling metropolis of thirty thousand, with an economy that was shifting from tobacco to manufacturing. After disembarking at Union Station, the three travelers took a buggy ride over the James River and arrived at the colony's front door.

Despite its somber mission of locking away people society had branded defective and dangerous, the Colony for Epileptics and Feeble-Minded had an undeniable rustic charm. Like many such institutions, it functioned as a working farm. There were cows, pigs, and chickens, and orchards and gardens that produced rich harvests of fruits and vegetables. The landscape was dotted with newly constructed residence halls, recreation buildings, light industrial factories, and medical facilities.

The "colony" system that gathered the feebleminded to live in settings of this kind served several purposes. The rustic surroundings were in keeping with the latest ideas about treatment of people with mental defects. Out in the country, the thinking went, far from the stresses of big-city life, inmates would be soothed by the "perfume of the pine and the cedar." At the same time, having a working farm and factories allowed the colony to keep its inmates productively occupied.

There were also financial advantages. Inmates were able to contribute to their own upkeep and reduce the burden on taxpayers. When states throughout the South first established colonies for the feeble-minded, legislators and administrators hoped they would become financially self-sufficient, which would allow them to expand and take in ever-larger numbers of mentally deficient inmates, but none achieved that level of economic success.

Carrie was admitted to the colony as patient 1692. Like her mother, she received a thorough examination, and the colony began to assemble a detailed file on her. The "History and Clinical Notes" drawn up on June 4, 1924, stated that Carrie was seventeen, in good general health, well nourished, and free of communicable diseases. She had no paralysis or deformity, talked distinctly, and had "good teeth and tonsils."

The next day, Dr. John Bell conducted a physical examination: Carrie was 5 feet 4¼ inches tall and weighed 134½ pounds. Dr. Bell noted her "low narrow forehead." A few days later, a Wassermann test for syphilis came back negative.

Carrie's admissions records repeated the critical assessments the Dobbses and others had made about her. They stated that "nothing is known of her birth or early development," but despite that lack of information the file went on to say that she "has always been subnormal." In a section on "social history and moral reaction," Carrie was described as "untruthful and dishonest" and labeled a "moral delinquent" for having given birth to an illegitimate child.

In evaluating Carrie's intellect, the colony noted that she had "attended school 5 years and attained the 6th grade," though her file did not mention her grades or other evaluations. The colony also observed that she took "proper notice of things" and "recognize[d] colors." The only mental assessment that mattered, however, was the Binet-Simon test that she was given on arrival, the same one her mother had taken. Based on it, the colony determined that Carrie had a mental age of nine, and it designated her a "Middle grade Moron."

The Binet-Simon test that Carrie was given was not an accurate measure of intelligence, and its creators never intended it to be. It had been invented in 1905 when the Paris school system commissioned Alfred Binet, director of the Sorbonne's psychology laboratory, to develop a way to identify mentally challenged children. Binet and another psychologist, Theodore Simon, devised a series of questions and tasks, such as describing how two objects were similar or repeating numbers from memory. Binet and Simon admitted to not putting a great deal of thought into deciding what to ask. "One might almost say, 'It matters very little what the tests are so long as they are numerous,'" Binet said.

Binet and Simon were attempting to create a test that would identify those children who could benefit from extra help in the classroom.

They established a scale to rank children's performance, identifying a "mental age" that could differ significantly from a child's chronological age. Binet insisted that the test was not an intelligence test, and that it should not be used to identify students who were inherently less mentally able. He intended his scale "to identify in order to help and improve," Harvard biology professor Stephen Jay Gould observed, "not to label in order to limit." Binet was troubled when teachers wrote off students as inherently unintelligent. "They have neither sympathy nor respect," he said, "and their intemperate language leads them to say such things in their presence as 'This is a child who will never amount to anything . . . he is poorly endowed . . . he is not intelligent at all.' How often have I heard these imprudent words."

When the Binet-Simon test arrived in the United States, it was transformed. The psychologists, academics, and institutional administrators who embraced it were not looking, as Binet and Simon had been, for ways to identify children who needed extra educational help. They wanted a method of sorting people into inflexible categories that could be presented with the trappings of science.

The man who launched this transformation was Henry Goddard of the Vineland Training School for Feeble-minded Girls and Boys. Goddard discovered the Binet-Simon test in Europe and brought it back to America. He began administering the test at the Vineland School, hoping it would be able to instantly assess and categorize students in the same way Vineland staff did after getting to know them over time. When he reviewed the results, Goddard was convinced he had found what he was looking for. "The tests," he said, "do come amazingly near what we feel to be the truth in regard to the mental status of any child tested."

Goddard championed the Binet-Simon and presented it as what it was not intended to be: a tool for measuring inherent intelligence. He used the test in its new, American form to create a "hierarchical, unidimensional vision of intelligence." Goddard argued that intelligence levels were characteristics that people were born with—and limited by. "Each human being has a potentiality for a definite amount of intelligence . . . and beyond that point all efforts at education are useless," he said.

Goddard redefined the field of mental disability in 1910, at a meeting of the American Association for the Study of the Feeble-Minded, when he unveiled a three-part hierarchy of mental defects. At the bottom of Goddard's pyramid were "idiots," people whose minds were developed below the level of a normal three-year-old's. Next were what he called "imbeciles," people whose mental level fell between ages three and seven. At the top were "morons" (a term he coined from the Greek word for "fool"), people with mental ages from eight to twelve. Goddard was most concerned about this final category, because they were the hardest to spot. "Morons are often normal looking with few or no obvious stigmata of degeneration," he said.

Goddard also promoted the rigidity of mental categories in another way: by arguing that they were strongly hereditary. He was not much interested in whether individuals had been raised in a deprived environment, where there was little access to education or proper nutrition, or if they were not good at test taking. Intellectual deficiencies, he insisted, were innate, and "no amount of education or good environment can change a feeble-minded individual into a normal one, any more than it can change a red-haired stock into a black-haired stock."

The Binet-Simon test was reconceived again when Lewis Terman, a Stanford psychologist, created a revised version, known as the Stanford Revision. Terman added new questions and dropped old ones, and he administered the test on California students to get more information about the validity and difficulty of particular parts. Terman also introduced the idea of the IQ, or intelligence quotient, which was calculated by dividing mental age by chronological age and multiplying by one hundred. A ten-year-old who tested at ten years would have a score of 100, and one who tested at eleven years would have a score of 110.

The Binet-Simon was presented as measuring innate intelligence, but many of its questions required specific knowledge or had class or cultural biases. It also left considerable room for examiners to make subjective evaluations. The unreliability of the Binet-Simon as a measure of intelligence was evident in the questions the colony posed to Carrie on her arrival. According to the "Record Sheet" in her files, Carrie was judged to be a "Middle grade Moron" on the basis of such questions as "What is the thing to do: (a) Broken something? (b) Danger of being tardy? (c) Playmate hits you?" Carrie was also asked questions about "Fables," including "Hercules and wagoners," "Maid and eggs," and "Farmer and stork." Her files do not reveal how she answered the questions, or what the colony would have accepted as intelligent responses.

While the Binet-Simon test was rapidly being adopted to decide whether to lock people up as feebleminded, a few skeptical voices were raised. Cyril Burt, a prominent British psychologist, objected that scores on these new "intelligence tests" might reflect environmental factors like "a prosperous history" or "the want of a cultured home" more than innate ability, leading to "gross distortion." Other critics questioned whether whatever it was the tests were measuring could be called intelligence at all. "Intelligence," an article in *Mental Hygiene* objected, "is defined in terms of the subject's ability to do the tests, *which is exactly the point to be proved!*"

The most damning evidence against the Binet-Simon test and others like it was what happened when they were actually administered. Reports were emerging about just how off the results were. J. E. Wallace Wallin, a St. Louis psychologist, gave an account of administering the test to a group of Iowa farmers. "Not a single one of these persons could by any stretch of the imagination be considered feeble-minded," he wrote. Yet based on the scores they received, "every one" of the people he tested "would be feeble-minded."

Goddard administered the Binet-Simon to newly arriving immigrants at Ellis Island in 1913 and got startling results. When he graded the tests, he found that 79 percent of Italians, 80 percent of Hungarians, 83 percent of Jews, and 87 percent of Russians were feebleminded.

After reworking the results, he came up with figures that still defied belief: he reported that between 40 and 50 percent of these groups were feebleminded—with a mental age of less than twelve.

At this point Goddard might have concluded that there were problems with the Binet-Simon test or with how it was administered. He could have considered the effect of weeks of travel across the ocean in steerage, or the disorientation of arriving in the chaos of Ellis Island, or the bewilderment many would have felt on being given a multiple-choice test by a stranger after, perhaps, never having taken a test before. He might have questioned the quality of the translations, or even how committed these preoccupied new immigrants were to correctly answering his questions. Instead, Goddard made a definitive pronouncement. "We cannot escape the general conclusion," he declared, "that these immigrants were of surprisingly low intelligence."

The most infamous intelligence testing of all came in 1917, when Robert Yerkes, a Harvard psychologist, administered a Binet-Simon-style test to 1.75 million U.S. Army enlistees. Yerkes worked with Terman, Goddard, and other experts to devise special mental tests for this group. Yerkes found that in this largely native-born group, fully 47.3 percent of the white test takers were feebleminded.

Yerkes's results were broadly accepted, even though they were no less absurd than Goddard's findings at Ellis Island. If more than 47 percent of white army enlistees were feebleminded that would make the United States, as one critic observed, "a nation of morons." It was, of course, far more likely that the overwhelming majority of army enlistees and newly arriving immigrants were not feebleminded—and that it was the tests and categorizations that had failed.

Carrie was assigned to live in Ward FB9. Every colony resident received a work assignment on the farm, in manufacturing, or with the institution's operations. Carrie was given kitchen duty, which meant making and serving meals for the roughly two hundred residents of her ward. Preparations for breakfast began early, and she spent much of the day cooking, serving, or cleaning up for one meal or another.

Carrie was reunited with her mother, who was by now a colony veteran. The two women became close for the first time in years. Carrie was a dutiful daughter, and helped to care for Emma, bringing her food from the kitchen and spending time with her. Carrie also kept in touch with her own daughter, arranging furloughs to visit Vivian at the Dobbses' home in Charlottesville.

Carrie had already been a victim of a great deal of bad luck in her short life, and it continued when she arrived at the colony. The Virginia legislature had just enacted a law authorizing state hospitals to perform sterilizations on their patients for eugenic purposes. Before sterilizing anyone, the leaders of the state hospital system wanted a ruling from the courts that the new law was constitutional. They were working to create a test case, which meant they needed an inmate to place at the center of it. Just as this decision was about to be made, Carrie had the misfortune of catching the eye of the man who would be making it—the colony superintendent, Dr. Albert Priddy.

Two

Albert Priddy

In the summer of 1924, Dr. Albert Priddy was in his fourteenth year as superintendent of Virginia's Colony for Epileptics and Feeble-Minded. The superintendent of a Virginia state hospital in the 1920s was a combination of chief medical officer, chief executive officer, and plantation master. Dr. Priddy, who was the colony's first superintendent, was all of these things. He was also something else: a social reformer, with a keen vision of the role he wanted the colony to play in improving society.

Dr. Priddy was a man of medicine who had dedicated his life to mental health. His institution housed many people with mental disabilities and epilepsy, and it was a source of frustration to him that, although there were therapies and regimens that could help, there was no cure for his inmates' disabilities. At the start of the twentieth century, however, the rapidly growing eugenics movement promised something even better than a cure: a way of ensuring that, over time, the conditions he was working to treat would completely disappear, and future generations would not suffer from them.

The answer to feeblemindedness, as Dr. Priddy saw it, lay not in treating the condition but in improving the gene pool and rooting out its hereditary basis. In many states, doctors were among the first to be drawn to eugenics because they were closest to the problems of disease and defect, and they saw it as their responsibility to find a cure. Dr. Priddy was one of these pioneers, among the earliest people in Virginia to advocate for state eugenic policies to stamp out feeblemindedness.

Dr. Priddy believed in one policy in particular: eugenic sterilization, which he was convinced could quickly and permanently cut off mental defect at its source. By the 1920s many people across the country had come to support sterilization, and more than a dozen states had adopted legislation to carry it out. Dr. Priddy had made it his mission to bring this eugenic cure to Virginia—and because of the position he had risen to in the state's medical establishment, and the tenacity with which he pursued his goals, he was in a good position to get his way.

Albert Sidney Priddy was born on December 7, 1865, on a farm in Lunenburg County, southeast of Lynchburg. The Civil War had ended just eight months earlier, when General Robert E. Lee surrendered at Appomattox Courthouse, about fifty miles from the Priddy farm. The Priddys soon moved to nearby Charlotte County, and it was there that Albert spent his childhood as one of a large farming family of nine.

Young Albert began his education in the small town of Keysville, in a four-room schoolhouse with the lofty name of the Shotwell Institute. When he exhausted the local educational opportunities, Albert, a gifted and driven student, traveled north to Baltimore to enroll in its newly established College of Physicians and Surgeons. He graduated in 1886, becoming a medical doctor at the age of twenty.

Dr. Priddy returned to Keysville and established a practice. Despite his relative isolation, he followed medical advances at the research hospitals in the big cities and overseas, particularly in his specialty of surgery. Dr. Priddy integrated the latest procedures into his own medical work: in 1888 he performed one of the earliest successful operations for a perforating injury of the intestines.

Despite having a thriving medical practice, Dr. Priddy was drawn to politics. He was elected to the Virginia House of Delegates and, while still treating patients, he represented Charlotte County, which contained Keysville, from 1893 to 1894 and again from 1899 to 1900. Dr. Priddy was a progressive force in the legislature. He helped draft a law requiring a secret ballot in Virginia elections, an important advance for the forces fighting political corruption in the state.

Dr. Priddy also was an advocate for an issue that was gaining attention in statehouses nationwide: improved care for the mentally ill. He arrived in the legislature at the start of the Progressive Era, a period of idealistic social reform in many areas, including mental health. The progressives had faith that state hospitals, if properly constituted, could make great strides in treatment. As a legislator, Dr. Priddy became a leading advocate for reforming the governance of the state's hospitals for the insane.

When his final term in the House of Delegates ended, Dr. Priddy decided not to return to the practice of medicine. His professional interest had turned to mental health, with an emphasis on reforming the way in which the mentally ill were cared for. Dr. Priddy closed up his medical office in Keysville and accepted a position at the Southwestern Lunatic Asylum in Marion, the newest of Virginia's mental health hospitals.

Virginia was not a leader on many social issues in the 1920s, but it had historically been a pioneer in mental health. In colonial times, the mentally ill were generally kept in almshouses or jails, or simply left to fend for themselves. The British governor of Virginia Colony, Francis Fauquier, who was the son of a Huguenot physician, believed more should be done for them. He proposed that "a hospital be constructed for the 'lunatics and ideots wandering helplessly around the country.'" The House of Burgesses agreed, and in 1773 the Publick Hospital for Persons of Insane and Disordered Mind opened in Williamsburg.

It was the first hospital for the mentally ill in the United States—older than the nation itself.

The hospital in Williamsburg, later renamed Eastern State Hospital, was Virginia's only hospital for the mentally ill until 1828, when the Western Lunatic Asylum—later called Western State Hospital—was established in the Shenandoah Valley. A third hospital, the Southwestern Lunatic Asylum—later called Southwestern State Hospital—was opened in 1887 in Marion. After the Civil War, Virginia established a separate hospital for mentally ill blacks, the Central Lunatic Asylum, which was later renamed the Central State Hospital for Negroes.

There were now mental hospitals in every part of Virginia, but the state had no hospitals for another group that needed special care: epileptics. Epilepsy was little understood at the time. The medical profession was just starting to move away from ancient prejudices—including the belief that epileptics were possessed by the devil—and it was discovering treatments to suppress seizures. Across the nation, interest was growing in creating new institutions for epileptics based on the "colony" model.

The move to institutionalize epileptics was in part for their own benefit. Without specialized facilities, epileptics were often sent to mental hospitals, even if they were not mentally ill, or to jails, even if they had not committed crimes. At a meeting of the National Conference of Charities and Correction in 1902, Dr. William P. Spratling, medical superintendent of an epileptic colony in western New York, made the progressive case for building more institutions like his own. Colonies, with their "vocations ranging from . . . weeding the cabbage patch or the making of brick" and abundant "amusements and recreation," offered "the highest treatment of the disease," he said.

The interest in building state institutions for epileptics was also driven by fear. In the early 1900s, America was still caught up in what has been called "the myth of the dangerous epileptic." There was a long tradition of regarding epileptics as—in the words of one epilepsy expert—"mad and bad, liable to explosive and unpredictable attacks of violence and insanity, perhaps murder or at least moral depravity." For those who feared epileptics, segregation in far-off institutions was an ideal solution.

There was interest in the Virginia legislature in establishing a special state hospital for epileptics, and in 1905 an unusual opportunity presented itself. A wealthy resident of Amherst County, southwest of Charlottesville, left two hundred acres of land to Western State Hospital so it could provide "extra Comforts" to its patients. Sidney R. Murkland had acted in gratitude for the treatment his son received at Western State. Even though the bequest was designated for the hospital's general use, supporters of an epileptic hospital saw an opening.

The legislature passed a bill authorizing Western State Hospital to erect on Murkland's land "all suitable buildings and appurtenances for the establishment of a colony for the reception, care, treatment and employment of three hundred epileptic patients." It also allocated $25,000 for building construction. The legislature noted that the new facility would serve dual purposes: providing specialized care for epileptics and reducing the overcrowding in "existing State hospitals for the white insane," which were filled to capacity.

It was now settled that Virginia would have an epileptic colony, but not everyone agreed the Murkland land was the right location. The State Hospital Board objected that it was "very inaccessible," a situation made worse by the fact that it would be hard to get a spur track on the site, which meant railroad travel would be difficult. The hospital board also insisted that an epileptic colony should have a working farm. The donated land was of poor quality and cut up with ravines, the board said, making it "of practically no value as farming land."

The State Hospital Board and the legislature began looking for a better site. Western State Hospital sued, arguing that it was the beneficiary of the Murkland bequest and if the land was going to be used for an epileptic colony, it should be part of Western State. Western State lost its suit, however, and the Murkland land was sold. The proceeds were used to buy a parcel about fifty miles away, two miles outside of Lynchburg, which would be the home for the state's first hospital for epileptics.

The Virginia State Epileptic Colony, as the new institution would be called, needed a superintendent. On April 8, 1910, the colony's board appointed Dr. Priddy of Southwestern State Hospital. As a medical doctor, a state hospital administrator, and a former member of the House of Delegates, Dr. Priddy brought a rare combination of skills to his new position. His first major responsibility, however, was an undertaking he knew little about. He had to build a facility for housing and treating hundreds of resident epileptic patients.

The State Hospital Board was proved right about the new location: nestled high above the James River, the wide and majestic tidal river that British colonists named after King James I, the colony sat on a lush 1,020-acre campus. There was considerable room for facilities, recreation, and, most important, farming. Dr. Priddy would soon put 350 acres, or more than one-third of the campus, under cultivation.

Though far better suited for a colony than the Murkland parcel would have been, the site was not without its drawbacks, starting with its remote location. In the colony's early days, the roads leading out to it could not be relied upon, particularly after it rained. The first time the governor visited, he got stuck in the mud and remained trapped until help arrived from Lynchburg. In the next legislative session, funds were allocated to pave the roads between the highway and the colony.

When he took charge, Dr. Priddy presided over a flurry of construction. Two buildings that were already on the grounds were renovated: one became executive offices and the other a residence. On March 1, 1911, the colony's first new structure, the Drewry-Gilliam Building, was completed. The first epileptic patients moved into the colony on May 16, a little more than a year after Dr. Priddy took over.

In its first year, the colony admitted about one hundred patients, all epileptic men. The first wave included thirty epileptics who had been inmates at Eastern State Hospital, thirty from Southwestern State, and forty from Western State Hospital. The very first patient to move in was a thirty-seven-year-old man who illustrated well why a specialized institution for epileptics was needed. Before arriving at the colony, he had been confined to a mental hospital for thirteen years, though he had no mental defects.

Epileptics were better off at the colony than they would have been at a mental hospital or a jail, but their situation was still far from ideal. The colony had little to offer epileptic patients in the way of medical treatment or therapy—or help in returning to society. The colony was necessarily "custodial in character," a history of the institution noted. "Lack of personnel and facilities restricted the operation to that level."

If the colony could not offer cures, it did provide modest recreations and diversions. There were weekly dances, Thanksgiving and Christmas dinners, and a summer watermelon feast. Inmates were given leaves to attend moving picture shows in Lynchburg, and every residential building had a phonograph for the inmates' use. For the more spiritually inclined, services were held in the colony's chapel every week, Methodist and Baptist on alternating Sundays.

In keeping with the colony model, inmates spent much of their time working out in the fields. They raised fruits and vegetables both to eat fresh and to be stored for the winter. Dr. Priddy would eventually be able to boast that the colony "has bought no canned goods for two years." The colony had its own cattle farm and the hog herd alone yielded twenty thousand pounds of pork a year, an amount that was "ample for supplying the institution with salt meat."

As an administrator, Dr. Priddy emphasized thrift in all things. He took satisfaction, he wrote in one "Report of the Superintendent," whenever he visited institutions in other states and compared "the condition of their inmates from the standpoints of health, comfort and death rate, and their cost of maintenance." He invariably found, he said, that Virginia was supporting its inmates "with practically as much comfort and at much less cost to the taxpayers than in most any other State."

Dr. Priddy had many ways of keeping expenses in check, which he enumerated in his public reports. His economizing touched on every aspect of the inmates' lives, and continued even after they died. Dr. Priddy found that funeral costs could be kept to a minimum if inmates were buried on the colony's grounds. If relatives insisted on holding their own services, they were required to pay the embalming and shipping costs.

The colony soon expanded its mission. After initially admitting only epileptic men, in 1912 it began to accept the feebleminded, and women inmates, both epileptic and feebleminded. The new admission policies helped to take some of the pressure off of the other state hospitals, which were filled beyond capacity. A few years earlier, the commissioner of state hospitals had warned in a report that if additional accommodations were not made available for housing the mentally defective and epileptics, some of them would have to be held in jails.

The colony began to fill up with inmates who had been adjudicated as feebleminded, many of them poor women who had run afoul of the police or government agencies. Dr. Priddy took a dim view of many of his female charges. In a 1914 annual report he described one group as unfortunate "creatures," who were "adept in the use of the vilest language and practices, common among women of their class." The women "morons" at the colony, Dr. Priddy would later say, "consisted for the most part of those who would formerly have found their way into the red-light district and become dangerous to society."

The colony continued to expand. Several new buildings opened in rapid succession: the Mastin-Minor Building, which housed feebleminded women; the Strode-Massie Building, home to one hundred epileptic women; and Lesner-Fletcher Hall, which had an auditorium on the first floor and classrooms below. Another residence, LeCato Cottage, added fifty-six more inmate beds.

It was no longer accurate to refer to the colony as simply a facility for epileptics. In recognition of its wider mission, on October 1, 1919, the name was officially changed to the State Colony for Epileptics and Feeble-Minded. Over the next few years, an increasing percentage of the new admissions were feebleminded. By 1925 more than two-thirds of the colony's inmates would be classified as mentally retarded.

Dr. Priddy carefully managed the inmate population. He insisted on housing feebleminded and epileptic inmates separately. And he drew the line at accepting idiots, the lowest level of Goddard's hierarchy. "Pitiful appeals in behalf of the admission of idiots continue to be received," Dr. Priddy lamented in a 1923 report, but "all such applications have to be rejected."

Dr. Priddy came to the colony at a time when opinions were changing about what to do with the feebleminded. In the early days of the Republic, there was little help available for people with mental difficulties. Unlike Virginia, with its Publick Hospital for Persons of Insane and Disordered Mind, most states left it to local communities to care for people with mental disabilities, who "commonly languished in local jails and poorhouses or lived with family and friends."

As the nation's population increased and became more urban, these informal approaches became outdated. States began to establish public mental hospitals: Massachusetts in 1848, New York in 1851, Pennsylvania in 1853, and Connecticut in 1855. This "cult of asylum" continued to spread, and by the start of the Civil War almost every state had one or more facilities for the mentally ill. It was a sign that the institutionalization movement had reached critical mass when, in 1877, administrators organized the Association of Medical Officers of American Institutions for Idiotic and Feeble-Minded Persons.

These institutions for the mentally defective began idealistically, with a commitment to "moral treatment and compassionate care—and a conviction that they could do a great deal to help their patients." In time, however, this therapeutic impulse began to give way. During the Gilded Age, the final three decades of the 1800s, it was increasingly replaced by a darker assessment of people with mental defects and where they fit in the social and biological order.

For nearly a century, social scientists had been reframing the history—and future—of humanity in biological terms. In 1798 the English political economist Thomas Malthus published *An Essay on the Principle of Population,* in which he offered a bleak vision of the implications of population growth. Malthus argued that the world's population would eventually outstrip the food supply, with only famine and disease to provide a counterbalance. "The power of population is so superior to the power in the earth to produce subsistence for man, that unless arrested by the preventive check, premature death must in some shape or other visit the human race," Malthus warned.

A half century later, in 1851, the English philosopher Herbert Spencer argued in *Social Statics* that rather than being guided by God, humans were evolving based on scientific rules. In that book, and several later ones, Spencer identified a natural sorting process that separated those who were strong enough to survive and those who were not. In his 1864 work *The Principles of Biology,* he gave this process a name: "survival of the fittest." As Spencer saw it, the healthiest humans lived and reproduced, while "nature's failures"—those with mental, physical, or moral deficiencies—did not. "Life has reached its present height," he said, under a universal law of nature: "that a creature not energetic enough to maintain itself must die."

Spencer believed this violent sorting out was not only natural but right. Intervening to help the unfit would weaken all of humanity, "and eventually the degenerate species would fail to hold its ground in presence of antagonistic species," he wrote. This compassionate course would, he insisted, be "fatal" to the human race. It was dangerous folly for reformers or the government to rescue the poor and weak from the "natural" forces that were defeating them, he insisted. "If they are not sufficiently complete to live, they die, and it is best they should die."

Spencer's pitiless view of the human condition would later be branded "social Darwinism," but his writings actually preceded Darwin's. It was eight years after *Social Statics* that Charles Darwin, the British evolutionary theorist, introduced his observations of the natural world into the discussion. In 1859, in his *On the Origin of Species,* Darwin argued that animal populations evolve over time through a process of natural selection. There was considerable interest in applying these evolutionary theories to mankind. Darwin would do this himself more than a decade later—but a relative of his did it first.

Francis Galton, Darwin's half cousin, turned the newly emerging ideas about evolution into a science of human improvement. In 1869 Galton published *Hereditary Genius: An Inquiry into Its Laws and Consequences,* a study of the families of some of history's most brilliant thinkers and athletes. Galton concluded—as his title gave away—that genius was hereditary, in the same way various traits were passed on in the animal world. Galton, who was intent on being taken seriously as a scientist, boasted that his analysis was the first to treat "the subject in a statistical manner."

Galton went on to turn the science of human improvement that he was developing into an intellectual movement. In 1883 he published *Inquiries into Human Faculty and Its Development,* the book in which he coined the word "eugenics." Derived from the Greek *"eu"* for "good" and *"genes"* for born, eugenics was, Galton explained, a "brief word to express the science of improving stock."

Galton called on humanity to take its future into its own hands by adopting eugenics programs that would promote "the more suitable races or strains of blood . . . over the less suitable." Through such efforts, he argued, "what Nature does blindly, slowly, and ruthlessly, man may do providently, quickly, and kindly." Having invented eugenics and set out its ambitious goals, Galton wrote and lectured on the subject extensively, becoming, the journal *Nature* observed, "indefatigable in his zeal to promote the cause."

For Galton, eugenics was not only a hard and indisputable science but also an ethical and spiritual movement. Eugenics exalted marriage, in his view, by bringing greater focus to the quality of the offspring a union would generate. He considered eugenic measures to be a form of philanthropy bestowed by the present generation on future ones. Galton was convinced that eugenics would lift humanity to glorious new heights—it was, he declared, "a virile creed, full of hopefulness."

In his writings, Galton described two kinds of eugenics: "positive" and "negative." Positive eugenics—the one that interested him the most—meant encouraging people with superior traits to have more children. In evaluating an individual's worth to the species, he believed there were three main considerations: physique, ability, and character. All were important, and he deemed "inferiority in any of the three" to "outweigh superiority in the other two."

At the same time, Galton saw a value in negative eugenics, which called for preventing reproduction of those with "undesirable" traits. Galton was convinced that England was "overstocked and overburdened with the listless and the incapable." He believed affirmative steps should be taken to address this drag on humanity—whether isolating the unfit so they could not reproduce, or through "some other less drastic yet adequate measure." Galton was vague about the specifics, but he insisted that "our democracy will ultimately refuse consent to that liberty of propagating children which is now allowed to the undesirable classes."

While his half cousin was building a movement, Darwin was doing his own work on humans and evolution, though of a more elevated, scientific sort. In 1871 he published a second work of evolutionary theory, *The Descent of Man, and Selection in Relation to Sex,* in which he applied many of the ideas he had laid out in *On the Origin of Species* to humanity. The book was wide-ranging in its subject matter, including extensive discussions of evolution of specific physical and mental traits in humans, the nature of racial distinctions, and division of labor between men and women.

Darwin touched on some of the issues Galton and the eugenicists were speaking to, including the popular debate over whether society should help its weakest members. Many eugenicists believed philanthropy was a threat to the human race. As the philosopher and reformer Jane Hume Clapperton complained, charities "deliberately selected the half-starved, the diseased, the criminals, and enabled them to exist and propagate." Many eugenicists and Tory politicians also opposed the widespread use of vaccinations, another intervention that, as they saw it, helped people survive who had been targeted by nature for illness and death.

Darwin understood why eugenicists objected to smallpox vaccinations. "There is reason to believe that vaccination has preserved thousands, who from a weak constitution, would formerly have succumbed to small-pox," he wrote in *The Descent of Man*. Through interventions like these, "weak members of civilized societies" are allowed to "propagate their kind." Anyone who had ever bred animals, he wrote, understood "this must be highly injurious to the race of man."

If Darwin had stopped there, he could have been mistaken for a hard-core eugenicist. He went on, however, to explain why humans should recoil at letting natural selection operate ruthlessly. The support that people gave "the helpless," he said, derived from "the instinct of sympathy"—a social instinct that had, over time, become "more tender and more widely diffused."

Darwin believed humans could not "check our sympathy," even at the urging of "hard reason, without deterioration in the noblest part of our nature." Refusing to help the weak might provide "contingent benefit," but it brought with it "a certain and great present evil." For this reason, Darwin insisted, "we must bear without complaining the undoubtedly bad effects of the weak surviving and propagating their kind."

The ideas of Galton and his contemporaries gained momentum as they crossed the Atlantic. The belief that some groups and individuals were inferior by nature was hardly a new one in the United States—a nation whose founding documents incorporated slavery based on race. The new thinking coming out of Britain, however, was giving human inferiority and superiority a modern, scientific orientation. Suddenly it seemed, as the historian Eric Foner noted, that "every serious thinker felt obligated to reckon with" Darwin's writing and the fundamental questions it raised about human nature.

In the United States, this reckoning was being done not through grand theories but through empirical, fact-based research. A new form of inquiry was emerging, one that would come to be called "criminal anthropology." The book that set this field in motion in the United States, and did more than any other to launch American eugenics, was *The Jukes: A Study in Crime, Pauperism, Disease, and Heredity: also Further Studies of Criminals,* which was published in 1877 by a prison reformer who opposed almost everything the eugenicists stood for.

Richard Dugdale was examining an upstate New York jail in 1874 when it struck him that six of the inmates he met were related. Dugdale investigated the family, which he called the Jukes, to find out whether there were high levels of criminality in its past, and what the causes were. He looked back five generations and discovered that of the 709 people he identified, more than half were criminals or prostitutes.

The Jukes resembled the eugenic family studies that Galton conducted but with one key difference: Dugdale concluded that the Jukes's problems were more due to environment than heredity. He argued that society should provide better education and other material support to families like the Jukes, which showed dysfunction over generations, to help them break the cycle of crime and poverty.

Eugenicists were quick to seize on *The Jukes.* They ignored Dugdale's conclusions about causation and focused instead on the facts he presented about the family. To the eugenicists, Dugdales's findings were evidence that bad traits were hereditary—and that these traits explained the persistence of social problems.

This interpretation of *The Jukes* was a clear perversion of Dugdale's work. When the book was republished after Dugdale's death, the sociologist who wrote the introduction lamented that the "impression quite generally prevails that 'The Jukes' is a thorough-going demonstration of 'hereditary criminality,' 'hereditary pauperism,' 'hereditary degeneracy,' and so on. It is nothing of the kind." But these objections could not stop people from saying, as many did, that *The Jukes* was evidence that delinquency ran in families, and that some people were born bad.

More studies of troubled families and communities soon followed, and the focus shifted from environmental factors to heredity. In 1878

Oscar McCulloch, a minister with the National Conference of Charities and Correction, began work on what would be one of the most influential post-*Jukes* studies. For a decade, McCulloch studied an impoverished extended family in the Indianapolis area, which he called the "Tribe of Ishmael." In *The Tribe of Ishmael: A Study in Social Degradation,* he described generation after generation of murderers, thieves, beggars, and prostitutes.

In his analysis of the Tribe of Ishmael's failings, McCulloch agreed with Dugdale that environmental factors were important. He described the harsh conditions in which they lived: "mostly out of doors in the river bottoms, in old houses." He believed the family's situation would be improved by "changed surroundings," and he advocated taking its children away and raising them under better conditions.

More than environment, however, McCulloch believed the Ishmaelites' problems were due to their "decaying stock." He urged his fellow reformers and philanthropists to stop trying to alleviate the poverty of people like the Ishmaelites. Their hereditary flaws were so serious, he argued, that the government and private aid that was directed to them by "the benevolent public" did not cure their "generally diseased" condition. It simply "encouraged them" in their "idle, wandering life," and in the "propagation of similarly disposed children."

This growing attention to the role of heredity in antisocial behavior received a significant boost in 1900, when the scientific world embraced the work of Gregor Mendel. Mendel, a monk who lived in a monastery in what is now the Czech Republic, discovered many basic laws of heredity in his experiments breeding pea plants. He died in obscurity in 1884, his research all but unknown, but at the dawn of the twentieth century his findings were rediscovered. His theories revolutionized genetics and had a profound impact on the emerging field of eugenics.

Before Mendel, it was widely assumed that heredity worked by blending; that is, a tall plant crossed with a short plant would produce a medium-height plant. Mendel found, instead, that when he crossed peas one trait dominated. When green peas and yellow peas were crossed, the first generation was all yellow—the dominant trait. In the next generation, however, the recessive trait would reassert itself, and one-quarter of the offspring would be green.

Mendel's work provided experimental precision, quantitative analysis, and certitude in a field that had so far been marked by mere speculation. This new science of heredity was precisely what the eugenicists were looking for. Eugenics argued that positive and negative traits were passed down from generation to generation, and with Mendel's pea plants, Galton and his followers now had, or so they believed, a scientific basis for saying so.

The eugenicists argued that just like traits such as height and color in pea plants—or blood type and color blindness in humans—the physical and mental qualities they focused on were inherited in predictable patterns. They created elaborate pedigrees showing how feeblemindedness, drunkenness, criminality, and moral degeneracy were inherited within families. In the eugenicists' view, Mendel's laws supported their belief that if the "socially defective" were prevented from having children, and the highest-quality people had more, bad traits could be bred out, and good traits would proliferate.

There were, of course, fundamental problems with the eugenicists' science. They were making the mistake of assuming that "like produces like"—that brilliant parents produce brilliant children, and criminals produce criminals. Intelligence, indolence, dependency, and other human qualities are not, however, "unit characters"—traits passed on in a single gene from parent to child. And as Mendel's work suggested, in reproduction genes combine and are expressed in complex ways, particularly for the sort of human qualities eugenics focused on. The eugenicists' plan of ending feeblemindedness simply by preventing the feebleminded from reproducing had no basis in genetics.

The eugenicists also failed to take environmental factors into account. There were many reasons people were poor or indolent—or scored low on intelligence tests—that were unrelated to biology. In a few years, Thomas Hunt Morgan, a Columbia University geneticist who would go on to win a Nobel Prize, would argue that many human deficiencies were more the result of "demoralizing social conditions" than heredity. Supporters of eugenics had little interest, however, in the effect of an impoverished childhood or a poor education on life outcomes.

The eugenicists stuck to their own beliefs about genetics. When Bleecker van Wagenen, a leading American eugenicist and a trustee of the Vineland School, addressed the First International Eugenics Congress in London, he listed groups whose flaws should be regarded as hereditary in origin. He included criminals, paupers, the blind and deaf, and "the deformed." Van Wagenen urged that they be "eliminated from the human stock."

The weakness of the science did not slow the spread of eugenics in the United States. While eugenics theoreticians continued to refine their views on "defective" groups, and criminal anthropologists kept up their fieldwork on what they regarded as hereditarily cursed communities, the movement's main focus in these early years was a practical concern: an obsession with what came to be known as "the menace of feeblemindedness."

Leading eugenicists were starting to warn that the single biggest threat to the nation's hereditary "stock" was feeblemindedness, and they were studying the problem intensively. Some of the most urgent warnings were coming from Henry Goddard of the Vineland Training School for Feeble-minded Girls and Boys, the inventor of the categories of "idiots," "imbeciles," and "morons." In 1912 Goddard published his own enormously influential work of criminal anthropology. Unlike many of its predecessors, which discussed a wide array of defects, Goddard's book concerned itself with a single problem: feeblemindedness.

In *The Kallikak Family: A Study in the Heredity of Feeble-Mindedness*, Goddard examined six generations of a New Jersey family and showed how it supported his theories of inherited mental defect. Goddard began his tale during the Revolutionary War, with "Martin Kallikak" (a fictitious name, like all the others in the book). Kallikak produced two lines of descendants, one through his wife, "a woman of his own quality," and another through a "feeble-minded girl" he met in a tavern. The line from Kallikak's wife, Goddard found, included generations of doctors, judges, and other successful men. The line from the "feeble-minded girl" was rife with prostitutes, criminals, and epileptics.

Goddard presented the Kallikaks as a "natural experiment in heredity," and he drew larger lessons from it. He was not concerned, he said at the outset, with the "low-grade idiot." Some had "proposed the lethal chamber," he noted, but he said somewhat wistfully that he saw "no probability" society would support mass executions of its least intelligent members. The "idiot" is "indeed loathsome," Goddard said, but fortunately, because he was unlikely to become a parent, "he lives his life and is done." The problem, he said, was what to do about the higher-level feebleminded.

Two years later, Goddard published *Feeble-Mindedness: Its Causes and Consequences*, a 599-page study that drew on cases he observed at the Vineland School. In his new work, he continued to warn about the menace of feeblemindedness. As much as 2 percent of the school population might be feebleminded, he said, and the causes were "mostly hereditary." Not only was feeblemindedness a problem in its own right, he argued, but it "underlies all our social problems." Marshaling questionable data, Goddard contended that as much as 50 percent of criminals, prostitutes, and almshouse residents were feebleminded. What was at stake in the war on feeblemindedness, he insisted, was nothing less than "the future welfare of the race."

Goddard was only one of many influential voices urging the nation to awaken to the threat posed by the feebleminded in their midst. Lewis Terman, the Stanford professor who revised the Binet-Simon test, warned urgently about feeblemindedness among the young. In his 1917 essay "Feeble-Minded Children in the Public Schools of California," he said feeblemindedness was "one of the most important factors in delinquency, crime, alcoholism, pauperism, prostitution, and the spread of venereal diseases." He estimated that more than 1 percent of California students were afflicted.

The nation's universities churned out large quantities of these reports, all expressing alarm. Samuel J. Holmes, a University of California zoology professor, warned in *The Trend of the Race: A Study of Present Tendencies in the Biological Development of Civilized Mankind* that the feebleminded were reproducing at a rapid rate. "The best blood of a nation is its most priceless possession," he insisted. Holmes ended his book with a plaintive question: "The race has its fate in its own hands to make or to mar. Will it ever take itself in hand and shape its own destiny?"

The government joined in, issuing its own stern reports on the tide of feeblemindedness. A study prepared for the California state legislature in 1915 said the problem had always existed "but only recently have we begun to recognize how serious a menace it is to the social, economic, and moral welfare of the state." The same year, Virginia's State Board of Charities and Corrections published a booklet on the problem, using the phrase that now seemed to be everywhere—"the menace of feeble-mindedness"—and assuring Virginians their state was taking steps "for the elimination and prevention of this evil."

The anxieties of these experts were mirrored in the general-interest media, which was engaged in its own mania. *Scientific American* warned in 1912 that the "reproduction of feeblemindedness" was "rife" in much of the country. An article the following year in *Life and Health: The National Health Magazine* helpfully explained that the time was approaching when feeblemindedness, which was a "definite, inheritable Mendelian unit" trait, could be eliminated, allowing society to "cultivate instead the valuable physical and mental traits and talents."

For sheer poignancy—mixed with a strong dose of alarm—few articles could rival "The Village of a Thousand Souls," published in the *American Magazine* in 1913. Arnold Gesell, who was then a junior professor at Yale, returned to his all-American hometown of Alma, Wisconsin. Gesell claimed to have found that about a quarter of the residents showed signs of feeblemindedness or insanity, and he called for eugenic measures, including isolating the feebleminded, to uplift his beleaguered hometown.

Eugenics and the mania over feeblemindedness arrived at a time when America was particularly receptive. The start of the twentieth century was an era of fast-paced, disruptive change. As rural residents fled farms and small towns, the United States was transforming from a predominantly rural nation to an urban, industrial one, and in the process community and family ties were breaking down. At the same time, immigrants were arriving in record numbers, dramatically altering the country's religious, cultural, and racial makeup.

These roiling changes caused considerable social anxiety and ushered in what the historian Richard Hofstadter called "the Age of Reform." Native-born, white, middle-class, Protestant Americans mobilized to put their own imprint on a nation in transition by uniting behind an array of causes. They fought corrupt urban political machines. They agitated for safer factories and against child labor. They campaigned for improved public education and for women's rights. These reform campaigns were, one history of the period explained, a "response" to the "crisis" caused by the great changes the nation was undergoing—"a *counter* to these movements that threatened to transform American society in more fundamental ways."

If the age of reform was about the native-born, white, Protestant middle class trying to build a nation in its own image, eugenics fit right into the ethos of the era. The reformers believed in using intellectual tools, including science, to uplift—and purify—society, and this was just the sort of promise eugenics was holding out. The old-stock reformers could not prevent the country from urbanizing or spawning teeming immigrant neighborhoods, and they could not prevent the nation's cultural and religious composition from changing. They could, however, do battle with what they were being told was an alarming rise in "the diseased, the deficient, and the demented."

The eugenicists matched the demographic profile of the reformers of the era. Both the leaders of the eugenics movement and the rank and file were largely middle-class, well educated, white, and Protestant. Hofstadter observed that professionals and intellectuals were in the forefront of the reform movements of the era: they were the sort, he noted, who "see the drift of events" and then "throw their weight on the side of what they feel is progress and reform." So it was with eugenics—it appealed, in particular, to academics and professionals, including lawyers, doctors, social workers, and journalists.

In the legal profession, support for eugenics came from the very top. When Connecticut enacted the nation's first eugenic law in 1895—a ban on certain marriages—the American Bar Association's president praised it as a necessary "practical deterrent." James C. Carter used his president's address that year to declare that government must "prevent unhealthy progeny" to protect "future generations from the evil operation of the laws of heredity."

The highest echelons of the medical profession also largely supported the eugenics movement. At the American Academy of Medicine's first meeting of the twentieth century, in June 1900, its president called for laws to prevent, as the title of his address put it, "Crime, Pauperism, and Mental Deficiency." Dr. G. Hudson Makuen argued that medicine as it was currently practiced was counterproductive. "We prolong the lives of weaklings," he said, "and make it possible for them to transmit their characteristics to future generations."

Many religious leaders actively promoted eugenics to their flocks and to the nation. The Very Reverend Walter Taylor Sumner, dean of Chicago's Protestant Episcopal Cathedral of Saints Peter and Paul, announced in 1912 that he would only marry couples with a "certificate of health" from a reputable physician. A few months later, the *New York Times* reported that two hundred Chicago clergy adopted a resolution "urging pastors to direct their energies toward creating public opinion indorsing Dean Sumner's plan." Other religious leaders offered their houses of worship. New York's West End Presbyterian Church was an organizing center, with the Reverend Dr. A. E. Keigwin convening his fellow Protestant clergy to "push a eugenics campaign."

Women were active in all of the movements during the age of reform and were well represented in the ranks of the eugenicists. Many influential feminists supported the cause, including the writer Charlotte Perkins Gilman and the birth control crusader Margaret Sanger. Sanger lectured to a Vassar College audience on the importance of reducing "the rapid multiplication of the unfit and undesirable."

Women were particularly influential at the grassroots level. In the early twentieth century, women were largely excluded from politics and public policy—they could not vote until the Nineteenth Amendment was ratified in 1920. Many legislators, however, considered eugenics, with its focus on reproductive issues, a proper realm for female guidance. Women were among the most active lobbyists for eugenic laws of all kinds. The historian Edward J. Larson, in his study of southern eugenics, concluded that in every state in the Deep South federated women's clubs played a decisive role in establishing eugenically segregated institutions for the mentally retarded.

Eugenics found support across the ideological spectrum. In addition to the feminists, some of the era's most outspoken progressives endorsed some manner of eugenics. Theodore Roosevelt, the most famous progressive of all, was characteristically unreserved in his beliefs. A few years after leaving the White House, he wrote a magazine article declaring, "I wish very much that the wrong people could be prevented entirely from breeding." He insisted that "feeble-minded persons" should be "forbidden to leave offspring behind them."

At the same time, eugenics exerted a strong appeal to conservatives. Many were drawn to its insistence that there was a natural elite, and that differences among people could not be eradicated simply by improving their environment. Eugenics offered what purported to be a scientific answer to the progressive argument that the disadvantaged could be saved if only they were provided with the right government programs. Conservatives could point to the writings of thinkers like Galton and Goddard, who believed that helping the genetically disadvantaged would only increase the number of criminals and welfare cases.

There was almost always a strong current of racism and anti-

Semitism to the eugenics movement, and bigots of all kinds were drawn to it. Many of the most prominent eugenicists were openly white supremacist and saw racism as central to their beliefs. In *Hereditary Genius*, Galton flatly asserted that whites were superior to the "African negro," a race that he asserted contained a particularly large number of "half-witted men," and he claimed that Jews were "specialized for a parasitic existence." Paul Popenoe, one of the American movement's leading theoreticians, wrote in his 1918 book *Applied Eugenics* that if races can be judged by their original contributions to the world's civilizations "the Negro race must be placed very near zero on the scale."

Although eugenics was popular with many southern racists, who saw in it a scientific rationale for the Jim Crow system, eugenicists in the South generally focused their attention on whites. Their primary interest was in "preserving" the white race from decline. Southern eugenicists were particularly concerned with the lowest economic class, people often disparagingly referred to as "poor white trash," who were seen as repositories of the worst of the white race's germplasm. One Louisiana doctor spoke for many white elites when he asked, in 1917, "What language can express the humiliation we should feel at seeing [our] race, physically, mentally and morally, slowly going to decay?" Whites were, he feared, "a race, proud of its lineage, boastful of its achievement, . . . and withal rotting at its roots!"

Blacks were victims of eugenics, and they were sterilized—in some cases in the worst way, by prison or hospital doctors operating without legal authority. But southern eugenicists in the early twentieth century were more concerned about keeping blacks as far as possible from whites. On the same day Virginia enacted its eugenic sterilization law, it adopted the Racial Integrity Act of 1924. Like other southern states, Virginia already prohibited sexual relations between races, but the new law was stricter. It defined every person in Virginia as either "white" or "colored" according to the "one drop" rule, which held that any nonwhite ancestry made someone nonwhite. Southern eugenicists believed that if they strictly policed the race line, any hereditary defects of blacks would remain with them—and not corrupt the white race.

Eugenics reached into every corner of the nation, and became a popular subject in the mass media—often intermixed with strong strands of "scientific" racism. Mass-market books spread the message to a vast reading audience, none more so than Madison Grant's *The Passing of the Great Race*, which argued in 1916 that the "Nordic" race was superior to other races—and responsible for all progress—but also in peril. "We Americans must realize that the altruistic ideals which have controlled our social development during the past century, and the maudlin sentimentalism that has made America 'an asylum for the oppressed,' are sweeping the nation toward a racial abyss." In 1920 Lothrop Stoddard published *The Rising Tide of Color Against White World-Supremacy*, which painted a portrait of the impending collapse of the superior white civilization in the face of the global rise of people of color. Stoddard invoked "the vision of a 'Pan-Colored' alliance for the overthrow of white hegemony at a single stroke—a dream which would turn into a nightmare of race-war beside which the late struggle in Europe would seem . . . child's play." He warned: "We stand at a crisis—the supreme crisis of the ages."

Grant's and Stoddard's racist eugenic arguments resonated strongly. In a 1921 speech in Birmingham, Alabama, President Warren G. Harding praised Stoddard's book, which had fourteen printings in its first three years. "Whoever will take the time to read and ponder Mr. Lothrop Stoddard's book on *The Rising Tide of Color*," the president declared, "must realize that our race problem here in the United States is only a phase of a race issue the whole world confronts." In F. Scott Fitzgerald's *The Great Gatsby*, the wealthy and brutish Tom Buchanan, husband of Daisy, holds forth on how "civilization's going to pieces" and cites "'The Rise of the Colored Empires' by this man Goddard." The reference is to *The Rising Tide of Color Against White World-Supremacy*, and critics have noted that the name "Goddard" is an amalgam of the names "Grant" and "Stoddard," as well as being the name of a prominent real-life eugenicist.

National magazines carried the eugenic message to a broader public and patiently explained the science of hereditary defects to a lay audience. A 1915 *Atlantic Monthly* article that ran under the headline "Some Misconceptions of Eugenics" instructed that by promoting the "most desirable" strains and "eliminating the inferior breeds," eugenics had the prospect of producing "untold benefits to society." In the early days of eugenics, such articles were ubiquitous: according to one survey, from 1910 to 1914, general-interest magazines ran more articles on eugenics than on three of the era's biggest social problems—slums, tenements, and living standards—combined.

Major newspapers covered eugenics no less extensively, on both their news and editorial pages. The *New York Times* gave respectful coverage to the eugenicists' agenda. "Courses in Eugenics Increase in Colleges of This Country," the paper reported, citing figures from the American Eugenics Society, an organization it described as having "for its aim the betterment of racial standards throughout the country." At times, newspapers were more expressly supportive. When Louisiana's legislature was considering a major eugenic law, the *New Orleans Times-Picayune* gave its endorsement. In several editorials, it insisted the bill was not a "wild eugenic scheme" or a violation of human rights. It was, the editorial board insisted, "simply a step to protect the community and the human race against the . . . unfit."

Religious leaders spread the word in articles for religious journals and through sermons from the pulpit, including ones they entered in the American Eugenics Society's popular Eugenics Sermon Contest. The Reverend Harry F. Ward, a founder of the Methodist Federation for Social Service and a professor of Christian Ethics at Union Theological Seminary, wrote in the magazine *Eugenics* that Christians and eugenicists were fighting a common battle because both were concerned with the "challenge of removing the causes that produce the weak."

The Reverend Phillips Endecott Osgood, the rector of St. Mark's Church in Minneapolis, used metallurgical imagery to urge people of faith to purge "the "dross" of humanity. "The Refiner's Fire" won the 1926 Eugenics Sermon Contest and was reprinted in the *Homiletic Review*. Many years later, the United Methodist Church would formally apologize for the prominent role its churches and pastors played in the eugenics movement. "As the Eugenics Movement came to the United States," it said regretfully, "the churches, especially the Methodists, the Presbyterians, and the Episcopalians, embraced it."

There were high-profile eugenics conferences, such as the Second International Eugenics Congress, which convened in 1921 at New York's American Museum of Natural History. The museum was a welcoming site for the gathering—its president, Henry Fairfield Osborn, was a cofounder, along with Madison Grant, of the eugenic Galton Society. On the opening day, Osborn instructed a standing-room-only crowd that "the selection, preservation, and multiplication of the best heredity is a patriotic duty of the first importance." The Museum of Natural History installed special eugenic exhibitions, including ones on race, which taught that "humanity is composed of many races differing widely in physical, mental and moral qualities."

There were eugenic presentations at less lofty gatherings as well, including state and county fairs. The Kansas Free Fair of 1920 had a contest that judged human families in the same way as animals, and soon the American Eugenics Society was sponsoring "fitter family" competitions at fairs across the country. A volunteer who helped organize the contests said that when fairgoers wondered about the word "Eugenics" over the entrance to a building on the fairgrounds, "we say, 'While the stock judges are testing the Holsteins, Jerseys, and White-faces in the stock pavilion, we are judging the Joneses, Smiths, and the Johnsons.'" Families who entered these competitions had to submit to medical and psychiatric examinations and take intelligence tests. Like the livestock, the winning families were awarded prizes. The "fitter family" contests were enormously popular and gave the movement a boost. "All the newspapers were glad to cooperate," a leader of the American Eugenics Society later recalled. "No activities of the society got so much publicity."

Eugenics even found its way into the nation's movie houses in the form of a feature-length horror film. In 1917 William Randolph Hearst's media company produced *The Black Stork*, a fictionalized version of the story of Chicago obstetrician Harry Haiselden. Haiselden became famous for allowing a baby with serious birth defects to die without treatment. In the film, in which the real Haiselden starred, a doctor saves the life of a "defective" baby, who grows up to be a disabled adult and returns to kill the doctor who "condemned" him to "this life of torture and shame." Fortunately, the baby's grim adulthood is only a vision from God, and the mother is able to allow her defective newborn to die before he grows up to be a threat to society.

While eugenics gained strength across the United States, a fundamental problem remained: it was not clear how the movement would achieve its goals. Galton and other eugenics pioneers talked about preventing the "unfit" from reproducing, but they were vague on the details. Early eugenicists in the United States were equally unclear about how to proceed—an imprecision that was driven in large part by the lack of good options.

The first tactic that eugenicists tried was one that struck many as barbaric: forced castration. In 1855 Gideon Lincecum, a Texas physician, drafted a bill to castrate criminals. Lincecum had no reservations about the procedure. "Did you never see [a] eunuch?" he wrote to a friend. Lincecum said he had known five, including one that he castrated himself, a "degraded drunken sot." Lincecum said that he performed the operation "in a kind of youthful frolic," but castration "cured him." The legislature did not take the matter so lightly. The bill "occasioned a smart amount of angry discussion," Lincecum later recalled, and was referred to the committee that supervised cattle issues, where it died.

In 1897 the Michigan legislature considered a bill authorizing "asexualization," as it called castration, of inmates of the Michigan Home for the Feeble Minded and Epileptic and certain classes of criminals. The bill's sponsors had great hopes, but castration struck too many members of the general public as unseemly and cruel.

Dr. W. R. Edgar, a Michigan state representative who sponsored the bill, blamed the state's "sentimentalists" for its defeat.

In the absence of laws, some doctors at state institutions started to perform castrations on their own authority. In the 1890s Dr. F. Hoyt Pilcher, head of the Kansas State Asylum for Idiotic and Imbecile Youth, castrated forty-four boys and men and performed hysterectomies on fourteen girls and women. Dr. Pilcher's methods drew opposition, including from a local paper that reported his activities under the headline "Mutilation by the Wholesale Practiced at the Asylum." In the end, public opposition forced Dr. Pilcher to stop.

With public opinion a seemingly insurmountable obstacle to castration laws, the eugenicists set their sights on a new approach: eugenic marriage restrictions. Connecticut, the first state to act, adopted an 1895 law barring "epileptic, imbecile, or feeble-minded" individuals from marrying if the woman was under forty-five. The penalty was up to three years in prison—and up to five years for anyone who aided in such a marriage. Other states soon followed. The majority had eugenic marriage laws by 1914, and forty-one states would by the mid-1930s.

Marriage prohibitions were a major advance for the eugenics movement: they were the first laws to endorse the goal of reducing reproduction by the "unfit." Many eugenicists insisted that they did not go far enough, however, and that defective people would continue to have children, with or without a marriage license. One of the nation's leading eugenicists was direct about it: "No cheap device of a *law* against marriage," he protested, was going to solve the problem of hereditary defects.

Eugenicists began to rally around a tactic they saw as more promising: "segregation" of the unfit. The idea was simple: identify the feebleminded and other people who should not have children, and place them in state institutions during their reproductive years. In *The Kallikak Family*, Goddard advocated "segregation and colonization"—locking away the feebleminded in state colonies. If such a system had been in place during the Revolutionary War and the "feeble-minded girl" that Martin Kallikak had children with had instead been "segregated in an institution," Goddard said, the defective line of the Kallikak family would not have existed.

Dr. Walter E. Fernald of Massachusetts spoke for many eugenicists when he wrote in a journal article that "institutional segregation of uncared-for feeble-minded persons . . . during the child-bearing period is probably the most potent plan for reducing the number of feeble-minded in succeeding generations." Goddard insisted that the most important thing was to get to the unfit while they were young. "Determine the fact of their defectiveness as early as possible, and place them in colonies under the care and management of intelligent people who understand the problem," he advised. "Train them, make them happy; make them as useful as possible, but above all, bring them up with good habits and keep them from ever marrying or becoming parents."

There was an obvious problem with the segregation model: cost. Locking people up for their entire reproductive cycle imposed a large burden on state taxpayers. The public might support a few colonies for the feebleminded, but it was unlikely they could be persuaded to pay to warehouse the number of people the eugenicists believed had to be locked away.

Supporters of segregation struggled to find ways to make the economics work. Goddard argued that if large numbers of the unfit were "colonized," many almshouses and jails could close, and the savings spent on more colonies. He also urged colonies to find ways to exploit child labor. If "feeble-minded children were early selected and carefully trained," he said, "they would become more or less self-supporting in their institutions, so that the expense of their maintenance would be greatly reduced." Even with all of Goddard's enterprising ideas, many eugenicists were convinced that "segregation and colonization" could not be done on a large enough scale to solve the problem posed by the unfit.

While eugenicists were desperately looking for a method of carrying out their program, new options were emerging—alternatives to barbaric castration, ineffective marriage laws, and expensive segregation—and they were coming from medical science. In 1899 Dr. Albert J. Ochsner, a surgeon at St. Mary's Hospital and Augustana Hospital in Chicago, published a paper, "Surgical Treatment of Habitual Criminals," in the *Journal of the American Medical Association*. He described a new procedure that rendered a man sterile by severing his vas deferens—what came to be known as a vasectomy. Unlike castration, it was not disfiguring and did not upset a man's hormonal balance. Dr. Ochsner advocated that the procedure be used to prevent criminals from passing on their hereditary defects.

Inspired by this work, Dr. Harry C. Sharp, a surgeon at the Indiana Reformatory, began performing vasectomies on inmates. In 1909 Dr. Sharp published "Vasectomy as a Means of Preventing Procreation in Defectives." He revealed that he had performed sterilizations on forty-two inmates under the age of twenty-six, and argued that many more such procedures were needed. Dr. Sharp called for sterilizations to be conducted in every "almshouse, insane asylum, institute for the feeble-minded, reformatory or prison," and he urged doctors to lobby their state legislatures to allow these institutions "to render every male sterile who passes its portals."

While medical researchers were perfecting the vasectomy, they were also making advances in sterilizing women. A German surgeon, Dr. M. Madlener, developed the salpingectomy, a procedure in which the fallopian tubes are cut and partially removed so a woman's eggs cannot travel from the ovary to the uterus to be fertilized. Early salpingectomies were far from safe. Of the eighty-nine operations Madlener performed from 1910 to 1920, three ended in fatalities. As they were done more frequently the mortality rate declined, but they remained major abdominal surgery.

As these new procedures became available, eugenicists had a new cause: laws mandating sterilization of people with hereditary defects. Eugenic sterilization had all of the advantages that previous techniques lacked: it was a modern medical procedure that was far less barbaric than castration; it was completely effective when done correctly; and it was relatively inexpensive—one procedure rendered a person infertile for life.

Eugenics supporters began to lobby for involuntary sterilization laws at the state level. Given its underlying values, it is not surprising that the eugenic sterilization campaign never became a mass movement. As the historian Carl Degler observed, eugenics was a "necessarily elitist" ideology, which was an impediment to building a truly grassroots movement. The drive for eugenic sterilization laws came largely from societal elites who had an outsize impact on public policy. One leading eugenics group conceded in a report that there were not great numbers of people across the country who were committed to the sterilization cause. The pressure, it said, came from a "very small energetic group of enthusiasts, who have . . . influence in the legislatures."

The most important elite advocating eugenic sterilization was the medical establishment. Major medical journals ran articles by prominent academics that endorsed sterilization, often in fiery terms. The normally staid *Journal of the American Medical Association* took an apocalyptic turn when Dr. William T. Belfield, a professor of surgery at Rush Medical College, took to its pages in 1908 to advocate sterilization laws. The title of his article, which urgently called for sterilizing criminals and mental defectives, was "Race Suicide for Social Parasites."

The medical establishment not only spoke out in favor of eugenic sterilization but did so with near unanimity. No prominent medical professors or surgeons publicly opposed the sterilization movement—or if they did, they were not being heard. One survey found that every article on the subject of eugenic sterilization published in a medical journal between 1899 and 1912 endorsed the practice.

One part of the medical establishment was particularly strong in its support for eugenic sterilization: doctors in state institutions for the feebleminded. The leaders and medical staff of these institutions, which had been founded with therapeutic care in mind, were rapidly joining the eugenics movement and coming to see sterilization as the most practical method of achieving its goals. At a meeting of the Association of American Institutions for the Feeble-Minded in 1905, Dr. S. D. Risley spoke for many in his field when he insisted that sterilization was the only way to save the nation from "the slough of degeneration."

Scientists were another group drawn to eugenic sterilization, and they were active in supporting it. Harry Laughlin, the most influential eugenic sterilization advocate, was a scientist, with a doctoral degree in biology from Princeton. The most prominent organization that promoted eugenic sterilization in the early days of the movement, the American Breeders' Association's Committee on Eugenics, had distinguished scientists as members, including its chairman, David Starr Jordan, an ichthyologist who was the first president of Stanford University.

Reformers and charity workers were among the biggest proponents of eugenic sterilization. Isabel Barrows, a prominent advocate for the mentally disabled, talked of the need for laws that would "as far as possible prevent the birth and reproduction of these imperfect creatures." Josephine Shaw Lowell, who helped found New York's Custodial Asylum for Feeble-Minded Women in 1878, was even more blunt. "Promiscuous and criminalistic" women carried a "deadly poison," she warned. Charitable institutions put society at risk when they allowed "men and women who are diseased and vicious to reproduce their kind."

There was no strong, national movement opposing eugenic sterilization. The group that was most organized in its opposition was the Catholic Church. The church had not yet issued an encyclical against eugenic sterilization—that would come in 1930, with Pope Pius XI's *Casti connubii* (On Christian Marriage). Even so, many Catholics believed sterilization violated natural law connecting sex to procreation, and they mobilized against sterilization laws. In many states with large Catholic populations, including Massachusetts and Louisiana, the church's opposition played a crucial role. Politicians in these states, one observer noted, "knew they faced political suicide by backing eugenic statutes."

In Louisiana, where half the voters were Catholic, reformers and public health leaders repeatedly backed sterilization bills, but without success. The New Orleans archbishop mobilized statewide opposition to what he called "unnatural legislation." One legislator, a grand knight in the Knights of Columbus, the Catholic fraternal organization, denounced eugenic sterilization, saying, "God created these poor unfortunates just the same as he did legislators."

The rest of the opposition to eugenic sterilization was more scattershot and did not fall into neat categories. Oregon had an Anti-Sterilization League, led by a woman who was hostile to the medical profession after the death of her young son. In other states, the primary obstacle to enacting sterilization laws was a general belief, on the part of legislators and the public, that eugenic sterilization was morally wrong or deeply distasteful. Many opponents agreed with the federal judge who struck down Iowa's sterilization law, saying it was fraught with "humiliation" and "degradation" and "mental suffering" that "belong[ed] to the Dark Ages."

There were a significant number of lawsuits around the country challenging sterilization laws—many successfully—but they did not necessarily represent grassroots opposition. New Jersey's eugenic sterilization law was struck down when it was challenged by a lawyer appointed to represent an epileptic woman who was to be sterilized. New York's law was challenged in a test case brought in large part to resolve a dispute among state officials who disagreed about sterilization.

Even with influential forces in favor of eugenic sterilization, and relatively little organized opposition, state legislatures did not rush to enact legislation—at least, not right away. In 1897 the Michigan legislature considered a bill introduced under the name "An Act for the Prevention of Idiocy." It authorized the state to castrate criminals and "perverts." Support for sterilization was not strong in Michigan, and the bill ran into opposition from lawyers who said it was unconstitutional. The legislature declined to pass it, and it would be another sixteen years before Michigan adopted a eugenic sterilization law.

In 1905 a sterilization bill was introduced in Pennsylvania. One of its main advocates was Dr. Martin Barr, the chief physician of the Pennsylvania Training School for Feeble-Minded Children. Dr. Barr had been an outspoken supporter of Dr. Pilcher, who had been performing castrations at the Kansas State Asylum. Dr. Barr argued in a scientific journal that an advantage of castrating inmates was that "some nice male soprano voices could be obtained for the institutional choir." The Act for the Prevention of Idiocy provided that if a state institution for the feebleminded believed it was "inadvisable" for some of its inmates to reproduce, it could "perform such operation for the prevention of procreation as shall be decided safest and most effective." Pennsylvania's legislature passed the bill, becoming the first legislature in the nation to support eugenic sterilization.

Governor Samuel Pennypacker, however, refused to sign it. Pennypacker used his veto message to deliver a stern rebuke to the eugenic sterilization movement. "It is plain that the safest and most effective method of preventing procreation would be to cut off the heads of the inmates," he said, "and such authority is given by the bill." The legislature failed to realize, Pennypacker said, that "scientists, like all other men whose experiences have been limited to one pursuit . . . sometimes need to be restrained." The fundamental problem with the bill, he said, was simple: it would "inflict cruelty upon a helpless class in the community, which the State has undertaken to protect."

With his veto, Pennypacker—a progressive reformer and an opponent of child labor—became one of the most prominent figures in any field to stand up to the eugenics movement. Despite his serious concerns, Pennypacker was able to keep a sense of humor. Toward the end of his term, when he was addressing a loud and unruly gathering of reporters, he raised his arms to ask for silence and declared: "Gentlemen, Gentlemen! You forget you owe me a vote of thanks. Didn't I veto the bill for the castration of idiots?"

It was not long before the tide began to turn. In Indiana, Dr. Sharp, who was sterilizing inmates at the state reformatory, was strongly lobbying the legislature to legalize eugenic sterilization. With his support, a bill was introduced aimed at "confirmed criminals, idiots, rapists, and imbeciles." Under the bill, state institutions would be allowed to sterilize inmates who were medically certified as having "no probability of improvement."

To help make the case to the legislature, Dr. Sharp submitted testimonials from the young men he had operated on, attesting that the procedure could be beneficial for those who were sterilized. This time, the eugenicists prevailed: the legislature passed the bill and the governor signed it. In 1907 Indiana became the first state in the nation to legalize compulsory eugenic sterilization.

Other states soon followed. In 1909 California enacted a sweeping sterilization law. Once again, a doctor with expertise in the field played a key role. Dr. F. W. Hatch, secretary of the State Lunacy Commission, helped draft the California statute, which authorized prisons and state hospitals to carry out sterilizations. People eligible for the procedure included mental defectives, criminals, "moral degenerates," and "sexual perverts."

In Oregon, another doctor, Bethenia Owens-Adair, one of the first female physicians in the West, was the driving force behind eugenic sterilization. With backing from other doctors in the state, Dr. Owens-Adair promoted a bill to allow sterilization of criminals, epileptics, the insane, and the feebleminded. She succeeded in getting a bill through the legislature in 1909, but not in persuading the governor to sign it. Although she failed in her home state, Dr. Owens-Adair, who has been called eugenic sterilization's "pioneer advocate in the Pacific Northwest," was influential in getting a similar law enacted the same year in neighboring Washington State. Eight years later, she would succeed in Oregon as well.

More states adopted sterilization over the next few years until, by 1913, the first legislative wave was complete. At that point, twelve states—Indiana, Washington, California, Connecticut, Nevada, Iowa, New Jersey, New York, North Dakota, Michigan, Kansas, and

Wisconsin—had enacted sterilization laws. The laws varied in who could be sterilized, and in what processes had to be followed. Some were especially broad. Iowa allowed sterilization of "criminals, rapists, idiots, feeble-minded, imbeciles, lunatics, drunkards, drug-fiends, epileptics, syphilitics, moral and sexual perverts, and diseased and degenerate persons." Kansas's law made it a crime for the managing officer of any state institution to fail to recommend sterilization for any inmate who was deemed unfit to procreate. A supervisor who neglected to have someone sterilized who was covered by the law could be imprisoned for up to thirty days. Taken together, these new sterilization laws established a legal regime of eugenic sterilization that covered a significant portion of the country.

The first wave of sterilization laws did not reach Virginia or any states in the Deep South. Eugenics was promoted largely by progressives, intellectuals, and professionals, and in the South of that era all of these were in comparatively short supply. H. L. Mencken exaggerated outrageously in his famous 1917 essay "The Sahara of the Bozart," in which he called the American South "almost as sterile, artistically, intellectually, culturally as the Sahara Desert." Nevertheless, it was true that the South trailed the nation by many measures, particularly in the sciences. In the 1910s and 1920s, not a single university in the Deep South offered a Ph.D. in chemistry.

When eugenics did gain traction in the South, it largely began in the Upper South, in states like Virginia and North Carolina, which were most exposed to influences from the North. The strongest support came from these states' most progressive sectors: medical doctors, university professors, and reform-minded lawyers. Many members of these groups followed developments outside of the South closely, and they were "anxious for their region to 'catch up with' the more enlightened North and West"—and to prove critics like Mencken wrong.

In Virginia, one of the main centers of eugenic thought was the University of Virginia. In 1903 it hired a new president, Edwin Anderson Alderman, a leading progressive educator. He modernized the medical faculty, bringing in experts in genetics, many of them eugenicists. Under Alderman, the historian Gregory Michael Dorr has observed, the university became "an epicenter of eugenical thought, closely linked with the national eugenics movement . . . and tied to the state mental health professionals who promoted eugenic sterilization."

Among the most prominent of the University of Virginia eugenicists was Harvey Ernest Jordan, who would go on to become dean of the medical school. Jordan, who had extensive ties to eugenics groups nationwide, helped organize Virginia scientists and laypeople to promote eugenic policies, including sterilization. Forced sterilization was, Jordan believed, necessary "for the protection of society against distressing economic and moral burdens and racial decay."

Ivey Foreman Lewis, a professor of biology who rose to become a top university administrator, was one of the nation's most influential eugenics educators. Starting in 1915, he taught generations of Virginians biological science from a eugenic perspective. In his course Biology C1: Evolution and Heredity, Lewis lectured his students: "In the 20th century an abundance of experimental evidence proves that the large part ascribed to environment was mostly imaginary and that the capacity and natural bent of an individual are due to heredity."

Not surprisingly, "scientific racism" was a central part of the university's eugenics instruction. Lewis, who admired Madison Grant and Lothrop Stoddard, was outspoken on the issue of immigration. The idea of the melting pot was "simply and perilously false," he said, and the nation's openness to foreigners was endangering the "purity of the white race." In some parts of the university, the racial "science" was cruder. Robert Bennett Bean, who came to the school as an anatomy professor in 1916, researched the biology of race and propounded the idea that differences in brain size made whites and blacks "fundamentally opposite extremes in evolution."

The University of Virginia's eugenic teachings were influential because its graduates played such an important role in the state. Many served in the legislature and on the courts, and they carried their educations with them. One alumnus, Lemuel Smith of Charlottesville, voted for both the sterilization and racial purity laws as a state legislator; thirty years later, as a justice on the state's highest court, he voted to annul a "miscegeneous" marriage between a white woman and a Chinese man.

The university's faculty became an important force in support of eugenics in the state, the nation, and even the world. Harvey Ernest Jordan attended the First International Eugenics Congress in London in 1912 and presented a paper, "The Place of Eugenics in the Medical Curriculum." Robert Bennett Bean would become a national leader in racist eugenics, inspiring generations of white supremacist scientists with his research on subjects like, as the title of one of his papers expressed it, "Some Racial Peculiarities of the Negro Brain."

Another center of support for eugenics in Virginia, as in other states, was the charitable community. In Virginia, the leader in this sector was Joseph Mastin, a Methodist minister who headed the state's Board of Charities and Corrections. The legislature created the board in 1908 to be Virginia's first government-funded social welfare system. When Mastin was appointed, he made clear he was interested not only in helping Virginia's disadvantaged but also in using biological tools to reduce their number.

One of Mastin's first acts in office was to survey the scope of the "problem." He enlisted doctors across the state to help him determine the number of "epileptics, idiots, feeble-minded, and cripple children." Mastin issued reports that emphasized the size of this population, and he used his platform to argue that these disabilities had hereditary origins. "The child of normal parents may be feeble-minded, but it is impossible for the children of feeble-minded to be mentally normal," he wrote.

Mastin propounded the common eugenic refrain about the "differential fecundity" of the feebleminded: they reproduced at a dangerous rate, he advised in one report—"about twice as rapidly as normal stock." Mastin called on Virginia to protect itself from what he saw as a looming threat. He advocated a law barring the feebleminded from

marrying, as well as broader, unspecified legislation "for the prevention of the procreation of the feeble-minded."

Doctors were another sector of Virginia society that—as in other
parts of the country—was particularly drawn to eugenics. In the early
1900s, physicians from across the state took to the pages of the *Virginia Medical Semi-Monthly* to argue that "defectives" should be barred
from marrying. Dr. A. Einer, from Rural Retreat, a small town in the
southwest part of the state, made the case in a 1905 article, "Medical
Supervision of Matrimony." He called on the state to create panels of
doctors to conduct eugenic examinations of couples before they were
granted marriage licenses. It was the only way, Dr. Einer insisted, to
prevent unions that would produce "diseased and degenerate progeny"
who would lead to "national degeneration."

Other Virginia doctors went further, arguing in favor of eugenic
sterilization. Dr. H. W. Dew of Lynchburg was alarmed by the growing ranks of "feeble-minded women" who were "notoriously immoral."
They were prone to give birth out of wedlock, he warned, citing one
feebleminded woman he said he knew who had "two illegitimate children by her own father." Dr. Dew called for a program of "sterilization
of the confirmed criminal and the mentally defective."

Dr. L. S. Foster of Richmond addressed a meeting of the Medical
Society of Virginia about the threat posed by defective members of
the population. Using case studies from state hospitals, he argued that
feeblemindedness, syphilis, and immorality all had a hereditary basis.
His answer was emphatic: "We must have a sterilization law."

Though there was as yet no law in Virginia authorizing eugenic
sterilizations, doctors in the state had already begun performing them.
The subjects were blacks and poor whites—people on the margins of
society with little ability to resist. In 1908 Dr. Charles Carrington, a
surgeon at the Virginia State Penitentiary in Richmond, told a National
Prison Association conference that he was "unreservedly of the opinion
that sterilization of our habitual criminals is a proper measure" and he
mentioned having sterilized two black men. Using the crude racial imagery of the time, Dr. Carrington described one of his unfortunate

subjects as "a debased little negro . . . a notoriously lusty, boastful Sod-omist and masturbator."

Another physician, Dr. Bernard Barrow, reported in the *Virginia Medical Semi-Monthly* in 1910 that he had sterilized five mentally de-ficient black men. Dr. Barrow was blunt about the role his racist views played in his decisions to sterilize. "The negro" was "a savage race" that could not solve its own "social and sanitary problems," he said. The responsibility lay with "the stronger race—the white man." Dr. Barrow got around the absence of a law authorizing sterilization by asserting, improbable though it was, that the men had agreed to the procedure. He underscored that claim in the title of his article: "Vasectomy for the Defective Negro with His Consent."

During the first national wave of sterilization laws, there was an effort in Virginia to get a law passed. In 1909 Dr. Carrington told a meeting of the Medical Society of Virginia that he intended to push the legislature to adopt a eugenic sterilization statute. A few months after Dr. Carrington's presentation, the Virginia legislature was con-sidering a bill he had drawn up, based on the Indiana law, "to prevent procreation by confirmed criminals, idiots, imbeciles, and rapists."

The Medical Society of Virginia endorsed the bill, and Dr. Carrington personally lobbied for it, offering his scientific expertise to legislators who knew little about the subject. Dr. Carrington's bill failed, however, in the House of Delegates. The *Virginia Medical Semi-Monthly* reported that it ran into "much blind sentiment" in the lower house, among delegates who did not understand the issue. Dr. Car-rington's bill was not introduced again.

The next push for a eugenic sterilization law in Virginia came from a group that had been active in campaigns in other states: the superin-tendents of the state mental hospitals. Dr. Priddy, the superintendent of the Colony for Epileptics and Feeble-Minded, was a prominent member of the group of Virginia superintendents who emerged to pro-mote eugenic sterilization—but he was not the first.

That distinction belonged to Dr. Joseph S. DeJarnette, the super-intendent of Western State Hospital. Dr. DeJarnette came from a family whose Virginia roots traced back to colonial times. His father was a Confederate army captain, and he had an uncle who served in both the United States House of Representatives and its Confederate counterpart. His mother was a writer whose stories appeared in popular magazines, many of them written in a version of "Negro dialect." Dr. DeJarnette had no doubt that his own high station in life was due, in large part, to what he considered to be his exalted lineage.

Dr. DeJarnette graduated from the Medical College of Virginia in 1888 and then worked for a year at the Robert E. Lee Camp Confederate Soldiers' Home, a retirement home and poorhouse for Civil War veterans. He then joined the staff of the Western Lunatic Asylum, which would later be renamed Western State Hospital, and quickly took to the work of ministering to the "lunatics," developing a particular interest in the intersection of mental illness and criminality. A large and imposing man, Dr. DeJarnette was a stern authority figure at the asylum. He was also a moralist who opposed the use of alcohol. When he rose to superintendent, Dr. DeJarnette was a force for modernization and reform. He phased out the use of physical restraints and constantly sought out more modern approaches to therapy.

Like many mental health reformers of his time, Dr. DeJarnette was drawn to the promise of eugenics. Writing in his hospital's annual report in 1908, he argued that it was important for Virginia's future to get rid of the "defectives and weaklings." He urged the state legislature to enact a eugenic marriage law, as Connecticut and other states had.

In the same annual report, he advocated eugenic sterilization. Dr. DeJarnette was the first state hospital superintendent in Virginia to endorse it, and he would later claim to have been the first person in Virginia to publicly call for it. He compared sterilization laws with laws against spitting that were passed to prevent the spread of tuberculosis—which had also once been ridiculed, but came to be widely accepted. As a doctor, he insisted that the case for sterilization was simple: "In the treatment of all diseases, it is an established fact that prevention is far better than cure."

Dr. DeJarnette became an outspoken advocate for eugenic sterilization legislation. He lectured to medical associations, spoke to elected officials and political groups, and made efforts to educate the general public. In his hospital's 1911 annual report, he repeated his call for eugenic sterilization in even more emphatic terms: "Sterilization of all weaklings should be legally required," he wrote.

To make his case, Dr. DeJarnette even composed a pro-sterilization poem. He was enormously proud of "Mendel's Law: A Plea for a Better Race of Men," which he published in the *Virginia Medical Monthly* on three separate occasions. In it, Dr. DeJarnette urged:

> Oh, you wise men, take up the burden
> And make this your loudest creed,
> Sterilize the misfits promptly—
> All not fit to breed.

Dr. DeJarnette may have been the first Virginia superintendent to endorse eugenic sterilization, but it was Dr. Priddy, the superintendent of the Colony for Epileptics and Feeble-Minded, who ended up leading the campaign for it. Dr. Priddy would work with Dr. DeJarnette to get Virginia to enact a sterilization law, and then Dr. Priddy became the driving force behind the legal campaign to defend the law. There was no cause in his life that Dr. Priddy fought for more passionately—and he would pursue it, quite literally, until his dying breath.

Three

Albert Priddy

In his first annual report as superintendent of the Colony for Epileptics, as it was then called, Dr. Albert Priddy enthusiastically endorsed the eugenics movement. In the report—the colony's official annual statement to government officials, the medical profession, and the public at large—he was blunt about why he supported eugenics. He saw it as the best way to rid the world of the sort of patients he spent all of his days ministering to. Epileptics were, Dr. Priddy declared, among "the most pitiful, helpless, and troublesome of human beings." Of all the known causes of epilepsy, he said, "that of bad heredity is the most potent." He recommended marriage restrictions on epileptics to prevent them from increasing their kind.

The next year, Dr. Priddy went further and used his annual report to endorse eugenic sterilization. He warned of an impending rapid increase in "epileptics and mental defectives." It was time, he said, "to call the attention of our lawmakers to the consideration of legalized eugenics for the prevention of this growing blight on [Virginia's] population." Dr. Priddy once again urged restricting marriages of epileptics—as well as of the insane, the feebleminded, and "confirmed alcoholics." This time, however, he also suggested permitting sterilization of inmates "in such cases as it is deemed proper."

Dr. Priddy returned frequently to the subject of eugenics. In his 1915 annual report, he warned that without "radical measures . . . to curb" the feebleminded from reproducing it would "be only a matter of time before the resulting pauperism and criminality" would "be a burden too heavy . . . to bear." Until the state sterilized defective people, Dr. Priddy saw institutionalization as important to protect society. In a 1916 letter, he argued that segregating epileptics could prevent reproduction by "these afflicted and troublesome burdens on our population."

As much as Dr. Priddy supported segregation of defective people, he believed it was not an adequate response to the threat they posed. There were not enough institutions in Virginia to hold them all, in his view—and it was not likely there ever would be. Without a "great increase in tax rate," he said, the state could not afford to institutionalize all the "anti-social women and girls" in the state who were likely to produce defective children.

Dr. Priddy argued for a combination of segregation and sterilization, which he called the "clearing house" model. In this approach, young women with hereditary defects would be identified and sent to institutions like the colony. When they arrived, they would be given "educational, industrial and moral training." Once they were properly instructed, the young women would be sterilized and then safely released into society again. By sterilizing and releasing many women, rather than holding a few women until their reproductive cycle ended, Dr. Priddy argued, his model would lead to many more women being sterilized, relieving the state of an "enormous financial burden."

There was a third superintendent who joined in Dr. Priddy and Dr. DeJarnette's campaign. Dr. William F. Drewry, who ran the Central State Hospital for Negroes in Petersburg, publicly endorsed sterilization in 1912. Dr. Drewry, who was white, added a racial element to the discussion, by focusing on what he regarded as the particular threat posed by feebleminded black people. He warned that feebleminded blacks were increasing in numbers and that "the presence of such individuals is a perpetual menace, a constant source of trouble and danger." Dr. Drewry believed the answer lay in preventing the feebleminded from reproducing "by the relentless hand of science, under sanction and authority of law."

Like other doctors across the country, Dr. Priddy appears to have sterilized people before it was authorized by law. In his first few years at the colony, he began performing procedures that were, as the legal historian Paul Lombardo has argued, almost certainly eugenic sterilizations, even though they were not described that way. In his 1915 annual report, Dr. Priddy said the colony had performed an operation on a young woman "for relief of a chronic pelvic disorder, which sterilized her." The woman was then permanently discharged from the colony. In the next few years, an extraordinary number of women at the colony were diagnosed with vague "pelvic diseases" and ended up being sterilized.

In 1916 Dr. Priddy and Dr. DeJarnette began a campaign to persuade the state legislature to enact a eugenic sterilization law. They had missed the first national wave, which peaked in 1913, when six state legislatures adopted sterilization statutes, four of which were signed into law. Now, however—six years after Dr. Carrington's bill failed— there was growing support in Virginia, particularly at the University of Virginia and among administrators of the state's mental hospitals. Dr. DeJarnette and Dr. Priddy approached a state senator they believed would be sympathetic and asked if he would draft a bill.

The state senator, Aubrey Strode, was a friend of Dr. Priddy's who had been pivotal in founding the colony. He drafted a bill, but it was not the kind of bold eugenic sterilization law other states had passed. Strode's bill, which became law, did not directly authorize sterilization or mention eugenics. Instead, it gave superintendents of state hospitals for the feebleminded authority to provide inmates "such moral, medical and surgical treatment" as they deemed "proper."

The "moral, medical and surgical treatment" language in Strode's law was vague, but it left superintendents room to claim that any sterilization they performed was authorized. Dr. Priddy was quick to do just that, asserting that "a logical and plain construction" of the newly enacted statute permitted him to sterilize feebleminded inmates at the colony. His reading was, as even Dr. DeJarnette conceded, a "broad and liberal interpretation" of the law.

When the 1916 law took effect, Dr. Priddy began openly performing sterilizations. In his next annual report, he made reference to a group of feebleminded women who had been sterilized. They had been released, he said, and were almost without exception doing well in the outside world.

The next year, Dr. Priddy sterilized thirty women, and he offered up the same excuse. "We have continued the policy of sterilizing young women and girls of the moron type," he reported. "In nearly all cases sterilized, the pelvic disease was found in a greater or lesser degree, such as to make the removal of the tubes necessary for the relief of physical suffering."

Colony records suggested another reason for the sterilizations. Dr. Priddy described most of the women as "feebleminded," but he generally also included a reference to their being overly sexual. They were "immoral," "over-sexed," or "man-crazy," in his words—and he made references to their purported histories of prostitution or promiscuity. The women's clinical diagnoses included such conditions as "sexual degeneracy" and "nymphomania." These were traits, Dr. Priddy believed, that had to be eugenically removed from the population.

It was only a matter of time before Dr. Priddy's aggressive program of sterilization under the vague authority of the new law got him into trouble. The source of the trouble was Willie Mallory, a thirty-eight-year-old mother of nine. Willie had come to the colony after being arrested at home in Richmond and charged with running a house of prostitution. The Mallorys had experienced setbacks over the years, but at the time of her arrest, her husband, George, was working at a sawmill, and Willie had a factory job. Willie was also generally acknowledged to be a good mother. When she was arrested, she had a baby in her arms.

Willie's arrest led to her being brought before a Commission of Feeblemindedness with two of her daughters, Jessie and Nannie. Willie would later testify that the hearing was anything but scientific. The doctor who examined her asked "foolish" questions, she said, such as whether she could tell if there was salt in bread and if she knew how to tie her shoes. When Willie was found to be feebleminded, she insisted that the hearing was rigged.

The Commission of Feeblemindedness ordered that Willie and her daughters be sent to the colony. Willie escaped and went back home to take care of her children. The police found her in Richmond and brought her back to the colony. About six months after she arrived, Dr. Priddy sterilized Willie and her daughter Jessie. The colony released them, but Dr. Priddy imposed a particularly cruel condition on their freedom. Neither could return to live with her family. Willie had to stay with her eldest daughter, Bessie, who lived with her own family more than twenty miles outside Richmond. Jessie went to live with Mrs. J. W. Murphy, who was even farther away.

Dr. Priddy had sterilized about eighty inmates with no resistance, but Willie Mallory was different. In November 1917 she sued him for "wrongful and illegal assaults, and batteries." Specifically, she charged that Dr. Priddy placed her "under ether, or other anesthetic," and then performed an operation "sterilizing her, and unsexing her, and destroying her power to bear children." It caused Willie "great physical and mental pain," the suit said. She also filed a motion to have Nannie discharged from the colony and returned to her family.

Dr. Priddy mounted a spirited defense. He claimed, as usual, that he had operated not to sterilize, but to treat unrelated medical problems. From his examination of Willie, he said, "it was determined that an operation was not only desirable, but absolutely necessary." Dr. Priddy did not give any details about Willie's condition or why she had to be sterilized. He insisted, however, that the 1916 law authorized him to operate. Dr. Priddy also claimed that Willie had consented— that the procedure was explained to her and she "expressed not only a willingness, but a desire to have the operation performed."

While the parties awaited a verdict, Willie's husband wrote to Dr. Priddy, demanding Nannie's release. George Mallory said he feared she would be the next Mallory woman sterilized. "I want to know when I can get my child home again," he wrote. "She is not feeble minded." He ended with a threat. "I have told you not to" operate "on my child," he told Dr. Priddy, and warned there would be "trouble" if he did.

Dr. Priddy was neither intimidated by George Mallory's threats nor moved by his plea for his daughter. He responded with a letter full of self-confidence and condescension. Willie and Jessie had been sterilized, he said, "because they asked me to do so and it was done for diseases they had." He warned George that if he sent another letter like his last one "I will have you arrested."

Even with the new authority in the 1916 law, Dr. Priddy was on uncertain legal ground. Courts were beginning to recognize the importance of patient consent, and they were increasingly ruling against doctors who operated without it. In 1914 New York's highest court had issued an influential ruling that supported Willie. In *Schloendorff v. Society of New York Hospital,* the eminent judge Benjamin Cardozo had declared that a "surgeon who performs an operation without his patient's consent commits an assault, for which he is liable in damages."

Despite the rise of informed consent, Dr. Priddy prevailed in the lawsuit. The jury, which delivered its verdict in March 1918, accepted the defense's argument that Dr. Priddy had acted within his medical discretion. It was, however, far from a complete victory. The judge warned Dr. Priddy not to sterilize any more inmates until the law changed.

Willie's lawsuit had a significant impact on sterilization in Virginia. After the judge's warning, it was clear the 1916 law would not protect state hospitals that sterilized inmates. Superintendents were now on notice that if an inmate sued they could be held personally liable for damages. The Mallory case "frightened all the superintendents in the State," Dr. DeJarnette later recalled, "and all sterilization was stopped promptly."

D r. Priddy was unsettled by his near loss in the Mallory lawsuit. It made him more intent than ever on getting Virginia to enact a law that would give him and his fellow superintendents legal authority to perform sterilizations. There was reason to believe such a bill might now have a good chance. The eugenic sterilization movement had been gaining strength across the country. By 1920, thirteen years had passed since Indiana enacted the nation's first eugenic sterilization statute, and about a third of the states had adopted such laws. The movement had even made inroads in the South. In 1919, North Carolina and Alabama had become the first southern states to enact eugenic steril- ization laws.

Dr. Priddy and Dr. DeJarnette had a eugenic sterilization bill drawn up and introduced in the legislature. The members of the Virginia leg- islature, however, were not ready for it. When the bill was introduced, it was "was laughed out of committee," Dr. DeJarnette later recalled. One of the reasons for the laughter was the legislators' concern over who would be sterilized. "They might get all of us," the lawmakers joked.

If Dr. Priddy could not get Virginia to enact a eugenic sterilization law—and for now, it was clear he could not—he wanted some kind of legislation to protect him from lawsuits like the Mallorys'. He went to Aubrey Strode, who was now out of the legislature, and asked him, working as a private lawyer, to draft bills that would protect state hos- pitals and superintendents.

Strode wrote two bills for the 1920 legislative session. One required inmates challenging their detention to sue in the county in which they were being held. Willie had been able to sue in Richmond, which meant Dr. Priddy had to travel from the colony for the lawsuit and defend himself on her home turf. The bill, which became law, would mean that lawsuits by prisoners seeking to be released would be tried before judges in the same community as the state hospital—judges who were presumably well known to the superintendents and their lawyers.

Strode's second bill decreed that all inmates who were sent to a state hospital by either a court or a commission were "lawfully committed." Dr. Priddy and his fellow superintendents were worried about having to defend against more lawsuits like Nannie Mallory's, challenging their confinement. With a single law, the legislature acted to block such suits.

Dr. Priddy and Dr. DeJarnette did not give up on their hopes for a eugenic sterilization law. In 1921 Dr. Priddy went back to Strode, in his capacity as attorney for the colony. Dr. Priddy told Strode that the State Hospital Board, which supervised all five of Virginia's mental hospitals, wanted his advice on the possibility of enacting a law authorizing eugenic sterilization.

Strode agreed to investigate the matter. He researched the law of eugenic sterilization in other states. In every case he could find where such a law had been challenged in court it had been struck down on equal protection, due process, or other constitutional grounds. Strode thought it was likely that if Virginia passed a sterilization law, it too would be invalidated. Strode also mentioned that he had been in the legislature when it voted down Dr. Carrington's sterilization bill. It had been rejected, Strode advised, because of "public sentiment" against eugenic sterilization.

In advising the board not to pursue a eugenic sterilization law, Strode may simply have been doing his job, urging his client not to try to enact a law that would likely not win the support of the legislature—and, if it did, would only be struck down by the courts. Strode's advice may also, however, have indicated his own lack of enthusiasm for eugenic sterilization. Had he been a true believer, as Dr. Priddy and Dr. DeJarnette were, he might have considered it worth the risk. After his discouraging legal assessment, Strode recalled later, the board "for the time dropped the matter so far as I know."

Dr. Priddy continued to use the colony annual reports to argue for a sterilization law. Reflecting Strode's words of caution, he said that any new law would have to be carefully drawn, but he insisted that for some mentally defective women sterilization was the "only solution of the problem." He reported that a bill was being prepared for the next legislative session. "It is to be hoped that with the best legal talent to draft such a bill," he wrote, it will be written with the appropriate "constitutional limits," and it will be "enacted into a law." He noted that the governor supported the law, and the State Board of Public Welfare "has always favored it."

In the midst of his work to get a eugenic sterilization law enacted, Dr. Priddy married for the first time. In October 1923 the fifty-seven-year-old superintendent wed Mamie Hardy Mitchell of Alexandria, Louisiana. As it turned out, the marriage was destined to be short-lived, and—like a good number of the leading advocates for eugenic sterilization—Dr. Priddy would not have any children of his own.

On the eve of the 1924 legislative session, Dr. Priddy and Dr. DeJarnette "carried" their "troubles" to "A. E. Strode" once again, as Dr. DeJarnette later recalled. They told Strode that the State Hospital Board had asked that Strode draft a eugenic sterilization bill. The board believed that in the time since it last considered the matter, public understanding of heredity and eugenics had increased, and that changes in popular opinion made it more likely the legislature and the courts would now support such a law. The superintendents also said Governor Elbert Lee Trinkle supported a eugenic sterilization law and would sign a bill if the legislature passed it.

This time, Strode agreed to draft a bill, but once again some of his actions suggested he might not have been enthusiastic about eugenic sterilization. Strode researched eugenic sterilization laws in other states, and he consulted a legal treatise Dr. Priddy had given him, *Eugenical Sterilization in the United States,* by Harry Laughlin, the assistant director of the Eugenics Record Office in Cold Spring Harbor, New York. Laughlin's book included a "Model Eugenical Sterilization Law" to help states in drafting effective laws that would also survive legal challenge. Strode made a "diligent effort," he would later say, "to avoid the defects that have brought disapproval from the Courts" of other eugenic sterilization laws.

Strode's bill borrowed liberally from Laughlin's model law, but he narrowed its scope in significant ways. Strode included three of the categories of defect Laughlin had in his model: "hereditary forms of insanity," "feeble-mindedness," and "epilepsy"—and he added "imbecility" and "idiocy," which in the model law were simply covered by "feeblemindedness." Strode rejected several of the model law's "socially inadequate" categories: "blind (including those with seriously impaired vision)," "deaf (including those with seriously impaired hearing)," "deformed (including the crippled)," "criminalistic (including the delinquent and wayward)," "diseased (including the tuberculous, the syphilitic, the leprous, and others with chronic, infectious, and legally segregable diseases)," "inebriate (including drug habitués)," and "dependent (including orphans, ne'er-do-wells, the homeless, tramps and paupers)."

Strode's decision on what to include—and what to omit—was significant. Laughlin's model law sought to usher in an era of mass sterilization, in which anyone who was in any way "defective"—including people who were merely poor or who did not hear or see well—could be involuntarily operated on to prevent them from reproducing. Strode's bill made many fewer Virginians subject to eugenic sterilization.

Strode added another major limitation to his bill: it authorized sterilization only when the state could show it was in "the best interest of the patients." The eugenics movement generally did not concern itself with the interests of the people it wanted sterilized. Neither Laughlin's model statute nor any other sterilization law in the country had this condition. When Virginia's law was challenged, its defenders would boast that theirs was the only law limited to cases in which "the welfare of the patient will be promoted." This was a provision that could have created legal difficulties for Strode's clients, because it gave inmates a legal basis to challenge sterilization orders. But it may also have been an indication that Strode was concerned about the human costs of the eugenic sterilization program he was helping to bring about.

On one point, Strode followed Laughlin's advice closely: he put strong procedural protections into his bill in an attempt to protect it from constitutional challenges. Like Laughlin's model, Strode's bill created an expert body to make decisions about who should be sterilized. Laughlin vested this power in a state eugenicist, while Strode gave it to the people who were paying his bills—the boards of the state's mental hospitals. Following Laughlin's guidance, Strode provided that people facing sterilization had a right to a hearing and to be present at it. He also included, as Laughlin had, a right to appeal the decision to the local county court and as high as the U.S. Supreme Court.

Strode also limited his bill in one more important way. Laughlin's model statute applied to everyone in the state, whether they were inmates of a state hospital or not. Laughlin urged other states to draft their statutes in this way, for legal reasons. Eugenic sterilization laws had been struck down in three states—New York, New Jersey, and Michigan—as a violation of the equal protection clause of the Fourteenth Amendment because they applied only to hospital inmates, and not to people with the same conditions who were not confined to hospitals. Laughlin emphasized that it would be an enormous strategic mistake to draw up any new laws that applied only to inmates. In his treatise, Laughlin called writing a law that applied only to a narrow part of the population "the only great stumbling block" eugenic sterilization had met, and he instructed that "new laws must take great pains to avoid similar disaster."

Despite this emphatic warning, Strode did precisely what Laughlin advised him not to do: he drafted the Virginia law to apply only to inmates of the five Virginia hospitals for the feebleminded: Western State Hospital, Eastern State Hospital, Southwestern State Hospital, Central State Hospital for Negroes, and the Colony for Epileptics and Feeble-Minded. Strode, who was a highly skilled lawyer and had researched the issue extensively, knew that limiting the law in this way would make it vulnerable to an equal protection challenge.

The question is why he did it. It is possible that Strode was simply acting as an advocate for his clients. He represented the state hospitals, and he drafted a law to let them do all of the sterilizing. It would not help them, however, if the law he drafted were struck down as unconstitutional. Another possibility is that Strode did not believe the legislature would pass a law that applied to everyone in the state, but he thought it might accept his narrower version. But that was unlikely, given how little opposition there would prove to be in the legislature.

There are two more possibilities, which suggest degrees of reluctance on Strode's part about eugenic sterilization. One is that Strode thought a sterilization law that applied to the whole population of the state would go too far. He may not have been comfortable with making every Virginian eligible to be sterilized by the state. By limiting his bill to inmates of the state's five mental hospitals, Strode ensured that only a few thousand people would be eligible for eugenic sterilization, rather than millions.

A final, intriguing possibility is that Strode may not have supported eugenic sterilization, and might have intentionally written the law in a way that made it vulnerable to being struck down. Strode was the brother of six sisters, and a champion of women's rights. He was also someone who, as a member of the legislature, had not spoken out in favor of eugenic sterilization or introduced a bill of his own. In fact, on the day Dr. Carrington's eugenic sterilization bill came up for a vote, Strode was present in the legislature, and voted on thirty other bills. He was, however, apparently absent for the vote on the sterilization bill—hardly the act of a man who thought the state desperately needed eugenic sterilization to save itself from ruin.

If Strode was trying to undermine his own bill, he did one more unusual thing that could have helped to prevent it from ever taking effect. Strode strongly advised the State Hospital Board that if the eugenic sterilization bill passed, the state hospitals should not carry out any sterilizations until the law was tested in the courts—all the way up to the Supreme Court, if the case got that far. It was unusual advice: states generally act on laws once they are passed, rather than wait for them to be tested in the courts, perhaps for years. Strode might have given this advice out of an abundance of caution, or he might have wanted to give the law he was hired to draft every chance to fail.

Strode gave his bill—formally titled An Act to Provide for the Sexual Sterilization of Inmates of State Institutions in Certain Cases—to the chairman of the Senate Committee on Courts, Marshall Booker, to introduce in February 1924. Dr. Priddy and Dr. DeJarnette both testified in favor of it. Governor Trinkle also used his influence in the legislature in support of the bill.

Whether or not there was a change in popular opinion, as Dr. Priddy had said, there had clearly been a change in legislative opinion. Strode's bill became law on March 20, 1924, after passing the state senate unanimously, and the House of Delegates by a vote of 75–2. Dr. Priddy's and Dr. DeJarnette's years of persistence had paid off. "This proves Abraham Lincoln's theory that 'nothing is ever settled until it is settled right,'" Dr. DeJarnette would later say.

Even though eugenic sterilization was now the law in Virginia, no sterilizations were being scheduled. The State Hospital Board accepted Strode's advice, and it decided that none would be carried out until the law could be reviewed by the courts. Proceeding as Strode advised required that a challenge be brought to the new law's constitutionality. It was unlikely opponents of the law would emerge to do this on their own. There was no organized opposition in Virginia to eugenic sterilization, and there were no national advocacy groups working against such laws. Nor was there reason to expect any of the inmates in Virginia's state hospitals would be as assertive about their rights as the Mallorys had been. It would be up to the new law's supporters to put together a test case—and one that they could win.

Dr. Priddy became the architect of the case challenging the constitutionality of the law he had just worked years to enact. In taking on the assignment, he was thrusting himself onto a larger stage. When he began, Dr. Priddy was only seeking the legal authority to carry out sterilizations at his own institution without the risk of being sued. Now he was putting together a case that could go as far as the United

States Supreme Court. Dr. Priddy, who had been born in rural Lunen-burg County and educated in a four-room schoolhouse, might be help-ing to establish eugenic policy for the whole nation—and, given the role the United States played in setting eugenic policy, for the world.

True to his methodical nature, Dr. Priddy moved deliberately through a checklist of necessary steps. He began by obtaining the ap-proval of the colony's Special Board of Directors and the State Hospi-tal Board, and he persuaded the hospital board to finance the litigation. Dr. Priddy had to retain a lawyer, but there was no real doubt about who that would be. Strode had been critical to founding the colony, and he had done its legal work for years. Dr. Priddy and Strode were also friends of long standing. And Strode knew more about Virginia's sterilization law than anyone.

The next big task was choosing someone to sterilize and to put at the center of the case. Dr. Priddy and his allies had a large pool to choose from. The law applied to all inmates of the state's five mental hospitals who were afflicted with "hereditary forms of insanity that are recurrent, idiocy, imbecility, feeble-mindedness or epilepsy." Based on the statutory criteria, there were thousands who qualified.

It mattered a great deal, however, who was chosen. As Strode had explained, eugenic sterilization laws were meeting with considerable resistance in courts across the country, and it was far from certain that the Virginia law would survive. The law's supporters needed a subject who would make the best possible case for their side—someone a court would decide was well deserving of eugenic sterilization. Dr. Priddy had hundreds of his own inmates to choose from: male and female, young and old, epileptic and feebleminded.

It did not take him long, however, to set his sights on Carrie, who had been at the colony for less than two months. There were many reasons she was ideal. To begin with, she presented a strong record of feeblemindedness, and Dr. Priddy had the medical records to prove it. Carrie had been legally designated as feebleminded by a Commission of Feeblemindedness, after a hearing conducted by a judge and two doctors. The colony had then made its own assessment that Carrie was a moron. If called on to testify, Dr. Priddy could personally vouch for her mental defects.

Dr. Priddy also had what he believed was strong evidence of mental deficiency in her family. Not only had her mother been declared a moron, but his own staff had done the diagnosis, and again Dr. Priddy could personally testify to it. He also knew about eight more Bucks and Harlowes at the colony, all from Albemarle County, and more inmates with those names from nearby counties. Dr. Priddy was not certain of Carrie's relation to these people, but he believed they created a picture of a family with hereditary feeblemindedness.

As an unwed mother, Carrie also embodied the nightmare vision the eugenicists were promoting of feebleminded women—that they were oversexed and excessively fertile. Having already given birth once before the age of eighteen, the eugenicists could argue, there was no telling how many more feebleminded children she would bring into the world if she was not sterilized.

Carrie's youth was also an advantage. With so many childbearing years ahead of her, Carrie would have to be locked up at the colony for years if she was not sterilized. That would be costly for the taxpayers and it would be burdensome for Carrie, who would be denied her liberty far longer than a woman toward the end of her reproductive years.

After settling on Carrie for the test case, Dr. Priddy began taking the steps the law required to sterilize her. He petitioned the circuit court in Amherst County, the county in which the colony was located, to appoint a legal guardian. On July 21, 1924, the court named Robert G. Shelton, a local lawyer. Shelton was authorized to bring a challenge to the law on Carrie's behalf, and the court decreed that he be compensated at the rate of $5 a day, not to exceed a total of $15.

Shelton would prove to be Carrie's guardian in name only. The requirement that a guardian be appointed was supposed to ensure that an adult with full mental capacity would vigorously protect Carrie's interests in the upcoming proceedings, but that was not how it worked out. Shelton, who was likely well known to Dr. Priddy and Strode, became an active participant in the test case the two men were putting together. He would hire a good friend of Dr. Priddy and Strode's to represent Carrie, and he would stand by as Carrie's interests—her ability to have children and her bodily integrity—were sacrificed to the eugenic cause.

With the guardian appointed, the next step was for Dr. Priddy to formally request authorization to sterilize Carrie. The law required him to submit a petition to the colony's Special Board of Directors "stating the facts of the case and the grounds of his opinion" that sterilization was warranted. The board was then required to hold a hearing to receive testimony and consider evidence. The law specified that the inmate had to be given advance notice and had a right to be present.

On July 24, Dr. Priddy petitioned the colony's board for permission to perform a salpingectomy on Carrie. Tracking the language of the new law, he said he believed it was in society's interest and her interest that she "should be sexually sterilized, she being afflicted with feeble-mindedness." It was in society's interest because if she reproduced, "by reason of the laws of heredity" she would "in all probability . . . transmit to her offspring some form of mental defectiveness." It was in Carrie's interest because she could then be released to "enjoy the liberty and blessings of outdoor life." Dr. Priddy also said, without explaining how he knew it, that Carrie "desires" that the sterilization "be performed."

The colony's Special Board of Directors set a hearing for September 10, 1924. Carrie, her mother, and her guardian were notified of the date and time, as the law required, and invited to attend. The colony was scrupulous about following the law's procedural protections, which were designed to protect the rights of the person being considered for sterilization. There was only one problem: Carrie had no idea what was going on.

On September 10, the colony hosted Virginia's first eugenic sterilization hearing. The Special Board of Directors convened and sat in judgment. Dr. Priddy attended as petitioner, represented by his counsel, Strode. Carrie was present, accompanied by her guardian, Shelton.

The chairman of the colony's board swore in Dr. Priddy and the testimony began. Under questioning by Strode, Dr. Priddy recited his qualifications, including his years at Southwestern State Hospital. During his tenure as superintendent of the colony, he said, he had observed and treated more than six hundred mentally defective female inmates.

Strode quickly moved to the heart of the matter. What was it about Carrie Buck's situation, he asked Dr. Priddy, that led him to the "opinion that it would be better both for her and for society" if she were sterilized? Dr. Priddy said Carrie had been under his care and observation since she arrived at the colony on June 4. He had administered the Binet-Simon test, he said, and had "ascertained that she is feebleminded of the lowest grade Moron class." While her chronological age was eighteen, Dr. Priddy said, her mental age was just nine. Dr. Priddy also testified that Carrie was a "moral delinquent," apparently a reference to her having given birth out of wedlock.

Dr. Priddy's claim that Carrie had tested as "the lowest grade Moron class" was one of a number of false or misleading statements he made at the hearing. In the "History and Clinical Notes" he prepared when she arrived, Dr. Priddy stated that Carrie was a "Middle grade Moron," not the "lowest grade," as he now testified. He did not inform the board of his previous evaluation.

Dr. Priddy also failed to provide the board with information in the colony's records that contradicted the claim that Carrie was mentally defective. He did not mention that she had successfully reached the sixth grade, a fact that he had recorded in the "History and Clinical Notes" just a few months earlier, when Carrie arrived. Nor did he tell the board that Carrie's "practical knowledge and general information" were "about up to that of her class and opportunity," which he had also written in his notes on Carrie's arrival, before she was at the center of his test case.

As Strode continued his questioning, Dr. Priddy made his case that

Carrie belonged to a line of mentally and morally defective people. He testified that Carrie was, according to the sworn depositions that were part of her commitment papers, "of unknown paternity." He said that Carrie's mother, Emma, had been a "feebleminded patient" at the colony for several years, and "of low mental grade." And he told the board that "according to the depositions" that had been used in committing Carrie to the colony, she had "one illegitimate mentally defective child."

Once again, Dr. Priddy's testimony contained critical falsehoods. Saying that Carrie's paternity was "unknown" cast further aspersions on the family—but it was not true. The depositions of John and Alice Dobbs at the time of Carrie's commitment stated that Carrie's father was "Frank Buck." In his "History and Clinical Notes," Dr. Priddy had recorded on Carrie's admission that her father was "Frank Buck," who had been "accidentally killed." Dr. Priddy did not tell the board this, or explain why his account of her parentage had changed.

Dr. Priddy's testimony about Carrie's daughter, Vivian, was particularly egregious. By presenting her as feebleminded, it strengthened the colony's case that Carrie was part of a defective line and had to be sterilized to prevent more feebleminded offspring. The testimony, however, was false. At the time of Carrie's commitment hearing, on January 23, 1924, Vivian had not yet been born, so there could have been no depositions attesting that she was mentally defective. When Dr. Priddy testified at the sterilization hearing, Vivian was less than six months old, and no one had attempted to test her for mental defects.

Dr. Priddy then delivered his main appeal to the board: that it would be best for both society and Carrie if she was "protected against child-bearing by sterilization." When Strode asked for his expert recommendation, Dr. Priddy said unequivocally: "I am of the firm belief and opinion that to prevent Carrie Buck bearing offspring is a duty to her and society." Without the operation she would have to remain in the custody of an institution for the next thirty years. If she was sterilized, he testified, "she could leave the institution, enjoy her liberty and life and become self-sustaining."

When Strode was done, Shelton offered a brief, spiritless cross-examination. He did not challenge any of Dr. Priddy's inaccuracies: the misstating of his client's level of mental disability, the failure to mention her academic success, the false statement that her paternity was unknown, or the outrageous statement about her daughter. He made no attempt to introduce Carrie's colony files, or even Dr. Priddy's "History and Clinical Notes" on Carrie, which were at odds with much of his testimony.

Shelton's few questions were instead so poorly composed that they allowed Dr. Priddy to strengthen the colony's case. Shelton asked what assurances could be given that the operation would not be dangerous. Dr. Priddy was able to respond that "salpingectomy is as harmless as any surgical operation can be" and that he had performed or assisted in eighty to one hundred sterilizations of women who needed their tubes removed due to pelvic disease with no ill effect.

Shelton asked if there was a course of training Carrie could be given, instead of sterilization, that would allow her to be released from the colony without harming society or herself. Dr. Priddy was able to respond that it would be "an impossibility" since her "self-control and moral conception" were "organically lacking." Shelton let the answer stand uncontested.

Carrie's sterilization hearing ended with a single question posed directly to her. "Do you care to say anything about having this operation performed on you?" Strode asked, pointedly not saying what "this operation" was. "No, sir," Carrie responded. "I have not, it is up to my people."

It was poignant response. It suggested that Carrie thought she had "people" looking out for her. She may have believed Dr. Priddy and the other staff at the colony had her best interests at heart, even though they were trying to forcibly sterilize her. She might have thought Shelton was fighting for her, though his performance at the hearing suggested otherwise. Despite Carrie's apparent confusion about the situation, neither Shelton nor Strode followed up to clarify what she was thinking.

No one made any effort to determine that Carrie understood that the operation being contemplated would make it impossible for her to have children—not Strode, not Shelton, not Dr. Priddy, and not the members of the Special Board of Directors. The one question put to her at the hearing appeared to be intentionally phrased to avoid informing her of what was being done to her. Nonetheless, the official record the colony created after the hearing stated that "this girl" was "desirous of taking advantage of the Sterilization Law."

The Special Board of Directors rendered its decision on September 30. It determined that "by the laws of heredity" Carrie was "the probable potential parent of socially inadequate offspring." The board also found that Carrie could be sterilized without harming her health, and that performing the operation would promote her welfare and the general welfare of society. The board granted Dr. Priddy's petition, and ordered him to have Carrie sterilized by salpingectomy.

As the new law required, the board gave Carrie thirty days to appeal its order. The law's supporters wanted Carrie to appeal, so they would have their test case. The decision about whether to appeal, however, lay not with Dr. Priddy and Strode—who had prevailed before the board—but with Carrie and Shelton. If Carrie really was "desirous of taking advantage of the Sterilization Law," as the colony claimed, there would be no reason for Shelton to appeal. But Shelton did appeal the board's ruling, in a motion filed on October 3, 1924, with the Amherst County Circuit Court.

In filing the appeal, Shelton was creating a test case—exactly what Dr. Priddy and Strode wanted. In a letter to an expert witness, Dr. Priddy was open about the collusion. Carrie's "guardian at our request is taking an appeal from the action of the Board," he wrote, "in order that we may test the constitutionality through our State Courts, even to the Supreme Court of the United States."

In his appeal, Shelton objected to the board's decision to sterilize Carrie as not supported by the evidence. More significantly for the purpose of the test case, Shelton also objected that Virginia's new eugenic sterilization law was unconstitutional. The appeal claimed that the statute did not provide due process of law, denied inmates of state institutions equal protection of the law, and imposed cruel and unusual punishment. While the appeal was pending, the sterilization order was automatically stayed.

Shelton hired Irving Whitehead, a lawyer with deep roots in Amherst County, to handle the appeal. The choice of Whitehead was another indication that Dr. Priddy and Strode were likely making all of the major decisions in the case—both for their side and for Carrie's. Whitehead had extraordinarily close personal and professional connections to the colony and to the people trying to sterilize Carrie, and it would soon become clear that he was working for them, not for his nominal client.

Whitehead's most long-standing ties were to Strode, and they went back to childhood. The two men had been boyhood friends growing up on neighboring farms in Amherst County, and their bond continued into adulthood, when they practiced law in the same swath of west-central Virginia. Whitehead and Strode were both involved in founding the colony—in its early years Whitehead served on the Special Board of Directors while Strode handled its legal work.

Whitehead became close to Dr. Priddy through his association with the colony. He served on the colony's board when it selected Dr. Priddy to be the first superintendent, and the two men worked together on colony business, including taking a joint trip to Indiana to investigate its eugenic sterilization program. In April the colony had recognized Whitehead's role in its history by co-naming a new facility for male inmates, the Dew-Whitehead Building, in his honor. Whitehead had moved to Baltimore to take a position with a bank, but he remained in contact with Dr. Priddy.

Although he would be representing Carrie in her challenge to the sterilization order, Whitehead had a long record of support for sterilization. He had been chairman of the colony's board in 1916, when Dr. Priddy was sterilizing inmates without benefit of a state statute. Whitehead had supported the superintendent's expansive reading of existing Virginia law, and the following year, his final one as a board member, he strongly supported Dr. Priddy in his battles with the Mallory family.

The litigation over Carrie's sterilization presented a more complicated geometry than the usual situation of two legal adversaries facing off in court. Dr. Priddy, Strode, and Whitehead all had close social, political, and financial ties. Further complicating the relationships was the fact that it was Dr. Priddy who would be paying Whitehead's legal fees. Carrie was, in every way, the odd woman out—and Whitehead's performance would reflect this. His representation of Carrie in the trial and subsequent appeals would turn out to be, as the legal historian Paul Lombardo has observed, "not merely incompetent" but "nothing less than betrayal."

The Amherst County Circuit Court scheduled a trial on Carrie's appeal for November 18, 1924. That did not leave Strode and Dr. Priddy much time to put together their case. The hearing before the colony's board had been a relatively simple matter. Strode and Dr. Priddy had offered their uncontroverted account of the facts and showed that they had met the law's conditions. The board, whose members all knew Dr. Priddy and Strode well, had been inclined to defer to their medical and legal conclusions, and it granted Dr. Priddy's petition unanimously.

The trial would be more challenging. A county judge was different from a member of a state hospital board. He had no institutional loyalty to the hospital or to the superintendent—his mandate was more broadly to ensure that justice was served. Even if the judge who heard the case in Amherst County had close ties to Strode and Dr. Priddy, which seemed likely, the case would ultimately be heard by the Virginia Supreme Court of Appeals in Richmond, and perhaps even the U.S. Supreme Court. Dr. Priddy and Strode would ultimately not be able to rely on their connections to the decision makers to prevail.

The biggest difference, however, would be in the law. The colony's board had accepted the validity of the Virginia sterilization statute and only inquired into whether its provisions were being met. A state court would start with the question of whether the eugenic sterilization law itself was valid, and it might not be an easy one for Dr. Priddy and the colony to prevail on. As Strode had discovered when he researched the matter, when courts across the country had reviewed eugenic sterilization laws, almost without exception the laws had been struck down.

The eugenicists had won the first such challenge in 1912, when Washington's sterilization law was upheld by the Washington Supreme Court. The tide, however, had turned quickly. New Jersey, home to the Vineland Training School for Feeble-minded Girls and Boys, had enacted a sterilization law, which had been signed by Governor Woodrow Wilson, the former president of Princeton, and future president of the United States. In 1913 the New Jersey Supreme Court ruled that the law violated the equal protection clause because it applied to individuals who were in state institutions but not to people in the general population with the same conditions.

The next year, a federal district court in Iowa struck down a law that authorized sterilization of criminals. The court ruled that it was a "bill of attainder"—a law that pronounced people guilty without a trial—because it said certain categories of criminals had to be sterilized, leaving nothing "for the prison physician to do but to execute" the order. The decision was not directly relevant to Virginia's law, which required individualized determinations of who should be sterilized. But it was another ruling against sterilization, and one in which the court had expressed particular outrage at the barbarism of the procedure.

In 1918 the courts in two more states—New York and Michigan—had struck down eugenic sterilization laws. The grounds were the same as in New Jersey: that the laws violated equal protection because they applied only to inmates of state institutions. Those rulings were relevant to Virginia, because Strode had included the same limitation, and they were not helpful to the eugenic cause. The latest legal setback—and in some ways the most discouraging one for the eugenicists—occurred where the movement began. In 1921 the Indiana Supreme Court had struck down that state's first-in-the-nation eugenic sterilization law. The court ruled that the 1907 law violated the due process clause.

In all, from 1913 to 1921, eight laws were challenged, and after the success in Washington, the eugenicists had lost in the next seven states: New Jersey, Iowa, Michigan, New York, Nevada, Indiana, and Oregon. State and federal courts decided these cases on a variety of constitutional grounds: equal protection, due process, and cruel and unusual punishment. The rulings pointed to a range of problems with the laws—that they applied only to a portion of a state's population or did not provide sufficient procedural protections. Read on their own terms, the decisions suggested that the specifics of the statutes mattered a great deal, and laws that were not drafted properly would be struck down.

There was another way of reading the cases, however: as an expression of general societal unease with eugenic sterilization. There had been enough enthusiasm for sterilization that in a short period of time laws were adopted across the country. Nevertheless, it was now clear that not everyone was caught up in the eugenic mania, and the resistance was not just coming from the courts. In several states, governors vetoed eugenic sterilization laws and delivered strongly worded indictments. Nebraska's governor insisted his state's sterilization bill seemed "more in keeping with the pagan age than with the teachings of Christianity," and he declared in his veto message that "man is more than an animal."

The landscape for eugenic sterilization, which had been so promising in 1913, was now decidedly less so—and the judicial momentum was strongly against it. Dr. Priddy and the other supporters of the Virginia sterilization law would need to create the strongest possible case. They had drafted the law with considerable care, drawing on expert advice on how to make it resistant to constitutional challenge. Then they had chosen, in Carrie Buck, a plaintiff they believed demonstrated particularly well why eugenic sterilization was necessary.

Now they needed a eugenic sterilization expert—a respected aca-

demic authority—who could persuade skeptical judges that the law
and the sterilization order were necessary. In a letter to Dr. Priddy,
Strode explained that they needed someone who could bolster their
arguments with the most credible and convincing scientific evidence.
Dr. Priddy agreed, and there was one name at the top of both men's
lists. It was the man who had written the treatise on eugenic sterilization, and the model statute, that Strode had relied on in drafting the
Virgina law: Harry Laughlin.

Four

Harry Laughlin

I n 1924 the drive to enact eugenic sterilization laws was a truly national movement. It had begun in the Midwest, in Indiana, in 1907, and quickly spread to the East and West Coasts—the next two states to adopt laws were Connecticut and California. The states that followed over the next seventeen years were in every region of the country: they included South Dakota, New Jersey, Nevada, Kansas, Maine, and Alabama. The sterilization movement was national in other ways as well. It had prominent citizens in its ranks, drawn from the worlds of science, medicine, law, and politics, and it was receiving extensive attention in newspapers and magazines.

This large national movement had an undisputed nerve center: the Eugenics Record Office in Cold Spring Harbor, New York. The Eugenics Record Office was a gathering place for eugenics scientists and a training ground for eugenics field researchers. It was a clearinghouse of public education materials and, as its name suggested, a repository for eugenics records. It was also, above all else, a force for eugenics advocacy and propaganda.

The Eugenics Record Office had been founded by Charles Davenport, a onetime Harvard zoology professor, but it was managed day to day by Harry Laughlin, who was arguably the nation's most influential eugenicist. Laughlin had just won the greatest victory of his career: helping, as a special adviser to Congress, to enact an immigration law that made eugenic principles the guiding force in admitting—and, more important, excluding—new Americans.

Now Laughlin was returning to the issue he cared about above all others: eugenic sterilization. He had been working for years to increase the number of sterilizations carried out nationally, through his prolific writings and energetic advocacy. As many as fifteen million Americans would need to be sterilized, he insisted, to save the nation from the looming threat of hereditary disaster.

Laughlin hoped the nation was headed toward this goal, but he could not be sure, in part because the legal landscape was so uncertain. It was not clear that, in the end, eugenic sterilization would be held to be constitutional. Laughlin had made affirming the constitutionality of eugenic sterilization a personal crusade—he had recently published a lengthy book intended to persuade the courts to uphold sterilization laws. If the United States adopted a national program of mass eugenic sterilization—as now appeared possible—there would be no one more responsible than Laughlin. He had arrived at this lofty perch from far away—and from very humble origins.

Harry Hamilton Laughlin was born on March 11, 1880, in the small college and coal-mining town of Oskaloosa, Iowa. Laughlin's father, George Hamilton Laughlin, taught ancient languages at Oskaloosa College, a small school affiliated with the Disciples of Christ. Shortly after Harry's birth, George Laughlin became the college's president.

George Laughlin was a charismatic man. A biographical sketch noted his "excellent physique" and "dark brown eyes" that had not "lost any of their original fire and expressiveness." He embodied the two great passions of the Laughlin family: knowledge and deeply felt religious faith. When he was not working as a professor or a college administrator, he was a clergyman in the Disciples of Christ Church.

The family moved frequently, following George Laughlin's peripatetic academic career. When Harry was three, they settled in Hiram, Ohio, where the elder Laughlin became president of Hiram College, another Disciples of Christ–affiliated school. Next, they moved to Wichita, Kansas, where George Laughlin once again taught ancient languages, this time at Garfield University. The family finally settled in Kirksville, Missouri, where Harry's father took positions as chairman of the English Department at the First District Normal School and pastor of Kirksville Christian Church.

Laughlin's parents had met as college classmates at Abingdon College in Illinois—his mother was valedictorian, while his father had to settle for salutatorian. Deborah Ross Laughlin was the family's flinty moral center. When she was not busy raising her five sons and five daughters in a series of rough-and-tumble towns on the American frontier, she was active in her church and an array of moralistic causes.

Deborah Laughlin was an advocate for women's suffrage and temperance, and a strong supporter of Christian missionary work. A compelling public speaker, she regularly addressed church congregations, women's groups, and, on occasion, political rallies. She was especially drawn to the Woman's Christian Temperance Union, which was founded in Cleveland in 1874. The group, whose motto was to "Agitate, Educate, Legislate," organized housewives to kneel down in prayer outside establishments that sold liquor. Deborah Laughlin led antidrinking "pray-ins" in front of saloons, and at her urging Harry signed a temperance pledge, which he kept his entire life.

The Laughlin family was proud of its lineage. Laughlin's background was English, Scottish, Irish, German, and French—the northern European stock he would later insist was superior to other nationalities. His mother's ancestry qualified her for the Daughters of the American Revolution. His father's family claimed kinship to President James Madison.

After attending the local Kirksville schools, Laughlin enrolled at the First District Normal School, which would later be renamed Truman State University, where his father taught. Even as a college student Laughlin was convinced of the critical importance of ancestry. In "Cosmopolitanism in America," a paper he wrote in 1899, he declared that it was "generally conceded that . . . science and invention are preparing every portion of the globe for the happy and prosperous abode of the white man." It was, he insisted, "an established law of Ethnology that races inferior in intellect morals and action recede before the expansive march of superior blood." In later life, Laughlin would often be described as a eugenics evangelist who combined his father's academic inclinations and his mother's religious fervor. That intellectual moralism was already evident during his student days in Kirksville. In "Cosmopolitanism in America," Laughlin predicted that "eventually the world will be inhabited by an enlightened race, Caucasian in blood, Christian in religion and free in government."

Laughlin remained in Kirksville after graduating from college in 1900. He became a teacher at, and then principal of, Kirksville's small high school. In 1902 he married Pansy Bowen, the daughter of a teacher at the school. After his marriage, Laughlin moved to Iowa, where he accepted a better-paying job as principal of a larger school, Centerville High School. Laughlin came home three years later to become superintendent of the Kirksville Public Schools. In 1907 he moved into higher education, joining the faculty of his alma mater, the First District Normal School, where he became the sole member of the Department of Agriculture, Botany, and Nature Study.

Laughlin's academic interest was breeding. He did not limit his study to books and scholarly articles. A profile in a local newspaper reported that he was involved in "many interesting experiments in chicken raising." In his first year at the college, Laughlin wrote to a prominent East Coast genetics expert named Charles Davenport to discuss crossbreeding of long-tailed Yokohama and other varieties of chickens. Davenport, the director of the Department of Experimental Biology of the Carnegie Institution in Cold Spring Harbor, New York, and Laughlin, the small-town agriculture professor, struck up a friendly correspondence about their shared interest in poultry breeding.

Davenport decided he had found a kindred spirit. He arranged to meet Laughlin in person in January 1909, when he would be in Missouri for a meeting of the American Breeders' Association, an organization that brought animal and plant breeders together with academic experts on heredity. Laughlin persuaded Davenport and his wife to add a visit to Kirksville to their trip. The couple stayed with the Laughlins and Davenport spoke to a local audience on his area of expertise. "Your visit here has aroused great interest in the subject of heredity," Laughlin wrote Davenport afterward. "Your lectures were greatly appreciated."

The two men continued their correspondence and Davenport sponsored his new friend for membership in the American Breeders' Association. The next year, Davenport invited Laughlin to attend a summer session at Cold Spring Harbor. Laughlin traveled to New York, and the two men continued to bond over animal breeding. When he returned to Missouri, Laughlin wrote to Davenport to say that the summer had been "the most profitable six weeks that I ever spent." Laughlin had found in Davenport a mentor who would set his life in a whole new direction.

Charles Benedict Davenport was born in Stamford, Connecticut, in 1866, into a family with elite roots in Puritan New England. The Davenports traced their American chapter back to the Reverend John Davenport, a prominent Puritan clergyman who left his native England to help build a new world. Reverend Davenport, who co-founded the colony of New Haven in 1638, was considered "the most puritan of New England puritan leaders"—a man whose biography reported that he died "waging a desperate struggle to preserve the old New England Way."

Charles Davenport's father, Amzi Benedict Davenport, was a

deeply religious man who tried mightily to impress upon his twelve children the extraordinary quality of their ancestry. After intensive research of the family tree, he published *History and Genealogy of the Davenport Family* in 1851, and an enlarged edition in 1876, which traced the Davenport lineage back to England in 1086. The book—the title page of which attributed authorship to "A. Benedict Davenport (of the twenty-fourth generation)"—was described as "the most elaborate work of that sort ever published in this country."

Charles Davenport attended Harvard University, from which he received an A.B. in 1889 and a Ph.D. in biology in 1892, and then began teaching zoology, briefly at Harvard and later as an assistant professor at the newly established University of Chicago. As part of his research, Davenport wanted to breed relatively large animals, which the university lacked the farming facilities to support. He began to look for a new academic home that would allow him to carry out his breeding work.

Davenport decided to establish his own academic center. He approached the Carnegie Institution, which had recently been founded by the industrialist Andrew Carnegie, with a sizable endowment. Davenport secured annual funding for an institution to study "hereditary evolution, more particularly by experimental methods." In 1904 he founded the Station for the Experimental Study of Evolution in Cold Spring Harbor, New York, on the north shore of Long Island. Davenport left academia to become its first director, and to do his own scholarly research.

The Station for the Experimental Study of Evolution's focus was the study of nonhumans. Davenport, however, was becoming increasingly interested in human heredity. He wrote a paper—coauthored with his wife, Gertrude, a fellow zoologist—on heredity in human hair traits, and other papers on inheritance of skin and eye color. Davenport suspected that mental traits, such as personality and a disposition toward delinquency, followed hereditary patterns of inheritance as much as physical traits did, and he was eager to research the question.

Davenport had traveled to England years earlier and met Francis

Galton, emerging from the audience as a disciple. Davenport pursued his interest in eugenics at the American Breeders' Association. The organization, which would be the setting of his historic meeting with Harry Laughlin, had an unusual mission and unconventional membership. It sought to bring together academic genetics scholars like Davenport with "practical breeders" who had developed their insights "at the feeding trough, at the meat, butter, and wool scale, on the race track, and at the prize ring."

The Breeders' Association's members believed they were on the brink of achieving something great. "Science is taking hold of the forces of heredity as it has hold of the forces of mechanics," an editorial in *American Breeders Magazine* declared, "and the Twentieth Century bids fair to be the century of breeding." The organization's interest, like that of so many people working in the field, was rapidly moving toward the genetics—and breeding—of humans.

The American Breeders' Association became one of the first prominent American organizations to study eugenics. It formed a Committee on Eugenics with a distinguished membership. The committee chairman was David Starr Jordan, Stanford University's first president, and its members included the inventor Alexander Graham Bell, who was conducting research on hereditary deafness. Davenport served as secretary, and in that capacity he organized a subcommittee on the heredity of feeblemindedness.

Increasingly, Davenport was leaving animal breeding and shifting his focus to eugenics research and advocacy. At a Breeders' Association meeting in Omaha in 1909, he delivered a speech arguing for government policies to improve the nation's genetic stock. Rational, scientific measures were needed, he insisted, "to dry up the springs that feed the torrent of defective and degenerate protoplasm." Davenport persuaded the Breeders' Association to elevate the Committee on Eugenics to a "section," putting it on an equal footing with the Animal and Plant Sections.

In that same year, Davenport published his first major book on eugenics. In *Eugenics: The Science of Human Improvement by Better*

Breeding, he contended that "three or four percent of our population is a fearful drag on our civilization." Once again, he called for strong government action. "Society must protect itself," he wrote. "As it claims the right to deprive the murderer of his life so also it may annihilate the hideous serpent of hopelessly vicious protoplasm."

Davenport ended his short book with a "Plan for Further Work," which included a plea to the nation's philanthropists to fund increased research. "Vastly more effective than ten million dollars to 'charity' would be ten millions to Eugenics," he insisted. Any wealthy person who contributed his money to "redeem mankind from vice, imbecility and suffering," he wrote, "would be the world's wisest philanthropist."

Davenport's appeal was strategically timed. He was in the process of trying to raise money to create a center for eugenics, and he was looking for what he regarded as wise philanthropists. Davenport approached Mrs. E. H. Harriman, the widow of the railroad magnate, who had inherited a sizable fortune. Davenport had a connection to the family: Harriman's daughter Mary, a Barnard undergraduate, had spent part of a summer at the Cold Spring Harbor Biological Laboratory. As it turned out, Harriman was herself a strong believer in the eugenic cause, as she would show with her financial contributions and her own supportive words. "What is the matter with the American people?" Harriman would later exclaim at a public meeting. "Fifteen million must be sterilized!" When Davenport left a meeting with Harriman at which she had pledged significant financial support, he could barely contain his excitement. In his diary, he declared it to be nothing less than "a red-letter day for humanity." Harriman became the main patron of Davenport's new project, an offshoot of the Station for Experimental Evolution that would be known as the Eugenics Record Office. Over the next five years, she would donate more than $500,000, a white frame house, and about seventy-five acres of land.

Davenport recruited a prestigious Board of Scientific Directors. Alexander Graham Bell, his colleague from the Breeders' Association Eugenics Section, agreed to serve as chairman. Bell, who was the son of one deaf woman and the husband of another, was studying eugenic solutions to the problem of deafness. In a paper presented to the National Academy of Sciences, "Upon the Formation of a Deaf Variety of the Human Race," he expressed his fear that if the deaf reproduced unchecked they would produce a "defective race of human beings" that would be a "great calamity to the world."

Davenport recruited other scientists from leading universities. William Welch, the dean of Johns Hopkins School of Medicine, agreed to be vice chairman, and E. E. Southard, a Harvard psychiatrist, signed on as a board member. Irving Fisher of Yale, perhaps the most prominent economist of his time, also joined the board. Fisher's main intellectual interest, aside from economics, was eugenics. In 1909 he wrote *A Report on National Vitality: Its Wastes and Conservation,* anticipating a proliferation of eugenic laws. "Humanity will probably submit in the future to communal restriction of the right to multiply with as good grace as it has given up the right to rob and to rape," he predicted.

Davenport also persuaded John D. Rockefeller Jr., the world's richest man, to underwrite fellowships at the Eugenics Record Office. Rockefeller, who was troubled by the human defects he saw all around him, was creating his own organization, the Bureau of Social Hygiene, to end prostitution, venereal disease, and other societal ills. An organization affiliated with the bureau, the Criminalistic Institute, conducted eugenic investigations of women criminal defendants.

Davenport intended for the Eugenics Record Office to do more than conduct research and collect records. He wanted it to explore practical ways of addressing the threats that people with hereditary defects posed. Davenport wrote to Galton to inform him of the office's founding. It would, he said, promote both positive and negative eugenic measures in pursuit of Galton's vision: "weeding out" humanity's worst traits.

Davenport knew whom he wanted to head up his new organization. He had been impressed with Laughlin from their first correspondence about poultry, and since then their professional relationship had developed into a strong meeting of the minds. They shared undeniable common ground, as one history of the Eugenics Record Office observed: both men were "highly energetic and serious about their work, utterly humorless and rigid in their approach to life, and totally dedicated to the cause of social reform through eugenics."

Davenport offered to make Laughlin the first superintendent of the Eugenics Record Office, and Laughlin accepted without hesitation. "As rapidly as we can, we are settling our business affairs," Laughlin wrote to Davenport on September 2, 1910. "Mrs. Laughlin also anticipates with pleasure the making of a new home." Davenport responded a few days later to say that he had ordered filing cases, a typewriter, and office furniture, and there would be letterhead on hand when Laughlin arrived.

The Laughlins arrived in Cold Spring Harbor in mid-September. They moved into the large house Harriman had donated, sharing the ground floor with office space. On October 1, 1910, the Eugenics Record Office formally opened, and it was on its way to becoming—as one history would call it—a "center for research in human genetics and for propaganda in eugenics."

While his new creation took shape, Davenport published another book. *Heredity in Relation to Eugenics*, which was released in 1911, quickly became one of the most authoritative texts of the eugenics movement. It was assigned reading in many of the eugenics courses that were springing up at colleges and universities across the country, and it was cited by more than one-third of the high school biology textbooks of that era. In his new book, Davenport explored the way in which various human traits were inherited. He argued that qualities like "criminality," "narcotism," and "pauperism" were genetically determined. With pauperism, Davenport conceded the environment was important, but he still insisted it was largely hereditary. "When both parents are shiftless in some degree," he wrote, only about 15 percent of their children would be "industrious."

In keeping with the bigotry that was rarely far from the surface of

American eugenics, *Heredity in Relation to Eugenics* offered Davenport's views about the hereditary deficits of various racial and ethnic groups. America's earliest immigrants had been "men of courage, independence, and love of liberty; and many of them were scholars or social leaders," he wrote. The newer immigrants, he insisted, fell short.

Jews had positive attributes, Davenport allowed, including literacy and earning capacity, but "the hordes of Jews" who were "now coming" were inferior to the English and Scandinavians, "with their ideals of community life in the open country, advancement by the sweat of the brow, and the uprearing of families in the fear of God and the love of country." On personal care, he wrote, the "recent Hebrew immigrants occupy a position intermediate between the slovenly Servians and Greeks and the tidy Swedes, Germans and Bohemians."

Heredity in Relation to Eugenics was equally opinionated about Italians. Davenport began by noting that Italians in America came mainly from southern Italy and were darker than northern Italians, "doubtless" having "derived part of their blood from Greece and Northern Africa." He credited Italian immigrants with "thrift," "careful attention to details," and capacity for hard work, particularly monotonous labor, but he was troubled by their lack of initiative and "tendency to crimes of personal violence."

Davenport credited the Irish with "sympathy, chastity and leadership of men." He cautioned, however, that they brought "alcoholism, considerable mental defectiveness and a tendency to tuberculosis." The Irish also tended to "aggregate in cities and soon control their governments, frequently exercising favoritism and often graft," he said. Davenport had an even lower opinion of the black Portuguese who were coming to New England as agricultural workers. He pronounced them "illiterate and neither resourceful nor intelligent."

Heredity in Relation to Eugenics concluded that the nation's demographic changes were a genetic crisis. Northern European stock was steadily being replaced by people of lesser genetic worth. The "great influx of blood from South-eastern Europe" was likely, Davenport warned, to rapidly turn the nation "darker in pigmentation, smaller in stature, more mercurial, more attached to music and art, [and] more given to crimes of larceny, kidnapping, assault, murder, rape, and sex-immorality." In addition, he said, "the ratio of insanity in the population will rapidly increase."

For Davenport, it all came down to regulating "germplasm," the eugenicists' term for the genetic inheritance individuals carried. Nations also had germplasm—the sum total of the germplasm of all of their citizens—and this national store varied considerably based on the racial, ethnic, and other characteristics of the population. It was this national stock of germplasm—its quality, and its likelihood of preserving and enhancing America's greatness—that was at stake, Davenport believed, in the eugenics movement.

The views that Davenport and other American eugenicists were expressing were ones that, in a couple of decades, would be associated with German racial theorists. In the 1910s, with the founding of the Eugenics Record Office, and the publication of books like *Heredity in Relation to Eugenics,* the United States was on a parallel track with Germany. Decades before the Nazis, German "racial hygienists" were already in the forefront of the eugenics movement. The Germans established the world's first eugenics journal, the *Archiv für Rassen- und Gesellschafts-Biologie* (Archive for Racial and Social Biology), in 1904, and, the following year, the world's first eugenics professional organization, the Deutsche Gesellschaft für Rassenhygiene (German Society for Racial Hygiene). Germany was also a leader in international eugenics. In 1907 the Gesellschaft für Rassenhygiene became a global organization, and four years later Germany hosted its first international meeting of eugenicists, in Dresden.

For all of their early success, German eugenicists were becoming worried that their American counterparts were surpassing them. The German Society for Racial Hygiene circulated a flyer noting "the dedication with which Americans sponsor research in the field of racial hygiene and with which they translate theoretical knowledge into practice." It pointed, in particular, to Harriman's generous donations to the Eugenics Record Office. The society asked, with evident envy,

"Can we have any doubts that the Americans will reach their aim—the stabilization and improvement of the strength of the people?"

Under Laughlin's leadership, the Eugenics Record Office became a vital arm of the American eugenics movement. One of its central functions was the training of eugenics field-workers to help establish the standards and protocols for what the eugenicists hoped would become a new science of human evaluation and improvement. The trainees attended classes taught by Laughlin, Davenport, and an array of guest lecturers with special expertise in areas like hereditary science and the social structure of rural communities.

The Eugenics Record Office emphasized the collection of eugenic information, a focus that was in keeping with the times. Jane Addams, the founder of Hull House in Chicago, noted that when new workers arrived at settlement houses like hers in the 1890s, they said, "We must do something about social disorder." After 1900, they said, "We want to investigate something." The Eugenics Record Office instructed its staff and students in investigation, imparting what it maintained were the scientific methods of eugenic fieldwork.

Eugenics Record Office trainees were taught how to conduct eugenic investigations of communities, families, and individuals. They learned how to interview a subject's neighbors, and to discern "community reactions" by asking if a subject was law breaking, inclined to the overconsumption of alcohol, or simply "silly." Depending on the answers, individuals and families could be labeled "feebleminded" without any intelligence testing or educational records. The researchers were also taught practical skills, such as measuring brain size by assessing cranial capacity.

The trainees, who were overwhelmingly young women—in the first few years, 131 out of 156 trainees were female—were deployed to mental hospitals, poorhouses, and other institutions across the country. They were also sent to Ellis Island, where they were instructed on how to identify feebleminded people trying to enter the country. The data that the researchers collected, which was stored in fireproof cabinets and intricately indexed, became the basis for studies of the heritability of various traits.

As part of its "clearinghouse" function, the Eugenics Record Office staff produced manuals to help other organizations and individuals conduct their own eugenic fieldwork. *The Family-History Book* advised researchers on how to map out family trees and trace hereditary connections between generations. *The Trait Book* assigned numerical codes to a wide array of human qualities, from beauty to criminality. The codes allowed researchers to systematically track these traits when they appeared in family lines.

The Eugenics Record Office also provided more individualized information. An admiring profile that appeared in the *New York Times* in 1913 under the headline "Social Problems Have Proven Basis of Heredity" called attention to a service the *Times'* readers could take advantage of. The Eugenics Record Office staff was available to help members of the public with "advice as to the suitability of marriages." In a report released that year, Laughlin said the Eugenics Record Office was getting a steady stream of requests from couples considering marrying but uncertain of the eugenic implications.

The subject matter at the Eugenics Record Office was serious, and the workload heavy, but there were also more carefree times to be had on the rustic Cold Spring Harbor campus. A drama club produced plays performed by the field-workers, which were put on in the surrounding community, for entertainment and edification—though as with much of the organization's work, the lessons were often unsettling. Pansy Laughlin wrote "Acquired or Inherited? A Eugenical Comedy in Four Acts," a lighthearted romp in which various characters, including a eugenics field-worker and a wealthy merchant, pursue their attractions for one another. By the play's end, the young women have learned, among other things, that Felix Rosenfeld, a money-hungry Jewish peddler, is not an appropriate eugenic choice.

Laughlin's position at the Eugenics Record Office immediately elevated him to the highest ranks of the eugenics movement. He continued to conduct his own research on the subjects he cared about most, especially eugenic sterilization and the threat posed by immigrants with hereditary defects. He also investigated some of the scientific issues eugenicists were most focused on, such as "differential fecundity," the claim that certain groups like the feebleminded reproduced at a higher rate than "normal" people.

Laughlin was also becoming a larger presence in national eugenics organizations. When the American Breeders' Association established a high-profile committee with an unwieldy name to recommend eugenic policies, Laughlin was at the center of it. The Committee to Study and to Report on the Best Practical Means of Cutting Off the Defective Germ-Plasm in the American Population was chaired by the Breeders' Association president, Bleecker Van Wagenen. Laughlin was named secretary, which meant that when the committee decided to prepare a major report on eugenic sterilization, he was designated its main author.

In January 1914, while Laughlin was hard at work on the Breeders' Association's eugenic sterilization report, he was invited to address the First National Conference on Race Betterment, another high-profile platform. The conference, which was being held at the Battle Creek Sanitarium in Michigan, was organized by Dr. John Harvey Kellogg, the director of the sanitarium and the brother of W. K. Kellogg, the inventor of cornflakes and founder of the Kellogg Company.

Kellogg promoted many eccentric health regimens and causes, and his newest one was eugenics. It was, for him, a matter of urgency. He made this clear in his own paper for the conference, which he titled "Needed—A New Human Race." In it, Kellogg declared that "all serious-minded men and women should join in making known to every human being in every corner of the globe the fact that the human race is dying, and to discover and apply the remedies necessary for salvation from this dismal fate."

The Race Betterment conference was the largest eugenics conference ever held in the United States. More than four hundred delegates and thousands of members of the general public descended on the

Battle Creek Sanitarium. Attendance at the first session "so far exceeded the expectations of the organizers," the official proceedings reported, "that some two hundred people were unable to enter the auditorium."

There were exhibits on subjects ranging from "Open-Air Sleeping" to home cleanliness, the latter including an unmade bed with dirty clothes on it and a squalid kitchen with moldy pickles on display. There were also "Mental and Physical Perfection Contests," in which schoolchildren and babies were given extensive tests and evaluations. The winners were awarded gold medals stamped with the official insignia of the First National Conference on Race Betterment.

The heart of the conference was the sessions on eugenic theory and practice, with addresses from leaders in the field. In Laughlin's presentation, "Calculations on the Working Out of a Proposed Program of Sterilization," he spoke about the same subject he had been working on so intently for the Breeders' Association. He came to Battle Creek with a powerful message: to save the nation from the threat posed by "defective" people, there would need to be millions of sterilizations.

Laughlin put a precise percentage on how much of the nation was genetically unworthy. The "lowest ten percent of the human stock are so meagerly endowed by Nature that their perpetuation would constitute a social menace," he told the conference. Laughlin brought charts that provided examples of the sort of people he was talking about. One chart showed the "Poorhouse Type of Source of Defectives" and was illustrated with a feebleminded woman living in an almshouse, whose children were feebleminded and, in one case, an "epileptic imbecile." Another showed the "Hovel Type of Source of Defectives," in this case a family beset by feeblemindedness, alcoholism, epilepsy, sex offenses, and criminality.

In his speech to the conference, Laughlin laid down a marker on how many eugenic sterilizations would be needed. To rid the nation of what he called the "lowest one-tenth" of the population would require fifteen million people to be sterilized over the next two generations. There had so far been fewer than one thousand eugenic sterilizations, he said, and that was not nearly enough. Current sterilization regimens were little more than a "slight palliative," he said, and "[a] halfway measure will never strike deeply at the roots of the evil."

Laughlin called for a new, more methodical approach to sterilization. He argued for identifying "defective" people and sending them to institutions, sterilizing them, and then quickly releasing them. "The shorter the periods of commitment," he explained, the more rapidly the whole population of "individuals possessing hereditary potentialities for defective parenthood" could be rendered sterile.

The costs of such a sweeping program would be considerable, Laughlin conceded, but he urged states not to be discouraged. He argued that the increased expenditures could be made up for by forcing the people who were institutionalized to work in the fields or in factories. In any case, the expense was well worth it, he insisted, because "the germ-plasm of a nation is always its greatest asset, and . . . the expense of such measures would be paying investments—not only in dollars and cents, but in the inborn qualities of future generations."

In February, not long after his return from Battle Creek, Laughlin's American Breeders' Association report was released. It was published as *Eugenics Record Office Bulletin No. 10* under the title *Report of the Committee to Study and to Report on the Best Practical Means of Cutting Off the Defective Germ-Plasm in the American Population*. Writing on behalf of the committee, Laughlin expanded on many of the themes he had discussed at the Race Betterment conference. The report was the most thorough argument to date for using eugenic sterilization to save the nation from a tide of mental and physical defects.

Laughlin examined the problem of "defective germ-plasm" from a variety of scientific perspectives, including medicine, biology, anthropology, and thremmatology (the science of animal and plant breeding). With his usual precision, Laughlin set out ten problems and ten solutions. The problems were ten defective classes that were the source of the defective germplasm of the report's title. These included the feebleminded, the pauper, the inebriate, the deformed, and the criminalistic. He then considered ten "suggested remedies," ranging from "laissez-faire," doing nothing, to what he called "euthanasia," which he defined as killing off people with undesirable traits.

In evaluating the options, Laughlin rejected killing those with defective germplasm. Any eugenic advantages it would bring about, he said, would come at too high a moral price. Laissez-faire, on the other hand, posed too great a threat to the hereditary stock of the nation, because people with defective germplasm were increasing as a percentage of the population. "There must be selection not only for progress, but even for maintaining the present standard," he insisted.

The report put the rate of "great anti-social human varieties" at about 10 percent of the population, the same number as Laughlin used in Battle Creek. It offered two main recommendations: "life segregation" and sterilization. Unlike Laughlin's presentation in Battle Creek, the report put greater emphasis on segregation. It called for greatly increasing the number of "defectives" held in state institutions, starting as early as possible in their reproductive years. "Life segregation" of this kind should, the committee urged, "be the principal agent used by society in cutting off its supply of defectives."

Sterilization was also an option, the report said, but it noted that "there is a wide range of opinion as to the extremity to which society itself should go in applying" it. The report called for using sterilization primarily as a backup to institutionalization, to be used only when "life segregation" failed to "function eugenically." It stated that "society must, at all hazards, protect its breeding stock," but it argued that segregation was "equally effective eugenically, and more effective socially."

Although Laughlin was the author, the report was far more skeptical about sterilization than he had been, just a month earlier, in Battle Creek. The critical difference was that in the report Laughlin was bound to reflect not only his own opinion, but the views of the whole American Breeders' Association committee. Evidently, they did not share his enthusiasm for mass sterilization, and believed that the eugenic goals that they all shared could be achieved in less intrusive ways.

The report included a second part, titled "The Legal, Legislative and Administrative Aspects of Sterilization," also written by Laughlin. It included a model eugenic sterilization law that the committee "respectfully commended[ed]" to the states as a "probably efficacious" way of addressing their "practical eugenical problems." The model law called for eugenics commissions to be established at the state level that would examine institutionalized people and members of the general public and determine which ones should be sterilized.

In its list of categories of "defective" people who should be sterilized, the law did not include all ten of the "problem" categories that appeared in the first part of the report. It recommended sterilization for the "feeble-minded, insane, epileptic, inebriate, criminalistic and other degenerate persons." It exempted other groups, however—the "crippled, the blind, the deaf, and the tubercular." The committee believed that these groups could be educated "voluntarily, from a sense of social duty, to refrain from having offspring in the interest of national welfare and vigor." As a result, it said, "eugenical training rather than enforced sterilization, should apply to them."

If Laughlin had to be more restrained than he would have liked in some of the report's policy recommendations, he had no such limitations on the use of soaring rhetoric to describe the problem—and he took full advantage of this freedom. "If America is to escape the doom of nations generally, it must breed good Americans," the report warned. "The fall of every nation in history has been due to many causes, but always chiefest among these causes has been the decline of the national stock."

For all of his new prominence in the eugenics movement, Laughlin lacked the graduate training in science that Davenport and the academic members of the American Breeders' Association had. Laughlin's formal education had ended years earlier, with his undergraduate degree from the First District Normal School. With the research he was now conducting, and the highly credentialed circles he was traveling in, that was becoming a handicap. At Davenport's suggestion, Laughlin took a leave of absence to pursue a doctorate in biology at Princeton.

Laughlin moved through the doctoral program rapidly, earning a master's degree in 1916 and a doctor of science in 1918. He studied with Edwin G. Conklin, a prominent biology professor with a strong interest in eugenics, who encouraged his students to fill out family records that could be ued for eugenic research. Laughlin focused on science, not polemics, however, in his doctoral thesis, "Determining the Relative Duration of the Several Mitotic Stages."

On his return to Cold Spring Harbor, Laughlin added a new role to his duties: editor. The Eugenics Record Office launched a new journal that Davenport and Laughlin jointly ran. The *Eugenical News* quickly became the house organ of the American eugenics movement. It published research on popular eugenics subjects, such as the rising tide of feeblemindedness and the dangers of race mixing. In keeping with the views of the editors, the articles were often xenophobic and racist, and when the Nazis began their rise in Germany, the *Eugenical News* would report on German eugenic and racial policies with considerable sympathy.

The years after his return from Princeton were among the most productive of Laughlin's career. He conducted his research with a single-minded intensity, rarely stopping for weekends, holidays, or vacations. Laughlin had long been trying to gain access to U.S. Census Bureau records of institutionalized Americans, but he was told the information was confidential. He finally succeeded in persuading the bureau to designate him as a "special agent of the Bureau of the Census" and let him conduct his own study of the populations of all of the nation's custodial institutions.

Laughlin used his access to create a database on the national origins and racial backgrounds of prisoners and institutionalized mentally ill people across the country. His work was slowed by World War I, but in 1919 he wrote the *Statistical Directory of State Institutions for the Defective, Dependent, and Delinquent Classes.* Laughlin would go on to use the data, in testimony before Congress and elsewhere, to argue that certain nationalities had higher levels of mental and physical defects than others.

Laughlin was increasingly building alliances with leading eugenicists. He became close friends with Madison Grant, the author of *The Passing of the Great Race*. Grant was an upper-class New York lawyer and writer, whose family had roots in pre–Revolutionary War America. A big-game hunter and an environmental activist, Grant helped to preserve the California redwoods, played a major role in creating the Denali and Glacier National Parks, and drew up the legislation that created the Bronx Zoo.

Grant was also a leader of the emerging eugenics establishment. He was a cofounder of the American Eugenics Society and of the Galton Society, a New York–based eugenics organization that emphasized scientific racism and espoused the superiority of Northern Europeans. Grant served as treasurer of the Second International Eugenics Congress, which was held in New York City. Like Laughlin, Grant believed that the nation was under siege by defective people, and that the answer lay in a system of "negative eugenics." The two men even agreed on the percentage of the population that was unworthy: in a letter to Davenport, Grant said that it was necessary to eliminate "the submerged tenth" of the population.

Grant was particularly focused on what he saw as the threat posed by "inferior races." He was contemptuous toward "the negroes," on whom, he complained in a letter to Davenport, "so much sentimentalism has been wasted." Grant was also fixated on Polish Jews, "whose dwarf stature, peculiar mentality, and ruthless concentration on self-interest," he said, were "being engrafted upon the stock of the nation."

In his book *The Passing of the Great Race,* Grant had argued that a white, northern European "native American aristocracy" supplied "the leaders in thought," and controlled capital, education, and "the religious ideals and altruistic" inclinations of the community. This hereditary elite rested, he said, upon "layer after layer of immigrants of lower races."

Grant introduced a disturbing typology of the world's races. He divided the people of Europe into Nordic, Alpine, and Mediterranean races, and he warned that Nordics, the most exalted in his view, was in peril. Grant's vision of the Nordic race in many ways anticipated the Nazis' idealization of the Aryans. Grant extolled the Nordic race, which "in its purity has an absolutely fair skin," as "the white man par excellence." In a chapter on the Nordic Fatherland, he warned of the danger race mixing posed to Nordic people. "Races must be kept apart by artificial devices," he wrote, "or they ultimately amalgamate and in the offspring the more generalized or lower type prevails."

Grant's proposed responses to these issues also anticipated Nazism. Readers might fear there was "little hope for humanity," he wrote, "but the remedy has been found, and can be quickly and mercifully applied." He advocated a "rigid system of selection through the elimination of those who are weak or unfit." With an aggressive program of forced sterilization, society could do away with "an ever widening circle of social discards," starting with "the criminal, the diseased and the insane" and gradually extending to "weaklings" and "perhaps ultimately to worthless race types."

Grant's theories about racial superiority and the need for dealing firmly with the weak and defective greatly influenced the Nazis, who translated his writings into German. Parts of *Mein Kampf,* and of the racial policies Germany put in place, appeared to borrow directly from *The Passing of the Great Race.* The book would later be discovered in Adolf Hitler's personal library, and Hitler is said to have written Grant a fan letter, in which he said "the book is my Bible."

Laughlin and Grant corresponded frequently and enthusiastically. In their letters, the two men freely exchanged opinions about eugenics— and racist and anti-Semitic views. Laughlin had to be circumspect in public, because the Eugenics Record Office relied on financing from organizations and individuals who might not want to be associated with virulent racism and anti-Semitism. He also served on committees with Jews and others who might find such views offensive. Laughlin had already been the subject of at least one complaint, from a trainee who had reported to a Eugenics Record Office funder in 1914 that Laughlin had discriminated against him because he was Jewish.

In his private correspondence with Grant, however, Laughlin could express himself more freely. In one letter, written shortly before the Nazis took power in Germany—but well after their agenda was known—Laughlin cautioned that America faced a "Jewish problem" of its own. "The Jew is doubtless here to stay and the Nordics' job is to prevent more of them from coming," he wrote. Laughlin's disdain extended to a wide range of groups. In another letter, he betrayed both his support for racial segregation and where he ranked Hindus and blacks on his personal racial hierarchy. It was good, he told Grant, that so few Hindus had immigrated to the United States. "The Hindu, although a colored man," is "more intelligent than the Negro, and claim[s] 'Aryan descent,'" he wrote. As a result, Hindus in America "would be more insistent in . . . trying to destroy the barriers to mixture between the white and colored races than would any other nonwhite race which has come to our shores."

Laughlin and Grant collaborated on their eugenics work. The wealthy Grant helped fund the Eugenics Record Office. Laughlin, for his part, helped Grant with his writing. He reviewed a prepublication manuscript of Grant's next major book about race, *The Conquest of a Continent*, and provided not only technical and stylistic advice, but help in identifying the most offensive parts. In one letter to Grant, Laughlin flagged a passage that he said had "a tinge of 'Damn Jew' about it."

When *The Conquest of a Continent* was released, Laughlin wrote to the publisher, Charles Scribner's Sons, urging that the book be sent to high school and college history departments. He also wrote letters to prominent people urging them to read it. "The wide and continuous distribution" of *The Conquest of a Continent* was, he insisted, "important."

Laughlin remained close to Grant throughout the older man's life. Shortly before Grant died, Laughlin conducted an unsuccessful letter-writing campaign to members of the Yale Committee on Honorary

Degrees, urging them to award Grant a doctorate of law. Laughlin was effusive in his praise. "No Yale graduate more definitely than Madison Grant is an exemplar of American ideals," he wrote. "As a painstaking student in American history . . . Grant has thrown great honor upon Yale University."

In the years after World War I, Laughlin increasingly turned his attention to immigration. War-weary Americans were in an isolationist mood, and popular opinion was turning against the new arrivals who were flooding into the nation's cities. In 1900 the foreign-born were nearly 14 percent of the population, and immigrant families, including American-born children, were more than one-third. In the years since, immigration had continued at record and near-record levels, with as many as one million new immigrants arriving each year.

The demographics of immigration had changed considerably from the early days of the Republic. In the eighteenth century, and much of the nineteenth, large numbers of immigrants came from the United Kingdom, Scandinavia, and Germany. The new waves of immigrants were predominantly from eastern, central, and southern Europe, with large numbers of Asians on the West Coast. Since 1896 Protestants had ceased to be the majority of immigrants, with Catholic, Jewish, Russian and Greek Orthodox, Hindus, and Muslims making up more than half of the new arrivals.

An anti-immigrant backlash was forming. Many native-born Americans resented the immigrants' customs and dress, languages, religions, and skin colors. They were disturbed that teeming immigrant neighborhoods, like New York's Lower East Side and East Harlem, seemed to be bringing the Old World to America. Grant expressed these resentments in 1916 in *The Passing of the Great Race*, complaining that Nordics like him were being "elbowed out of . . . [their] own home":

> The man of old stock . . . is to-day being literally driven off the streets of New York City by the swarms of Polish Jews. These im-

migrants adopt the language of the native American; they wear his clothes; they steal his name; and they are beginning to take his women, but they seldom adopt his religion or understand his ideals.

Along with this general dislike of foreigners and their un-American ways, immigration opponents had more specific concerns. Conservatives objected to the politics of the newcomers, many of whom were viewed as radical, or at least pro–labor union. Unions worried that immigrants would be a source of cheap labor, undermining wages and degrading working conditions. Protestant church leaders were troubled that the influx of Catholics and Jews was changing the nation's religious character.

There was also a new kind of objection, though it may have been an indirect expression of all the other anxieties: that the immigrants were of inferior genetic stock. This complaint was first raised by the Immigration Restriction League, a small group of Harvard alumni who met in Boston in 1894 to push for closing the nation's borders, particularly to Italians and Jews. The league persuaded Massachusetts senator Henry Cabot Lodge to introduce a bill requiring a literacy test for immigrants. The bill passed Congress, only to be vetoed by President Grover Cleveland. In 1917, after sustained lobbying by the anti-immigration forces, the literacy requirement became law.

The Immigration Restriction League directly injected eugenics into the debate. Its members, who communicated with newspapers across the country and spoke directly to elected officials, insisted that immigrants were bringing genetic defects with them. "The same arguments which induce us to segregate criminals and feebleminded and thus prevent their breeding apply to excluding from our borders individuals whose multiplying here is likely to lower the average of our people," a leader of the league, Prescott F. Hall, argued. Hall helped to form a Committee on Immigration under the American Breeders' Association's Eugenic Section, and used it as another platform for raising his eugenic objections.

These anti-immigration organizations spread the ideology that Grant had set out in *The Passing of the Great Race*. They argued that to protect American racial stock, it was necessary to drastically reduce the number of immigrants coming from southern and eastern Europe. If there was to be immigration, they insisted, it should come from Nordic nations. Their arguments were buttressed by avowedly anti-Semitic and anti-Catholic organizations and publications. In Michigan, Henry Ford's *Dearborn Independent* was demonizing Jews, arguing that they were parasitic and bent on world domination. The Ku Klux Klan, whose membership reached a record two and a half million in 1923, made fulminating against immigrants a new focus. It distributed literature such as *The Menace of Modern Immigration* and warned against the nefarious "Roman Catholic hierarchy" and "International Jew."

There were a few lonely voices raised against the eugenic turn the immigration debate was taking. Representatives of Jewish, Italian, and Slavic communities challenged how those groups were being described. Franz Boas, a respected Columbia University anthropologist, was a rare establishment figure who strongly defended immigrants. Boas, who was a member of the Breeders' Association's Committee on Immigration, dissented from a report calling on Congress to be guided by eugenic considerations in setting immigration policy—and resigned from the committee. Anyone who stood up in this manner risked reprisal. Madison Grant attacked Boas in a letter to a North Carolina senator as "a Jew" who represented "a large body of Jewish immigrants, who resent the suggestion that they do not belong to the White race." Grant tried to use his influence at Columbia University, as a prominent alumnus of the law school, to get Boas fired from the Department of Anthropology.

The forces demanding immigration restrictions found a powerful ally in Albert Johnson, the new chairman of the House Committee on Immigration and Naturalization. Johnson, a Republican, represented a Tacoma, Washington, district that was seeing an increasing number of Japanese immigrants. The main reason Johnson had come to Congress, he said, was to bring about "a heavy reduction of immigration by any method possible."

The blond, blue-eyed Johnson, who traced his family back to the Revolutionary War, fully subscribed to the eugenic arguments against the current immigration system. He was looking for "scientific testimony" to help make a case for broad-based new immigration legislation that would not have to rely solely on xenophobia and bigotry. Johnson, who was an admirer of *The Passing of the Great Race*, met with Madison Grant to seek advice. Grant introduced Johnson to Laughlin and the work of the Eugenics Record Office.

Johnson invited Laughlin to appear before the House Committee on Immigration and Naturalization as an expert adviser. On April 16 and 17, 1920, Laughlin testified on the subject of "biological aspects of immigration." He opened with a simple assertion: "The character of a nation is determined primarily by its racial qualities." He went on to explain in detail how current immigration patterns were threatening "the hereditary physical, mental, and moral . . . traits" of the United States.

Federal immigration policy had so far largely been based on economic factors, Laughlin said, but it was now "high time" for "the eugenical element" to "receive due consideration." The "biological aspects of immigration" that Laughlin promised in the title of his testimony had several components. One key part was identifying prospective immigrants who had particular hereditary defects and excluding them before they could enter the country and debase the nation.

Laughlin proposed a new program of eugenic screening. He argued that prospective immigrants should be examined in their hometowns, because only there would it be possible to get the necessary "eugenical facts," including family history and information like whether a prospective immigrant "comes from an industrious or a shiftless family." Laughlin testified that if the individual in question was a "potential parent"—that is, a "sexually fertile person"—he or she should only be admitted on a showing that their "family stock" contained "such physical, mental, and moral qualities as the American people desire to be possessed inherently by its future citizenry."

Laughlin also told congress that more attention should be paid to what nations immigrants were arriving from. He argued that non–northern European immigrants were a problem for the country. Laughlin said that because the United States' "foundation stock is largely from northwestern Europe" it was easier for the country to assimilate immigrants from there than from other places. He also introduced data he had on the population of institutions for the criminally insane in New York State. "Careful studies have shown that the frequency of Insanity in our foreign population is 2.9 times greater than in those of native birth," he informed the committee. Laughlin provided data purporting to show that the biggest problem lay in immigrants from southern and eastern Europe. He testified that Italy furnished 23.1 percent of the inmates, and Russia and Poland 12.6 percent, while England and Wales supplied 5.5 percent, and Scandinavia just 1.8 percent.

Johnson was so pleased with the testimony that he appointed Laughlin the official "Expert Eugenics Agent" for the House Committee on Immigration and Naturalization. This newly created position gave Laughlin and his testimony greater stature in the immigration debate, and it also brought more practical benefits. As Expert Eugenics Agent, Laughlin could invoke federal authority when he wanted to collect data for his research. He also had access to the congressional franking privilege, which he could use to send out eugenics literature without paying postage. Laughlin returned Johnson's warm feelings, calling his new benefactor "the great American watchdog whose job it is to protect the blood of the American people from contamination and degeneracy."

After Laughlin's appearance, Congress began to adopt the "biological" approach to immigration that he advocated. It passed the Emergency Immigration Restriction Act of 1921, which for the first time imposed national immigration quotas. The total number of immigrants was scaled back, and the number from any country was capped at 3 percent of that nationality's foreign-born population in the United States in 1910. Under this new quota system, fewer people would be admitted from countries like Italy, Russia, and Poland, whose nationals were a smaller percentage of the population in 1910. More would be let in from countries like England and Germany, which had been the main sources of older waves of immigration. The impact was dramatic. The number of immigrants from Europe fell from more than 650,000 in 1921 to 216,000 in 1922, with the sharpest declines coming from southern and eastern Europe.

Laughlin testified twice more on immigration reform. In November 1922 he made a presentation titled "Analysis of America's Modern Melting Pot," a report that included work he did as the committee's official Expert Eugenics Agent. Laughlin's view of the melting pot was a grim one. Covering the committee room walls with charts and photographs, including ones of Ellis Island immigrants, he was more emphatic than he had been in his earlier testimony that the newer immigrant groups would dangerously degrade the nation's gene pool. "Making all logical allowances for environmental conditions, which may be unfavorable to the immigrant, the recent immigrants, as a whole, present a higher percentage of inborn socially inadequate qualities than do older stocks," he told the committee.

Laughlin's "Analysis of America's Modern Melting Pot" was enormously influential. At a critical moment, when Congress was considering making even more profound changes in the nation's immigration policy, Laughlin supplied what purported to be irrefutable quantitative proof that the changes were necessary to protect the nation from a tide of hereditary defectives. Johnson, who played a major role in rounding up the votes for new immigration legislation, called it "one of the most valuable documents ever put out by a committee of Congress."

Laughlin's data was deeply flawed. Despite his insistence that he had made "all logical allowances for environmental conditions," much of the disparity he claimed to have found among different groups could be traced to environmental factors. It made little sense to compare Russian and British immigrants on measures like criminality or mental illness without taking into account the many nonbiological ways in which these groups differed. Russian immigrants in America had arrived more recently, were poorer, and were less likely to be able to speak English—all facts Laughlin was not interested in. The committee, however, accepted his testimony and sought more of it.

In March 1924 Laughlin testified before Congress a third time. In his report, "Europe as an Emigrant-Exporting Continent and the United States as an Immigrant-Receiving Nation," he went even further in arguing that immigrants from the "wrong" countries were dangerously eroding the nation's intelligence. Laughlin had prepared a chart of nationalities ranked by intelligence, relying on U.S. Army testing. At the top he placed England and Scotland. At the bottom, Russia, Greece, Italy, Belgium, and Poland.

Since his last visit, Laughlin's rhetoric had become more vehement. "Immigration is an insidious invasion just as clearly as, and works more certainly in national conquest than" an "invading army," he told the committee. If immigrants were closely related racially to the native stock and had "inborn talents" of a higher level, the immigration could work out well, he said. If, however, "the racial type is not assimilable, and the inborn traits of character are less ideal than those of the foundation stocks, then immigration works toward ultimate disaster."

Once again, there were serious problems with Laughlin's data. The Russian, Polish, and Italian immigrants who scored relatively low on the U.S. Army tests were recent arrivals, with limited ability to speak English, while the groups that scored higher had been in the country far longer. Laughlin failed to mention this—or the fact that the scores of foreign-born test takers rose with their years of residence in the United States, suggesting that what was holding them back was language skills and knowledge about America, not any inherent lack of intelligence.

The scientific community largely remained silent about Laughlin's misrepresentations, but a few prominent scientists did speak out. Herbert Spencer Jennings, a geneticist from Johns Hopkins, reanalyzed the data and, writing in the *Survey*, the national social workers' magazine, refuted Laughlin's claim that "recent immigrants are inferior in their inherited qualities." Joseph Gillman, a professor at the University of Pittsburgh, published a paper pointing out serious errors in the testimony. Laughlin "attempted to conceal his preconceptions in the elusiveness of technical statistical inaccuracies," Gillman wrote.

The great majority of members of both houses of Congress, however, eagerly embraced Laughlin's eugenic arguments for immigration restrictions. Representative Robert Allen, a West Virginia Democrat, put the matter bluntly in a statement on the House floor. The "primary reason for the restriction of the alien stream," he said, "is the necessity for purifying and keeping pure the blood of America."

Laughlin's biological arguments buttressed the ordinary xenophobia and bigotry that were already rampant in Congress. The floor debates were filled with racial and ethnic disparagement and outright falsehoods. Senator J. Thomas "Cotton Tom" Heflin of Alabama, a notorious white supremacist, presented as fact the story of "the arrest of a negro in New York." According to Heflin, the "negro" spoke Yiddish, the Irish policeman who arrested him spoke Yiddish, and the judge "also tried him in Yiddish." Heflin warned his Senate colleagues: "We are coming to a pitiful pass in this great country when it is unpopular to speak the English language, the American language."

Representatives of districts with large immigrant populations did their best to hold back the "biological immigration" tide, but they were badly outnumbered. New York congressman Samuel Dickstein, a Jewish immigrant from what is now Lithuania, protested that members of Congress were "infected with the germ of the Nordic superior race theory." Adolph Sabath, a Czech-Jewish immigrant who represented Chicago's West Side, explained on the House floor why Congress was about to enact new restrictions on immigrants like him:

They believe these people are inferior. They have been fed by misinformation; they have been fed by new dope, as I may term it, by unrelated statisticians, and by Professor Laughlin's eugenic and anthropological false tests, until they themselves believe there is some foundation for the unjustifiable conclusions contained in the so-called Laughlin report.

While Laughlin was delivering his scientifically couched pleas to Congress, the eugenics movement took its case directly to the public. A new edition of Madison Grant's *Passing of the Great Race* was released in 1921, and hard-line eugenicists began whipping up anti-immigrant sentiment. Major magazines clamored for a eugenic approach to immigration policy. In 1921 *Good Housekeeping* published an article by Calvin Coolidge, the vice president–elect, titled "Whose Country Is This?" In it, Coolidge made an appeal for racial purity for the "Nordic" race. "Biological laws tell us that certain divergent people will not mix or blend," he wrote. "The Nordics propagate themselves successfully. With other races, the outcome shows deterioration on both sides."

The *Saturday Evening Post*, whose weekly circulation of over two million made it one of the nation's most popular magazines, concurred. In a 1923 article, the journalistic voice of middle America, famous for its homespun Norman Rockwell covers, endorsed Laughlin's biological approach to immigration. "If America doesn't keep out the queer, alien, mongrelized people of Southern and Eastern Europe, her crop of citizens will eventually be dwarfed and mongrelized in turn," the article insisted.

After Laughlin's final testimony, Congress adopted the Immigration Act of 1924, a far more severe restriction on immigration than the 1921 revision. The new law reduced the national immigration quotas from 3 percent to 2 percent, and it changed the base year for national quotas from 1910 to 1890. In 1890 there were few immigrants from eastern Europe or Italy, and this change ensured that going forward, there would again be few. The new formula would help the nation to remain, as one congressman said on the House floor, "the home of a great people: English-speaking—a white race with great ideals, the Christian religion, one race, one country, one destiny."

With the passage of the Immigration Act of 1924, the eugenicists had their long-sought victory. Representative Johnson called the new law "America's Second Declaration of Independence." Madison Grant hailed the Immigration Act as "one of the greatest steps forward in the history of this country," and declared that the nation had "closed the doors just in time to prevent our Nordic population being overrun by the lower races." The following year, in *Mein Kampf*, Adolf Hitler offered his own praise for the new immigration law. In contrast to Germany, whose borders he found disturbingly open, the United States was making an effort to impose reason on its immigration policies, Hitler said, by "simply excluding certain races from naturalization."

The Immigration Act of 1924 had its intended effect. Under the new regime that it established, the demographics of American immigration changed dramatically. Southern and eastern Europeans, who had been about two-thirds of immigrants in 1920–21, fell to about 10 percent, and the percentage of immigrants from northern and western Europe soared. Jewish immigration fell from 190,000 in 1920 to 43,000 in 1921, and just 7,000 in 1926.

For European Jews, the timing could hardly have been worse. In just a few years, Nazism would begin its rise, and with violence and genocide sweeping across the continent, millions of Jews would be searching for a safe haven. The "biological" immigration policies that Harry Laughlin championed blocked almost all of them from entering the United States, even ones who were in imminent danger. Among the many victims of Nazism who would be turned away was the Frank family of the Netherlands. In 1941, Otto Frank wrote desperate letters to a U.S. government official, which became public many decades later, pleading without success to secure American visas for his wife, Edith, and his daughters, Margot Frank and Anne Frank.

Five

Harry Laughlin

After his triumph in helping persuade the nation to adopt a biological approach to immigration, Harry Laughlin shifted his attention to his other main prescription for improving America's genetic stock: eugenic sterilization. In Laughlin's view, restricting immigration from nations with high rates of hereditary defects reduced the foreign threat to the gene pool, but it did nothing about the equally serious domestic threat posed by defective Americans reproducing more of their own kind.

Laughlin had been promoting sterilization for more than a decade. In 1914, in his address to the First National Conference on Race Betterment in Battle Creek, he laid out his ambitious goal of sterilizing fifteen million people to save the nation from its "lowest one-tenth." That same year, with the report he drafted for the American Breeders' Association, Laughlin helped give the sterilization movement the imprimatur of a respected organization, whose members included some of the nation's leading biological scientists.

After that early start Laughlin had been pulled in many directions. He went to Princeton to obtain his master's degree and doctorate, and he worked on his study of institutionalized populations for the Census Bureau. In 1921, while he was working on immigration policy, Laughlin also helped to organize the Second International Eugenics Congress at the American Museum of Natural History in New York. Laughlin was in charge of exhibitions. The exhibits at the congress addressed a wide range of eugenic subjects, from "the relation between natural hereditary qualities and national greatness" to the "differences between white and Negro fetuses."

Through it all, Laughlin maintained his interest in eugenic sterilization and, in his indefatigable way, continued studying the subject. When he finished his research, he had an epic 502-page treatise. Laughlin's study of eugenic sterilization was the most comprehensive analysis ever done of the subject. It contained analyses of the history and texts of state sterilization laws and discussions of bills that had been vetoed. It included descriptions of particular methods of sterilization—seven for men and ten for women. It had family histories of individuals who were the subjects of eugenic sterilization, with capsule descriptions such as "Alice Smith, epileptic and feebleminded, New Jersey" and "Peter Fellen, moral pervert, Washington." And Laughlin had drafted a highly detailed model eugenic sterilization statute.

The only thing the sprawling treatise did not have was a publisher. It was by now well known that Laughlin was an outspoken advocate for eugenic sterilization, and there was little doubt that his new study would be a brief for the expanded use of sterilization. This presented a problem. Although there was little in the way of organized opposition to eugenic sterilization, people in influential positions were quietly expressing their unease about it. Laughlin observed this firsthand on the American Institute of Criminal Law and Criminology's sterilization committee, on which he served. The committee initially supported sterilization, but before long it became divided on the subject, and it stopped issuing reports.

When Laughlin tried to enlist an organization to fund publication of his book, he found that many potential funders did not want to be publicly associated with advocating mass sterilization. The Carnegie Institution would not underwrite it. The Bureau of Social Hygiene, the nonprofit organization created by John D. Rockefeller Jr., also turned him down. The bureau conceded the information could be valuable, but it was unwilling to support Laughlin's "direct propaganda favoring sterilization legislation."

Laughlin eventually turned to the Municipal Court of Chicago, which was a national leader in developing innovative approaches to social problems. Harry Olson, the court's chief justice, believed strongly that criminality had a hereditary basis, and that it required eugenic solutions. A year earlier, the court's Psychopathic Laboratory had appointed Laughlin a eugenics associate. Now the same organization agreed to publish Laughlin's book. In 1922, *Eugenical Sterilization in the United States* was released by the Chicago Municipal Court, with an introduction by Chief Justice Olson.

As the prospective funders anticipated, *Eugenical Sterilization in the United States* made no pretense of being a neutral analysis. The chief justice set the tone, declaring in his introduction that America needed "to protect herself against indiscriminate immigration, criminal degenerates, and race suicide." He insisted the crisis was an urgent one. If "racial degeneracy" continued, Chief Justice Olson warned, it would only be "a question of time when popular self-government will be impossible, and will be succeeded by chaos, and finally a dictatorship."

In the book itself, Laughlin expanded on the themes he struck in the American Breeders' Association *Report of the Committee to Study and to Report on the Best Practical Means of Cutting Off the Defective Germ-Plasm in the American Population.* Now that he was speaking for himself rather than writing for a committee, Laughlin took on a more emphatic tone and called for a sweeping eugenic sterilization program. *Eugenical Sterilization in the United States* sounded more like his Battle Creek address than his Breeders' Association report.

Laughlin made clear in his new treatise that he was interested in eugenic sterilization on a mass scale. He did not believe—as the model statute in the Breeders' Association report had provided—that sterilization should be limited to inmates of "state institutions for the so-cially inadequate," a small subset of the population. Writing now on his own, Laughlin argued that sterilization should be used on people who because of "degenerate or defective hereditary qualities" were the "po-tential parents of socially inadequate offspring" whether they were "in the population at large or inmates of custodial institutions."

Laughlin also proposed a more expansive list of "socially inade-quate classes" who should be candidates for sterilization than he had included in the Breeders' Association report. The model law in *Eu-genical Sterilization in the United States* called for sterilizing the feeble-minded, insane (including the psychopathic), criminalistic (including the delinquent), epileptic, inebriate (including both alcoholics and drug users), diseased (including the tubercular, syphilitic, and leprous), blind (including those with serious vision impairment), deaf (including those with serious hearing impairment), deformed (including the crippled), and dependent (including orphans and paupers). The Breeders' Asso-ciation model law had omitted a number of these categories, including the "crippled," "blind," "deaf," and "tubercular." When the decision was up to Laughlin alone, he wanted to make many more Americans sub-ject to sterilization.

There was one item on Laughlin's list of "degenerate or defective hereditary qualities" that had a striking, if hidden, significance. Laughlin recommended that eugenic sterilization laws apply to people who were "epileptic." What made his inclusion of epileptics of particu-lar note is that Laughlin himself was epileptic, though it is unclear whether he knew at the time that he had this particular "degenerate or defective hereditary quality." He had his first reported seizure in 1923, the year after the book was published, at the age of forty-three.

When Laughlin's first seizure struck, he was on a trip to Europe and suffering from a severe tooth infection. In his later years, while driving in Cold Spring Harbor, he would have a seizure that caused a near-fatal accident; after that his wife would not let him drive. Laugh-lin could have changed his belief that epileptics should be sterilized, but he did not. There is no record of his ever questioning the idea that he and others like him were defective and unworthy of reproducing. Laughlin and Pansy did not have children, but it is not known whether they intentionally avoided reproducing for eugenic reasons.

When Laughlin's book was released at the start of 1922, the eugenic sterilization movement was losing force. The legal tide had begun to turn in 1913, and from then to 1921 courts in seven states had struck down sterilization laws, mainly on due process or equal protection grounds. The year before *Eugenical Sterilization in the United States* came out, Indiana—the state where eugenic sterilization had gotten its start in 1907—had seen its own law struck down by the Indiana Supreme Court. Eugenicists were worried that even if they prevailed in state legislatures, they would lose the battle in the courtroom.

In his book, Laughlin put great emphasis on defending eugenic sterilization from legal challenges. He did two things to try to hold back the legal onslaught. First, he attempted to make the case for why the recent court decisions had been wrong—and why eugenic sterilization legislation should be upheld. Laughlin argued that sterilization laws represented the "prevention of social menace," which was "an essential purpose of law." When states sterilized people with hereditary defects, it was not any different from requiring residents to get vaccinations, quarantining the sick, or imprisoning criminals, he insisted. All were examples of the law acting "to prevent . . . conduct inimical to the welfare of the community."

To bolster this argument, Laughlin included expert opinions endorsing eugenic sterilization laws. Justice Olson provided Laughlin with a written opinion stating that properly drawn eugenic sterilization laws would be "held constitutional by the courts." The California attorney general, the Connecticut attorney general, and a prominent New York lawyer submitted detailed analyses of why eugenic sterilization laws should be upheld. In an unconvincing gesture toward balance, Laughlin included a one-paragraph summary of a speech given by a New York lawyer contending that sterilization laws were unconstitutional, and referred readers interested in more detail to an article in a criminology journal.

The second thing Laughlin did to fight the wave of court rulings was to write a model eugenic sterilization law designed to survive judicial scrutiny. The courts that were striking these laws down on due process grounds were objecting to the lack of procedural protections for people at risk of being sterilized. To insulate against such claims, the model statute called for states to designate a "State Eugenicist" whose office would conduct careful investigations of whether particular individuals should be sterilized. The model law also contained the sort of trial procedures the courts were looking for, including ensuring that people who might be sterilized were given formal hearings, advance notice of the hearings, the right to a jury trial, and the right to appeal.

Laughlin also had suggestions for protecting eugenic sterilization laws against equal protection challenges. Courts had been striking sterilization laws down on equal protection grounds when they applied only to inmates of state institutions and not to members of the general population. Laughlin strongly advised the states to make all of their residents eligible for eugenic sterilization "regardless of whether" they were members of "the population at large or inmates of custodial institutions."

Eugenical Sterilization in the United States was hailed as "epoch-making" and praised for its enormous influence. Laughlin's treatise spread the eugenic sterilization message to legislators, opinion makers, and grassroots activists nationwide. It also helped its author to further cement his position as one of America's most prominent eugenicists and its leading expert on sterilization. In February 1923, Laughlin was invited to join the Galton Society, which was one of the nation's most elite eugenics organizations. Its charter members included Laughlin's good friend Madison Grant, his boss Charles Davenport, and his old Princeton professor Edwin Conklin. With the invitation, Laughlin was being ushered into the intellectual leadership of American eugenics.

As his reputation rose, Laughlin's interests were becoming more international. In 1923 the Department of Labor named him a "Special Immigration Agent to Europe," courtesy of a labor secretary who shared his biological views of immigration. In the second half of 1923, he and Pansy traveled extensively throughout Europe, including visits to Germany, Sweden, Denmark, and Belgium, to observe his favorite racial groups in their native habitats. In a letter from Sweden to Harry Olson, Laughlin extolled the ability of the hardy Nordic people to survive in the unforgiving climate of northern Europe. "The strenuous struggle for existence seems to have eliminated the weaklings," Laughlin said. As a result, as "a breeding ground for racial stocks for exportation" to other parts of the world, "Sweden is exceedingly successful."

In January 1924 Laughlin went to London to deliver a lecture titled "Eugenics in America" at Burlington House. In his remarks, which were reprinted in the *Eugenics Review,* a publication of the Galton Institute in England, Laughlin told his audience the story of eugenics' rapid rise in the United States, including the founding of the Eugenics Record Office. His larger, flattering message to his British audience was that his goal in his eugenics work was to make America more like England.

The United States and the "white British colonies"—Canada, Australia, New Zealand, and South Africa—were, he warned, being threatened by immigrants from the "races of Southern Europe and Eastern Europe and the Oriental races" who were "crowding on the borders." If America and the white British colonies acted wisely and admitted "only emigrants who are of assimilable races and of good family-stocks," he said, they had a chance to reproduce in their countries "a civilization of the type which has developed in Britain."

For all of Laughlin's research, writing, and lecturing, his work to get eugenic policies adopted remained his greatest focus. During this era Laughlin was, as one observer put it, "a zealot for passing laws." He provided extensive assistance to eugenics supporters across the country as they organized and lobbied in favor of sterilization laws.

Laughlin's cause was meeting with considerable success in state legislatures. Washington, which had adopted a sterilization law in 1909 that applied only to certain criminals, enacted a law in 1921 aimed at preventing "the procreation of feeble-minded, insane, epileptic . . . moral degenerates" and other groups. Other states followed in rapid succession: Oregon, Montana, Delaware, and Michigan in 1923, and Virginia in March 1924. Laughlin took pride in his role in this new wave of legislation. He would soon boast in an annual report that these laws were in important ways "based upon the researches of the Eugenics Record Office."

As well as things were going in state legislatures, the eugenicists still had reason to worry about the courts. There had been a deluge of rulings since 1913 striking down sterilization laws in New Jersey, Iowa, Michigan, New York, Nevada, Indiana, and Oregon, where a predecessor to the 1923 law had been held to be unconstitutional. For the eugenicists, losses in the courts were more dangerous than legislative defeats. A political fight, if lost, could be resumed immediately. With the stroke of a pen, however, a judge could deliver a setback to eugenics that would last for years.

Some eugenicists dreamed of a way out: a United States Supreme Court decision upholding eugenic sterilization. If the justices ruled that sterilization laws did not violate the Fourteenth Amendment equal protection or due process clauses, all of the nation's lower courts would have to follow its lead, leaving them few legal bases on which to rule against sterilization. The eugenicists believed they had reason for cautious optimism: the newest laws had been written after publication of Laughlin's treatise, and with knowledge of the objections courts were raising. These laws, they hoped, would be better able to survive constitutional challenge. It was at just this moment, with eugenic sterilization at a legal crossroads, that a letter arrived for Laughlin from Lynchburg, Virginia.

On September 30, 1924, Aubrey Strode wrote to Laughlin to invite him to be an expert witness in a case testing the constitutionality of Virginia's new eugenic sterilization law. Strode said he and his colleagues believed Laughlin could play an important role. Both in drafting the Virginia law and in preparing for trial, Strode said, they had found *Eugenical Sterilization in the United States* "very helpful."

In his letter, Strode, who identified himself as the lawyer for the State Hospital Board, explained the case and where Laughlin would fit in. It would begin in about six weeks, most likely in the circuit court in Amherst County, Virginia. Whichever way the court ruled, an appeal would be taken to the Virginia Supreme Court of Appeals, and then to the United States Supreme Court. His client was "unwilling to proceed under the Act," Strode said, "until it shall be sustained by the highest court."

The law's defenders were looking for an expert who could help them "in making up a proper record for the test case." They wanted to put on testimony from "some authority who has made a study of the hereditary considerations involved in such cases," Strode said. They were seeking expert testimony to support two critical arguments: that the "patient is the probable potential parent of defective offspring" and that "considerations both of public welfare and of the welfare of the individual patient counsel the performance of the operation."

Strode gave Laughlin a brief synopsis of the facts of the case, but, as would be true at every stage of the proceedings, there were significant inaccuracies. Strode told Laughlin that the case concerned the sterilization of a "feeble-minded young woman nineteen years of age," even though Carrie was not feebleminded, and she had just turned eighteen in July. He said Carrie's mother was "also feeble-minded"—a dubious assertion, given the quality of the intelligence testing used to make that determination. And Strode told Laughlin that Carrie was "the mother of a feeble-minded child"—another falsehood, because Carrie's daughter, Vivian, was just six months old and had never been tested in any way.

Laughlin wrote back to Strode on October 3, his letter brimming with professional enthusiasm. He said he was "much interested" in hearing about the test case involving Virginia's sterilization law. Laughlin noted that there was a similar challenge being posed to a statute in Michigan, and he provided the name of a lawyer in Detroit who had just completed a legal brief in the case. But Strode's case appealed to him more because the Virginia eugenic sterilization law was newer and had been built "upon a thorough consideration of all previous legislation and litigation on the subject."

Laughlin made clear from the outset his hope that the Virginia case would reach the Supreme Court. The nation's highest court could settle once and for all "just what a state can do in reference to enacting eugenical sterilization laws," he said. If the case got that far, Laughlin was optimistic their side would prevail. The pro-eugenics forces had "thrashed out the matter so thoroughly"—and they had learned so much in the process about what was acceptable—that the Supreme Court "would sustain the essential elements of the Model Statute."

The facts of the Virginia case struck Laughlin as particularly "well selected." He agreed with Dr. Priddy that Carrie and her family were just the sort of people who would help the state make its case for "the hereditary factor in the production of feeblemindedness." The key, Laughlin told Strode, was that "both the immediate ancestor and the immediate offspring" were "feebleminded." In his review of the eugenics literature, and the Eugenics Record Office fieldwork investigations of many hundreds of families, he could not "recall a single instance in which feeblemindedness appeared in the grandmother, the mother (the patient) and the child (three generations), by environmental or accidental causes."

Strode did not think it was necessary for Laughlin to travel to Virginia. It would be enough to submit written answers under oath to a set of questions sent to him by the lawyers. Laughlin agreed to do that—without meeting or examining Carrie or her family. To begin the scientific study necessary to offer his expert opinion, however, Laughlin wanted a more detailed description of the young woman's lineage.

Laughlin sent a memorandum outlining the sort of "first-hand field material" he would need for his eugenic analysis. He asked Strode for information on Carrie and her siblings, parents, aunts, uncles, cousins, grandparents, children, nephews, and nieces, as well as any "consorts who have married into this stock and who are the parents of any of the blood kin above mentioned." For each of these, he wanted to know about parents, physical and mental development, literacy and mental test records, and a final quality: "social status with particular reference to the question of whether the individual has constituted a debit or credit to the social order."

Laughlin sent two tools the Eugenics Record Office had developed, a "Family Tree Folder" and a set of "Single Traits Sheets" for collecting and organizing the data. "If this material could be sent to me," he said, "I should be very glad to analyze it in light of the present existing knowledge of the inheritance of mental defect." Strode wrote to Dr. Priddy and asked him to collect the information Laughlin requested.

After Laughlin signed on, Dr. Priddy followed up with a letter of his own on October 14. He offered Laughlin his assistance in assembling the necessary information. Dr. Priddy reminded Laughlin that the two men had previously been in contact. Virginia's sterilization law had been drafted with the help of a copy of *Eugenical Sterilization in the United States*, "which you kindly gave me," Dr. Priddy wrote.

Dr. Priddy offered an idealized account of how Virginia's sterilization law had come about. In his telling, it had not been the culmination of years of persistence by him and Dr. DeJarnette in the face of skepticism and rejection. Dr. Priddy told Laughlin the impetus had come from the top. At a meeting of the State Hospital Board the previous year, Dr. Priddy said, the governor had instructed him "to prepare and have pushed through the General Assembly of Virginia a Sterilization Law." Dr. Priddy had then gone to Strode to draft a bill.

In his letter, Dr. Priddy shared his philosophy about eugenics, sterilization, and the feebleminded, which was similar to Laughlin's. Dr. Priddy explained his hope that he would be able to operate the colony on what he called the "clearing house" model: taking in feebleminded women, sterilizing them, and then setting them free to make room for more mentally defective women. It was a conception that closely tracked what Laughlin had recommended in his Battle Creek speech.

As for the genealogical information Laughlin requested, Dr. Priddy's attempts to trace Carrie's lineage had proved frustrating. He had begun investigating Carrie's family before Laughlin signed on as an expert. In mid-September, Dr. Priddy had written to Caroline Wilhelm, the Red Cross social worker who brought Carrie to the colony, asking for her help with eugenic fieldwork. He asked Wilhelm if she would "take Carrie Buck and her allied kin and get up the names of all defectives connected with the two sides" of the family "and make a report to me."

The investigation did not go as Dr. Priddy hoped. It got off to a slow start when the nurse assigned to the project phoned her supervisor to say she had lost Dr. Priddy's letter. "'Thought maybe it went down the back seat of the car,'" the supervisor informed Dr. Priddy of the news with evident irritation. She asked Dr. Priddy to send another copy of the letter.

When the fieldwork finally began, it did not turn up much. "I have had the Red Cross people at work making these investigations but have gotten little more information than I already had," Dr. Priddy told Strode. Dr. Priddy wrote to Laughlin that he was "very sorry" he could not "make you out a genealogical tree as you would like to have." He offered a simple explanation for the lack of information. "This girl comes from a shiftless, ignorant and moving class of people," and as result it was "impossible to get intelligent and satisfactory data."

What Dr. Priddy came up with was a tangle of relationships and possible relationships. He told Laughlin there were several inmates at the colony named Buck and others named Harlow (Emma's maiden name was Harlowe). Dr. Priddy said "all of the Bucks and Harlows we have here descen[d] from the Bucks and Harlowes of Albemarle County" and that he believed "they are of the same stock." There was "considerable doubt," Dr. Priddy said, about whether Carrie was biologically a member of the Buck family. But he was more certain that Carrie was a Harlowe, through her mother. That "line of baneful heredity seems conclusive and unbroken," he wrote.

The picture of Carrie's immediate family was not much clearer.

Dr. Priddy told Laughlin that Carrie had two or three half brothers and half sisters, but they had been taken from Emma and adopted by non–family members. All he was able to learn, he said, about Richard Harlowe, Emma's father, was that he had died of spinal trouble.

Dr. Priddy offered more specific information about Carrie and Emma. Carrie, he reported, had been adopted by the Dobbses at age four, but was given up when her "moral delinquencies culminated in the illegitimate birth of" her daughter. Carrie attended school up to the sixth grade, and was "fairly helpful to the domestic work of the household under strict supervision." Dr. Priddy said that as far as he understood, "there was no physical developmental or mental trouble" in "her early years." He reported that Carrie had a "mental age of nine years," and that she was "incapable of self support and restraint except under strict supervision." He also offered his opinion, belied by photographs, that Carrie had a "rather badly formed face."

Laughlin did not get all of the information he wanted, and his elaborate eugenics research forms were never filled out. He did not personally meet Carrie or Emma or any other members of their family. He was satisfied, however, that based on the questionable information he received from Dr. Priddy, he knew enough to provide an expert opinion about Carrie and her family's hereditary worth, and about whether Carrie should be sterilized.

In a formal legal document that he signed before a notary public in Cold Spring Harbor on November 6, Laughlin answered Strode's interrogatory questions. In response to the preliminary questions, Laughlin listed his credentials: assistant director of the Eugenics Record Office of the Carnegie Institution of Washington, and immediate supervisor of the office since it opened in 1910; supervisor of the annual Training Corps for eugenics field-workers; Expert Eugenics Agent for the House Committee on Immigration and Naturalization; Eugenics Associate of the Psychopathic Laboratory of the Municipal Court of Chicago; and author of *Eugenical Sterilization in the United States*, "a book of 502 pages," he noted.

After the background questions, Laughlin was asked to "give a short analysis of the hereditary nature of Carrie Buck." He made clear that he was relying on "the truth of the following facts which were supplied by Superintendent A.S. Priddy." With that qualification out of the way, he proceeded to explain why Carrie was mentally deficient, the probable parent of deficient children, and an appropriate subject for sterilization.

Laughlin's description of Carrie, based as it was on the sparse and not entirely accurate information Dr. Priddy had provided, was disconnected from her actual life. He testified that she had "mental defectiveness, evidenced by failure of mental development," with a chronological age of eighteen but a mental age of just nine, according to the Stanford Revision of the Binet-Simon test. He described her history as having been marked by "social and economic inadequacy," and stated that she had never been "self-sustaining." Laughlin also testified that Carrie had a "record during life of immorality, prostitution, and untruthfulness," though he did not back up these charges with any particulars. In a final disparaging detail, Laughlin included Dr. Priddy's contention that Carrie, whom he had not met, had a "rather badly formed face."

Laughlin described Emma, whom he referred to by the archaic legal title "Mother of Propositus," in even more negative terms. He reported that her chronological age was fifty-two and her mental age seven years and eleven months, based on the Stanford Revision of the Binet-Simon. Like her daughter, Emma had a record of "social and economic inadequacy," Laughlin said, and had never been "self-sustaining." Employing the same trio of disparaging words he used to describe Carrie, Laughlin said Emma had a record of "immorality, prostitution and untruthfulness." He also said she had syphilis and at least one, but more likely three, illegitimate children.

In his section on Carrie's family, Laughlin offered another description taken from Dr. Priddy. "These people belong to the shiftless, ignorant, and worthless class of anti-social whites of the South," he testified. Laughlin included the jumbled descriptions Dr. Priddy had given him of the Buck and Harlowe families and their possible relation to Carrie. He also repeated Dr. Priddy's claim that Carrie might not be a Buck, and tracked his language about her Harlowe lineage, asserting that "the line of baneful heredity seems conclusive and unbroken on the side of her mother."

Laughlin's most dubious assertions, again taken from Dr. Priddy, concerned Carrie's daughter. He said Vivian, who was "about six months old," was "considered feebleminded." As support, Laughlin included a parenthetical that stated: "According to depositions of the Red Cross nurse, Miss Caroline E. Wilhelm, of Charlottesville, Va., in the proceeding committing Carrie Buck to the State Colony, Carrie Buck's illegitimate baby gave evidence of mental defectiveness at an early age."

Laughlin's statement was similar to the false claim that Dr. Priddy made at Carrie's sterilization hearing, at which he had said that "according to the depositions" used in committing her to the colony, Carrie had "one illegitimate mentally defective child." Wilhelm had said no such thing in the depositions used to commit Carrie to the colony— for the simple reason that when Carrie was committed, her daughter had not yet been born. It was a useful inaccuracy, however, because it allowed Laughlin to testify that there were three consecutive feebleminded generations in the Buck family, a pattern that he said in his first letter to Strode was, in his experience, always associated with hereditary mental defect.

In the "Analysis of Facts" section of his interrogatory responses, Laughlin gave his opinion that Carrie's feeblemindedness was hereditary. Feeblemindedness can be caused by environmental factors, he allowed, but he believed Carrie's defect was "due, primarily, to inheritance." In his experience, he said, a single feebleminded child appearing in an "apparently normal family" might be a result of environmental factors. However, "if the same mother has more than one feebleminded child, then, even in the absence of a more detailed pedigree record, the evidence weighs very heavily against the primary cause being environmental." It was an odd analysis, because it bore no relation to the facts of Carrie's case as he had just presented them. Laughlin was uncertain how many siblings Carrie had, but he did not say that any of them were feebleminded—and there was, at this point, no evidence that they were.

Laughlin also purported to find evidence of Carrie's feeblemindedness in her limited educational achievements. He noted that at the age of four she had been taken from "the bad environment furnished by her mother" and "given a better environment by her adopted mother, Mrs. J.T. Do[bb]s." Despite this improvement in environment, Laughlin said, Carrie was "able to attain only to the 6th grade in school." Her failure to do better in school was, Laughlin testified, "typical . . . of a low-grade moron."

It was, once again, an odd and misleading analysis. Laughlin's statement that Carrie "was able to attain only to the 6th grade in school" suggested that the failure to proceed further was hers. The truth was that Carrie was performing perfectly well in school, and only stopped her education because the Dobbses would not let her continue. There was, in fact, nothing about Carrie's educational history that pointed to feeblemindedness.

Laughlin then addressed a critical question under the statute: whether Carrie was likely to give birth to defective children. Carrie was clearly a "potential parent," he said, because she had already given birth to a child. Given her own "feeblemindedness and moral delinquency," and the evidence from her family history that her defects were hereditary, Laughlin said, she had to be considered a "potential parent of socially inadequate or defective offspring."

Another interrogatory question asked Laughlin to "give in brief outline the results of scientific investigations tending to show that feeblemindedness is likely to be transmitted to offspring from a feebleminded parent," and to include illustrative cases if he desired. Laughlin presented the court with a sizable list, starting with chapter 8 of his own book, *Eugenical Sterilization in the United States*, in which he had "analyzed, so far as data would permit, the hereditary nature of the particular social inadequacy from which the subject of the particular test case was suffering." In every case he analyzed in the chapter, he said, the evidence showed "beyond a reasonable doubt" that "the particular inadequacy was inborn."

In another question, Strode asked about a key provision he had written into the Virginia sterilization law: the requirement that sterilization be in the interest of both the patient and society. Laughlin gave his opinion that salpingectomy and vasectomy "have but little physiological effect other than sexual sterility." On the positive side, he said, eugenic sterilization provided a clear benefit to society. The state had to prevent individuals who were fertile and "socially inadequate because of feeblemindedness" or "other constitutional defect" from reproducing. There were, Laughlin said, two ways of doing this: (1) segregating them in an institution where they would be prevented from having intercourse; and (2) eugenic sterilization. "Modern eugenical sterilization," he concluded, "is a force for the mitigation of race degeneracy which, if properly used, is safe and effective."

Finally, Laughlin was asked to "give any other information or testimony in regard to the general subject" he thought might be helpful to the court. Laughlin took the opportunity to say he had closely examined sterilization laws that had been enacted around the country. Virginia's statute was "one of the best laws thus far enacted," he said. It "avoided the principal eugenical and legal defects of previous statutes, and has incorporated into it the most effective eugenical features and the soundest legal principles of previous laws."

It was agreed from the beginning that Laughlin would not have to travel to Virginia to research the case or to testify. His participation would be limited to the interrogatories he mailed in from Cold Spring Harbor. It would clearly help the case, however, to have an expert witness appear in court. In a letter to Strode, Laughlin suggested a colleague, Arthur Estabrook, who might be willing to make the trip. Strode was enthusiastic about the recommendation, and told Dr. Priddy he would write to Estabrook.

Arthur Estabrook was a thirty-nine-year-old eugenics field researcher. He was not as prominent as Laughlin, but he was beginning to make a name for himself with his studies of hereditary defects in communities and individuals. Like Laughlin, Estabrook had come to eugenics from an academic background. He was born into a middle-class family in Leicester, Massachusetts, and earned bachelor's and master's degrees at nearby Clark University. After receiving a Ph.D. in biology from Johns Hopkins in 1910, Estabrook joined the Eugenics Record Office as one of its first employees. Estabrook quickly became adept at the art and science of eugenics research. He was on his way to becoming, as one study of his work pronounced him, "the most prolific eugenics field worker in the history of the movement."

Soon after his arrival in Cold Spring Harbor, Estabrook embarked on his first major eugenics research project. With financial support from Mrs. E. H. Harriman, he went off to study what he would later describe as a "highly inbred rural community of New York State." He found the community to be plagued by alcoholism, sexual misbehavior, and other social inadequacies.

In August 1912 Estabrook and Davenport jointly published *The Nam Family: A Study in Cacogenics*. The "Nam" of the title was a bit of eugenics wordplay: it was "man" spelled backward—a linguistic expression of the backwardness the authors believed they had found. *The Nam Family* was the latest in the line of "criminal anthropology" books that traced back to Richard Dugdale's *The Jukes: A Study in Crime, Pauperism, Disease, and Heredity: also Further Studies of Criminals,* which had been published thirty-five years earlier. In keeping with their positions at the Eugenics Record Office, Estabrook and Davenport injected more eugenic "science" than earlier books of this sort had included. They insisted that the role of heredity in determining the "indolence," "alcoholism," and "licentiousness" in families like the Nams "cannot be doubted." The book's subtitle was an attempt to drive this point home: "cacogenics" was a combination of the Greek words for "bad" (*caco*) and "gene" (*genics*).

In *The Nam Family,* Estabrook and Davenport wrote about a rural New York community that was, the authors explained, the product of the union of a "roving" white patriarch of Dutch lineage and an "Indian princess." That union led to generations of men and women, they said, with unusual levels of alcoholism, lack of ambition, and other dysfunction. Although the authors said their primary aim was to present "bare facts" about the Nam family, they also offered advice. Doing nothing about the Nam family's problems was not a viable option, they said. "No State can afford to neglect such a breeding center of feeble-mindedness, alcoholism, sex-immorality, and infanticide as we have here," they wrote. "A rotten apple can infect the whole barrel of fruit."

Estabrook and Davenport considered the possibility of using trained nurses to teach members of the community housekeeping skills and hygiene, but they decided it would not work. Such efforts would, they said, be nothing more than "supplying a veneer of good manners to a punky social body." The authors also raised the idea of scattering the Nam community, but concluded that would just create more "centers of indolence and alcoholism—for like seeks to mate with like wherever it finds itself."

There was one solution Estabrook and Davenport believed could solve the problem of the Nam family: mass segregation. The children and youth whose family history suggested they would produce inferior offspring could be institutionalized for thirty-five to forty years, until there was no danger of their reproducing. It was, the authors conceded, "perhaps the most expensive" solution, but if it were done the Nams "would leave no progeny" and "the worst of the strain would . . . be brought virtually to an end."

Estabrook and Davenport were open to the idea of sterilizing all the Nams. "Asexualization," as they called it, would have the same effect, they noted, of ending all Nam progeny. It was doubtful, however, that "public sentiment would favor such treatment," they said, even though sterilization of the community was "quite within the province of the State."

In 1916 Estabrook released his second book, *The Jukes in 1915*, a follow-up to Dugdale's 1877 classic. Working from family records in the New York Prison Association archives, Estabrook identified more than two thousand descendants of the same family Dugdale had made famous. Estabrook had traveled to places where Jukes now lived and conducted eugenics research. "It has been persistently carried on for three years in fourteen States of the Union," he reported. "Every Juke possible to see has been personally visited."

Estabrook discovered that over time the Jukes had improved their status, becoming more intelligent and less socially isolated. But there were still high rates of defects of all kinds, and he cataloged them meticulously in the style of eugenic fieldwork. In a typical entry, Estabrook described one member of the family, the "second child of VI 7," as "mentally incapable of work in school." The woman "became a harlot, later married, had one child, continued her harlotry, and was finally divorced by her husband," he wrote. "Her neat and well-dressed appearance does not give the impression of the character she has become."

Estabrook reported finding elaborate hereditary patterns of such defects as feeblemindedness, laziness, and "harlotry." In one eugenic analysis, he examined the grandchildren of Althea, described as "of an erotic make-up," and her mate, Otto, "a steady, industrious, plodding man" who died in an accident while intoxicated. After assessing the grandchildren's varying degrees of sexual proclivity, Estabrook concluded that it was "probable" that the "eroticism" exhibited by two of them was a remnant of "the licentiousness . . . of their ancestors."

Estabrook found that decades after Dugdale first discovered them, the Jukes were still defective. There were, he conceded, family members who were "perhaps normal mentally and emotionally," but there were many more who were not. "One half of the Jukes were and are feeble-minded, mentally incapable of responding normally to the expectations of society," he wrote, "satisfied with the fulfillment of natural passions and desires, with no ambition or ideals in life."

The conclusions of *The Jukes in 1915* were very different from those of the 1877 original. Dugdale, the prison reformer, had traced the Jukes' problems to their poor environment and argued for greater efforts to ameliorate their conditions. Estabrook, the eugenics field worker, insisted their problems were largely bad genes: "No matter what the degree of perfection to which we raise the standard of environment, the response of the individual will still depend on its constitution and the constitution must be adequate before we can attain the perfect individual, socially and eugenically."

Estabrook also disagreed with Dugdale on what should be done. As he had in *The Nam Family,* Estabrook called for eugenic solutions. Once again, he argued that the two most effective approaches would be segregation and "asexualization." He still believed sterilization was not practical because public sentiment was against it. But if the six hundred living feebleminded and epileptic Jukes could be segregated, he said, "at the end of fifty years the defective germ-plasm would be practically eliminated."

For his next major study, Estabrook traveled to Indiana, which held a special status in the eugenics community for having enacted the nation's first eugenic sterilization law. Once again, he did a follow-up to a famous field study—this time, Oscar McCulloch's investigation of the extended family he had called "the Tribe of Ishmael." McCulloch had focused on the family's purported high levels of criminality and pauperism. In his follow-up, Estabrook investigated the family's intelligence levels and blamed their low status on high rates of feeblemindedness. As he had with the Nams and the Jukes, Estabrook concluded that most of the Ishmaelites were still "cacogeneic folk" who "spread the anti-social traits of their germ plasm with no check by society."

Estabrook's work on the Ishmaelites had some notable weaknesses. His claim that much of the family was feebleminded was undermined both by the fact that they had not been given intelligence tests and by the fact that so many of them were employed in respected trades and professions. Members of the family had also assimilated into the surrounding society to the point where it was not clear they could legitimately be considered a distinct class. In the end, despite his years of work and the considerable expenses incurred, Estabrook's study of the Ishmaelites was not published in book form, likely because leaders of the eugenics movement "considered the work to be highly problematic."

After his Indiana project, Estabrook studied a mixed-race community of about five hundred people near Lynchburg, Virginia. He published his fieldwork in 1926, with Professor Ivan McDougle of Sweet Briar College, under the title *Mongrel Virginians: The Win Tribe*. The community's ancestors were white, black, and Native American, and the "Win" of the title was an acronym for White-Indian-Negro.

Estabrook was "among the American eugenicists most obsessed with race," and in *Mongrel Virginians* his crude prejudices were on full display. The authors described one member of the community, whom they called "Ichabod Ross," as having "much the appearance of a 'darky with thick lips.'" Another was said to have "no characteristics of an Indian whatever" but rather "the appearance of 'a mean white woman with a little Negro in her.'" The authors invoked an array of racial stereotypes, which they put forth as science, such as their casual assertion that "as is well known, the negro is 'full' of music."

Mongrel Virginians was a classic example of the type of fieldwork the Eugenics Record Office championed, but critics pointed out how flawed its techniques were. Writing in the *Annals of the American Academy of Political and Social Science*, Abraham Myerson, a neurology professor at Tufts University, called the book "absolutely unscientific in method." *Mongrel Virginians* was "an exposé of small community moral depravity recorded from the lips of neighbors," he wrote, in which "the most trifling morsels of gossip, with arbitrary interpretations, with no possibility of verification since many of the characters are dead, form the basis of judgment." Driving his point home, Myerson concluded his review by calling *Mongrel Virginians* a "really absurd and useless book!"

Mongrel Virginians appeared to have a specific racial agenda. The authors began the fieldwork in January 1923, just as a campaign was under way to strengthen Virginia's laws against race mixing. While they were researching the book, segregationist elected officials were in the process of adopting the 1924 law that established the "one drop" rule in the state. The publisher of *Mongrel Virginians* promoted it as providing answers to the racial issues Virginia and the rest of the South were wrestling with. "What Happens When White, Indian, and Negro Blood Intermingles?" the headline of a publicity pamphlet asked. According to the publisher, the book would answer such questions as "Is it a fact that any white race subject to continuous contact with the negro, ultimately becomes mongrelized?"

The authors' answer to this question was "yes." Whites, they argued, became "mongrelized"—a word taken from dog breeding—when exposed to other races. And it was Estabrook and McDougle's opinion, as a review in the *Journal of Negro History* explained, that "the result of this race admixture has been to produce an inferior stock." In a letter to the *Richmond Times-Dispatch* on February 22, 1926, McDougle argued that the intermingling of the races was dragging Virginia down. "While many of the better white families of the State have been sending their sons and daughters into other parts of the country to make fame for themselves, these mongrel groups have remained for the most part in their native habitat and have increased biologically at a much more rapid rate," McDougle wrote. "As a result it is to a great extent true that there are portions of the State which are rapidly becoming mongrelized."

Estabrook was working on *Mongrel Virginians* when the Virginia trial team decided to invite him to become an expert witness in the case. He was doing eugenic fieldwork in rural Kentucky in the fall of 1924, and Strode had difficulty contacting him. With the trial scheduled to start in a few weeks, Strode appealed to Laughlin for help, and Laughlin asked Estabrook's wife to send a telegram. "Superintendent Priddy Lynchburg Virginia wants expert witness sterilization test trial," Jessie Estabrook wired to Kentucky on October 23. "Can you attend."

In a November 3 letter to Strode, Estabrook accepted the assignment and said he would attend the trial, which was scheduled to begin on November 18. Strode asked his new expert to come to Virginia a few days in advance, so he could meet Dr. Priddy, Carrie, and Emma. On November 8, Estabrook said he would do his best to adhere to Strode's schedule, but he warned that his remote location might delay him.

"I am a days [sic] ride on horseback from the railroad," he wrote, "and hence may not make exactly the train I desire."

Estabrook's assignment was a critical one. The proceeding in the Amherst County Circuit Court would be the only chance for the colony to create a factual record about the Buck family and the reasons for sterilizing Carrie. If the trial court's ruling was appealed, future courts—all the way up to the United States Supreme Court—would make their decisions based on the facts presented at the trial in Amherst County. So far, however, Strode and Dr. Priddy had not been able to turn up much information about Carrie's family. Strode was direct in his instructions to Estabrook. "We wish to present in this test case as strong a showing of facts as possible, both for the trial court and for the appellate courts," he said. "We shall not have another opportunity."

As the trial drew near, it was beginning to look like a small courthouse in Amherst County, Virginia, could become the center of the roiling national debate over eugenic sterilization. And there was a real chance that what happened at trial there—and on appeal—could settle the issue for the entire nation. The testimony of the fact witnesses and expert witnesses, and the legal arguments that were made, in the Amherst County Courthouse would resonate widely. That meant that to a significant degree, the future of eugenic sterilization was now in the hands of a single man: Aubrey Strode.

Six

Aubrey Strode

I n its early days, the campaign for eugenic sterilization in Virginia had involved public education and legislative lobbying. Dr. Albert Priddy and his fellow superintendent Dr. Joseph DeJarnette had been the driving forces. But now that Virginia had a eugenic sterilization law, the focus had shifted. True to Alexis de Tocqueville's dictum that "scarcely any political question arises in the United States which is not resolved, sooner or later, into a judicial question," eugenic sterilization had been transformed into a legal case. As a result, Aubrey Strode, the well-respected trial lawyer who represented the state's hospital board, would now play the largest role.

Strode was, in one critical respect, an unexpected person to be leading the charge. Unlike Dr. Priddy and Dr. DeJarnette—and Harry Laughlin—he was not a eugenics true believer. As a member of the state legislature, he had worked for better public schools, the right of women to attend college, and other progressive causes. But he had never shown any interest in eugenic sterilization until Dr. Priddy approached him and and asked him to draft legislation on behalf of the colony.

Even now, as Strode worked on the case, it was not clear how committed he was to sterilizing the "defective." The first time Dr. Priddy approached him to draw up a law in 1916, he drafted such a weak statute that it soon became clear—when the Mallory family sued—that it did not authorize superintendents to perform sterilizations at all. The second time Dr. Priddy approached Strode, after having gotten the support of the hospital board for a sterilization law, Strode talked the board into dropping the matter.

When Strode was finally prevailed upon to draft sterilization legislation, he wrote a narrow bill, one that was considerably more limited than the model statute Dr. Priddy had given him. Strode omitted whole categories of defective people. He wrote the bill to apply only to inmates of state mental hospitals, so it covered thousands of people instead of millions. And he advised the board not to allow any sterilizations to be performed until a challenge could be taken all the way to the Supreme Court—a process that could take years, and that might lead to the law being struck down before it could be used.

Strode might not have been a sterilization enthusiast, but he was a dedicated advocate for his clients. When he accepted a case, he was driven to win. Because of the time and place in which he was born, and the friends and associates he had made over the course of his career, Strode was handed the case of a lifetime—a chance to litigate eugenics on a grand stage and to become a part of legal history. Unfortunately for Carrie, Strode was a highly intelligent man and a skilled litigator who was more than up to the task.

Aubrey Ellis Strode was born in Amherst County, Virginia, on October 2, 1873. He was the scion of two old Virginia families who took considerable pride in their ancestry. The Strodes traced their lineage to England in 1066, when Sir John Strode accompanied William the Conqueror on the Norman Conquest. The American branch of the Strode family settled in Virginia, where they built Strode Fort Farm to protect themselves from Indians. Strode's mother, Mildred

Ellis Strode, was part of another family, the Ellises, who were among the state's earliest settlers. Her ancestor John Ellis was granted land in the second charter of the Virginia Company.

Aubrey Strode arrived in the world just eight years after the Civil War ended. His family lived at Kenmore, an antebellum tobacco plantation with a two-story brick Greek revival home. With the end of slavery, Kenmore had been transformed into an elegant, if rustic, homestead. It was "one of the most charming old Southern homes that it has ever been my pleasure to see," one visitor would later recall, a place "flowing with milk and honey" that represented "the best of the South."

Strode's family was deeply connected to the Confederate cause. His father, Henry Aubrey Strode, joined Braxton's Battery of the Fredericksburg Artillery at the age of sixteen and fought with it until the South surrendered. Strode's maternal grandfather, John Thomas Ellis, abandoned his position of commissioner of revenue in Amherst County to join the Confederate cause. He was serving as a lieutenant colonel at Gettysburg when, in a Union bombardment just before Pickett's Charge, he was decapitated by a cannonball. Aubrey Strode keenly felt the weight of his family's war history. He would later say that "as the son and grandson of Confederate soldiers I both inherited and have cultivated a reverence for those who wore the gray."

Strode's father, Henry, attended the University of Virginia, where he won a medal in mathematics. After graduation, he taught high school and then moved into higher education, becoming an assistant professor of mathematics at Richmond College, in the state capital. In 1872 Henry Strode married Mildred Powell Ellis and bought Kenmore Plantation from her grandfather. He established Kenmore University High School, a preparatory school for boys, on the plantation. While he served as principal of the new school, he and Mildred began a family. Aubrey was born in 1873, and six daughters and another son would follow.

The Kenmore School took a progressive approach to education. It focused on science rather than the classics that most southern schools favored. It also emphasized the health of its students, engaging them in a wide array of physical activities on the plantation grounds. The school became a respected training ground for talented young men from the region, and sent many of its graduates on to the University of Virginia.

Aubrey attended the Kenmore School, studying under his father and living with his family in the antebellum plantation house. He graduated in 1887, one of a class of about a dozen boys. Aubrey enrolled at Washington and Lee, in nearby Lexington. Washington and Lee was a revered southern institution. After the Civil War, Confederate General Robert E. Lee had served as president of the college, which was then called Washington College. When Aubrey attended, Lee's son was president of the school.

Henry Strode closed the Kenmore school in 1889 and became a professor of mathematics at the University of Mississippi. The following year, he moved to South Carolina, to become the first president of Clemson Agricultural College, a small school that would become Clemson University. His presidency ended abruptly in 1893, but he stayed on as a mathematics professor.

While his father was moving up in academia, Aubrey continued his own travels through secondary and higher education. He left college to teach high school in South Carolina, and a year later he enrolled at the University of Virginia. Aubrey studied political economy and moral philosophy and won a medal for oratorical excellence. When he graduated, he went back to South Carolina to be a high school principal.

In 1896 both father and son returned home to Kenmore. Henry Strode, who was in poor health after several strokes, came back to retire. Aubrey, who was twenty-two, reopened the Kenmore School with a college friend, J. Thompson Brown Jr., so he could continue to work as an educator while being closer to his family, which needed him.

Under Aubrey's stewardship, the Kenmore School advertised itself as a quality preparatory school. The 1897–98 catalog trumpeted its location "in one of the most beautiful as well as most salubrious sections of Piedmont Virginia." And it emphasized that boys who lived on campus would be under the supervision of "Mrs. H.A. Strode," who would impart "the refining influences of a Christian home." The school promised to protect its students from "those whose society would be contaminating."

In promoting the quality of the education at Kenmore, the catalog emphasized Aubrey's erudition and teaching skills. It contained an enthusiastic endorsement from George F. Holmes, a professor of Historical Science at the University of Virginia: "Mr. Strode has been familiarized from boyhood with the duties, best methods, and habits of teaching—his father having been one of the most eminent instructors in Virginia."

While he was running the school, Aubrey began to study law. He enrolled in a course with the Sprague Correspondence School of Law in Detroit, which advertised, "Instruction by mail adapted to everyone . . . Takes spare time only." It was not surprising that after studying political economy and moral philosophy at the University of Virginia, and winning a medal for oratory, Strode would be drawn to the law. But given his early interest in education, he may well have been attracted to a legal career because he was looking for a more financially rewarding and secure profession, especially as more of the responsibility of caring for his family was falling to him.

In 1898 Strode enrolled in the University of Virginia School of Law. While he was there, he was not able to escape the burdens he had left behind at Kenmore. Strode's father ruptured a blood vessel and declined into paralysis and dementia. Around the same time, his mother began her own decline. Strode had to commit his parents to mental institutions, and both died shortly after his arrival at law school.

Strode rushed through his studies, and after less than half a year of classroom instruction, in January 1899, he was admitted to the Virginia bar. Strode closed the Kenmore School and dedicated himself completely to his new profession. He set up a law office near the Amherst County Courthouse and sent out cards announcing that he was available to take on legal work.

Strode's legal career got off to a fast start, and before long he opened a second office, in Lynchburg. In 1903 he married the former Rebekah

Davies Brown, the sister of his college classmate and Kenmore School colleague J. Thompson Brown Jr. The daughter of a local judge, Rebekah was also an educator who had taught at girls' schools.

After the wedding, Rebekah moved in with Strode at Kenmore. Even as he was starting his own family, Strode continued to help care for his seven younger siblings. With both parents deceased, Strode was now the mainstay of the family. He helped his sisters and brother pay tuition and other expenses with the income from his thriving law practice.

Strode's practice covered legal matters large and small. He took on run-of-the-mill commercial cases, trust and estates work, and personal injury litigation. In one case, he wrote a letter for a client who was injured while walking down the street: "Miss Alice Burke thinks she is aggrieved because of your having a vicious horse hitched and standing on the sidewalk . . . causing her to leave the sidewalk for the street and then being bitten by the horse." In her attempt to escape, Burke fell and injured herself on a pile of stones, causing her considerable pain and forcing her to miss more than two months of work. Strode informed the horse's owner that if he did not compensate Burke she would sue.

In 1903 Strode participated in a high-profile prosecution of a judge accused of grave misconduct. The Reverend C. H. Crawford, the superintendent of the Anti-Saloon League in Virginia, had written a newspaper article accusing Judge Clarence Campbell of taking bribes from businesses that applied for liquor licenses. Campbell did not take the accusations lightly. He had the minister hauled into court and demanded an apology. When Crawford refused, the tall and athletic judge followed the elderly minister into the street and declared: "I gave you an opportunity to apologize and you would not, now I give you this." Campbell proceeded to beat the clergyman with a horsewhip. According to a news story headlined "Judge Cowhides a Minister," Campbell inflicted "painful injuries and caus[ed] blood to flow from the head and face of the minister."

Crawford sued, but Campbell appointed a friend to sit as judge and arranged for a sympathetic jury. When Campbell was acquitted, local bar associations asked the legislature to impeach him. Strode helped represent the bar associations in the proceedings, which resulted in Campbell's being removed by the legislature. The victory helped establish Strode's reputation as an up-and-coming lawyer and a crusader against public corruption.

While he was burnishing his reputation as one of the region's most capable lawyers, the charismatic and well-connected Strode was also becoming a force in local politics. He gave his first political speech in 1896, to the Amherst County Democratic Club, and the following year he served as a delegate to the state Democratic convention. In 1904 Strode increased his influence by teaming up with a friend, Stickley Tucker, to purchase a local newspaper, the *Amherst Progress*. Tucker did most of the day-to-day work, while Strode wrote editorials and commentaries.

In 1905 Strode announced his candidacy for the state senate from a district that included Amherst and Nelson Counties. He printed up campaign leaflets with a picture of himself in an elegant suit and tie, which showed off his natural good looks. Strode billed himself throughout his career as a "Progressive Democrat," and when he ran for office he presented himself as someone who believed in the power of government to solve problems and improve society. His campaign literature offered up a platform that included electoral reform and increased spending on highways. It also had a detailed discussion of "Rotation in Office," which explained why he believed it was now the turn of a candidate from Amherst County, rather than Nelson County, to hold the seat.

As a former teacher and school principal, it was not surprising that Strode made education a major issue. His campaign literature noted that the illiteracy rate among white male Virginians was one in eight, no better than it had been in 1850, and it pointed out that teachers' salaries had stagnated since the founding of the state school system in 1870. Strode found both situations deplorable. "We are reaping in illiteracy what we have sown," he warned. Although he had run an elite private school, Strode was a strong supporter of public education. He argued for increasing taxes on the wealthy to improve education for poor children, and he insisted that "the present demand upon the part of our people for better free school facilities should be promptly met."

Strode also called for improving Virginia's roads, a popular progressive cause. Better roads required increased government spending, but they would help the state to move forward—a trade-off that progressives like Strode considered worthwhile. Strode argued for redirecting convict labor from private contracting projects to building and repairing roads and highways, which would keep the cost of road improvements down. Strode also supported election reform, or "purer elections," as he called it in his campaign leaflets.

Strode presented himself to the voters of Amherst and Nelson counties as a progressive on every major issue except one: race. In early-twentieth-century Virginia, white politicians, whether progressive or conservative, supported the Jim Crow system, and Strode was no exception. His fidelity to the old southern racial codes, which built subjugation of blacks into every aspect of daily life, was evident in every part of his life—even his professional correspondence. When a black man named Charles Clark, whose son was killed in a railroad accident, tried to retain Strode to represent him in a negligence lawsuit, Strode turned down the case. He addressed his letter to "Chas. Clark, Colored"—staying true to the Jim Crow rule that "you don't use Mister to a Negro even on an envelope."

Strode was firmly opposed to civil rights for his black neighbors and constituents. When he was running for office, there was a debate over the "grandfather clause," a legal subterfuge being used to prevent blacks from voting. During the Reconstruction Era, Virginia adopted a state constitution that gave blacks the vote—much to the regret of Virginia's white power structure. In 1902, when Reconstruction was over and supporters of political rights for blacks had lost power, Virginia adopted a new constitution that imposed poll taxes and literacy tests for the express purpose of disenfranchising blacks. The 1902 constitution had a grandfather clause that guaranteed citizens the right to vote if their fathers or grandfathers had voted before the abolition of slavery. It was a loophole that ensured that poor and illiterate whites could still vote without paying a poll tax or taking a literacy test—but poor and illiterate blacks could not.

The grandfather clause was an ugly reassertion of white supremacy, but Strode supported it. In his campaign leaflets, he noted that he had "always advocated and favored" the new constitution's electoral rules, through which "the negro vote has been practically eliminated from Virginia politics." He put a reform gloss on this mass disenfranchisement. As Strode saw it, denying blacks the vote made it easier to clean up elections—at least for white voters. When blacks went to the polls in large numbers, he argued, there was a considerable amount of corruption, including blatant attempts to buy black votes. And white political operatives rigged the system to reduce the influence of black voters. With the electorate essentially all white, Strode insisted, there was "no longer a vestige of excuse for doubtful election methods."

Strode won the primary and general election, and in 1906, at the age of thirty-three, he became a member of the state senate. Because his legislative duties were part-time, Strode was able to continue his law practice and his work for the *Amherst Progress*. Shortly after he joined the legislature, Strode suffered a great loss. His and Rebekah's first child, William Lewis Strode, died of pneumonia at the age of two.

One of the first issues Strode focused on in the legislature was mental health policy. It was a natural subject for him to champion. Progressives across the country considered the mental health system to be a troubled area, and they were bringing a "grand sense of mission" to reforming and improving it.

Strode may also have been drawn to the issue for more personal reasons. Both of his parents had spent their final days in institutions for the mentally ill: his father in Western State Hospital in Staunton, and his mother in Southwestern State Hospital in Marion. Even though neither of Strode's parents had suffered from classic mental illness, their hospitalizations had given him firsthand exposure to the institutions that few other Virginians had, and he had an opportunity to see just how deplorable conditions were.

Strode was a strong advocate for establishing a state hospital for epileptics. He introduced a bill in the legislature—An Act to Establish an Epileptic Colony on Land of the Western State Hospital, in Amherst County—that made a powerful case for why a facility for epileptics was needed. According to the bill, "existing State hospitals for the white insane are now taxed to their fullest capacity" and contained 250 epileptic patients. Strode noted that the commissioner of state hospitals had recently issued a report saying that unless more accommodations were provided a large number of epileptics would have to be held in jails.

Strode also emphasized that an epileptic colony could bring about improved treatments, more hygienic surroundings, and better employment opportunities, making it "the most economic, beneficial, and satisfactory method of caring for epileptics." Strode's bill passed the legislature and became law on February 20, 1906.

Strode may have been sincerely concerned about the plight of epileptics, a cause that appealed to many progressives. There were also, however, political reasons for him to support the new facility. A colony for epileptics would provide a major boost to the economy of the area in which it was located, and there was a good chance it would end up in Strode's district.

The most likely site for the new facility was Amherst County. The legislature was looking at building it on land that Sidney R. Murkland had donated to Western State Hospital. Murkland was an Amherst County resident, and the land he left in his bequest was also in the county. When the Murkland land parcel turned out to be poorly suited, the state hospital board urged the legislature to sell it and find a new site. At Strode's urging, in March 1908, the legislature amended the authorizing legislation to allow the epileptic facility to be relocated, on the condition that it remain in Amherst County. Strode helped to arrange the purchase of a new site in Madison Heights, just outside Lynchburg, keeping the new facility in Amherst County and in his legislative district.

In 1907 Strode was involved in another high-profile legal case involving a local judge—and this one proved even more notorious than the Judge Campbell affair. On April 22, Judge W. G. Loving of Nelson, one of the two counties Strode represented, killed Theodore Estes, a twenty-six-year-old man from one of Virginia's most prominent families. Estes, who was the son of the Nelson County sheriff, had taken the judge's twenty-year-old daughter, Elizabeth, on a buggy ride during which she had gotten drunk on whiskey.

Estes dropped Elizabeth off at the home of a friend later than she was expected. She told her father that Estes had drugged her on the buggy ride and assaulted her. Loving went out with his loaded shotgun and angrily confronted Estes, a short and slight young man who was described by those who knew him as intelligent, hardworking, and—in the words of one neighbor—"the most innocent boy I ever knew." Loving asked Estes if he had been out buggy riding and, according to an eyewitness, after Estes denied it, Loving shot and killed him. Loving said no power in heaven could have prevented him from taking Estes's life.

Loving was quickly arrested, and he turned to Strode to represent him. Whatever Strode might have thought of the facts of the case, the battle between Loving and Estes had strong political overtones. Estes was affiliated with the Martin Organization, a conservative Democratic machine that dominated politics in Nelson and Amherst counties, and across the state. The Martin Organization, led by Thomas S. Martin, a powerful U.S. senator from Charlottesville, supported business interests and was frequently accused of corruption. Loving and Strode were part of the antimachine opposition, which promoted more progressive, reform-minded policies. Loving, a Nelson County power broker, had played an important role in Strode's election to the state senate in 1905—and the Martin Organization had not. "As might be supposed," a local newspaper observed, "the Democratic machine leaders do not sit up at night trying to help the Senator from Amherst."

Strode was joined by lawyers from Lynchburg and Fairfax, a group one news account described as "three of the strongest criminal lawyers practicing in Virginia." Loving's attack on Estes was not entirely out of character—the judge was known for his temper. And he may have been motivated not only by what he believed was done to his daughter, but by the antipathy he had long harbored for the Estes family. Strode and the rest of the legal team decided early on, however, that to prevail they needed to present a simple case about fatherly duty—and the "unwritten law" that a man could not be condemned for rising up to defend the honor of his wronged daughter.

Early news reports were sympathetic to Loving, and repeated his account: that Estes had gotten Elizabeth drunk and had sexually assaulted her, and that the judge had been forced to respond. It was believed at the time that a woman compromised as Elizabeth had been might be unable to marry or find a respectable place in society, making her father's outrage, his supporters insisted, thoroughly justified. The *Charlottesville Daily Progress*'s headline captured this sentiment: "Father Invoked Unwritten Law/Loving Slays Author of Daughter's Ruin."

As the trial approached, the Estes family's version came out. They insisted the idea of drinking whiskey had been Elizabeth's. They denied an assault had taken place, and they said that when she returned from the buggy ride Elizabeth had not mentioned one. Loving, they charged, was a "heartless" killer, who had shot Estes without allowing him to give his version of events. Some news reports said Elizabeth had denied that Estes attacked her, and put the blame on her father, who, she said, was angry that she was dating a member of the Estes family.

Popular opinion in Nelson County had begun to turn against Loving. To avoid a hostile jury, Strode and the other defense lawyers asked for a change of venue, which the presiding judge granted, moving the trial south to Halifax County. When the procedings began, reporters descended from across the country to watch the drama unfold. The testimony went well for Loving. Elizabeth helped her father considerably by taking the stand and talking about having been attacked by Estes.

In his closing argument, Strode made an emotional, honor-based appeal to the jurors. He invoked chivalry and reverence for southern womanhood, and he talked about the agony the judge went through on learning what had been done to his daughter. "I do not undervalue life, but there is something sweeter to all Virginians—the purity of our women," Strode said. "We have written in our laws that if a man attempts to attack one of our daughters he has forfeited his life." Strode's performance received good reviews. "Mr. Strode spoke with much fervor," a newspaper reported, "and two or three of the jurymen seemed to be not a little moved." After deliberating less than an hour, the jury returned a verdict of not guilty.

The Loving case was a professional success for Strode, and it won him points with some of his most important political supporters. But it was hardly a great moral victory. Many newspapers and local observers objected to the decision of the Halifax County jury, rejecting the idea that an "unwritten law" justified killing a young man in cold blood. One news report was particularly blunt, declaring the jury's verdict "a menace to human life."

In 1907 Strode ran for reelection to the state senate. In his campaign, he emphasized his advocacy for progressive causes during his first term. His campaign literature noted that he had gotten a bill passed in the senate to strengthen the state's Pure Election Law, which allowed for elections to be voided when voting rules were violated. Strode had also supported new laws that created a state highway commission and a state convict road force, an inexpensive way of improving the roads. He reported that he had worked for a bill to allocate an additional $300,000 for public schools, though it did not pass. He did, however, succeed in lowering the entrance fee at the University of Virginia from $40 to $10. Strode continued to promote greater educational opportunity for underprivileged Virginians. "I believe that appropriations to colleges should be made only if they reduce the cost of attendance so that aspiring poor boys and girls can attend them at the least expense," he said.

Strode also ran on increasing pensions for Confederate veterans. In his campaign literature, he stated that with his support funds available for Confederate pensions had been increased to $50,000 more than had ever been appropriated before. This was still, he said, "far less than I thought their due." In a letter to a Confederate veteran, Strode promised to work for further increases, and to raise the property caps, so veterans and their widows would not need to be "paupers" to get benefits.

Strode was becoming an influential force in the state capital, but he had larger political ambitions. He left the legislature to campaign for Congress in 1912. Amherst County was represented by Henry D. Flood, a Democratic machine loyalist Strode accused of "aligning . . . with reactionary interests and forces." Strode had considerable success running in Amherst and Nelson Counties, but his progressive, reform-minded politics did not play well in much of the larger congressional district. His hopes for higher office thwarted, in 1915, Strode ran for his old state senate seat. On August 3 he won the election and was returned to the legislature. The following year, Strode again announced his interest in the congressional seat, and received "a good deal of urging" to enter the race, as he told one supporter. As before, he had little success in taking on an entrenched incumbent and the powerful political machine that was propping him up.

In the 1915 state senate campaign, the issue of grandfather clauses reemerged, and the passage of a decade had done nothing to alter Strode's views on the subject. That June, months before the election was to be held, the Supreme Court struck down grandfather clauses as a violation of the Fifteenth Amendment, which barred federal or state governments from abridging the right to vote on the basis of race, color, or previous condition of servitude. When it appeared that whites would have to pay the poll tax, there were calls for eliminating it entirely, but Strode was opposed to doing so. Given the "rapid education of the colored races," he warned, literacy tests soon would not be enough to prevent blacks from voting. There was hardly any price, he said, "too much to pay if necessary to prevent the return of the negro vote to politics in Virginia."

For all of his progressive beliefs, Strode never abandoned his allegiance to Jim Crow. Toward the end of his career, however, there would be times when he pushed in modest ways to moderate an ugly racial system. In 1940, when he was a municipal judge, blacks complained that the segregated Lynchburg courthouse had a single bathroom for black men and women, while white men and women had separate facilities. Strode told the city manager that the complaint was "well founded" and he directed the city manager to provide separate men's and women's rooms for blacks "without delay."

Around the same time, members of Lynchburg's black community objected to the restriction on black doctors who treated black patients at the city hospital. They were allowed to see their patients' charts but not to prescribe drugs, which only white physicians could do. Strode was told that Lynchburg was not unusual in this regard—and that, in fact, no hospitals in Virginia allowed black doctors to treat their patients in hospitals. Strode investigated the matter and found that to be true, but he argued in a letter to the State Department of Public Welfare that the city should still change its policies. "I should like to see Lynchburg pioneer in extending what I would regard as fairer treatment at the City Hospital to the colored physicians," he wrote.

In his letter urging the new policy, Strode went on to give his views on race relations. "We have here in the South some several million negroes destined perforce to remain with us," he said. Strode believed there must be "social separation . . . if we are to preserve as we must our racial integrity." But he also advised that "justice to fellow human beings as well as promotion of the general welfare counsel that they should have full opportunity to develop their capabilities."

Strode was more enlightened, and well ahead of his times, with respect to the rights of women. He was an outspoken advocate for greater educational opportunities for Virginia women, which was perhaps not surprising, given that he was the son of one female educator, the husband of another, and the brother of six sisters. Strode was particularly intent on opening up the University of Virginia. In a letter setting forth his views, he wrote that "it would be impossible within a reasonable limit for a letter to state all of the grounds upon which I think the State, when able, should begin to share with its women the benefit of its really great University."

Virginia was one of the few states that did not make any provisions for women to attend college. Not only was the University of Virginia all male, but it refused to open a "coordinate college" like Radcliffe at Harvard, Barnard at Columbia, or Newcomb College at Tulane. In 1910 Strode introduced a bill to establish a coordinate college at the University of Virginia, but it failed to pass. There was substantial opposition among faculty, alumni, and students. Many did not believe women had the intellectual capacity, and they worried women would upset the school's traditions, including its honor system.

Strode's opponent when he ran to reclaim his state senate seat in 1915 was one of the critics. Bland Massie, who had served four years in the state senate, had opposed the senate bill to create a coordinate college for the University of Virginia. In a campaign leaflet, Strode attacked Massie for resisting. "We have seen the good effect" of higher education for women, Strode insisted. After he was elected, Strode declared in a letter that he hoped the day was "not far distant when the girl of talent in Virginia, even though she may be poor, will find that the very best education that the State gives anybody is open to her too . . . if she be willing to strive for it."

Strode and the other supporters of a coordinate college for the University of Virginia came close in 1916. They succeeded in getting a bill passed in the state senate, but after six hours of debate lost 48–46 in the House of Delegates. Two years later, the legislature voted to open the University of Virginia graduate schools, except engineering and law, to women. It also decided that the College of William & Mary, another state-supported school, would be open to men and women equally. It would take many years, but Strode lived to see the legislature vote in 1944 to designate Mary Washington College a women's college affiliated with the University of Virginia.

When Strode returned to the state senate, he kept up his ties to the Colony for Epileptics and Feeble-Minded. He continued to serve as its counsel, working on a variety of legal matters, many of them routine. When Dr. Priddy wanted to buy a used Ford for the colony, Strode checked that the seller owned it free and clear, and he provided a form bill of sale. When Dr. Priddy had trouble with a company he had contracted with to supply coal, he called on Strode. When Dr. Priddy wanted advice on how to help an inmate protect her small farm from her brothers, who wanted to take it over and appropriate the rental income, he again turned to Strode.

In the state senate, Strode continued to work with Dr. Priddy on legislation of interest to the colony. He sponsored bills that expanded the power of state hospitals to identify people as feebleminded and to commit them, and, at Dr. Priddy's request, the bill that began to lay the groundwork for eugenic sterilization by authorizing "medical and surgical" treatment of inmates at facilities for the feebleminded.

In May 1918, in the waning months of World War I, Strode applied to the U.S. Army Judge Advocate General's Corps. Strode, who was now forty-three, was too old to be a regular enlistee, but the JAG Corps would give him a chance to use his professional abilities to aid the war effort. He secured the appointment with the help of Congressman Flood, who was not only supporting a highly qualified applicant, but sending a potential electoral challenger out of the country indefinitely.

Strode began his service in Washington, D.C., where he got his introduction to the military justice system. He also traveled across the South on a mission to recruit lawyers. In January 1919, two months after World War I ended, Strode was sent to France, where he served under General John J. Pershing in the American Expeditionary Forces headquarters. In May Strode was promoted from major to lieutenant colonel, and a few months later, he was discharged from the army.

Not long after Strode returned home, Dr. Priddy approached him for help in drafting legislation to protect superintendents from lawsuits like the one brought by the Mallory family. Strode drew up two bills— one requiring inmates challenging their detention to sue in the county in which they were being held, and one declaring that all inmates who were sent to a state hospital by a court or a commission were "lawfully committed." These bills became law, though they did not provide Dr. Priddy all of the protection he wanted.

In 1922, Strode made one last attempt to win political office. Congressman Flood had died unexpectedly of heart disease, at the age of fifty-four, in December 1921. The Democratic Party scheduled a special convention to choose a nominee, and within days of Flood's death Strode began reaching out to his political allies for support. He now had, in addition to his legislative and legal work in Virginia, a war record to run on. Strode's old allies lined up behind him, including Dr. Priddy and Irving Whitehead—the former colony board chairman who would later represent Carrie Buck—but once again, it was not enough. When the special convention met in Roanoke, Strode failed to win the nomination.

In July 1922, tragedy again struck Strode's family. His wife, Rebekah, died in an automobile accident. Strode was left to raise their four young children, all under the age of eighteen. It was not long before he married again. Strode had gotten to know Louisa Dexter Hubbard, a Red Cross nurse from nearby Bedford County, when she made her rounds on horseback in the region, surveying families of returning veterans of the world war. Hubbard had moved to North Carolina for her Red Cross work, but she remained in contact with the Strode family.

After Rebekah's death, Hubbard returned to Virginia. In a letter to the clerk of the Circuit Court of Bedford County, Strode requested a marriage license, enclosing $2 and stating: "I am widowed and she is single." On December 31, 1923, in the bride's hometown of Forest Depot, Aubrey Ellis Strode, age fifty, and Louisa Dexter Hubbard, age twenty-seven, were wed.

It was at just this time, when he was about to start his new life, that Strode drafted Virginia's sterilization law. Within Virginia, the law would be the culmination of years of effort by eugenicists, going back to 1909, when Dr. Charles Carrington of the Virginia Penitentiary in Richmond first lobbied the legislature. The last fifteen years had been difficult ones for the supporters of eugenic sterilization in Virginia, but times had changed.

Strode delivered An Act to Provide for the Sexual Sterilization of Inmates of State Institutions in Certain Cases to an ally in the state senate, Marshall Booker, who introduced it in February 1924. The bill became law, with little opposition, on March 20. Dr. Priddy and Dr. DeJarnette—the superintendent of Western State Hospital, and the first person in Virginia to advocate for eugenic sterilization—had finally achieved their dream.

With the new law, all five Virginia state mental hospitals were now authorized to conduct eugenic sterilizations. All they were required to do was to follow the statute's procedures, including holding hearings and offering a right of appeal, before they performed any sterilizations. Dr. Priddy was finally free to turn the Colony for Epileptics and Feeble-Minded into the "clearing house" he hoped it would become: admitting the feebleminded, sterilizing them quickly, and releasing them to make room for new arrivals.

Strode, however, had a different idea. He had recommended that the state hospitals not proceed with sterilizations until the law could be tested in the courts, up to and including the United States Supreme Court. Instead of preparing to sterilize inmates, the state hospitals were now helping to assemble a test case to determine whether the eugenic sterilization law was constitutional—a case that was now on the brink of going to trial.

Seven

Aubrey Strode

I n the fall of 1924, Aubrey Strode was one of Virginia's most distinguished lawyers—scion of some of the state's most established families, graduate of the University of Virginia's college and law school, and a former state senator. In his twenty-five years in the Virginia bar, he had become a seasoned litigator, with considerable expertise in bringing complicated cases to trial. Strode knew the importance of preparation: of developing a compelling theory of the case, and assembling the most favorable evidence and witnesses. He put all of his well-honed skills to work getting ready for the upcoming trial in *Buck v. Priddy*.

The recruitment of expert witnesses had gone remarkably well. Strode had enlisted Harry Laughlin, the nation's leading expert on eugenic sterilization, whose written interrogatories could hardly have been more favorable to the colony's position. Laughlin had stated his opinion that the Virginia eugenic sterilization law was among the best that had ever been enacted, and he had offered his strong support for the specific decision to sterilize Carrie Buck.

Arthur Estabrook, one of the nation's leading eugenics researchers, had signed on to provide eugenic fieldwork. As he had promised, Estabrook had come to Virginia to investigate Carrie's family. He visited the colony, where he examined Carrie and Emma, and traveled across their home county, Albemarle, and met with as many family members as he could locate.

Based on his research, Estabrook was prepared to offer up some definitive opinions. He had concluded that Carrie was a "feebleminded person," bringing her within Virginia's eugenic sterilization statute. And it was Estabrook's opinion that Carrie's family had hereditary defects—located, in particular, in the "Dudley germ plasm" of her maternal grandmother, Adeline Dudley Harlowe.

Estabrook would also provide a critical missing piece in Strode's case: a mental evaluation of Carrie's daughter, Vivian. Dr. Priddy had been insisting that Vivian was feebleminded, attributing that assessment to Caroline Wilhelm, the Red Cross nurse—and Laughlin had repeated the assertion in his interrogatory answers. Now that claim was falling apart. In an October 15 letter, Wilhelm had instructed Dr. Priddy that she should not be cited on the subject of Vivian's mental abilities. "I do not recall and am unable to find any mention in our files of having said that Carrie Buck's baby was mentally defected," she wrote. All she could find, she said, was "a letter of May 5th" in which "I said that we should not want to take the responsibility of placing so young a child, whose mother and grandmother are both mental defectives."

Wilhelm's disavowal had not had the effect it should have. Although she wrote to Dr. Priddy on October 15, Laughlin was still citing her as the source for his contention that Vivian was mentally defective in the interrogatories that he signed before a notary on November 6. Apparently, after Dr. Priddy received Wilhelm's letter, he had not bothered to tell Laughlin not to include the information about Vivian in his interrogatories. And apparently he had not advised Strode not to submit the interrogatories to the court—even though it was now clear that they contained inaccuracies.

It was critical for Strode to come up with expert testimony about Vivian's mental abilities before trial. There would have to be someone other than Wilhelm who could testify that Carrie's daughter was feebleminded. Estabrook, who had arrived in Virginia on the eve of trial, was now prepared to do this. He had examined Vivian, who was nearly eight months old, on his hurried eugenic fieldwork rounds. And he had reached the conclusion that Strode hoped he would: that she was mentally defective.

Strode also had two compelling expert witnesses within the ranks of his own trial team. Dr. Priddy was prepared to testify about eugenic sterilization, a subject with which he had great familiarity, and about Carrie and Emma Buck, who were living under his supervision. Dr. Joseph S. DeJarnette, who had decades of experience in treating Virginia's mentally ill and defective, would also testify in support of the sterilization law he had worked so hard to enact.

The expert witnesses would be a cornerstone of Strode's case, but they would not be enough. As he knew well, fact witnesses who could testify about Carrie and her family—and help make the case that Carrie was the sort of person who fell under the sterilization law—would be necessary. In a letter to Dr. Priddy, Strode explained that they would particularly need witnesses from the Charlottesville area "to give first hand testimony as to Carrie Buck's kinpeople" because they would "not be allowed in a case of this sort to have hearsay testimony upon that point."

In the days leading up to trial, Strode and Dr. Priddy—and Estabrook, out in the field—had worked energetically to assemble a witness list. They had succeeded in locating schoolteachers, social workers, and neighbors who knew Carrie and her family—on both her mother's and her father's sides. Once Strode had identified his witnesses, he sent out word: their presence was required at the Amherst County Circuit Court on Tuesday, November 18 at 10:00 a.m. "to testify and the truth to say in behalf of the Defendant in a certain matter of controversy."

The Amherst County Courthouse fell short of the southern ideal of the imposing judicial edifice, towering magisterially over the town square. In William Faulkner's *Requiem for a Nun* the courthouse was "the center, the focus, the hub . . . tall as cloud, solid as rock, dominating all." In Amherst County, Virginia, it was a drab brown brick building, perched precariously on a small hill. Its most prominent ornamentation was a monument, installed by the United Daughters of the Confederacy, in tribute to the men of the county who had risked their lives for the "noble cause."

Anyone who saw in this homage to the slaveholding South an augury of how the Amherst County Circuit Court would rule on eugenic sterilization might also have considered the court's own name. Lord Jeffrey Amherst, the British royal governor of Virginia, was famous for his bloody wars against the Indians—and for the idea of giving them smallpox-laced blankets. "You will Do well to try to Inoculate the Indians, by means of Blankets," General Amherst wrote to one of his officers, "as well as to Try Every other Methode, that can Serve to Extirpate this Execrable Race."

On the blustery fall morning of November 18, 1924, with Judge Bennett Gordon presiding, Strode started the testimony in *Buck v. Priddy* by calling the colony's first witness, Anne Harris. Harris was a district nurse from Charlottesville who purported to know a good deal about the Buck family. Harris testified that she had known Emma Buck for more than a decade. When asked what she knew about her, Harris responded with a fusillade of negative recollections. Emma was "on the charity list for a number of years, off and on—mostly on." She was "living in the worst neighborhoods." And she "was not able to, or would not, work and support her children." They were, Harris said, "on the streets more or less."

Emma was, in Harris's opinion, "absolutely irresponsible." "Numerous charity organizations" gave Emma and relief "at different times," Harris testified. In response to Strode's question about "what the trouble was with" Emma, Harris said: "She didn't seem to be able to take care of herself. She would not work."

When Strode asked about Emma's children, Harris said, "Well, I don't know anything very definite about the children, except that they don't seem to be able to do more than their mother." Despite her disclaimer about knowing little, Harris went on to say a great deal about the children, including casting doubt on their legitimacy. Emma's husband was absent, Harris testified, but she continued to have children. There was "no question," Harris said, "of them being her husband's."

Harris also had definite views on the intellectual capabilities of Emma's children. Asked if they were "mentally normal children," Harris responded, "No sir, they are certainly not." She guessed that Emma had a mental age of twelve, and that her children had the mentality "of a child four or five years younger."

Strode wanted to know about Carrie's sister, Doris. In response to his question about whether Doris was "a full sister," Harris replied, "I should say not," attributing her opinion to "hearsay" and "general reports." Asked what else she knew about Doris, Harris said she was "a very stormy individual" and a "very violent child." She had been placed in a children's home and spent time with "some people in the country," Harris said, "and they had a very stormy time with her, and they could not do anything with her."

When Harris's direct testimony was over, Carrie's lawyer, Irving Whitehead, rose to cross-examine her. There were many points he could have pursued. Harris had testified that Carrie had a mental age of about seven or eight, without offering any basis for her opinion. Whitehead could have pressed Harris on whether, in her experience, seven- or eight-year-olds generally successfully reached sixth grade, as Carrie had. He might also have asked if Emma's difficulties could have stemmed from poverty and lack of support rather than mental deficiency—and whether Doris's "stormy" personality might have been a result of growing up in poverty on the streets and being separated from her mother at a young age.

Instead, Whitehead cross-examined Harris in a way that actually bolstered the colony's case. In her direct testimony, Harris had not mentioned any bad behavior by Carrie, but under Whitehead's questioning, she recounted how a school superintendent had called and told her Carrie was misbehaving. "She told me that Carrie was writing notes, and that sort of thing, and asked what should she do about it," Harris said. Could Carrie's notes have been considered "anti-social"? Whitehead asked. "I should say so," Harris replied.

Strode then called a series of educators to testify about the academic deficiencies of Carrie's relatives. First was Eula Wood, Doris's teacher for the prior six weeks. Wood said she knew "very little about" Doris, but she testified that Carrie's half sister had been demoted from second grade because she had not been able to do second-grade work. Wood testified that even though Doris was eleven or twelve, she was "still in the first grade." Asked by Strode if Doris was "a dull child," Wood testified that she was "dull in her books."

Wood's testimony left many openings for cross-examination. There were, no doubt, other possible explanations for why Doris might have had trouble with second grade. Wood could have been asked about the possible impact of growing up on the streets and then being taken from her mother and put in a children's home. She could have been pressed on her odd answer to the question of whether Doris was a "dull child"—that she was "dull in her books," which could have meant she was not studying rather than that she lacked innate intelligence. But Whitehead chose not to cross-examine Wood.

Another teacher, Virginia Beard, testified that she taught Roy Smith, Carrie's half brother. He was fourteen and did not do passing work in the fourth grade, she said. His problem was that he "tried to be funny—tried to be smart." She also said he was "below the grade of the other boys of his age in school." When Strode pressed Beard on whether Smith was "weak-minded," she responded, "Well, I don't know."

Whitehead's brief cross-examination of Beard, like his questioning of Harris, did more harm than good. He asked Beard if it was usual for a fourteen-year-old like Smith to be in the fourth grade. No, she said, a fourteen-year-old would normally be in the eighth grade. With this question, Whitehead did a better job than Strode had of eliciting testimony from Beard that Carrie's half brother was mentally deficient.

Strode also called the superintendent of the County Home, John W. Hopkins, whose testimony was especially odd. Hopkins testified that he knew Roy Smith, slightly, from his occasional stays at the facility. Hopkins said he did not know "anything particular" about Smith, but that in their brief encounters the boy had struck him as being "right peculiar." His basis for his diagnosis was a single, brief conversation they had, in which he found Smith's answer to a question about who he was waiting for to be odd. Hopkins testified about another relative of Carrie's, Richard Dudley, who also struck him as "right peculiar," and Richard's son Arthur, who he believed was "a little peculiar."

There was one kind of educator missing from Strode's lineup: anyone who had taught Carrie. It was a notable omission, because Carrie's mental abilities were of far greater legal significance than those of her relatives. Carrie had made it as far as the sixth grade, so there were likely a number of educators available who would have remembered her as a student. Strode's failure to call any of them suggested that none was prepared to testify in the way he would have liked.

Next, Strode called Caroline Wilhelm, the Red Cross social worker who had accompanied Carrie to the colony, who was now Albemarle County's secretary of public welfare. In her testimony, Wilhelm made what seemed to be an accidental admission that the Dobbses had lied to have Carrie sent to the colony. Wilhelm testified that it all began when John Dobbs approached Mary Duke, who was the secretary of public welfare at the time, and reported that Carrie "was pregnant and that he wanted to have her committed somewhere." In their petition to the Juvenile and Domestic Relations Court, they had claimed Carrie was feebleminded and epileptic—not that she was pregnant. If the problem had been that Carrie was pregnant, she should have been offered services related to her pregnancy—not sent to a colony for the feebleminded and selected for eugenic sterilization.

That troubling admission aside, Wilhelm followed the colony's script in her testimony. She agreed with Strode that if Carrie was released from the institution while still capable of childbearing she was "likely to become the parent of deficient offspring." She also said she believed Carrie was likely to give birth to illegitimate children, based on "her past record" and her mother's "three illegitimate children." Strode asked Wilhelm if, based on her personal dealings, she regarded Carrie as "obviously feeble-minded." Wilhelm said that she did, "as a social worker," though she did not explain the basis for her opinion. Carrie was a "distinct liability" to society, Wilhelm said.

Strode asked Wilhelm if she had any impressions of Carrie's baby, Vivian. On October 15, barely a month earlier, Wilhelm had written to Dr. Priddy protesting that she had not reached any conclusion about whether the baby was mentally defective. Now, however, she gave Dr. Priddy the opinion he was looking for. She said she had examined Vivian two weeks earlier, and the baby, who was just under eight months old, had seemed like "not quite a normal baby."

The only explanation Wilhelm offered for her diagnosis was that she had seen Vivian at the same time as she saw the Dobbses' grand-child, who was three days older, and there was "a very decided differ-ence in the development of the babies." When Strode pressed further, Wilhelm said there was "a look about it that is not quite normal, but just what it is, I can't tell." Wilhelm conceded that her opinion about Vivian might have been prejudiced by her "knowledge of the mother."

In cross-examining Wilhelm, Whitehead once again elicited im-portant information that undermined his own case. Wilhelm had been unconvincing in explaining how she had concluded Vivian was feeble-minded. Whitehead asked her an open-ended question that allowed Wilhelm to elaborate. "Mrs. Dobb[s's] daughter's baby is a very respon-sive baby," Wilhelm said in reply to Whitehead's question. "When you play with it, or try to attract its attention—it is a baby that you can play with." Carrie's baby, Wilhelm said, "seems very apathetic and not re-sponsive."

Whitehead's cross-examination allowed Wilhelm to make several more points that were harmful to Carrie's case. In response to a ques-tion, Wilhelm explained—as she had not before—that Carrie's pregnancy was further evidence of her feeblemindedness. A "feeble-minded girl is much more likely to go wrong," Wilhelm told Whitehead. In her direct testimony, Wilhelm had not called Carrie "immoral," but in his cross-examination, Whitehead got the witness to lodge that accusation at his client. "Now, this girl, according to your viewpoint she has an immoral tendency?" Wilhelm replied: "Certainly."

Whitehead ended his cross-examination of Wilhelm by offering a concise summary of the eugenicists' rationale for sterilizing his client. "Your idea," he asked Wilhelm, is that Carrie would become "less of a liability" if she was sterilized—"she could be turned over to somebody and under careful supervision be made self-supporting?" Wilhelm said that was just what she believed.

Strode's next witness was Mary Duke, who had been Wilhelm's predecessor as superintendent of public welfare when the Dobbses were looking to remove Carrie from their home. Duke described having met Emma Buck, whom she visited as part of her charitable duties. Duke said she "understood at the time she was of bad character" and that attempts were being made to institutionalize her, but she had lost track of what became of Emma.

Duke recounted how John Dobbs approached her to do something about Carrie, who he said was feebleminded. In her testimony, Duke did not mention what Wilhelm had just told the court: that Dobbs had come to report that Carrie was pregnant. Duke said that she then went to meet with Alice Dobbs, who told her that Carrie "was a good worker when watched" but that she was inclined to get into trouble. Alice Dobbs told Duke that they had sent Carrie to church and Sunday school, but they still could not trust her. When the Dobbses left Carrie for a few days over the summer, Alice Dobbs said, "they did not watch her closely enough."

Duke had extremely limited contact with Carrie. She saw Carrie when she was being committed to the colony, but, she said, "I never had any dealings with her." Despite this lack of familiarity, Duke did not hesitate to give an opinion about Carrie's mental ability. "She didn't seem to be a bright girl," Duke testified.

Next, Strode moved on to his expert witnesses. The first to testify was Dr. Joseph S. DeJarnette, the Western State Hospital superintendent who had worked with Dr. Priddy to get the eugenic sterilization law passed. Dr. DeJarnette testified that he had been affiliated with Western State, the largest of Virginia's four state mental hospitals for whites, for thirty-six years. He estimated that in that time he had treated more than eleven thousand "mental defectives."

With Dr. DeJarnette's expertise established, Strode moved on to Virginia's sterilization law. Dr. DeJarnette testified that when a feebleminded person was sterilized, it was "the best thing" that could be done for "the patient and for society." Strode asked if feeblemindedness was a definite condition that was "judicially ascertainable," and Dr. DeJarnette insisted it was. He agreed with Strode's assertion that there were "well recognized tests that may be applied that would safely classify those that are feebleminded."

In explaining the need for sterilization, Dr. DeJarnette offered support for "differential fecundity," the eugenicists' claim that feebleminded women were more likely to reproduce. They will have "three children to every one child a college graduate will have," he said with scientific precision. Feebleminded women were "easily over-sexed," Dr. DeJarnette testified. "It depends on their looks as to how the boys or men will take advantage of them."

Dr. DeJarnette also testified that feeblemindedness was hereditary. "That is, if the parents are feebleminded and the children are feebleminded, you have every right to believe it is from inheritance," he said. There were occasional cases in which a child might become feebleminded due to an injury. But in the overwhelming number of cases, Dr. DeJarnette testified, feeblemindedness was "inherited." "I think Mendel's law covers it very well," he said.

Dr. DeJarnette delivered a discourse on Mendel's hereditary theory in response to a question, moving from pea plants to animals to humans in a muddle of scientific ignorance. He had "never worked the law out" and had "no accurate knowledge of it because inheritance is such a complicated thing," he conceded. Still, he told the court that if a feebleminded woman had children, it was likely "one fourth of them will be feebleminded." When "both parents are feebleminded," he said, "it is practically certain that the children will all be feebleminded."

The Virginia law required that sterilization promote the "best interests" of the patient. When Strode asked how, in Dr. DeJarnette's opinion, sterilization would promote Carrie's interests, he gave the same answer Dr. Priddy routinely did: if a patient in a state hospital was sterilized, he or she could be released from the hospital—"liberated," as Dr. DeJarnette put it—to take a job in the outside world, live independently, and marry "without bringing children into the world."

The law also required a showing that sterilization was in the interest of society. In response to a question from Strode, Dr. DeJarnette explained how, in his opinion, widespread eugenic sterilization would benefit the entire country. The overall "standard of general intelligence would be lifted," he said, and "it would lower the number of our criminals."

Finally, Dr. DeJarnette gave his opinion about Carrie. Strode asked if he had heard the evidence that Carrie was feebleminded, that her mother was also, and that Carrie had an illegitimate child "who, though only eight months old, does not appear to be normal." Strode then asked if he thought Carrie was the "probable potent[ial] parent of socially inadequate offspring." Dr. DeJarnette said she was. In his final question to Dr. DeJarnette, Strode asked if he thought Carrie's "welfare and the welfare of society would be promoted by her sterilization." Dr. DeJarnette answered, "I do."

On cross-examination, Whitehead had many clear openings. An obvious place to start would have been the fact that Dr. DeJarnette had said he did not understand Mendelian theory, but proceeded to apply it to Carrie's case—and give his opinion that she would give birth to defective children. Whitehead, however, did not press Dr. DeJarnette on his weak knowledge of the science he was testifying about. Instead, once again, Carrie's attorney simply asked a series of questions that did little to weaken the colony's case—and much to help it.

In his most unusual line of questioning, Whitehead demonstrated that he had an even lower opinion of his own client than Dr. DeJarnette did. Whitehead challenged the idea that sterilization was good for inmates because, once it was done, they could be freed to live independently. He suggested that "the bulk of" prostitutes are "more or less feeble-minded," an assertion Dr. DeJarnette agreed with. Whitehead also got Dr. DeJarnette to agree that many prostitutes had venereal disease. Well, Whitehead then asked, if Carrie was—hypothetically speaking—feebleminded, and if she had an "immoral tendency," and she was sterilized with an operation that did not reduce her sexual desires, would it not be more likely that she would contract venereal disease if she was released from the colony? DeJarnette agreed it was.

Using an archaic phrase, Whitehead asked if Carrie was not at risk of becoming a "fire-ship"—a woman infected with a venereal disease who has sex with unsuspecting men. The "man contracting syphilis" from such a woman "ultimately gets married to a normal, sound woman," Whitehead said. Then, he would pass the "syphilitic taint" on to his descendants. "How can you say," Whitehead asked, "that society would be benefited by turning this girl out?"

It was an odd, and disturbing, way for Whitehead to talk about Carrie. He was not arguing that she was too mentally healthy and too good to be sterilized. He was, rather, suggesting she was too mentally defective, and too overcome with "immoral tendencies," to ever safely be given her freedom. The colony's sterilization program was, Whitehead was proposing, too good for his client.

Strode's next witness was Arthur Estabrook, Harry Laughlin's associate at the Eugenics Record Office, who had done hasty fieldwork in the previous week investigating Carrie and her family. Strode began by asking him for his background. Estabrook put a scientific gloss on his position, omitting the name "Eugenics Record Office" and describing himself as "on the scientific staff of the Carnegie Institution of Washington, at Cold Spring Harbor, Long Island, New York." When asked to describe his position further, he said he worked in the "department of genetics" where he studied "heredity in humans, animals and plants." He made no mention of eugenics.

Under questioning from Strode, Estabrook described the work he had done in his fourteen years "with the Carnegie Institution." He discussed the Nams, the Jukes, and the Tribe of Ishmael. He was interested, he said, in "inheritance of feeble-mindedness." Estabrook said he had not been involved in sterilization legislation. His interest had been purely scientific, he said, "investigating the family histories in connection with the working out of information, and the education previous to the carrying out of such laws."

Strode asked Estabrook to "very briefly explain to the Court" how the science of human heredity worked. Estabrook's answers were not brief, and they were no more explanatory than Dr. DeJarnette's had been. Estabrook talked in a roundabout way about how a person with six fingers might or might not pass that trait on to future generations— being six-fingered was, he said, a "dominant" hereditary condition. It was a confusing account, and it was unlikely Strode or anyone else in the courtroom followed it. "Doctor, we are not interested in fingers," Strode said finally. "I should have narrowed my question to what have you discovered as regards to feeblemindedness."

After a forty-five-minute lunch break, Strode turned from trying to explain the laws of heredity to the specific case of Carrie Buck. Estabrook told the court he had visited the colony and observed Carrie and her mother firsthand, making a "brief study" of the two women, and read their case histories. He then proceeded to Albemarle County, where he visited the Dobbses and as many of Carrie's relatives as he could. He administered an intelligence test to Doris, and gathered information about Roy and five or six other relatives, most on Carrie's mother's side.

Estabrook began his analysis with Emma. "The evidence," he told the court, "points to the fact that Emma Buck is a feebleminded woman." He then offered up the results of his eugenic fieldwork on the family. Emma had "three feebleminded children by unknown fathers," he said. Estabrook further reported that his investigations in Albemarle County had turned up, on Emma's side of the family, "a sufficient number of cases of defective make-up mentally" to lead him to conclude that the "Dudley germ plasm," which passed through Emma's mother's family, carried "a defective strain in it."

Estabrook was less clear about Emma's paternal line. He suspected Emma's father, Richard Harlowe "was of a defective make-up," but he was not prepared to label him feebleminded. There were other cases in the Harlowe line, he testified, that made it "reasonable" to assume the Harlowe family strain also carried "feeblemindedness—that is, the germ plasm." Estabrook concluded that Emma's mother was mentally normal, but her father "was at least a border-line case within the classification of a feeble-minded stock." Given Emma's parents, Estabrook said, it made sense that all three of her children would be feebleminded.

Estabrook then gave his expert opinion that Carrie was feebleminded, but he was less than clear about his basis for it. When Strode asked, "Did you give Carrie Buck any mental tests to determine her mental capacity?" Estabrook responded:

> Yes, sir. I talked to Carrie sufficiently so that with the record of the mental examination—yes, I did. I gave a sufficient examination so that I consider her feebleminded.

It was a cryptic answer. Estabrook responded "yes" to having given Carrie "mental tests," but it appeared that what he meant was that he talked with her and looked at the record of her previous intelligence test. If that was all Estabrook did, the accurate answer to the question of whether he gave "Carrie Buck any mental tests to determine her mental capacity" was "no."

Estabrook expressed similar certainty, on an equally thin record, about Carrie's daughter. Strode asked Estabrook if he had seen Vivian, and whether he had been able to form any judgment about her. Estabrook responded in the affirmative to both questions. "I gave the child the regular mental test for a child of the age of six months, and judging from her reactions to the tests I gave her, I decided she was below the average for a child of eight months of age," he said. Estabrook did not explain what the "regular mental test" was for a six-month-old. Strode did not ask any follow-up questions about how Estabrook tested Vivian, which was likely an indication of just how unimpressive his testing methods were.

On cross-examination, Whitehead once again did little to advance his client's case. He did not ask Estabrook to admit that he had labeled Carrie feebleminded without administering an intelligence test, and did not press him on why he did not test her. It is hard to conceive why Carrie's lawyer would not aggressively challenge a witness who offered an expert opinion his client was feebleminded, given that feeblemindedness was the basis for sterilizing her. Whitehead, however, did not make Estabrook defend his assessment.

Whitehead also failed to challenge Estabrook's evaluation of Vivian. He did not try to find out what "the regular mental test for a child of the age of six months" was, or how Vivian had performed. He also did not press Estabrook on what he could conclude from the fact that, as he said, Vivian was "below the average for a child of eight months of age." Many people score below average on intelligence tests—half of all test takers are in the bottom half—but not all of them are feebleminded. Whitehead also did not ask Estabrook if there was some natural variation in babies' development that might cause some eight-month-olds who would grow up to be perfectly normal to appear "below average" at a particular point in time. Whitehead's failure to question Estabrook's evaluation of Vivian was particularly egregious because his testimony provided the crucial "third generation" of mental defect in Carrie's family. Estabrook was the only person ever to claim to have given Vivian an intelligence test.

Whitehead also failed to question Estabrook about his fieldwork methods, even though his techniques were highly questionable. Estabrook had designated Carrie's half brother, Roy, to be feebleminded despite never having met him—Estabrook had simply "gathered information." Estabrook diagnosed other relatives who were not even alive. It was the sort of scientific methodology that had led Abraham Myerson to criticize *Mongrel Virginians* as "absurd and useless."

Strode's final witness was Dr. Priddy, his client and old friend. Dr.

Priddy began by reciting his credentials: more than fourteen years as superintendent of the colony, roughly two decades working for Virginia state hospitals, and observation of four to five thousand state hospital inmates.

Without further delay, Strode got to the critical question of the trial: "I wish you would state to the Court why you moved to have this girl sterilized under this act?" Dr. Priddy responded that he came to the conclusion Carrie "was a highly proper case for the benefit of the Sterilization Act" by studying her family history, personally examining Carrie, and then observing Carrie during her months of living at the colony.

Strode asked for more specifics. After requesting permission to consult his notes, Dr. Priddy testified that Carrie had turned eighteen in July, which meant she would have to be kept in custody for three decades to ensure she was isolated during her reproductive years. That would cost the state of Virginia about $200 a year for thirty years, and it would mean denying Carrie "all of the blessings of outdoor life and liberty." If she was sterilized, she could move into her own home under supervision, get a good-paying job, and "probably marry some man of her own level," he said. Dr. Priddy argued that Carrie would be able to "do as many whom I have sterilized for diseases have done—be good wives—be producers, and lead happy and useful lives in their spheres."

Strode asked what it was in Carrie's "personal history" that led Dr. Priddy to decide she was feebleminded and "the probable potential parent of socially inadequate offspring." Dr. Priddy testified that Emma Buck was feebleminded, with a mental age of about seven years and eleven months, based on the colony's testing. He said Carrie had also tested as feebleminded—with a mental age of nine, making her a "middle-grade moron." That meant, he said, "two direct generations of feebleminded." He added that there were "about eight Bucks and Harlowes, all coming from the Albemarle stock" at the colony, though he said he could not "vouch for their relationship—I don't suppose they know." Dr. Priddy said he believed Carrie would be the parent of defective offspring based on "the generally accepted theory of the laws of heredity."

Moving through the sterilization law's provisions, Strode asked whether Dr. Priddy believed Carrie's welfare would be promoted if she was sterilized. He was convinced that it would. "Every human being craves liberty," Dr. Priddy said, and "she would get that, under supervision." As for whether society would benefit, he responded, "unquestionably." Carrie would no longer be society's responsibility, because she could be released from the colony, he said. Beyond that, sterilizing Carrie would remove a potential source of an "incalculable number of descendants who would be feeble-minded." It would, Dr. Priddy said, be "a blessing."

Strode asked whether people who were to be sterilized generally objected. On the contrary, Dr. Priddy insisted, they "clamor for it." That was only natural, he explained. They "know that it means the enjoyment of life and the peaceful pursuance of happiness . . . on the outside of institution walls." And they understood that as a result of sterilization "they have the opportunity of marrying men of their mental levels and making good wives in many cases."

Dr. Priddy said he had seen things work out well for women who were sterilized. Between 1916 and the winter of 1917, he said, the colony sterilized about eighty women for medical reasons. About sixty were given good homes, and others returned to their families. They were able to earn a living, and in some cases to marry, and none had to return to the colony. Strode asked who was better off: the women who remained at the colony or those who were sterilized and released. Dr. Priddy insisted that the sterilized women were "of course, much better off."

Dr. Priddy said he had kept in touch with some of the inmates he had sterilized and released. He told the story of one boy "of the imbecile class" who was sterilized and then ran off with a woman from the colony who had also been sterilized. They did well as a couple, he said. Dr. Priddy then looked to an unusual place for support for his account of the happily sterilized couple—opposing counsel. "Mr. Whitehead knows them both," Dr. Priddy told Strode. Without being sworn in, Whitehead testified against his own client: "Yes, put in there that

I know them," he said, explaining that he had encountered them through his service on the colony board. Whitehead's willingness to support Dr. Priddy's story about inmates who thrived after sterilization was a stark example of how allied he was with the opposing side.

Whitehead's cross-examination of Dr. Priddy—perhaps the most important witness against his client—was a short, aimless interrogation that once again bolstered the colony's case. Whitehead helped Dr. Priddy to underscore the relatively minor nature of the operation, allowing him to note that it involved nothing more than cutting the fallopian tubes without removing the ovaries. In his questioning, Whitehead referred to Carrie, his client, as "this girl here."

In brief redirect questioning, Strode asked Dr. Priddy if it was true that if Carrie was sterilized she could return to live with the Dobbses. Dr. Priddy said it was. "I understand," he said, "they want her back." If true, that meant that if Carrie was sterilized, she would be allowed to live in the same home as her only child, Vivian, and help to raise her. If Carrie remained at the colony for the rest of her life, her daughter would grow up without her. Even for a woman who did not want to be sterilized, this offer would likely exert a powerful pull. Unfortunately, it was not true.

When Dr. Priddy stepped down from the witness stand, the live testimony was over. All that remained was to introduce Laughlin's interrogatory answers, which Strode read aloud to the court. When he was done, Strode asked that the judgment of the colony's Special Board of Directors be affirmed. On the same day it started, the trial was over.

There was a great deal about the trial that was odd or wrong, but one thing stood out above all: only one of the two sides put on a case. Whitehead, who was challenging the colony's sterilization order on Carrie's behalf, did not call a single fact or expert witness, or introduce a single piece of evidence. In the face of all of Strode's witnesses about Carrie and her family, and his experts testifying that she was feebleminded and likely to produce feebleminded offspring, he offered nothing. If there was one fact that revealed how Whitehead, Strode, and

Dr. Priddy were allied against Carrie, it was that the court was never presented with a case for why she should not be sterilized.

Whitehead could have put on a strong factual case. On the question of whether Carrie was feebleminded, he could have presented evidence that she had reached the sixth grade, something children generally do at the age of eleven or twelve, and had performed well academically. This achievement could have cast considerable doubt on the colony's claim that she had a mental age of nine. He could have introduced her school assignments, which were good enough to get her promoted each year, into evidence. And he could have called her teachers as witnesses—something Strode notably did not do.

Whitehead could also have called Carrie's friends, neighbors, and employers to testify about her mental abilities. Later in life, people who lived and worked with her would tell interviewers that she was an intelligent woman and clearly not feebleminded. It is likely that people who knew Carrie at the time of the trial would have had similar things to say.

Most of all, Whitehead could have had Carrie testify on her own behalf. She was in the courtroom for the trial. If she had been allowed to speak in her own voice, she could have demonstrated her intelligence directly, rather than being reduced to a Binet-Simon test score and a barrage of expert opinions. By keeping Carrie silent, Whitehead allowed Dr. Priddy, Laughlin, and Strode to define her for the court as an example of that dreaded menace: the feebleminded young woman intent on reproducing.

If Carrie had taken the witness stand, she could also have challenged another critical part of the colony's case: that sterilization was in her own best interest, something the Virginia sterilization law required the colony to prove. Carrie could have put on the record something she would speak about later in life: how much she wanted to have children. Without her testifying, it was impossible to know whether Carrie even understood that she was in danger of being sterilized. Years later, she would say she had never been told.

There were also many respected academics and medical practitioners Whitehead could have called as expert witnesses. J. E. Wallace Wallin—the St. Louis psychologist who had described the Binet-Simon test's unreliability when he administered it to a group of Iowa farmers—was writing about how intelligence testing was being misused to label people as mentally deficient. He told of a superintendent of a state institution who labeled a boy feebleminded based on the Binet-Simon. The boy was released and became a top student in his preparatory school class, then went on to college. Wallin wondered how many "non-feeble-minded children" were wasting away in institutions to which they had been erroneously consigned.

In addition to authorities like Wallin who could have challenged the reliability of intelligence testing in general, Whitehead could have had an expert examine the tests given to Carrie and her family. He could have evaluated whether her answers to questions like what to do when "Playmate hits you" were so deficient as to label her a "Middle grade Moron." An expert could also have reviewed the basis for Estabrook's and Wilhelm's opinion that young Vivian was mentally deficient. He could also have administered his own intelligence tests.

Expert witnesses could also have challenged the spurious hereditary science that the colony's case relied on. Dr. DeJarnette and Laughlin insisted that conditions like feeblemindedness were distinct traits that were inherited according to Mendelian principles—and that anyone who had them was the "probable parent" of a child who was similarly afflicted. There were scientists at the time who knew this claim to be false, including Laughlin's own boss.

Charles Davenport considered feeblemindedness to be a "lumber room" of different mental defects, all inherited separately. He understood that it was not a single trait, or "unit character," that was inherited according to Mendelian principles. Davenport had testified to this as an expert witness in a case challenging New York's eugenic sterilization law, in which he argued that feeblemindedness was "a social term," not a medical one. Whitehead could have introduced evidence on this point—perhaps even testimony from Davenport—to undermine the colony's claim that feeblemindedness was inherited directly from parents.

There was another problem with the colony's science: it relied on the eugenicists' claim that if every feebleminded person were sterilized feeblemindedness could be wiped out. This was an argument Laughlin had long been making. In his 1914 American Breeders' Association report, he had said it was possible "to sterilize wholesale those individuals thought to carry defective hereditary traits, and thus at one fell stroke cut off practically all of the cacogenic varieties of the race." Laughlin repeated the claim in his interrogatory answers. One of the pieces of expert writing he included, "Sterilization of Mental Defectives" by Dr. R. A. Gibbons, insisted that through sterilization of people who gave evidence of being defective "we can get rid of this class, the mentally deficient."

The science was questionable, however. By the time of the trial, geneticists had already discovered that inherited traits cannot be removed from the population so easily. Even if feeblemindedness were a unit character, sterilizing every feebleminded person would not eliminate feeblemindedness. Most of the genes for "mental defects," geneticists understood, "would be hidden in apparently normal carriers." The reality was "even *if* the 'mentally deficient' did not reproduce, the frequency of mental deficiency in the population would decrease only slightly, if at all." Whitehead could have found experts to testify that even if Laughlin and Dr. Priddy had been able to turn state hospitals into "clearing houses," sterilizing the feebleminded and then releasing them, the effect would have been limited.

There were more eugenic assumptions Whitehead could have challenged, including the often-repeated claim that the feebleminded were a menace to society, a crucial justification for eugenic sterilization. Carl Murchison, a psychologist at Clark University, was doing extensive research on criminals and finding that they had high intelligence levels, casting doubt on the claim that feeblemindedness and criminality were inextricably linked. Even Henry Goddard, the champion of Binet-Simon testing, who had done so much to demonize the feebleminded, had revised his thinking. Goddard now believed that it was a mistake to view all feebleminded people as a threat to the national gene pool. "I am willing to say," he declared, "that if we educate properly" the mentally defective "we may very safely neglect this question of eugenics and marriage for a large proportion of them."

Whitehead's failure to put on a case would have an impact that went beyond the circuit court's ruling. If *Buck v. Priddy* was appealed, the judges who considered it would have to rely on the legal record that Strode and Whitehead created at trial. If the eugenicists won in a higher court, perhaps even in the United States Supreme Court, the foundation for their victory would have been laid by the very one-sided proceeding that had just concluded in Amherst County.

Now all that remained was to wait for Judge Gordon's decision. Dr. Priddy and Strode were both optimistic, and they believed the judge had already foreshadowed how he would rule. In a letter reimbursing Wilhelm for trial expenses, Dr. Priddy said he was "well satisfied with the way in which we presented our case." He added that there was a good chance Judge Gordon would rule in the colony's favor "if his views expressed at the close of the case that evening, are not changed." Strode's assessment was similar. On December 11, he wrote to Estabrook that the judge had said in open court that week that he had not yet had a chance to prepare his opinion, but "intimated that he would probably decide it in our favor."

With the trial behind him, Strode returned to his legal practice. Over the summer, the *Virginia Law Review* had invited him to write an article, and Strode had proposed two possible subjects: "Indemnity to Bail" or "Enforced Sterilization of Defectives," in that order. It could be interpreted as another sign of Strode's lack of enthusiasm for eugenic sterilization that, in the midst of a historic case, his first suggestion for a legal subject he wanted to write about was "indemnity to bail." Strode ended up writing about sterilization—a topic that was, the editor in chief told him, "such a popular one that, I am certain, it will please our readers." In late November, Strode submitted his draft of an article titled "Sterilization of Defectives." He told the law review it should use it "as you think proper."

Dr. Priddy was in poor health before the trial began. In a November 2 letter, he had indicated he was not well enough to travel from the colony to Lynchburg to meet Strode to discuss the case. He was only going to town, he said, for X-rays and hospital visits. In the months after the trial, Dr. Priddy's health declined further. When he wrote to Whitehead in mid-December to send him a $250 check for his work representing Carrie, Dr. Priddy told his old friend, "I still continue very unwell." He had had a "little spell of coughing" a few days earlier, he said, and "as a result of it, one of my vocal chords has since then refused to work." Dr. Priddy said he would be traveling to Philadelphia in a few days for medical treatment.

The decline in Dr. Priddy's health continued. On January 13, 1925, he succumbed to Hodgkin's disease. After all of his work in getting a eugenic sterilization law enacted, constructing a test case, and arguing for the law in court, Dr. Priddy died without knowing if his law would be upheld.

Strode was traveling and returned too late to attend the funeral. In a memorial tribute for the colony's board, Strode noted that Dr. Priddy had continued serving as superintendent—and, he might have added, kept working on the eugenic sterilization test case—"undeterred," even as his health was fading. In particular, Strode lauded his old friend and collaborator for his years of kindness toward the mentally ill. Dr. Priddy "took a profound personal and humanitarian interest" in "amelioration of the condition of these most afflicted of God's creatures," Strode wrote.

Dr. Priddy would be remembered in the annals of Virginia medicine as both an institution builder and a champion of Virginia's feeble-minded. Even after his friends and colleagues had faded from the scene, his reputation endured. Dr. Priddy did "exceedingly well in creating the foundation for a sound program of care and treatment for his patients," a history of the colony written in 1960 noted. His era was, the history said, one devoted to "humane custodial care."

In early February 1925, just weeks after Dr. Priddy's death, the Amherst County Circuit Court issued a decision upholding the eugenic sterilization statute and affirming the colony board's order that Carrie be sterilized. The law was a valid and constitutional enactment, Judge Gordon ruled. And Carrie was an appropriate subject of the law, he said, as someone who was both feebleminded and the probable potential parent of socially inadequate offspring. The court stayed its ruling to allow Robert Shelton, Carrie's appointed guardian, to appeal on Carrie's behalf.

With Dr. Priddy's death, a new defendant had to be added to the case. Strode wrote to Dr. John Bell, who was to succeed Dr. Priddy as superintendent, asking if he would take his predecessor's place. Dr. Bell signed on immediately. "It is agreeable with me," he wrote Strode, adding that he was "in entire sympathy with the effort being made to reach a final conclusion as to the legality of this sterilization procedure." New court papers were drawn up and, when the Amherst County Circuit Court formally approved the request on April 13, the case took on the name *Buck v. Bell*.

Dr. Bell's background was in many ways similar to Dr. Priddy's. A native Virginian, Dr. Bell had practiced medicine in private practice before joining the state hospital system. He spent a year as an assistant physician to Dr. DeJarnette at the Western Lunatic Asylum, and then transferred to the colony, where he effectively acted as Dr. Priddy's deputy.

After Dr. Bell took over Dr. Priddy's position at the colony and his status as defendant in the case, he also assumed his role as one of Virginia's most outspoken sterilization advocates. Dr. Bell brought a fresh enthusiasm to the cause, and his apocalyptic vision went beyond anything Dr. Priddy had expressed. In "The Protoplasmic Blight," an address to the Medical Society of Virginia, Dr. Bell warned of "a world peopled by a race of degenerates and defectives, a world gone topsy-turvy, and sunk into the slough of despond, the great edifices of our present civilization . . . falling in decay." As Dr. Bell saw it, eugenic sterilization was necessary to save humanity from the abyss.

On June 1, 1925, Whitehead filed a Petition for Appeal to the Virginia Supreme Court of Appeals, as the Virginia Supreme Court was then known. There would be no further evidentiary hearings or witnesses—the appeal would be evaluated entirely on the legal papers submitted by the two sides. The Petition for Appeal served as an opening legal brief, and in it Whitehead summarized the case so far and made his main legal arguments to Virginia's highest court.

Whitehead insisted that the Amherst County Circuit Court had "erred in its judgment and order," and he raised three constitutional objections: that the sterilization order against his client violated the due process clause of the Fourteenth Amendment; that it violated the equal protection clause of the Fourteenth Amendment; and that it imposed cruel and unusual punishment in violation of the Eighth Amendment. Whitehead's comprehensiveness in asserting Carrie's constitutional rights may have had an ulterior motive. For the test case to fulfill its purpose of affirming the constitutionality of Virginia's eugenic sterilization law, the main constitutional challenges would have to be raised and then rejected by the Virginia Supreme Court of Appeals.

Whitehead wrote that "for the purposes of this petition it is not deemed necessary to go into all of these matters at length," and he was true to his word. His petition was just eight pages long, and the arguments he offered up for his constitutional challenges were superficial. In the case of the equal protection claim, Whiteside accurately explained the weakness of the law. It applied only to inmates of state hospitals, which created two classes of "defective" people in Virginia: inmates like Carrie, who were eligible for sterilization, and people who had not been committed to hospitals, who could not be sterilized. Whitehead held back, however, in providing legal support for this claim. He cited one major case in which a state court struck down a eugenic sterilization law for violating equal protection—a 1913 ruling by the New Jersey Supreme Court. Whitehead failed, however, to cite cases in two other states, New York and Michigan, in which the courts had struck down sterilization laws on equal protection grounds.

The Petition for Appeal did not offer legal arguments in support of the two other constitutional challenges it raised, due process and cruel and unusual punishment. There was a case to be made for why the Virginia law, and the hearing Carrie was given, violated due process, but Whitehead did not make it. To support the cruel and unusual punishment claim, Whitehead could have cited federal district court rulings from Iowa and Nevada that struck down sterilization laws. These precedents would have been of limited value—the Iowa and Nevada laws that were struck down were criminal laws, not civil eugenics statutes like Virginia's. But they would have offered at least some support for the cruel and unusual punishment argument.

Whitehead also submitted a legal brief to the Virginia Supreme Court of Appeals, but it was a paltry document. A mere five pages long, it focused entirely on whether the Virginia law and the sterilization order violated the due process clause of the Fourteenth Amendment. Whitehead argued that before the state could do something as significant as sterilize someone it had to provide a hearing with strong procedural protections, something he said Carrie's did not have. In the scant space he devoted to the argument, he was not able to flesh out the argument. He also made some odd claims. One of his main due process objections was that at the trial Carrie had not had sufficient opportunity to confront the evidence against her or to challenge the conclusions of the state's expert witnesses. There was no little irony in Whitehead's objecting to these failings when he himself had made so little effort to cross-examine the witnesses against her, and no effort at all to put on evidence of his own.

Strode's legal brief was a far more impressive document. In forty-four pages, Strode offered a comprehensive case for why the statute and the sterilization order against Carrie should be upheld. He recited the most damaging factual findings against Carrie—including that she was feebleminded and the mother of an illegitimate child, that Emma had a mental age of seven, and that Vivian was mentally defective. Strode summarized the expert witness testimony from trial, including Laughlin's conclusion that Carrie's family and personal history presented "a typical picture of a low grade moron." The brief quoted Dr. Priddy, "an eminent p[sy]chiatrist and surgeon," explaining why sterilization would be in the interest of both Carrie and of society.

Strode's central legal argument was that the state's "police power"— its authority to protect the health, safety, and welfare of its residents— gave it the right to adopt a program of eugenic sterilization. Strode compared compulsory sterilization to state laws requiring people to be vaccinated, and he cited a Supreme Court case from 1905, *Jacobson v. Massachusetts*, upholding one such law. He may have come across this analogy—and the *Jacobson* case—in Laughlin's treatise *Eugenical Sterilization in the United States*, which Dr. Priddy had given him when he drafted the sterilization law. Laughlin argued in his book that eugenic sterilization was a "parallel case" to compulsory vaccination: "Vaccination protects the individual and his associates from a serious and loathsome disease in the more immediate future" while "eugenical sterilization protects society from racial degeneracy in the more remote future."

Strode went on to address each of the constitutional challenges Whitehead raised in the Petition for Appeal. He dispensed with the claim that the law violated the bar on cruel and unusual punishment by arguing that the sterilization order against Carrie was not a punishment. It was done, he said, for eugenic reasons, not because of any crime Carrie had committed. And since it was not punitive, the Eighth Amendment did not apply.

In response to Whitehead's due process claim, Strode enumerated the various procedural protections in the Virginia law—protections he had put there himself when he drafted it. Given such provisions as the right to notice of a sterilization hearing and the right to be present, the right to an appointed guardian, and the right to appeal the hospital board's decision to the circuit court, Strode insisted that "all the requirements of due process of law have been fully complied with."

Strode also responded to Whitehead's equal protection argument. Strode should have felt a personal responsibility for leaving the Virginia law vulnerable on this score. He had written the statute to apply only to state hospital inmates, which created two classes of "defectives" who were treated differently, despite the warning in Laughlin's treatise that it would be a mistake to do so.

In his defense of the law, Strode argued that he had not in fact created two unequal classes. Invoking the "clearing house" model that Dr. Priddy and Laughlin spoke of so often, Strode insisted that "defective" people who were not inmates of a state hospital could be committed to one later and thereby become subject to sterilization. Because anyone in Virginia could at some time be a state hospital inmate, Strode insisted that the eugenic sterilization law was "part of a general plan applicable to all feeble-minded."

Strode included one especially audacious argument in his brief. He insisted that since Carrie was under age, her father was dead, and her mother was mentally incapacitated, the decision about whether she should be sterilized should be made by the State—by the very people lined up against her in the lawsuit. "Poor the Commonwealth in powers and helpless in authority," Strode wrote, "if she be incompetent thus to act for her afflicted children."

Strode's final argument was about the role of the courts: he made a plea for judicial restraint. The question of the "expediency and wisdom" of permitting eugenic sterilization, he insisted, was a matter for the legislature alone. He urged that the court resist any impulse it might have to strike down the law. "We are not permitted to approach a legislative enactment with an adverse mind as to its constitutionality," he wrote. "A large discretion is vested in the legislature to determine what the interests of the public require."

On November 12, 1925, the Virginia Supreme Court of Appeals affirmed the Amherst County Circuit Court's decision. Justice Jesse West, writing for a unanimous court, ruled that the colony had the legal authority to sterilize Carrie. It rejected all of Whitehead's constitutional objections, holding that Carrie had no rights that would be violated if she were sterilized.

The Virginia Supreme Court of Appeals, like all appellate courts, relied on the record developed at trial. As a result, it accepted as fact the entirety of the uncontroverted case the colony presented. The court stated that Carrie was feebleminded, with "the mind of a child nine years old." Because Whitehead had made no attempt to challenge Laughlin's claim that feeblemindedness was generally inherited, the court accepted that "by the laws of heredity" Carrie was "the probable potential parent of socially inadequate offspring."

Accepting the colony's description of the physical act of sterilization, the court stated that salpingectomies do not impair the health of the patient. It added that "in the hands of a skilled surgeon," the operations "are 100 per cent successful in results." It also asserted that the operation, "practically speaking, is harmless and 100 per cent safe"—an improbable percentage.

The court also accepted Strode's claim that salpingectomy was in Carrie's interest—something the statute required if the procedure was to be approved. If Carrie was not sterilized, the court said, she would have to remain at the colony for thirty years. With the operation, "she could be given her liberty" and released to a good home. The court's reasoning was in conformity with Dr. Priddy's testimony—left unrebutted by Whitehead—that inmates were better off being sterilized and freed, and in fact "clamored" to be sterilized.

On the constitutional questions, the Virginia Supreme Court of Appeals again accepted Strode's analysis. The Virginia law did not violate due process because it contained procedural protections, including the right to appeal the colony's order to a circuit court. In Carrie's case, the "hearing was conducted strictly in accordance with the provisions of the statute," the court said, and the statute "complies with the requirements of due process of law." The court also rejected Whitehead's equal protection challenge. It accepted Strode's notion that the law did not discriminate against people who were inmates of state hospitals, even though they could be sterilized, and people just as feebleminded who were not institutionalized could not.

The court also insisted that the sterilization law was a proper exercise of the state's police power. On this point, it accepted Strode's analogy to the Supreme Court's compulsory vaccination decision, *Jacobson v. Massachusetts*—or, more precisely, Laughlin's analogy. The court said that, as with the requirement of vaccines during a smallpox outbreak, the sterilization law fell within the legislature's prerogative to pass laws to "'protect the public health and the public safety.'"

The Virginia ruling came just a few months after the Michigan Supreme Court upheld a state eugenic sterilization law, after having struck down a different one seven years earlier. For the eugenic sterilization movement, these were two important victories. Following a long string of losses in the courts, the Michigan and Virginia decisions lifted the spirits of sterilization advocates and increased their hope that they might prevail if these or any other sterilization cases made it to the United States Supreme Court.

After Virginia's highest court issued its ruling, Strode and Whitehead attended a meeting of the colony's Special Board of Directors on December 7, 1925. According to the official minutes, the two old friends together "outlined the present status of the sterilization test case" and "presented conclusive argument for its prosecution through the Supreme Court of the United States." Strode and Whitehead told the board the case "was in admirable shape to go to the court" and said that the board "could not hope to have a more favorable situation than this one."

Whitehead's appearance before the board was, on one level, not unexpected. He had close ties to the colony, and had at one time been chairman of the same board he was now addressing. Nevertheless, it was highly unethical, given his representation of Carrie. At the precise moment when he should have been protesting the ruling upholding a sterilization order against his client, he was celebrating and strategizing with the very people who were trying to sterilize her. Instead of viewing the United States Supreme Court as the last chance to obtain justice for his client, his attendance at the board meeting suggested that he shared the hope of Strode and the colony that the court would uphold the Virginia statute and the sterilization order.

Whitehead's representation of Carrie at the trial and on appeal was an extraordinary case of malfeasance. Not only did he violate well-established ethical rules about the duty of loyalty to a client—which would, for example, have prohibited him from helping the opposing side plan its appellate strategy—but his entire representation of Carrie, in a case of enormous importance to her, was a fraud. To advance the interests of the colony, an institution to which he had close personal ties, Whitehead played the role of Carrie's lawyer and fooled her into believing he was protecting her interests. He was an impostor.

In some ways, though, Strode's betrayal was even greater. He was not simply a litigator for hire but one of Virginia's most eminent lawyers. He was the scion of two of Virginia's oldest families, in a time and place in which that carried enormous weight. He was a distinguished graduate of both the college and law school of the University of Virginia, Mr. Jefferson's great institution of enlightenment. He was also both the son of a college president and an educator himself. And as a member of the Virginia legislature, Strode had been one of the state's most progressive voices for the past two decades. He had fought for higher education for women and better schools for poor children—white ones, at least. In his later years, he would continue a life of service by becoming a judge.

Strode was just the sort of lawyer who should have understood implicitly that what was being done to Carrie was wrong, and he should not have gone along with it. He must have known that Carrie was not aware of what was at stake in the proceedings, yet he phrased his own question to her at trial in a way that kept her in ignorance. As a pillar of the Virginia bar, he should have found it intolerable that the lawyer who represented Carrie at trial in the circuit court, on a matter of great importance to her, did not call a single witness or present any evidence. And when that same lawyer joined Strode in briefing his client, making clear that his loyalties were not with his own client, Strode's inherent sense of justice should have been offended. Strode, however, went along with it all.

Dr. Priddy, Dr. DeJarnette, Dr. Bell, and Laughlin were eugenics true believers, intent on doing everything in their power to begin a program of mass sterilization. Strode, however, was different. He never sought out the sterilization cause on his own—not as a legislator and not as a lawyer—and when his clients brought it to him, he counseled them either not to act or to act slowly, and he drafted a far narrower law than the eugenicists wanted. He seemed to be drawn to eugenic sterilization out of a commitment to serve his clients—or perhaps just as paid legal work.

If anyone was in a position to try to bring it all to a stop—to say that eugenic sterilization was wrong, and that the way the legal system was treating Carrie was wrong—it was Strode. At the very least, he could have been a conscientious objector, and said he would not be part of the case if this was how it was going to proceed. He could have, but he did not. What he did continue to do, however, was what he had done all along: urge the most impassioned eugenic sterilization advocates to slow down.

When the Virginia Supreme Court of Appeals upheld the sterilization law, there were calls for eugenic sterilizations to begin right away, and they were coming from the top. "I notice from the paper the Sterilization Law has been declared constitutional by the Supreme Court," Governor Elbert Lee Trinkle wrote in a letter to the state hospital superintendents. "I do hope you people will get busy and use the law as fast as it can be used and help us get rid of our overcrowded conditions."

The State Hospital Board asked Strode if eugenic sterilizations could now be performed, but Strode still insisted it was too soon. He advised the board that the case raised federal constitutional questions that only the United States Supreme Court could resolve definitively. On Strode's advice, the hospitals held off and waited for Carrie's guardian to appeal the ruling, something they knew he intended to do.

Robert Shelton filed the necessary papers with the United States Supreme Court. By doing so, he was not only carrying out Strode's plan of seeking a ruling from the "highest court" before the Virginia state hospitals began sterilizations, but also creating the possibility of a landmark ruling on eugenic sterilization. With the stroke of a pen, the Supreme Court could resolve years of litigation over state sterilization laws and settle a contentious legal controversy for the entire nation.

By taking the case to the Supreme Court, Shelton was also, unwittingly, doing something else: putting his client on a collision course with a man whose life could hardly have been more different from her own. She was young and barely educated. He had reached a venerable age, and was among the nation's most acclaimed thinkers. She came from the bottom of the South's social hierarchy and from a family that had struggled for generations. He had been born into the highest caste in the North, with centuries of prominent and accomplished ancestors.

Most important, she was in a position of extreme weakness, a poor and unsophisticated inmate of a colony for the feebleminded, with a court order of sterilization against her. He was the highly respected intellectual leader of the most important court in the world. Unfortunately for Carrie, he was also someone who had, as he himself cheerfully admitted, dedicated his entire life to making himself the "supple tool of power."

Eight

Oliver Wendell Holmes

In the spring of 1927, eighty-six-year-old Oliver Wendell Holmes Jr. was the leading figure in American law. Holmes was regarded not only as a Supreme Court justice of profound wisdom but as a man of transcendent nobility. The praise that has been showered on Holmes knows few bounds. Charles Wyzanski, a prominent federal judge in Boston, declared that "like the Winged Victory of Samothrace," Holmes was "the summit of hundreds of years of civilization, the inspiration of ages yet to come." Felix Frankfurter, the Harvard law professor who later became a Supreme Court justice, pronounced Holmes the modern embodiment of Plato's ideal of the "philosopher become King."

Holmes was celebrated for his judicial rulings, the most famous of which were stirring defenses of civil liberties and individual freedom. He was admired not only for his legal views but also for the lyrical way in which he expressed himself. Holmes had a gift for epigrams, such as his contention that "the life of the law has not been logic: it has been experience." He also had a rare ability to reduce complex principles to simple truths, like his famous assertion that the "most stringent protection of free speech would not protect a man in falsely shouting fire in a theatre."

Holmes's reputation derived from more than his jurisprudential accomplishments, notable as those were. It was a product, above all, of biography. Holmes was a Boston Brahmin—a member of America's most rarefied social caste. To that august lineage, he added adventure and valor, having enlisted as a young man to fight in the Civil War and having been wounded three times in battle. Holmes was also handsome in a distinctive way, with a robust mustache and unruly gray hair that suggested both wisdom and a kind of all-American reasonableness. At this stage in his life, he had one more virtue: an enviable longevity, at a time when life spans were short. Holmes was not so much a judge, one writer observed, as a "favorite of the gods."

The Holmes cult of personality reached beyond the legal world. On the occasion of his eighty-fifth birthday, a year earlier, he had been featured on the cover of *Time* magazine. On his ninetieth, he would be celebrated in a national radio broadcast. After his death, Holmes would be brought back to life as the subject of a long-running Broadway play, *The Magnificent Yankee*, later made into a Hollywood movie. The title of a bestselling biography of Holmes years later would capture his immortal reputation: *Yankee from Olympus.*

Given his status as a living monument to American justice, it would seem that Carrie Buck could hardly have done better than to have her fate placed in Holmes's hands. What she could hardly have known— few Americans did—was just how wide the chasm was between Holmes the legend and Holmes the man. The mythical Holmes was a creation for mass consumption, a careful admixture of rigorous legal logic, progressive values, sympathy for the underdog, and generosity of spirit. This Holmes would have understood on a deep level the overwhelming injustice of allowing the state to take away a young woman's ability to bear children in the service of a misguided ideology.

The true Holmes, however, was a far darker force. He was not a progressive, despite what all the admiring magazine articles said.

One critic has bemoaned the "cherished American myth . . . that Oliver Wendell Holmes was a 'liberal,'" calling it as "baseless as the tale of Washington and the cherry tree."

In Holmes's view, life was naturally competitive and cruel, and he had little inclination to rein in its harsh injustices. H. L. Mencken, the acerbic journalist and editor, said Holmes was at heart not a jurist but a soldier, with a "natural distaste and contempt for civilians" and a "corollary yearning to heave them all into Hell." The Yale law professor who was commissioned to write Holmes's official biography was only slightly less hyperbolic, declaring after he abandoned the project that he had found "the real Holmes" to have been "savage, harsh, and cruel, a bitter and lifelong pessimist who saw in the course of human life nothing but a continuing struggle in which the rich and powerful impose their will on the poor and weak." Anyone who knew Holmes only from his public persona would not have guessed the truth: that he could only regard a claim such as Carrie's with active contempt.

Oliver Wendell Holmes Jr. was born on March 8, 1841, into the highest stratum of Boston society. Although it was only the nation's fifth largest city, with a population of less than one hundred thousand, Boston was widely considered to be the nation's literary, educational, and philosophical capital. It was also, at the time of Holmes's birth, in the midst of a great intellectual flowering.

In 1841 Ralph Waldo Emerson published *Essays: First Series*, which contained some of his most important writings, including "Self-Reliance" and "The Over-Soul." In religion, the Reverend Theodore Parker delivered "A Discourse on the Transient and Permanent in Christianity," his famous sermon challenging New England's religious orthodoxy. And Margaret Fuller was in her second year as editor of the *Dial*, the influential new voice of transcendentalism.

These intellectual pioneers were not merely a collection of talented individuals. They were all members of the same social class: the Boston Brahmins. Holmes's father, Dr. Oliver Wendell Holmes Sr., had coined the phrase "Boston Brahmins," and in the book in which he did, he described them as "an aristocracy, if you choose to call it so . . . a *caste*,—not in any odious sense,—but, by the repetition of the same influences, generation after generation." The Boston Brahmins were a tightly connected group of elite families. "Quincys, Cabots, Lodges, Lees, Lowells, Curtises, Higginsons, and Holmeses banded together," the historian Liva Baker observed. "They lived in the same neighborhoods, went to the same schools, read the same books, shared the same ignorances as well as knowledge, belonged to the same clubs, dined at the same houses, donated to the same charities, and married their cousins." They also promoted one another in business, nonprofit organizations, and government. It was a supremely influential network that Holmes would avail himself of throughout his career.

The Brahmins were not ostentatious about their wealth and privilege—an ethic of Puritan reserve prevailed. But they had an unmistakable air of superiority, which a famous Boston poem pointedly mocked:

> And this is good old Boston
> The home of the bean and the cod,
> Where the Lowells talk only to Cabots,
> And the Cabots talk only to God.

On her first visit in the 1830s, the British sociologist Harriet Martineau was struck by the smug self-satisfaction of Boston's elites, declaring it "perhaps as aristocratic, vain, and vulgar a city, as described by its own 'first people,' as any in the world." Holmes's father contributed to this perception of Boston as a place of supreme self-importance when he drolly dubbed Boston's statehouse the "hub of the solar system," a phrase his fellow Bostonians converted to "hub of the universe" and turned into the city's unofficial motto.

The Brahmins' politics were conservative and deferential to authority. Their Puritan ancestors' preferred form of government was theocracy, and the Massachusetts Bay Colony had banished freethinkers like Roger Williams and Anne Hutchinson for their "new and dangerous opinions." In the mid-1800s, Brahmin Boston was Republican, staunchly pro-business, and hostile to reformers, whom Dr. Holmes dismissed as "dingy-linened friends of progress." Elite Bostonians who drifted from orthodoxy were no longer exiled, but they were firmly rebuked. The Boston Athenæum, the city's aristocratic private library, revoked Lydia Maria Child's access to use its collection after she published her first abolitionist pamphlet.

The Holmes family was not wealthy, but it was "well born," which in Brahmin Boston mattered more. Holmes was descended from Cabots, Quincys, and Eliots, among others, and had three more Brahmin dynasties in his name—the Olivers, the Wendells, and the Holmeses. On both sides of his family, Holmes had no shortage of illustrious ancestors. He was a direct descendant of Anne Bradstreet, the noted seventeenth-century Puritan poet. His paternal grandfather, the Reverend Abiel Holmes, was a prominent Cambridge minister and historian, who wrote a biography of his own father-in-law, Ezra Stiles, the president of Yale, as well as a history of the Mohegan Indians. Holmes's maternal grandfather, Charles Jackson, was a justice on the Supreme Judicial Court, the highest court in Massachusetts.

If Boston in the mid-1800s was the hub of the solar system, Dr. Holmes stood close to its white-hot center. Dubbed "the Greatest Brahmin," he had been hailed as "the most successful combination . . . the world has ever seen, of the physician and man of letters." As a physician, Dr. Holmes was a pioneer in early medical science, credited with discovering that puerperal fever, which struck women who had just given birth, was caused by bacteria carried by doctors and nurses on their unclean hands and medical equipment. The paper he wrote, "The Contagiousness of Puerperal Fever," helped end the "black death of childbed," and saved many mothers' lives. Dr. Holmes, who was also credited with coining the word "anesthesia," became dean of the Harvard Medical School in 1847, at the age of thirty-eight.

In the literary world, Dr. Holmes was no less eminent. At the age of twenty-one, he wrote the poem "Old Ironsides" to protest the secretary of the navy's reported plans to scrap the USS *Constitution*, which had performed heroically in the War of 1812 and was then docked in Boston Harbor. Dr. Holmes's poem, which was widely reprinted, was often credited with saving the great ship.

As an adult, Dr. Holmes was part of a circle that included Emerson, Nathaniel Hawthorne, Herman Melville, and Henry Wadsworth Longfellow. In 1857, he joined a group of Boston's leading literary men in forming a new magazine, and he thought up its name, *Atlantic Monthly*. Dr. Holmes went on to write a popular column for the magazine. It is said that one of his readers, Sir Arthur Conan Doyle, named his hyperrational detective, Sherlock Holmes, after Dr. Holmes.

Dr. Holmes had enormous expectations for his first son. In a letter to his sister, written on the day after his son's birth, Dr. Holmes anticipated that his newborn, who had not yet been named, might one day "be addressed as _____ Holmes, Esq. or The Hon. _____ Holmes, M.C. or His Excellency _____ Holmes, President." The relationship between father and son, which began with such high expectations, would prove to be a complicated one.

It was a challenge for Holmes, who was preternaturally ambitious, to grow up in the shadow of a man who was so accomplished and famous. Adding to Holmes's difficulty was the fact that the two men shared a name, and he was forever being confused with his father, even after he joined the Supreme Court. The competitiveness ran in both directions, which made for tense relations—something not lost on those who knew them both. William James, the pioneering Harvard psychologist and a friend of the younger Holmes, noted after seeing the two Oliver Wendell Holmeses together that "no love is lost between W. *pere* and W. *fils*." Holmes had a warmer bond with his mother, Amelia, who devoted herself mainly to home and family. He would later say that he "got a sceptical temperament . . . from my mother."

Holmes attended two schools that attracted students from Boston's elite. He started out at a boys' school run by T. Russell Sullivan, a former Unitarian minister, in the basement of the Park Street Church. Then he attended the Private Latin School, presided over by E. S.

Dixwell, a lawyer-turned-classics-scholar who "had no patience with slovenliness of mind." In the summers, the Holmes family retreated to a 280-acre family farm in the Berkshires, not far from the homes of Melville and Hawthorne.

Holmes followed a well-worn path from Mr. Dixwell's school to Harvard College, where he entered with the class of 1861. Harvard had been the choice of centuries of Holmes's ancestors, who had been attending since Dr. James Oliver entered with the five-member class of 1680. Few young men had stronger familial ties to the college: a great-great-uncle had been Harvard treasurer; his maternal grandfather had been a member of the board of overseers; and former Harvard president Josiah Quincy was a cousin. For someone of Holmes's background, enrollment at Harvard was all but inevitable. Henry Adams—a friend of the Holmes family and a member of the class of 1858—explained in *The Education of Henry Adams* how people like him and Holmes ended up there. "Any other education would have required a serious effort, but no one took Harvard College seriously," Adams wrote. "All went there because their friends went there, and the College was their ideal of social self-respect."

In college, Holmes studied science, history, economics, foreign languages, and the classics. The instruction he received was uninspired; Henry Adams wrote that the Harvard College of his and Holmes's era "taught little, and that little ill." Holmes was, for his part, a solid but unremarkable student: at the end of junior year, he ranked thirteenth in a class of eighty-four. Much of his energy went into Harvard's student organizations and clubs, including two of the most prestigious: the Porcellian Club, which was founded in 1791, and the Hasty Pudding Club, which was nearly as old. As with almost everything in his life, Holmes's path to the Porcellian and the Hasty Pudding was eased by family members who had been there before him.

On April 12, 1861, in the waning weeks of Holmes's senior year, the Confederates fired on Fort Sumter, and the Civil War began. As President Abraham Lincoln issued a call for seventy-five thousand militiamen to put down the Southern insurrection, Boston was quickly swept up in Union fervor. "The heather is on fire," wrote the Harvard professor George Ticknor. "The whole population, men, women, and children, seem to be in the streets with Union favours and flags."

Holmes got caught up in the fervor, as many Harvard students did. He left college before the semester's end to join the Union army, reporting for duty at Fort Independence in Boston Harbor. Holmes spent several months in training, and was allowed to return to Harvard in June to graduate with his class. He had been elected class poet, a position his father held before him, and at Class Day ceremonies his poem implored his fellow graduates to "be brave, for now the thunder rolls."

Holmes joined the Twentieth Massachusetts Volunteer Infantry, which was known as the "Harvard Regiment" because so many of its officers were Harvard students or alumni. In September the Twentieth Regiment was ordered to deploy to Washington, and its 41 officers and 750 men were off to war. Holmes joined as a first lieutenant, and his rank allowed him to travel with a considerable amount of luggage and personal effects; he and another lieutenant shared a servant. On a stop in New York, Holmes and some of his Harvard friends—not liking the looks of the official army meal—went to dinner at Delmonico's, one of New York's finest restaurants.

When the Twentieth Regiment arrived in Washington, it joined the Army of the Potomac. The regiment was assigned to patrol the Potomac River in Maryland, the dividing line between the Northern and Southern positions. On October 20, orders came to cross the Potomac and engage the Confederates on the Virginia side. The Union troops claimed a bluff on the river, which turned out to be a tactical error. The Union men were caught in an open field and fired upon by Confederate troops. The Battle of Ball's Bluff was a rout, with losses that were among the worst, on a percentage basis, of any battle in the war. Of the 1,800 Union troops, 921 were killed, wounded, taken prisoner, or missing in action.

In his first battle, Holmes was shot in the chest, a feeling he compared to being kicked by a horse. Writing to his mother, the twenty-year-old Holmes said that the first night after being wounded, "I made up my mind to die." Holmes's will to live quickly returned, and he traveled to Boston to convalesce at his parents' home. Much of Boston's Brahmin elite stopped by to wish him a speedy recovery, including Massachusetts's senior United States senator, Charles Sumner, and the president of Harvard.

In March 1862 Holmes rejoined the Twentieth Regiment as a captain. The Army of the Potomac was now trying to invade Richmond, while General Robert E. Lee was attempting to continue his drive north. That fall, on September 17, Union and Confederate troops clashed at the Battle of Antietam, and the Twentieth Regiment was on the front lines. In the fighting at Antietam, a small creek in rural Maryland, more than 23,000 were killed or wounded, making it the single bloodiest day of the Civil War.

Holmes was once again a casualty. A bullet entered his neck, narrowly missing his windpipe and jugular vein. When Dr. Holmes got the news by telegraph, he headed south in search of his son, and eventually found him in Pennsylvania on a train arriving from Maryland. The elder Holmes later recounted his search in a famous article, "My Hunt After 'The Captain,'" in the *Atlantic Monthly*. Once again, Holmes returned home to convalesce.

Holmes was ordered back to the front lines in November 1862. He traveled from Boston with his old friend Henry Abbott, known as "Little Abbott," who had been recovering from typhoid. Holmes's outlook was now far darker than it had once been. He no longer believed the Union army, which struck him as badly managed and ineffectual, would prevail. "I've pretty much made up my mind that the South have achieved their independence," he wrote in a letter. "Believe me, we shall never lick them."

Holmes and Little Abbott arrived to find the Twentieth Regiment in Falmouth, Virginia, looking tired and discouraged. Holmes was soon injured again—the third and final time. He took a bullet to the heel on May 3, 1863, in the Battle of Chancellorsville. Holmes wrote his mother that he had "been chloroformed & had bone extracted—

probably shant lose foot." He was so despondent he hoped the foot would be lost, he later said, so he could avoid another return to battle.

This time, Holmes took his longest convalescence of the war. While he was recovering in Boston, the Twentieth Regiment fought in the Battle of Gettysburg, with grim results. Ten of its thirteen officers and half of its enlisted men were lost. Several of Holmes's close friends were among the dead, including Henry Ropes, whose body was so badly mangled that, as his brother informed Holmes, "nothing of the face can be seen but the chin, round which is a handkerchief."

When he returned in January 1864, Holmes took a position as General Horatio Wright's aide-de-camp, which kept him off the front lines. In May, at his relatively protected perch, word reached Holmes that Little Abbott had fallen in battle. The loss hit Holmes hard. Decades later, he would recall that "for us, who not only admired, but loved [him], his death seemed to end a portion of our life also."

In the summer of 1864, his three-year enlistment complete, Holmes left the army and returned to civilian life. The war's brutality had taken an unmistakable toll. Holmes's youthful enthusiasm for marching off to battle was by now long gone. He told his parents that he had witnessed "all of fatigue & horror that war can furnish." On July 17, 1864, he was formally discharged.

Holmes could have become an eloquent witness to the horror of war. With the passage of time, however, he became the opposite: an old soldier who romanticized the experiences he had abhorred when they happened. In middle age, Holmes gave a celebrated Memorial Day address to Harvard's graduating class of 1895, titled *The Soldier's Faith*. "War, when you are at it, is horrible and dull," he told the graduates. "It is only when time has passed that you see that its message was divine." In the most famous line of the address, he reflected that "through our great good fortune, in our youth our hearts were touched with fire." Not everyone was persuaded by Holmes's nostalgia for the blood-soaked battles of the Civil War. His college classmate Wendell Garrison, writing in the *Nation*, dismissed *The Soldier's Faith* as "sentimental jingoism."

The Civil War's deepest impact on Holmes may have been to instill in him a dark worldview—or deepen one already there. In a letter to his sister, Amelia, written after his neck wound, he declared that he "loathed the thick-fingered clowns we call the people." The critic Edmund Wilson, in his study of Civil War literature, *Patriotic Gore*, concluded that Holmes had emerged from the war with a newfound "bleakness." The miseries of battle contributed, in Wilson's view, to Holmes's cynical view of power. "The rights . . . in any society, are determined, after a struggle to the death, by the group that comes out on top," Wilson wrote. "Holmes is always insisting on the right to kill, to establish authority by violent means."

In the fall of 1864, Holmes enrolled at Harvard Law School. The decision was not unexpected. In a short autobiography that he wrote after enlisting, he had declared that if he "survive[d] the war," he "expect[ed] to study law as my profession or at least for a starting point." Holmes was once again following in the footsteps of prominent ancestors. In addition to his maternal grandfather, the Supreme Judicial Court justice, his paternal great-grandfather had been probate judge of Suffolk County, where Harvard Law School is located.

When Holmes enrolled, Harvard Law School was a modest institution with a faculty of three and few course requirements. Most students were not college graduates, and many were still teenagers. Years later, when Holmes was the coeditor of the *American Law Review*, it ran an unsigned article, which some people suspected him of writing, that decried conditions at Harvard Law School as "almost a disgrace to the Commonwealth of Massachusetts." To graduate, it said, required little more than showing up. "Just as a certain number of dinners entitled a man in England to a call to the bar, so a certain number of months in Cambridge entitled him to the degree of Bachelor of Laws."

In April 1865, in the final days of Holmes's first year of law school, the Civil War ended. As Boston filled with returning soldiers, some badly wounded, there were celebrations with somber overtones. Holmes attended Class Day this year not as an eager undergraduate poet, but in his war uniform, as a battle-weary veteran. He returned to law school in the fall, but that winter, a semester short of the usual two years' study, he left to apprentice with a lawyer in private practice. The time he had put in was enough to earn him a law degree with the class of 1866.

In April 1866 Holmes set sail for Europe. When he arrived his Boston connections gave him entrée to the upper reaches of British society. Holmes dined at the home of Lady Belper in London and talked financial policy with John Stuart Mill. He traveled on to Scotland, where he attended a ball at the castle of the Duke of Argyll and shot grouse with the duke's hunting party.

On his return, Holmes joined the Beacon Hill law firm of Chandler, Shattuck and Thayer. Its leaders were Boston Brahmins who shared many of his interests. George Shattuck, who was twelve years older than Holmes, was a well-regarded litigator and a fellow Harvard Law School graduate. James Bradley Thayer would later become Harvard's Royall Professor of Law. The firm had blue-chip clients, including the Boston Railroad Company and the National Bank of America.

Holmes's friends had always detected a burning ambition in him. William James, a keen observer of personalities, saw Holmes as "a powerful battery, formed like a planing machine to gouge a deep self-beneficial groove through life." Before long, Holmes's interest in his commercial legal practice began to wane. After a few years, he accepted a part-time position as a university lecturer in law at Harvard. He was also named coeditor of the *American Law Review,* the periodical, started recently by some of his friends, that published the negative review of Harvard Law School.

Holmes worked at a furious pace, on a diverse array of demanding projects. In these hard-driving years, he spent little time on frivolity—or helping the less fortunate. "It is noticeable," an early biographer pointed out, "that in a city where 'good works' were a traditional obligation of the elect, Holmes gave, so far as one can discover, no time or interest to civic or charitable activities." Holmes's lack of altruism was something his friends commented on. "The more I live in the world, the more cold-blooded, conscious egotism and conceit of people afflict me," William James wrote to his brother, the novelist Henry James. "All the noble qualities of Wendell Holmes, for instance, are poisoned by them, and friendly as I want to be towards him, as yet the good he has done me is more in presenting me something to kick away from or react against than to follow and embrace." As an adult, Holmes would make no secret of his lack of charitable impulses. In a letter to a friend, he railed against the philanthropy of Andrew Carnegie and John D. Rockefeller Jr., writing, "I think charitable gifts on a large scale are *prima facie* the worst abuse of private ownership."

At the age of thirty-one, Holmes became engaged to Fanny Dix-well, the daughter of E. S. Dixwell, his old schoolmaster. The Dixwells were not wealthy, but they were Brahmins in good standing. Like Holmes, Fanny Dixwell was descended from some of Boston's most prominent families, including the Pickerings, Ingersolls, and Sargents. Holmes had known Fanny most of his life, and in a letter at the time of the engagement he described her as "for many years my most inti-mate friend." Holmes's bride-to-be was not regarded as a great intel-lect, but she was attractive and had other suitors vying for her hand. She also had a saturnine demeanor that made the couple dour soul mates. One member of Fanny's extended family said that she had no close friends and "hated" most of her sisters. Holmes once said of his wife, "She is a very solitary bird, and if her notion of duty did not com-pel her to do otherwise, she would be an absolute recluse, I think."

Holmes did not let any joy he might have felt over his impending nuptials interfere with his legal career. As the wedding drew near, he continued his frenetic work pace. Shortly before the wedding cere-mony, Holmes's coeditor at the *American Law Review* stepped down, leaving him to edit it alone. Holmes's journal entry for June 17, 1872, the day he was married, indicates how near work always was to his mind: "[June] 17 *married*. Sole editor of Law Rev."

The Holmeses' marriage would prove to be a close and enduring one. The union did not produce children, an absence that prompted a fair amount of conjecture but no firm answers. Fanny, who suffered from rheumatic fever, may have had difficulty conceiving. Holmes suggested on more than one occasion that he and Fanny were childless by choice. He told his first biographer that he had come to the conclusion that this was not the sort of world into which he wanted to bring children. He offered up another perspective in a letter to a friend: "I am so far abnormal that I am glad I have" no children.

In 1874 Holmes took his wife to Europe, and they retraced some of the travels he had done on his own. The trip reminded Fanny, who often preferred to stay at home when Holmes went out, why she did not like to socialize. The two-week ocean voyage from New York to Liverpool irritated her, with its choppy seas and enforced proximity to people she disliked. On arriving in London, she was confronted with hosts she considered inhospitable and food she found odd. She dismissed Lady Belper, who invited Holmes back for dinner, as a "twinkling hippopotamus."

Holmes was now doing a considerable amount of writing about the law, and in his legal analysis he was beginning to express more of his views about the world. In 1873 he published an article titled "The Gas-Stokers' Strike" in the *American Law Review*. In it, he analyzed the recent prosecution of gas stokers' union leaders for an illegal strike that left London in darkness. Progressives insisted the law used against the union was "class legislation," but Holmes defended it. The "law of human existence," he argued, is "the struggle for life"—and that struggle is a selfish one. "In the last resort, a man rightly prefers his own interests to that of his neighbors." There was nothing unusual about the antistrike law, as Holmes saw it: all legislation is "class legislation" because it inevitably reflects the interests of the class in power when it was enacted. Legislation, "like every other device of man or beast," he argued, "must tend in the long run to aid the survival of the fittest."

Holmes's gas-stokers essay signaled that he was aligning himself with the ascendant social Darwinist movement. It was not just his use of the phrase "survival of the fittest," which Herbert Spencer had coined about a decade earlier, but the whole worldview Holmes expressed. His claim that the "law of human existence" was a selfish "struggle for life" was similar to Spencer's contention that nature was a battle in which the "creature not energetic enough to maintain itself must die."

Applying this principle to the London strike, Holmes saw a set of economic classes and subclasses, including the gas stokers and the companies that employed them, locked in a brutal, life-or-death battle. That was the law of nature, as he saw it: life produced winners and losers. Holmes made clear that his sympathies lay with the winners, and he had little patience for the utilitarian idea that the goal of legislation should be to promote "the greatest good for the greatest number." Holmes asked:

> Why should the greatest number be preferred? Why not the greatest good of the most intelligent and most highly developed? The greatest good of a minority of our generation may be the greatest good of the greatest number in the long run.

With this argument that favoring the "most intelligent and most highly developed" could yield rewards in future generations, Holmes began to veer subtly but unmistakably from social Darwinism to eugenics.

There was likely no single source for the pitiless worldview that Holmes was beginning to express. The cynicism instilled on the bloody battlefields of the Civil War was no doubt part of it. His Boston Brahmin upbringing may have contributed, with his family's and his class's conviction that they were the highest caste, perhaps even the closest to God, as the Brahmins of India were believed to be.

Holmes's dark vision may have had even deeper roots. After all, the friend who told his brother that he saw something profoundly wrong with Holmes's character was not just any companion of youth, but William James, who would later be called "the father of American psychology." James detected something "cold-blooded" in the young Holmes. Whatever its source, the personal philosophy Holmes was beginning to reveal was unsentimental and power centered. It held that whoever won dominance in the social order would naturally use their position in ruthless pursuit of their own interests—and they were right to do so.

In 1878 a federal district court judgeship opened up in Boston. It was a rare occurrence, and Holmes's social networks mobilized on his behalf. His old friend John Gray and his Harvard classmate Charles Cotesworth Beaman, among other prominent men, did what they could. But George Frisbie Hoar, a powerful Republican senator from Massachusetts, had his own candidate, and Senator Hoar's influence with President Rutherford B. Hayes proved decisive.

Holmes soon received an honor of a different sort when he was invited to give the prestigious Lowell Lectures. The Lowell Institute, which had been funded by the estate of the textile magnate John Lowell Jr., was one of Brahmin Boston's leading cultural organizations, offering programming on significant topics to enlighten the public. Holmes chose as the subject of his lectures the development of the "common law," the judge-made legal doctrines that existed in all areas of the law. Over twelve nights in the fall and winter of 1880, Holmes offered his interpretation of the common law, covering criminal law, torts, and other fields.

Holmes's Lowell Lectures were published as *The Common Law* the following March. The timing was fortuitous. Holmes believed a man should achieve distinction before he turned forty, perhaps influenced by the fact that his father had become the dean of Harvard Medical School at thirty-eight. It was likely no coincidence his book came out five days before his fortieth birthday. *The Common Law* was a bold break from the legal analysis of its time. Holmes rejected the widespread fascination with "natural law," the view that law reflected timeless, unchanging absolutes handed down from above. He insisted the law was not a "brooding omnipresence in the sky," as he would later express it, arguing instead that humans and their institutions had created it over time.

The Common Law also argued against what Holmes saw as the legal system's excessive reliance on logic and abstract legal rules. Law "cannot be dealt with as if it contained only the axioms and corollaries of a book of mathematics," he wrote. In the book's most famous line, he explained, "The life of the law has not been logic—it has been experience."

With the success of *The Common Law*—which would be hailed by its admirers as the most important legal book by an American, and "a landmark in intellectual history"—Holmes turned further away from the practice of law. In a few years, he would tell an audience of Harvard undergraduates what he really thought of the legal profession, calling it a "greedy watch for clients and practice of shopkeepers' arts" mixed with "mannerless conflicts over often sordid interests."

In 1882 Holmes finally left private practice to become a professor at Harvard Law School. The school did not have funding for the position, but Holmes's elite social class came to his aid once again. After being approached by Louis Brandeis, a public-spirited lawyer who was a friend of Holmes's, Samuel Weld, a Boston Brahmin whose family had strong Harvard ties, contributed the whole amount.

Holmes was glad to be out of the practice of law, but he found the life of a full-time professor less than he had hoped. If the law firm had been too grubby a part of the real world, as he told the Harvard students, academia was too far removed. He would later try to dissuade a friend from joining the law school faculty. "Academic life is but half life," he wrote. "It is withdrawal from the fight in order to utter smart things that cost you nothing except the thinking them from a cloister."

In December 1882, not long after Holmes arrived at the law school, another chance to become a judge presented itself. In the final weeks of Governor John Davis Long's term, a vacancy had opened up on Massachusetts's highest court. At the urging of Holmes's former law partner George Shattuck, the governor appointed Holmes, making him the Supreme Judicial Court's youngest member. Holmes's hasty departure from the law school in the middle of his first year left hard feelings. His former law partner James Bradley Thayer, who was now on the faculty, conceded that Holmes had the legal right to leave, but wondered "what shall be said of his sense of what is morally admissible—of his sense of honor."

On the Supreme Judicial Court, Holmes heard a wide variety of civil and criminal cases, and it did not take long for his views on the law to emerge. They were, it turned out, not far from the ones he expressed in his gas-stokers article. He generally sided with the most powerful organizations or individuals, on the theory that they should be allowed to use their power as they saw fit.

This philosophy often led Holmes to take conservative positions, but not always. In *Commonwealth v. Perry*, the court reversed the conviction of Josiah Perry, a textile mill owner, under a law that made it illegal to withhold weavers' wages for flaws in their work. The majority ruled that the conviction violated the constitutional right of freedom of contract, but Holmes dissented. In his view, the weavers had enough power to get the legislature to pass a law protecting them, and the courts should not interfere with its operation.

Holmes's *Perry* dissent looked, on the surface, like a liberal stand— one analyst even called it his "first blow for the Massachusetts trade unions." But Holmes had little sympathy for the workers, and he made clear in his dissent that, when it came to the substance of the weavers' dispute, "I know nothing about the matter one way or the other." His concern was for legislatures, and those who lobbied them successfully— and his instinct was to let them do what they wanted without judicial interference.

Holmes, who would later be lionized as a champion of freedom of expression, was no great protector of free speech in his years on the Supreme Judicial Court. In a major case about the speech rights of public employees, *McAuliffe v. Mayor of New Bedford*, Holmes was, characteristically, more interested in power than speech. A police officer sued when the city of New Bedford fired him for off-duty political activity. To Holmes, this was the sort of thing public employers had the right to do. In a much-quoted aphorism, Holmes said the officer "may have a constitutional right to talk politics, but he has no constitutional right to be a policeman."

The logic behind the decision was "the greater power includes the lesser." Holmes believed that since New Bedford had the right to fire the officer, it also had the right to do anything less—including preventing him from speaking. It was an approach Holmes would use often, though it has been criticized for giving the government almost limitless authority. If the city's power to fire includes every "lesser" power with respect to workers, that leaves workers with almost no rights at all.

Holmes's years on the Supreme Judicial Court were not a joyful time for him and Fanny. The workload on the court was heavy, and Holmes labored away on his cases, rarely taking time off to socialize. "I have known and done almost nothing but law," Holmes wrote to his British friend Sir Frederick Pollock. Fanny, who had suffered a serious bout of rheumatic fever, also stayed close to home.

In 1897 Holmes published his second book, *The Path of the Law*. In it, he argued that the law should not be a reflection of moral values, a belief he had been refining since his writings on the gas stokers. Holmes believed that in the legal system there was too much "confounding morality with law." Lawyers and judges were too inclined to use morally tinged words such as "rights," "duties," and "malice." Holmes argued for a new legal terminology that would "convey legal ideas uncolored by anything outside the law." He also argued that judges should not base their decisions on their sense of what would be best for society—or resort to what some would later call "judicial activism." He was troubled that "people who no longer hope to control the legislatures" were looking instead "to the courts as expounders of the constitutions."

Holmes was named chief justice of the Supreme Judicial Court in 1899. The promotion gave him administrative control over the court's workings, and a more prestigious title, but the cases remained what they had always been: disputes that mattered a great deal to the parties but generally lacked larger significance. Holmes described the caseload as "trifling and transitory," and the lawyers' arguments did not always hold his interest. "As we don't shut up bores, one has to listen to discourses dragging slowly along after one has seen the point and made up one's mind," Holmes complained in a letter to a friend. He noted that he was writing the letter from the bench "as I sit with my brethren"— adding, "I hope I shall be supposed to be taking notes."

Holmes had long dreamed of serving on the Supreme Court, something he confided to a cousin before his marriage. As the highest-ranking state court judge in Massachusetts, he would be a plausible nominee, but there was an obstacle in his way. The court already had one justice from Boston, Horace Gray, and it was unlikely a president would name a second one.

In 1901 word began to circulate that Gray was ailing and would soon resign. That was good news for Holmes, but the bad news was that President William McKinley was reportedly looking to his secretary of the navy, John Davis Long, the former Massachusetts governor, for guidance on filling the seat, and Long was promoting Alfred Hemenway, his former law partner. Hemenway was in fact offered the seat, and he accepted. Holmes was now sixty, and with the Boston seat about to be filled by a new justice, his chances of ever being appointed to the Supreme Court appeared to be over.

On September 6, 1901, before McKinley could nominate Hemenway, he was shot by an assassin. When Leon Czolgosz, a Polish American anarchist, fired on the president at the Pan-American Exposition in Buffalo, he revived Holmes's dreams of serving on the Supreme Court. It now fell to the new president, Theodore Roosevelt, to fill the seat. Roosevelt was part of Holmes's world, or close to it, and Holmes had the perfect emissary to reach out to him.

Once again, Brahmin Boston played a pivotal role in Holmes's rise, this time in the form of Massachusetts senator Henry Cabot Lodge. Holmes and Lodge were old friends, who had in many ways led parallel lives. Lodge had also attended T. Russell Sullivan's boys' school, Mr. Dixwell's Private Latin School, Harvard College, and Harvard Law School. The two men had spent summers together on the North Shore, the coastal towns north of Boston that *A Handbook of New England* called "the favorite residential resort of Boston 'Brahmins'" and a place where "one must dress for dinner." Holmes and Lodge were also, as it happened, distant relatives: both men's mothers were Cabots.

Lodge, in turn, was close to Roosevelt, and he lobbied the new president heavily on behalf of Holmes. Roosevelt was said to be an admirer of Holmes's writings, in particular *The Soldier's Faith*, which was in keeping with his own enthusiastic views about war. The close connections among all three men made Lodge's work a good deal easier. Roosevelt was not himself a Brahmin, but his beloved first wife, Alice, had been born in Chestnut Hill, Massachusetts, the daughter of George Cabot Lee, a wealthy Brahmin banker. Holmes, Lodge, and Roosevelt had something else in common, besides their ties to Brahmin society, and the Cabot family specifically: all three were alumni of Harvard's Porcellian Club.

Horace Gray, the ailing justice from Boston, held on until the summer, but he finally resigned in July. On August 11 Roosevelt announced that he was nominating Holmes to fill the vacancy. The choice of Holmes was not met with universal approval. Some observers objected to his idiosyncratic record. In an editorial headlined "Remaking the Supreme Court," the *New York Evening Post* said Holmes had "been more of a 'literary feller' than one often finds on the bench," with "a strong tendency to be 'brilliant' rather than sound." On August 12 the *Boston Evening Transcript* predicted "his striking originality will help . . . when it does not hinder." Holmes found what he saw as the "incompetence and inadequacy" of many of the reactions to his nomination to be "annoying." He did not need to worry about Senate confirmation: the vote to confirm him, on December 4, was unanimous.

To Holmes, ascending to the Supreme Court just felt right. In a letter to Lady Georgina Pollock, the wife of Sir Frederick, Holmes described "the president's choice of me" as "a reward for much hard work." There was more than a little self-flattery to that analysis. Though

Holmes had worked hard, Boston Brahmin influence had propelled his career at every turn, from the schools he attended, to the law firm he joined, to his Harvard professorship, to his judicial appointments. Perhaps Holmes could not see it, but *The Common Law* and *The Path of the Law* played less of a role in securing his seat on the court than the extraordinary influence of his social class.

Holmes put his Boston life behind him and moved to Washington. On December 8 he reported for work at the Supreme Court's dingy offices in the United States Capitol. He heard oral arguments in his first case and, since the justices did not have chambers in the court's crowded offices, brought his work home with him to the hotel room in which he and Fanny were staying.

Life as a Supreme Court justice proved much to Holmes's liking. He was a more important man in Washington than he had ever been in Boston, despite all of his intellectual accomplishments and family connections. Holmes and Fanny were soon fielding invitations from some of the city's most prominent officials. They were regularly invited to dine at the White House, and occasionally to accompany the president and first lady to the theater.

The docket of the Supreme Court was more interesting to Holmes than the "trifling and transitory" matters he had bristled at on the Supreme Judicial Court of Massachusetts. It was not long before Holmes heard his first major civil rights case. In the 1903 case *Giles v. Harris*, Jackson W. Giles sued, on behalf of more than five thousand Alabama blacks, to be added to the voting rolls. He charged that blacks in Alabama were systematically being prevented from registering—something that was happening across the South.

The Alabama Constitution of 1901 had adopted a set of new voting rules designed to prevent blacks from voting. These included a "grandfather clause"—much like the one in Virginia that was an issue in Aubrey Strode's political campaign—that allowed men who had fought in the Civil War, and descendants of people who had fought in designated wars, to register automatically. The rules were designed to make it easy for whites, but not former slaves and their descendants, to vote. Blacks were subjected to literacy tests administered by white voter registrars who did not want them to vote.

There was no doubt that the convention that produced the Constitution of 1901 intended to disenfranchise blacks. The convention delegates were all white men, although Alabama at the time had 1,001,152 whites and 827,545 blacks. The convention president also said bluntly that it was intended "to establish white supremacy in this State." Giles argued that the voting rules violated the Fourteenth Amendment, which guaranteed blacks equal protection of the law, and the Fifteenth Amendment, which expressly prohibited states from denying blacks the right to vote.

Holmes, writing for the majority, ruled against the disenfranchised black men from Alabama. He argued that if Giles were correct that Alabama's whole voting system was "a fraud upon the Constitution of the United States," the court could not become "a party to the unlawful scheme" by "adding another voter to its fraudulent lists." It was a strange analysis, because ordering disenfranchised blacks to be put on the voting rolls would have been an important step in curing the system's unconstitutionality.

Second, Holmes argued that whether Alabama blacks should be added to the voting rolls was the sort of political question courts should stay out of. It was clear, he said, that in Alabama "the great mass of the white population intends to keep the blacks from voting." To stop whites from doing this, Holmes said, would require the court to "supervise the voting in that state by officers of the court"—something it was not prepared to do.

Holmes's opinion in *Giles* was a major defeat for black voting rights, and a "decisive turning point" in the law, as one legal analysis explained. As conservative whites came back into power across the South with the end of Reconstruction and declared a war on black political rights, Holmes's decision made clear that the Supreme Court would not intervene. There was nothing inevitable about the court's antidemocratic ruling: three justices dissented from Holmes's opinion, including John Marshall Harlan, a former slaveholder from Kentucky, who argued that Giles had a right to register. Holmes's view that "political rights" of this sort were not enforceable in federal courts remained the law into the 1960s, rebuffing the hopes of generations of southern blacks who fought in the courts for the right to register and vote.

It seemed odd that Holmes, the thrice-wounded Union soldier from Boston, would not side with black citizens in the former Confederacy seeking the right to vote, particularly when the former slaveholder Harlan did. Holmes was, however, being consistent with his long-held philosophies. It was the gas stokers' strike all over again: in Holmes's view, all legislation was properly "class legislation," because the group in power used its influence to promote its own interests. If white southerners, like British opponents of labor unions, had the power to enact laws that favored their group, that was the natural order of things, and Holmes had no interest in interfering.

In 1905 the Supreme Court heard another case about the power of special interests to enact laws, and it would be one of the highlights of Holmes's career. New York had adopted legislation limiting the number of hours bakeries could make their employees work in a week. Limits on hours were a major progressive cause, and New York's law was an important victory for the labor movement. Joseph Lochner, a baker from Utica who had been convicted of making his employees work excessive hours, challenged the law as unconstitutional, and the Supreme Court agreed. Rufus Peckham, writing for the majority in *Lochner v. New York*, said the law violated the due process clause of the Fourteenth Amendment by interfering with the "right of contract between the employer and employees."

Holmes wrote a famous dissent arguing that New York's law was constitutional. He said the court had no right to impose its economic views—or as Holmes memorably put it, "The 14th Amendment does not enact Mr. Herbert Spencer's Social Statics." Holmes's dissent was hailed as a liberal triumph. Charles Beard, the progressive historian, called it "a flash of lightning" in the "dark heavens." But the praise from progressives was undeserved. Holmes did not break with the majority because he believed workers should be protected from abusive conditions that threatened their health. His sympathy lay with legislatures, not overworked bakers.

In Holmes's view, legislators should be free to do almost anything they want—whether it helps workers or hurts them. "The only limit I can see to the power of the lawmaker is the limit of power as a question of fact," he wrote in a letter to his friend Harold Laski. In other words, legislatures should be able to do anything they can find the means to enforce. "When I talk of law I talk as a cynic," Holmes wrote. "And I understand by human rights what a given crowd will fight for (successfully)." If someone did not want to be oppressed, Holmes believed, they should not go to court—they should find a crowd and fight the tyranny.

There was another dissent in *Lochner* that did take a strong progressive stand. John Marshall Harlan, who wrote the main dissent in the case, cited real-world evidence for why New York's law was necessary to protect bakers. The law applied only to "bakery and confectionary establishments," where "the air constantly breathed by workmen is not as pure and healthful as that to be found in some other establishments," Harlan wrote. He went on to quote from a treatise called "Diseases of the Workers": "'The labor of the bakers is among the hardest and most laborious imaginable, because it has to be performed under conditions injurious to the health of those engaged in it.'" Two other justices signed Harlan's dissent, but Holmes did not.

The Supreme Court heard a series of major civil rights cases in these years, and Holmes almost invariably found a reason to side against the black plaintiffs, as he had in *Giles*. In 1911, in *Bailey v. Alabama*, the court struck down Alabama's debt peonage law, which was slavery by another name. Black men who owed money had "iron manacles . . . riveted upon their legs" and connected by chains, one federal court noted. "They wake, toil, rest, eat, and sleep, to the never ceasing clanking of the manacles and chains of this involuntary slavery." A "whipping boss" lashed recalcitrant workers with a heavy, 2½- to 3-foot-long leather strap. The Supreme Court agreed with Alonzo Bailey, a victim of the system, that it violated the Thirteenth Amendment, which prohibited involuntary servitude.

Holmes dissented—one of only two justices to do so. He refused to see the unmistakable parallels between the southern peonage system and slavery. Holmes treated peonage as if it were just another financial arrangement. "Breach of a legal contract without excuse is wrong conduct, even if the contract is for labor," Holmes said.

The same year, the court also heard a challenge to legally mandated segregation in education. In *Berea College v. Kentucky*, a Kentucky college was found guilty of violating a state law that required private colleges to separate black and white students. The college challenged its conviction, but the Supreme Court upheld Kentucky's right to impose racial segregation on its colleges. Holmes voted with the majority.

Harlan, who had dissented in *Giles*, and in *Plessy v. Ferguson*, the notorious 1896 ruling upholding racial segregation, wrote an eloquent dissent in *Berea*. If the state could prohibit white and black students from learning together, Harlan wrote, "it is difficult to perceive why it may not forbid the assembling of white and colored children in the same Sabbath school, for the purpose of being instructed in the Word of God." Harlan held up a vision of a constitutional right to racial equality—a vision Holmes did not share.

Immigrants were another group who drew little sympathy from Holmes. In case after case, he found ways to reject the claims of people trying to enter the country. In *United States v. Ju Toy*, Holmes wrote the majority opinion holding that Ju Toy, a longtime United States resident returning from China, could be denied entry under the Chinese exclusion acts even though he had been found by a federal court to be an American citizen.

In March 1911 Holmes turned seventy. The world was changing, and he worried he was being left behind. "Fanny has got one of those dust-devourers that swallows everything into a bag," he wrote to a friend. "I suffer—[but] it must needs be." What gnawed at him more than the passage of time or the advent of new technologies like the vacuum cleaner was the feeling he had not achieved greatness. Supreme Court justices were not household names, and nothing he had produced—not *The Common Law*, not the *Lochner* dissent—had won him renown. He complained frankly in a letter to a friend, "I have not as much recognition as I should like." In a letter to another friend, he explained what he was hoping for. "I should like," he wrote, "to be admitted to be the greatest jurist in the world."

There was, as it happened, an influential group of mostly young progressives who were prepared to help Holmes achieve the recognition he sought. The group, many of whose members were associated with Harvard Law School or the liberal-leaning *New Republic* magazine, admired Holmes and thought he could be useful to their cause. Many of them lived in or frequented a row house at 1727 Nineteenth Street in Washington's Dupont Circle that "served as a kind of commune for young men in the government" and was known as the "House of Truth." The group's influence on Holmes's reputation was so great that one legal scholar dubbed it "the house that built Holmes."

At the center of the group were two men who were themselves close friends: Felix Frankfurter, a Harvard Law School graduate who would go on to join the law school faculty and then the Supreme Court, and Walter Lippmann, an influential columnist and the cofounder of the *New Republic*. The denizens of the House of Truth were unhappy with the Supreme Court's antilabor rulings, in particular, and were eager to push it in a more liberal direction. They were looking for a progressive champion on the court, and they decided they had found one in Holmes, who was himself a regular dinner guest.

Once this influential group adopted Holmes, the pages of the *New Republic* and the *Harvard Law Review* began to fill up with accolades for their new hero. On March 8, 1916, when Holmes turned seventy-five, the law review dedicated an issue to the occasion. When Holmes dissented in a pair of cases in which the Supreme Court struck down progressive labor legislation—a federal ban on child labor in *Hammer v. Dagenhart* and, a few years later, a federal minimum wage law for women in *Adkins v. Children's Hospital*—the *New Republic* lavishly praised his *Hammer* dissent, and reprinted the *Adkins* dissent in its entirety.

As World War I approached, Holmes enthusiastically supported the United States joining the fight. Few Americans understood war as intimately as Holmes, who still bore his Civil War scars. The horror he had once felt toward battle had long since been replaced by the reverence he had put on display in *The Soldier's Faith*, his Memorial Day address to the Harvard class of 1895, and he reserved his disgust for those who were trying to keep the nation out of war. In a letter to his friend John Wigmore, the dean of Northwestern University School of Law, Holmes berated the pacifists "who think that something in particular has happened and that the universe is no longer predatory." He put the matter bluntly: "Doesn't this squashy sentimentality of a big minority of our people about human life make you puke?"

Holmes's early years on the Supreme Court were a time when many intellectuals were drawn to eugenics, and Holmes was one of them. He was, in many ways, fertile ground for ideas about human superiority and inferiority. From early childhood, it had been impressed upon him that he had been born into an elite—one that defined itself by its bloodlines.

Holmes's father, a medical school dean and a man with immense pride of ancestry, was an early eugenics advocate. In 1861, in the same book in which he coined the term "Boston Brahmin," Dr. Holmes held forth on the superiority of the "aristocracy" of which he considered himself a member. Eight years before Galton published *Hereditary Genius,* Dr. Holmes described the "Brahmin caste of New England" as a hereditary elite, physically and mentally. They were identifiable, he said, by their appealing "physiognomy"—slender, smooth-faced, and quick-eyed. At the same time, they were natural-born scholars, whose "aptitude for learning" was "congenital and hereditary." Dr. Holmes contrasted his own elevated caste with a simpler class among whom they lived, people with "coarse" mouths and "clumsy" facial movements—a group who had "been bred to bodily labor."

In 1875 in an essay in the *Atlantic Monthly*, Dr. Holmes applied his ideas about the heritability of good and bad traits to crime—and praised Galton in the process. In "Crime and Automatism," Dr. Holmes wrote: "If genius and talent are inherited, as Mr. Galton has so conclusively shown . . . why should not deep-rooted moral defects and obliquities show themselves, as well as other qualities, in the descendants of moral monsters?" He examined the case of "Margaret, the mother of criminals"—the same woman whose descendants Dugdale studied in *The Jukes*—and concluded that "in most cases crime can be shown to run in the blood."

The younger Holmes shared his father's belief in the power of bloodlines, and he began writing about eugenic ideas well before they were popular in America. In 1873 he published his article on the gas stokers' strike, which was heavily infused with social Darwinist thinking, including its assertion that the law "must tend in the long run to aid the survival of the fittest." In *The Path of the Law*, in 1897, he put forward the possibility that criminality had a genetic basis, echoing Dr. Holmes. "If the typical criminal is a degenerate, bound to swindle or to murder by as deep seated an organic necessity as that which makes the rattlesnake bite," the younger Holmes wrote, "it is idle to talk of deterring him by the classical method of imprisonment."

Holmes not only believed that bloodlines exerted a strong influence—for good, as in the case of families like his, and ill, as in the case of the criminal. He also insisted, as the eugenicists did, that actions should be taken to increase the positive hereditary influences on society and to reduce the negative ones. He had hinted at the idea in *The Soldier's Faith*, which contained a passing reference to "a future in which science" would "take control of life, and condemn at once with instant execution what now is left for nature to destroy."

As eugenics became more popular, Holmes began to talk more directly about the affirmative role society could play in human breeding. Speaking to a Harvard Law School Association of New York dinner on February 15, 1913, about law and the court, Holmes veered into eugenic musings. "I think it probable that civilization somehow will last as long as I care to look ahead," he said, "perhaps with smaller numbers, but perhaps also bred to greatness and splendor by science."

Holmes was beginning to educate himself more on the issues the eugenicists were raising. In 1914 he bought a copy of a new edition of Thomas Malthus's *An Essay on the Principle of Population.* Holmes was thoroughly won over by the book's bleak vision of the future, in which human population outstripped the food supply. In a letter to his friend Frederick Pollock, Holmes wrote, "Malthus pleased me immensely—and left me sad." Malthus had "busted fallacies" a hundred years ago, Holmes said, "that politicians and labor leaders still live on." Holmes would later declare himself a "devout Malthusian." Malthus appealed to Holmes's cynical, misanthropic side. He later explained to a friend, "I look at men through Malthus's glasses—as like flies—here swept away by a pestilence—there multiplying unduly and paying for it."

In 1915, Holmes made his most direct plea yet for eugenics, in an essay in the *Illinois Law Review* titled "Ideals and Doubts." The way to achieve the "wholesale social regeneration" that forward-looking people wanted, he argued, was not through "tinkering with the institution of property"—as the communists were urging—but "only by taking in hand life and trying to build a race."

In his correspondence with friends, Holmes wrote as a eugenicist. In a 1920 letter to Holmes, Frederick Pollock said his "complaint against war" was not that it killed men but that it killed "the wrong ones." Wars took "an undue proportion of the strong and adventurous" and left "too many weaklings and shirkers, thus working a perverse artificial selection." Holmes agreed, telling Pollock the discussion made him inclined to believe "it would be possible to breed a race." In the five years since his *Illinois Law Review* article, his phrasing had become more biological: he had gone from wanting to "build" a race to wanting to "breed" one.

In a 1921 letter to Frankfurter, Holmes returned to the idea in his *Illinois Law Review* article that biology was a better route to reform than leftist economic measures. Holmes said he did not think "intelligent socialism" could accomplish much "by tinkering with property without taking in hand life." It would also require "restricting propagation by the undesirables and putting to death infants that didn't pass the examination, etc. etc." Holmes said he didn't "know enough to say that I want it," but he did not say he was opposed—leaving open the possibility of supporting infanticide to reduce the number of "undesirables."

As Holmes saw it, the legal system had a role to play in ensuring that the "right" people reproduced. He argued this most directly in the introduction he supplied to his friend John Wigmore's 1923 book, *The Rational Basis of Legal Institutions*. Holmes wrote favorably of "legislation that aims . . . to improve the quality rather than increase the quantity of the population," which sounded a lot like the eugenic sterilization laws many states had by then enacted. Holmes said that he could understand insisting that, "whatever the cost, so far as may be, we will keep certain strains out of our blood."

Holmes's support for eugenics was notable for the extremity of his views. Many prominent people supported eugenics, ranging from establishment figures, such as former president Theodore Roosevelt and professors from Yale and Stanford, to reformers and a few radicals. But as one legal scholar has observed, "No one of note . . . joined Holmes in writing approvingly of . . . 'putting to death infants that didn't pass the examination.'"

Holmes's support for eugenics was notable for another reason: he was not, in general, a supporter of causes. Many people in his intellectual circles, including those he saw regularly at the House of Truth, were fighting for minimum wage and maximum hour laws, bans on child labor, antitrust laws, and other progressive goals, but Holmes was indifferent to all of it. He was, as one scholar has observed, "deeply cynical about legislated reforms that were intended to make the world over." Eugenics was an exception to Holmes's overarching cynicism— it was a movement to reform the world that he actually believed in.

On the Supreme Court, the great issue of the moment was not eugenics but free speech. During the war years, the nation was torn by battles between radicals and the government. That conflict found its way to the court in the form of a series of First Amendment cases that did more than any others to establish Holmes's reputation.

In March 1919 the Supreme Court decided the case of *Schenck v. United States*. Charles Schenck, the general secretary of the Socialist Party, was appealing his conviction for interfering with military re-cruitment. Schenck had mailed leaflets to fifteen thousand potential military draftees urging them to oppose the war and the draft. When he was charged with conspiracy to violate the Espionage Act, he ar-gued that the leaflets were protected free speech under the First Amendment.

Holmes, writing for a unanimous court, upheld the conviction. In his opinion, he set out the "clear and present danger" test of free speech. The First Amendment, he said—using his famous aphorism—did not protect "falsely shouting fire in a theatre." It would become a famous free speech test, though Holmes's application of it was odd. There was no evidence that Schenck's pamphlets had persuaded anyone to resist the draft. But Holmes considered them the equivalent of a panic-inspiring shout in a crowded theater—posing a "clear and present danger"—and found them not to be constitutionally protected.

Two more speech cases followed a week later, and Holmes again wrote opinions, for unanimous courts, rejecting the speakers' appeals. In *Frohwerk v. United States*, the editor of a German-language news-paper in Missouri was convicted under the Espionage Act of publish-ing articles critical of the war and the draft and sentenced to ten years in prison. Holmes did not apply the "clear and present danger" test, perhaps because it would have been hard to argue Frohwerk's articles, which were not directed at draftees, met the standard. Instead, he invoked a test that was less protective of speech, and applying it affirmed the conviction and the ten-year sentence.

In *Debs v. United States*, Holmes wrote the majority opinion upholding the conviction of the socialist leader Eugene V. Debs for giving an antiwar, antidraft speech. Once again, Holmes did not mention the "clear and present danger" test. As in the *Frohwerk* case, it would have been hard to show that the standard had been met, since the government had not made any showing that Debs's speech posed any real danger to the country.

With these three opinions in quick succession, Holmes was developing a reputation as an opponent of free speech. In a letter to Frederick Pollock, he complained of the backlash. "I am beginning to get stupid letters of protest against a decision that Debs, a noted agitator, was rightly convicted of obstructing the recruiting service so far as the law was concerned," he wrote. "There was a lot of jaw about free speech, which I dealt with somewhat summarily in an earlier case—*Schenck v. U.S.* . . . also *Frohwerk v. U.S.*" In fact, Holmes's anti-speech rulings went as far back as 1892, when he briskly dismissed the claim of the New Bedford policeman fired for off-duty speech.

After his three major opinions hostile to speech rights, Holmes abruptly changed course. The court heard *Abrams v. United States*, in which Jacob Abrams, a Russian immigrant anarchist, challenged his conviction for distributing antiwar leaflets. In November 1919, the majority ruled that Abrams's actions violated the Espionage Act, but this time Holmes dissented. His dissenting opinion included some of the most eloquent words about free speech in American law, and introduced the metaphor of a marketplace for the "free trade in ideas," which would become influential in future discussions of the First Amendment. A few years later, Holmes would write another ringing dissent, in *Gitlow v. New York*, in which the majority upheld the criminal anarchy conviction of Benjamin Gitlow for publishing a socialist newspaper.

A Civil War hero, a Harvard law professor, and, in the estimation of many, the most distinguished Supreme Court justice in history, Oliver Wendell Holmes Jr. wrote the opinion declaring that Carrie Buck should be sterilized—and that "three generations of imbeciles are enough."

Dean of Harvard Medical School, an acclaimed Boston literary figure, and the coiner of the phrase "Boston Brahmin," Oliver Wendell Holmes Sr. impressed on his son, the future Supreme Court justice, the importance of good bloodlines.

Led by Chief Justice William Howard Taft, the former president, the Supreme Court in 1927 upheld eugenic sterilization generally—and Carrie's sterilization specifically—by an 8–1 vote. From left to right: James Clark McReynolds, Edward T. Sanford, Oliver Wendell Holmes Jr., George Sutherland, William Howard Taft, Pierce Butler, Willis Van Devanter, Harlan Fiske Stone, Louis Brandeis.

Harry Laughlin, the nation's leading eugenics advocate, insisted that fifteen million Americans had to be sterilized to save the nation from a looming hereditary threat. His wife, Pansy, an amateur playwright, wrote a light comedy in which the female characters learn that a money-hungry Jewish peddler is not an appropriate choice for marriage.

Carrie and her mother, Emma Buck, were both declared feebleminded on scant evidence and committed to the Virginia Colony for Epileptics and Feeble-Minded, where Carrie was sterilized for eugenic reasons.

Carrie's former foster mother, Alice Dobbs, raised Carrie's daughter, Vivian, whom the state falsely declared to be feebleminded—a key part of its claim that Carrie posed a eugenic threat.

Charles Davenport (right), the Harvard-educated founder of the Eugenics Record Office on Long Island, shared with Laughlin (left) a passion for the science of animal breeding and lured him from small-town Missouri to be the organization's first superintendent.

Dr. Albert Priddy, the founding superintendent of the Virginia Colony for Epileptics and Feeble-Minded, was the driving force behind the legal case to uphold eugenic sterilization in Virginia, and he chose Carrie to be at the center of it.

Irving Whitehead, Carrie's lawyer, was a former chairman of the colony's board and a close friend of the men lined up against her—and he consistently betrayed his client's interests in the litigation over whether she should be sterilized.

A center of eugenic sterilization, the Virginia colony, where Carrie was sterilized in 1927, likely performed the procedure on more women for eugenic reasons than any other institution in the country.

Aubrey Strode, the lawyer for the colony in its effort to sterilize Carrie, may not have been a strong supporter of eugenic sterilization, but he drafted Virginia's sterilization law, and his success in *Buck v. Bell* laid the legal groundwork for as many as seventy thousand Americans to be sterilized.

Exhibit I (a)

BIOLOGICAL ASPECTS OF IMMIGRATION

HEARINGS

BEFORE

THE COMMITTEE ON
IMMIGRATION AND NATURALIZATION

HOUSE OF REPRESENTATIVES

SIXTY-SIXTH CONGRESS
SECOND SESSION

APRIL 16-17, 1920

STATEMENT OF HARRY H. LAUGHLIN

WASHINGTON
GOVERNMENT PRINTING OFFICE
26402   1921

Laughlin's testimony to Congress as its officially designated "Expert Eugenics Agent" played a large role in the enactment of the Immigration Act of 1924, which shut the door on Jews, Italians, and other groups that he insisted posed a eugenic threat to the nation.

There are a number of theories for why seventy-eight-year-old Holmes changed his views on free speech so dramatically, and so quickly. One is that the repression of speech during the world war gave him a new appreciation for the importance of free expression. His thinking may have been influenced by an article, "Freedom of Speech in War Time," that Zechariah Chafee, a young Harvard law professor, published in the *Harvard Law Review*. Another theory is that he was persuaded by a group of friends—including Frankfurter, Harold Laski, Learned Hand, and Chafee—who lobbied him into changing his mind.

Holmes's change of heart may, however, have been more calculating. His progressive supporters had been outspoken in their criticism of his anti-speech rulings. Ernst Freund, a noted University of Chicago law professor, had attacked the *Debs* opinion where it no doubt hurt Holmes the most—in the pages of the *New Republic*. When Holmes switched positions in *Abrams,* Freund mailed the dissent to Frankfurter, Lippmann, and other members of his progressive circle. If Holmes's goal in championing Jacob Abrams's free speech rights was to win the progressives' approval, he succeeded impressively. The *New Republic* paid tribute to what it called "the remarkable dissenting opinion of Mr. Justice Holmes," and declared that it would be of critical importance to the future of First Amendment law. Frankfurter wrote to tell Holmes of "the gratitude and, may I say it, the pride I have in your dissent . . . you lift the voice of the noble human spirit."

With his eightieth birthday approaching, Holmes took time off from his Supreme Court work to compile a volume of his collected legal writings. Just as he saw *The Common Law* as the capstone to his first four decades, he viewed *Collected Legal Papers* as a summing up of his judicial achievements. Holmes said that assembling this "little basketful" gave him "a mild excitement at the rather old little boy going out in a new jacket and trousers." The book's reviews were largely positive, and critics used its release as an occasion for looking back on a career that was assumed to be near its end.

Holmes, however, showed no signs of slowing down. After the judicial highs of the World War I era, his next several years on the court were quieter. In 1921 Holmes wrote the majority opinion in a sharply divided 5–4 ruling upholding Washington, D.C.'s rent control laws. He sided with the liberals, to the consternation of the court's free-market conservatives, but as was so often true, for Holmes the case was largely about judicial passivity. As long as Congress acted within its authority, he wrote, "we have no concern, of course, with the question whether" its "means were the wisest . . . or will effect the result desired."

In May 1921 there was major change on the court when the chief justice, Edward Douglass White, died in office. Warren G. Harding, the newly elected Republican president, appointed former president William Howard Taft to the position. Taft, who had been the twenty-seventh president, became the tenth chief justice, making him the only person ever to lead both the executive and judicial branches. Holmes and Taft liked each other, and the new chief justice, who bought a house not far from Holmes's, walked the older man to work most mornings.

The Taft court was conservative and pro-business. In April 1923, in *Adkins v. Children's Hospital,* the court struck down a law passed by Congress that established a minimum wage for women and children in Washington, D.C. The majority ruled that the law interfered impermissibly with "liberty of contract." Taft and Holmes both dissented, but on different grounds. Taft argued that the minimum wage was similar to other economic regulations the court had upheld. He insisted the court must not strike down laws because they promote "economic views" that it "believes to be unwise or unsound." For Holmes, it once again came down to deference to the legislature. He had "doubts" about the law, he said, but it was within Congress's power to enact.

The court took this idea of "liberty" beyond purely economic rights. That same year, in *Meyer v. Nebraska,* the justices considered a challenge to Nebraska's ban on teaching in any language but English. A parochial school teacher who taught in German claimed the law, which was part of a World War I–era drive to ban German from public life, violated the right to liberty under the Fourteenth Amendment.

The court agreed. Liberty, it said, meant more than just "freedom from bodily restraint." It also included the freedom "to acquire useful knowledge, to marry, establish a home and bring up children," to worship as one wished, and "generally to enjoy those privileges" that have long been recognized "as essential to the orderly pursuit of happiness." These freedoms are not absolute, the court said, but the state cannot deny them through a law that is "arbitrary or without reasonable relation to some purpose within the competency of the State to effect." Even though Nebraska's law had a valid purpose, there was no emergency that justified its infringement on "rights long freely enjoyed."

Holmes dissented, joined by one other justice, George Sutherland. For Holmes, this was another case about the power of legislatures. "We all agree, I take it, that it is desirable that all the citizens of the United States should speak a common tongue," Holmes said. Looking at the Nebraska law, he could not say with certainty that it was not "a reasonable or even necessary method of reaching the desired result."

Two years later, in *Pierce v. Society of Sisters*, the court struck down another state law on liberty grounds. Oregon, acting out of anti-Catholic animus, had required parents to send their children to public school. Invoking *Meyer*, the court ruled that the law unreasonably interfered with parents' liberty "to direct the upbringing and education of children." This time, Holmes and Sutherland joined the opinion, which was unanimous.

On March 8, 1926, Holmes celebrated his eighty-fifth birthday and was, as usual, flooded with letters and telegrams of congratulations. His appearance that year on the cover of *Time* magazine brought him the sort of national acclaim he coveted—an honor that was, no doubt, only modestly diminished for Holmes by the caption under his portrait: "as venerable as his father." Holmes's progressive claque showered him with accolades. In a column that ran on Holmes's birthday,

Walter Lippmann wrote in the *New York World* that "in every high court and in every law school throughout the world he is known and studied and revered as one of the few greatest minds who have dealt with the law in the course of the last century." Felix Frankfurter, writing in the *New Republic*, was even more purple in his prose. He hailed "the tender, wise and beautiful being who is Mr. Justice Holmes" as "one of those unique gifts, whose response to life is so transforming that he vivifies life for all who come within his range."

After twenty-five years on the Supreme Court, Holmes's legal philosophy was clear. He did not, for the most part, believe judges should strike down legislative enactments, and except for his newfound interpretation of the First Amendment's free speech right, he had a narrow view of individual rights under the Constitution. Holmes had little interest in rescuing society's victims—the Alabama black man cheated out of the right to vote by the state's white majority or shackled until he paid off his debts, or the Chinese American citizen turned away at the border on account of his national origin.

Holmes had his activist moments, as Jacob Abrams and others could attest. Some years earlier, in the case of *Silverthorne Lumber Co. v. United States,* Holmes had written an opinion that struck an important blow for defendants' rights. It stated that when the government seized evidence from a criminal suspect illegally, copies of that evidence could not be used to prosecute him—a pro-defendant's rule that would later be immortalized as the "fruit of the poisonous tree" doctrine. And in a couple of years, he would notably dissent in *Olmstead v. United States,* in which the majority upheld a conviction for which prosecutors used evidence obtained by a warrantless wiretap.

Holmes's willingness to sit back and let society's various interest groups battle it out was, however, considerable. He acknowledged his own instinct for passivity, particularly when asked to second-guess legislatures. In a letter to his friend Harold Laski, he described the standard he applied in challenges to a legislature's decision in setting the price of gas. "We accept the judgment" of the legislature, Holmes said, "unless it makes us puke."

Holmes's approach to judging—one scholarly critic called it "the judge as spectator"—likely had several explanations. To some extent, it simply reflected the classic reserve of the Boston Brahmin social class he had been born into. Holmes's friend Henry Adams—a member of a family that had produced two presidents—described this ethos in "Buddha and Brahma." In that poem of resignation, a wise man describes himself as "content to tolerate what I cannot mend."

Another factor contributing to Holmes's judicial passivity was his lack of interest in making moral decisions. Holmes gave little thought to what the fair outcome would be in the cases before him, and he rarely cared whether the result would be good for society. He considered the Sherman Antitrust Act, a landmark statute reining in monopoly power, to be a "foolish law," but he insisted that this view did not affect how he interpreted it. "I have little doubt that the country likes" the act, he wrote to his friend Harold Laski, "and I always say, as you know, that if my fellow citizens want to go to Hell I will help them. It's my job."

Holmes's opinions that were hailed for having a progressive vision were almost always about something else—generally deference to legislatures or larger social forces. His fellow justices understood this. They knew "he didn't care a straw for the 'social' or 'progressive' legislation that he was said to be heroically defending," Chief Justice Charles Evans Hughes's biographer observed. They "were well aware of his scorn for any deviation from the result he thought the law required because that result might be 'unjust' to the individuals concerned."

Holmes's judicial philosophy was, however, ultimately about more than deference and moral neutrality. It derived from a deeply held belief that the hierarchies that arise in the world are part of the natural order, and worthy of respect and deference. One critic observed that in his jurisprudence Holmes "announced that law is the will of the stronger— 'the jungle-toothed realism . . . of what the crowd wants.'"

It was a harsh assessment, but not an inaccurate one. Holmes's approach to the law suited the interests of society's winners. It was a philosophy that accepted the worldly success of his own Brahmin social caste as right and good, and argued that people like him should be free to use their power as they wished. Holmes's philosophy left scant room for the disadvantaged and the weak, who hoped the legal system would soften society's blows. In particular it had little to offer a poor, uneducated young woman from the rural South, who wanted the court to protect her from the state hospital in which she was confined, the state of which she was a citizen, and the popular social movement that had caught her in its sights.

Nine

Oliver Wendell Holmes

In the spring of 1927, Carrie Buck's legal case entered its final phase, as it headed to the United States Supreme Court. The eugenicists would be arriving at the court with a degree of momentum. They had put together a strong test case. Dr. Priddy had carefully chosen Carrie to be at the center of it, and in many ways she seemed ideal: his own institution had examined her and declared her to be a moron, he could argue that she was part of a feebleminded family, and she was a woman in her early childbearing years. Strode had identified strong expert and fact witnesses and gotten their testimony on the record.

The case had gone well so far. The colony had won in the Amherst County Circuit Court, and the Virginia Supreme Court of Appeals had upheld the eugenic sterilization law and the order of sterilization against Carrie. Along with the victory from Virginia's highest court, the Michigan Supreme Court had recently upheld that state's eugenic sterilization law—the two biggest legal successes for the movement in more than a decade.

Even with these promising signs for the eugenicists, there were also gathering clouds. Despite the recent wins in Virginia and Michigan, the vast majority of court rulings had been hostile to their cause. Judges in New Jersey, Iowa, Oregon, New York, Nevada, and Indiana had struck down eugenic sterilization laws.

The judges in these cases had not only found constitutional infirmities in the laws. In some cases, they had been outspoken about their abhorrence for the whole idea of sterilization. The federal court that struck down Iowa's sterilization law had not merely pronounced it unconstitutional but also insisted that such "strange methods of repression" belong to "the Dark Ages." The New Jersey Supreme Court had warned that the "feebleminded" were "not the only persons" the legislature might seek to eliminate as "undesirable citizens."

The eugenicists' problems were not limited to the courts. Their movement, which had been gaining force during the Progressive Era, had begun to slow in the 1920s. Many of the societal elites that had been in the forefront of promoting eugenics and sterilization were beginning to express doubts.

Mental health experts, who had been among the biggest supporters of eugenics, had started to shift. Dr. Walter E. Fernald, who was arguably the nation's leading expert on mental disability, had done an about-face. In 1912, he had called the feebleminded a "parasitic, predatory class" that posed "a menace and a danger." At a 1919 meeting of the National Committee for Mental Hygiene, he recanted and said that he regretted saying "that the feebleminded were all of hereditary origin, that they were pretty much all vicious and depraved and immoral, that they were not capable of self-support."

Even Henry Goddard, inventor of the hierarchy of "idiot," "imbecile," and "moron," had come to disavow his views on feeblemindedness. After years of promoting the term "feebleminded," Goddard was now objecting to this "unscientific and unsatisfactory word." He had also begun to renounce reliance on the intelligence testing he was so closely associated with. To label people feebleminded for scoring low on exams like the Binet-Simon was, he now said, "an absurdity of the highest degree." In just a couple of years, Goddard would declare that he had gone over "to the enemy."

Geneticists, who had initially said little about eugenicists' misuse of science, were also beginning to speak out. In a 1924 book preface, Edward M. East, a prominent Harvard genetics professor, took aim at eugenicists' use of spurious science. Two years later, his Harvard colleague William E. Castle, who pioneered the use of the fruit fly in genetic research, wrote in *Encyclopedia Britannica* that much of the so-called scientific writing on eugenics "is probably of small value, since it is uncontrolled by experiment and is based largely on uncritical data." By 1927, scientists had made great strides in destroying "the myths that mental retardation and shiftlessness and 'laziness' were in the genes."

Scientists were not the only ones defecting from eugenics. The mass media, which had cheered the movement on at the outset, was increasingly raising questions. In 1922 Walter Lippmann, arguably the nation's leading public intellectual, wrote a series in the *New Republic* eviscerating intelligence testing. Exams purporting to find that large percentages of the adult population were deficient, such as the U.S. Army test, were "silly," Lippmann argued. They were producing false data that attracted "gross perversion by muddleheaded and prejudiced men," he said.

National magazines were also publishing direct attacks on the eugenics movement. In 1926, the *American Mercury* printed an article by Clarence Darrow on eugenics—or "the eugenics cult," as he called it. Darrow, who had attracted national headlines a year earlier for his role in the Scopes evolution trial, caustically sent up the eugenics movement and the "good old *Mayflower* stock" who were drawn to it. Of all "the schemes for remolding society," Darrow wrote, eugenics was "the most senseless and impudent that has ever been put forward by irresponsible fanatics."

Eugenics was now at a crossroads. In the decades since Francis Galton coined the word, it had become a global movement, with international conferences, national eugenics campaigns, and, in America, legally sanctioned eugenic sterilizations. The backlash, however, was growing where it mattered the most—in the United States, the world-wide leader in eugenics.

Buck v. Bell was likely to have an enormous impact. If the Supreme Court rejected Virginia's eugenic sterilization law, it could sweep away state sterilization laws across the country and give enormous moral support to Darrow, Lippmann, East, Castle, and all the other people who were starting to challenge the eugenicists. If the Supreme Court upheld Virginia's law—after all of the state courts that had struck down sterilization laws—it would completely change the legal land-scape. It would also give the eugenicists one of the greatest imprima-turs American society can offer—and inject new life into a waning movement.

I n advance of the Supreme Court oral argument, Irving Whitehead and Aubrey Strode submitted legal briefs. Once more, the quality of the advocacy was lopsided, something that was again evident just in the page counts. Strode submitted a forty-nine-page brief arguing that the Virginia Supreme Court of Appeals had decided the case correctly. Whitehead wrote only eighteen pages arguing that the Supreme Court should reverse the decision of two state courts and a state hospital board and declare Virginia's eugenic sterilization law unconstitutional.

Whitehead's brief to the Supreme Court was better than his brief to the Virginia Supreme Court of Appeals, but it was still woefully inadequate. As had been true of his work throughout the case, some of Whitehead's advocacy was helpful to his client and some less so. He once again argued that the Virginia law violated the equal protection clause of the Fourteenth Amendment, the claim that had proven most successful so far in state courts. He did not do it with particular enthu-siasm or skill, and he once again left out important precedents that could have been persuasive to the court.

Whitehead also argued that the sterilization order violated Carrie's "inherent right of bodily integrity" as guaranteed by the Fourteenth Amendment's due process clause. There was, he argued, a "right of mankind to go through life without mutilation of organs." This was another worthy argument, which took Carrie's case beyond the technicalities of who was covered by the law and into the substantive realm of whether eugenic sterilization was the sort of activity the government should be involved in at all.

Less helpful, the primary authority Whitehead cited for his due process argument was *Munn v. Illinois*, an 1877 commercial law case about the constitutionality of maximum rates for grain storage. Whitehead did not discuss *Meyer v. Nebraska* or *Pierce v. Society of Sisters*, the two recent cases in which the Supreme Court had begun to define an expansive conception of the right to liberty under the Fourteenth Amendment. In *Meyer*, just a few years earlier, the court had expressly included in the right of liberty the freedom "to marry, establish a home and bring up children." It was a precedent worth citing prominently—if Whitehead was interested in winning his case.

The oddest part of Whiteside's brief was a section on "Eugenic Laws and Regulations, Ancient and Modern," which argued that "the idea of selective breeding is as old as recorded history." Whitehead quoted a variety of classical sources that he said had endorsed eugenics, ranging from "The Twelve Tables of Rome" to Plato's *Republic*. It was a puzzling decision to include this history because it had the effect of making sterilization appear to be not barbaric or outlandish, but rather an integral part of Western civilization.

Whitehead did not challenge any of the false evidence that was used against his client at the original trial, nor did he present any of the growing body of scientific opinion challenging the underlying assumptions of the eugenicists. It might have been difficult for him to introduce new evidence at the Supreme Court stage—the court generally limits itself to the factual record created in the courts below—but he still had an opportunity to present the sort of expert opinion on eugenics that he failed to offer at trial.

Whitehead could have submitted a "Brandeis brief," named after Louis Brandeis, one of the justices who would be hearing the case. When he was an acclaimed "people's attorney," Brandeis invented a model of legal brief that included more expert opinion and social science data than law. In *Muller v. Oregon*, a challenge to an Oregon law setting maximum hours for women workers, Brandeis submitted a brief defending the law that was 113 pages long—with only two pages of legal analysis. The rest of the brief was an argument about the effects of excessive work hours on women, drawn from sources as varied as the Maine Bureau of Industrial and Labor Statistics and the British House of Commons.

There was a powerful Brandeis brief to be written on Carrie's behalf. It could have quoted extensively from experts who challenged the colony's positions: Lippmann on how the intelligence testing used on Carrie and Emma was "silly," Davenport on feeblemindedness being "a social term," not a medical one, and East disassembling Laughlin's and Estabrook's claims about heredity. The brief could have challenged the colony's claim that the sterilization was in Carrie's interest by raising medical questions about the procedure and discussing the negative aspects of being rendered infertile. It would have been an opportunity for Whitehead to address many of the issues he did not bring up at trial—but he did not take it.

Whitehead ended his brief with a rhetorical flourish. In a final one-paragraph section on "Danger of Legislation of this Character," he raised a dark specter of where laws like the Virginia statute would take the country: over time a "reign of doctors" would be established to add new categories of people for sterilization—perhaps "even races"—allowing for "the worst forms of tyranny." It was a stirring ending to a less than compelling brief that logged in at a little more than one-third the length of the brief for the other side.

Strode's brief for the Virginia state hospitals was much like the one he had submitted to the Virginia Supreme Court of Appeals. He presented the Supreme Court with an array of facts, taken from the trial in the Amherst Circuit Court, that helped to make the case for the sterilization law and the sterilization order. Strode wrote that Carrie had a mental age of nine, that Emma had a mental age of seven, and that Vivian had been "found to give evidences of defective mentality."

Strode quoted extensively from the expert witnesses he had called at trial. He invoked Laughlin saying that Carrie appeared to be a low-grade moron and cited his opinion that, based on the "hereditary nature of the feeblemindedness" and her moral delinquency, she was a "potential parent of socially inadequate or defective offspring." Strode also quoted Dr. Priddy, "Superintendent of the Colony, with twenty-one years of experience in this and similar institutions," stating that he had "arrived at the conclusion" that Carrie was "a highly proper case for the benefit of the Sterilization Act."

The main legal argument in Strode's brief, as it was in his brief for the Virginia court, was that eugenic sterilization was the kind of act government had the right to engage in. Strode argued that eugenic sterilization fell squarely within the state's "police power." Once again, he relied on the 1905 Supreme Court ruling in *Jacobson v. Massachusetts,* the compulsory vaccination case, including two full pages of quotes from it in the brief.

Strode carefully constructed responses to each of the constitutional objections Whitehead raised. On equal protection, Strode repeated the "clearing house" argument he made in the Virginia Supreme Court of Appeals. He maintained that even though the law allowed only inmates of state hospitals to be sterilized, what was important was that any feebleminded person in the state could at some point be institutionalized and sterilized. The statute was "part of a general plan applicable to all feeble-minded." On due process, Strode enumerated the protections that Virginia's sterilization law provided and once again insisted that based on them "all the requirements of due process of law have been fully complied with."

Strode included two more arguments he had made to the Virginia Supreme Court of Appeals. Once again, he made the audacious claim that because of Carrie's youth, her father's death, and her mother's mental incapacity, the state should be allowed to decide whether she consented to sterilization. Strode repeated the line he used in the lower court: "Poor the Commonwealth in powers and helpless in authority," he wrote, "if she be incompetent thus to act for her afflicted children."

Strode also repeated his plea for judicial restraint. The question of "whether it is better that feeble-minded women be kept in custodial care of institutions" or that they instead be sterilized and released was a "legislative" not a "judicial" question, he argued. Strode told the Supreme Court in direct terms that it should let Virginia decide for itself whether to engage in eugenic sterilization. "The question before the Court is one of power only," he wrote. "If it be found that the Legislature has the power to do what it has here done without running counter to clear constitutional prohibitions, the Court may only so declare and there the function of the Court ends."

In his statement of the facts, Strode repeated one of the colony's cruelest falsehoods. He explained that Carrie had "lived as a member of the household with a respectable family" who had "taken good care of her in return for the simple services she might render despite her affliction." If she were no longer a risk to have more children, Strode told the court, that family "would be glad to have her back again."

Strode was passing on what Dr. Priddy had testified at trial. This promise had special significance for Carrie because—although Strode's brief did not mention it—Vivian was currently living in the Dobbs household. Any hopes Dr. Priddy and Strode might have raised in Carrie about returning to her old home and being reunited with her only child would later be crushed. Despite what Strode assured the Supreme Court, the Dobbses would not take her back.

The Supreme Court set the case down for oral arguments on April 22, 1927. The chief justice who would preside, William Howard Taft, was an unusual leader of the court. He had been born in suburban Cincinnati, a scion of the powerful Taft Republican political dynasty, and had been imbued with political ambition from an early age. Taft's father had served as attorney general and secretary of war under President Ulysses S. Grant.

Taft attended Yale—where he was a member of Skull and Bones, the elite secret society his father helped found—and then returned home to Ohio. After graduating from the Cincinnati Law School, Taft was appointed to a local judgeship. President Benjamin Harrison named Taft solicitor general of the United States—the youngest in the nation's history. Taft returned to Ohio when he was nominated to the U.S. Court of Appeals for the Sixth Circuit.

Taft, who once joked that he always had his "plate the right side up when offices were falling," continued to be appointed to prominent positions. President William McKinley designated Taft chief civil administrator for the Philippines, and President Theodore Roosevelt named him secretary of war, his father's former position. Roosevelt chose Taft to succeed him as president, and the Republican Party nominated him in 1908.

Taft was elected handily, but his one term as president was not an easy one. He found himself trapped between the progressive and conservative factions of his party. When Taft sided with conservatives on several key issues, including keeping tariffs high, progressive Republicans formed their own party, and Roosevelt was its standard-bearer in the 1912 election. With the Republican Party divided, Taft lost to the Democratic nominee, Woodrow Wilson. He retired to a professorship at Yale Law School.

In his years at Yale, Taft wrote about the law and promoted his favorite causes, including world peace. For his whole life, Taft had aspired to be chief justice of the United States. He held out hope that the man who defeated him, President Wilson, would appoint him to the Supreme Court. Taft was disappointed when Wilson passed him over repeatedly—and, in particular, when Wilson nominated Louis Brandeis. In a letter to a friend, Taft decried the selection of Brandeis, whom he considered "unscrupulous" and a "muckraker," as "one of the deepest wounds that I have had as an American and a lover of the Constitution."

Taft finally achieved his lifelong ambition when Warren Harding reclaimed the White House for the Republicans. In May 1921, only months after Harding took office, Chief Justice Edward Douglass White died. Harding nominated Taft to succeed him. The *New York Times* would later say that chief justice was "an office which by both tempera-ment and training he was better fitted to hold than that of President."

Taft took to his new position with enthusiasm. As the Supreme Court's chief administrator, he went to work right away modernizing its operations. He traveled to England to study the workings of the British court system—in particular, how judges there managed to dis-pose of unimportant cases so quickly. The *Christian Science Monitor* observed that "As many men strive for riches, Mr. Taft strove for a clear docket."

When he returned home, Taft put his newfound knowledge to use. He was the driving force behind the Judiciary Act of 1925. The new law gave the court broad discretion over what cases it would hear, end-ing the days when 80 percent of its docket was made up of appeals that had to be accepted. It was a major change, which helped to usher in the modern era of the court.

As chief justice, Taft adhered to the same old-line conservatism he had espoused as president. He was concerned at first that Brandeis and Holmes might interfere with his ability to maintain a solid conserva-tive, pro-business majority. Several new appointments that came soon after his own, however, reassured Taft he would have the votes to keep the court firmly on the side of property rights and other core conserva-tive values. Not long after he joined the court, Taft wrote a strong pro-business opinion in *Bailey v. Drexel Furniture Co.*, a decision that augured well for Taft's conservative plans. The court struck down the Child Labor Tax Law, which Congress had imposed on companies that employed children. The ruling was 8–1, and both Holmes and Brandeis joined Taft in the majority.

Taft had preexisting connections to the issues presented in *Buck v. Bell*. Before joining the court, he had served as chairman of the board of the Life Extension Institute, which worked to prolong human lives through such measures as promoting physical exams and advocating for pure foods and drugs. The chairman of the group's Hygiene Reference Board was Irving Fisher, the Yale economist and prominent eugenicist. The Life Extension Institute's major publication, *How to Live*—which had a full-page photo of Taft in its opening pages—included a chapter on eugenics. It advocated "sterilization of certain gross and hopeless defectives, to preclude the propagation of their type."

The most prominent member of the court, after Holmes and the chief justice, was Louis Brandeis. Born in Louisville, Kentucky, Brandeis settled in Boston after graduating from Harvard Law School. It was during his work as a public-spirited attorney that he won fame as the "people's attorney" and invented the "Brandeis brief," which made sociological facts and expert opinions the primary part of Supreme Court advocacy.

Brandeis had strongly supported Wilson's 1912 presidential campaign, and became a close adviser to the administration, particularly on antitrust policy. In January 1916, President Wilson nominated Brandeis to the court, partly because of the high regard in which he held Brandeis, and partly to shore up liberal support for his reelection campaign.

There was considerable opposition to the choice of Brandeis. Members of the business and legal establishments argued that he was too radical. Adding to the anti-Brandeis sentiment was the reluctance of many people to see a Jew join the court for the first time. Seven former American Bar Association presidents came out against Brandeis, as did much of Brahmin Boston, including Harvard's president, A. Lawrence Lowell. Holmes, who owed his Harvard professorship to Brandeis's fund-raising, could not bring himself to support the nomination. It "was a misfortune for the Court," he wrote a friend, "because whichever way it went half the world would think less of the Court thereafter—but I expect [Brandeis] will make a good judge." Despite the opposition, the Senate confirmed Brandeis by a 47–22 vote.

Brandeis was considered a liberal on the court, though his vote with the majority in *Bailey v. Drexel Furniture Co.* demonstrated that he did not always side with the progressives. He generally supported civil rights plaintiffs, but he did not fundamentally challenge the racial order that prevailed at the time. Brandeis joined the majority in *Lum v. Rice*, rejecting the claim of a Chinese American girl in Mississippi who wanted to attend an all-white school. Segregated schools, a unanimous court held, did not violate the Fourteenth Amendment's equal protection clause.

Harlan Fiske Stone, a New Hampshire native and Columbia Law School graduate, had joined the court in 1925. A former Wall Street lawyer and attorney general under Republican president Calvin Coolidge, Stone was opposed by some progressives for being too close to big business. Once on the court, however, Stone quickly settled into the liberal bloc. In later years, he would be one of the justices most supportive of the New Deal when it came under conservative legal attack. Roosevelt eventually elevated Stone to be chief justice, the ultimate confirmation of his liberal record. Nevertheless, Stone was sympathetic to social Darwinism, an outlook he adopted at Amherst College, under the influence of Charles Edward Garman, a prominent philosophy professor.

The remaining justices ranged from moderate to extreme conservatives. James Clark McReynolds, another Kentuckian, had been attorney general under President Wilson, who appointed him to the court in 1914. In his legal practice, McReynolds had fought monopolies—a major progressive cause—but as a justice he was deeply conservative. He was also mean-spirited and bigoted: Holmes called him "a savage." McReynolds, who was virulently anti-Semitic, could not reconcile himself to Brandeis's presence on the court. When Brandeis spoke at the justices' meetings, McReynolds would often get up and leave the room, and there was no official court portrait in 1924 because McReynolds refused to follow protocol and sit beside Brandeis.

George Sutherland emigrated from England to Utah with his parents after they converted to Mormonism. Sutherland attended Brigham Young Academy, which later became Brigham Young University, where he came under the sway of its headmaster, Karl G. Maeser, who believed strongly in social Darwinism. From there, Sutherland moved on to the University of Michigan Law School, and after graduation to the practice of law in Provo. He was elected to the House of Representatives and the Senate, then President Harding appointed him to the court. As a justice, Sutherland was generally a reliable conservative vote. In the 1930s, he would become the intellectual leader of the "Four Horsemen of the Apocalypse," a bloc of justices who voted to strike down key parts of the New Deal.

Willis Van Devanter was born in Marion, Indiana, but he made his name in the Wyoming Territory, where he moved as a young man. He practiced law and served in the territorial legislature until President Benjamin Harrison appointed him chief justice of the Wyoming Territorial Supreme Court. President Theodore Roosevelt appointed Van Devanter to the U.S. Court of Appeals for the Eighth Circuit, and President Taft named him to the Supreme Court. When Taft joined him on the bench, Van Devanter was a reliable member of his pro-business majority. During the New Deal, Van Devanter was a stalwart member of the Four Horsemen.

Edward T. Sanford, a Tennessean and a Harvard Law School graduate, was a centrist—one who was, Holmes said, "born to charm." He was a federal judge in his home state before President Harding nominated him to the court. Sanford generally voted with Taft's pro-business bloc, but he was less doctrinaire than some. In 1923 he dissented from a ruling striking down Washington, D.C.'s minimum wage law for women. Sanford wrote the majority opinion in *Gitlow*, the anarchist speech case, from which Holmes so energetically dissented. Sanford upheld the conviction, but ruled for the first time that the core civil liberties in the Bill of Rights applied to the states. This principle, known as "incorporation," greatly advanced civil liberties by subjecting the states to federal free speech and other protections.

The final member of the court was Pierce Butler, an archconservative and the only Catholic justice. Butler was born in Minnesota to Irish immigrants who had fled the potato famine. He began his career as a successful railroad lawyer—or, as critics saw it, a tool of the railroad interests. He was also a regent of the University of Minnesota where, during World War I, he was a driving force in dismissing professors who held "unpatriotic" views. Butler was appointed to the court by President Harding, who was looking to name a Catholic.

On the court, Butler held to his principles, showing little interest in compromise. He was, like McReynolds, a bigot, though a less foul-tempered one. When Benjamin Cardozo was being considered for the court, Butler reportedly joined McReynolds and Van Devanter in asking President Hoover not to "afflict the Court with another Jew." Butler was a strong believer in market capitalism and feared the effect of "too much wet-nursing by the state" on "individual initiative and development." He held firmly to his Catholic faith, and his sense of morality infused his legal decision making. Butler liked to quote Archbishop John L. Spalding: "The end of all worthy struggles is to establish morality as the basis of individual and national life."

When the justices met in conference to discuss *Buck v. Bell*, Holmes doubtless played an outsize role. Many of the justices had some interest in the subject matter of the case. Taft had served on the Life Extension Institute board. Sutherland had had his brush with social Darwinism at Brigham Young, and Stone had a similar experience at Amherst. McReynolds, Van Devanter, and Butler believed in the inferiority of certain groups. Holmes, however, was the only member of the court who had given serious thought to the legal issues that eugenics raised.

Holmes had been considering eugenics at least since his 1873 article on the gas stokers' strike, and he had formed strong opinions on the direction in which he wanted the law to go. In his 1915 *Illinois Law Review* essay, he wrote of "taking in hand life and trying to build a race." In his 1923 introduction to Wigmore's treatise, he was more precise. Holmes favored laws "to improve the quality rather than increase the quantity of the population" and "keep certain strains out of our blood." That statement, written just four years before the court considered *Buck v. Bell*, could have been an endorsement of Virginia's eugenic sterilization law.

At conference, Holmes likely held forth on eugenics, and on why he thought the Virginia statute should be upheld. His views would have been highly influential with his fellow justices. As the court's senior member, Holmes would by tradition have been first to speak, after the chief justice, which would have amplified his words. More significant was the fact that Holmes, who was now more than halfway through his ninth decade, was revered for his wisdom about the law. Taft spoke for the court when he said of Holmes that it was a "great comfort to have such a well of pure common law undefiled immediately next to one so that one can drink and be sure of getting the pure article."

The justices' conferences varied in style over the years based on the court's membership and its leadership. Before Taft took over, when justices took different positions at conference it was regarded "as an invitation to a cockfight," Holmes recalled. Taft, however, cut off the debate over a case when the issues seemed clear. As a result, Holmes said, "never before have we gotten along with so little jangling and dissension."

Taft was known for trying to use the conference to build consensus. He liked unanimous rulings, and he had an aversion to sharply divided ones. When the majority view on a case became clear, Taft lobbied his fellow justices to join the majority—a charm offensive he called "massing the court." If Taft tried to mass the court in *Buck v. Bell*, he did well. Eight of the nine justices agreed to uphold the Virginia law and Carrie's sterilization, with only Butler dissenting.

Holmes was, in many ways, the obvious justice to write the majority opinion. Taft made it a practice to assign opinions to justices based on their "particular interests and expertise," a scholar of the court has observed—and no other justice came close to Holmes's interest and expertise in eugenics. It is also likely that Holmes expressed a desire to write the opinion, given his strong feelings on the subject, and because of his seniority, and the deep respect in which he was held, Taft would have been inclined to grant the request.

When Taft assigned the opinion to Holmes, he sent a note with some advice:

Some of the brethren are troubled about the case, especially Butler. May I suggest that you make a little full [the discussion of] the care Virginia has taken in guarding against undue or hasty action, the proven absence of danger to the patient, and other circumstances tending to lessen the shock that many feel over such a remedy? The strength of the facts in three generations of course is the strongest argument for the necessity for such state action and its reasonableness.

Taft's note was significant in a number of respects. It made clear that there were justices who were "troubled" by the case—who perhaps felt "shock" at the idea of sterilization—and they would still need to be persuaded, or at least convinced to stick with the majority. It also suggested that the work Laughlin had done with his model eugenics statute, and that Strode had done in drafting the Virginia law, had made a difference: the procedural protections against "undue or hasty action," and the protections for the health of the "patient," or inmate, made a real impression on the chief justice.

Perhaps most interesting, Taft—who was in a position to know—said that the strongest argument in winning over wavering justices would be "the facts in three generations." This was something Dr. Priddy believed when he selected Carrie to be at the center of the test case, and something Laughlin said right away when he reviewed the facts of the case. It meant that Dr. Priddy and Strode were right, as a matter of trial strategy, to work as hard as they did to produce "evidence" that the less-than-eight-month-old Vivian was mentally defective. It may have been the most important fact—or, more accurately, falsehood—in the whole case.

Holmes took to his writing assignment with great enthusiasm, and he quickly produced an opinion for the ages. Holmes's first book, *The Common Law*, has been hailed by some as "the greatest work of American legal scholarship," though others have sharply disagreed. His *Lochner* opinion has been called "the greatest dissent of all time"—mistakenly, a good number of people would insist. There is greater agreement, however, about the superlative quality of his *Buck v. Bell* opinion. One critic spoke for a vast consensus in saying it "could represent the highest ratio of injustice per word ever signed on to by eight Supreme Court Justices."

Holmes's opinion was a mere five paragraphs in length, and there can be no doubt that he devoted far less thought to it than the subject deserved. The opinion began the way most judicial opinions do: with a brisk recitation of the facts. If Holmes's statement of the facts was inadequate, it is not surprising given how he felt about facts in general.

Holmes was the first to say that facts did not interest him. He did not read newspapers, which he considered to be "wasting time." Holmes also boasted of not caring about details. "I never know any facts about anything," he told an English friend, "and always am gravelled when your countrymen ask some informal intelligent question about our institutions or the state of politics or anything else." Holmes's "intellectual furniture" consisted, he said, of "an assortment of general propositions which grow fewer and more general as I grow older."

Holmes's summary of the facts of the case was consistent with this lack of interest. It was brief, and he relied on the information presented at the trial—where Whitehead had not put on any facts to help Carrie's cause—and on the Virginia sterilization law itself. On some key points, he simply made things up, or rounded out the actual facts with his own "assortment of general propositions."

Holmes began by stating flatly that Carrie and Emma were "feeble minded" and that Vivian was an "illegitimate feeble minded child." If he had been more skeptical, and more willing to probe the factual record, he could have raised questions about the designation of Carrie and Emma, based as it was on the Binet-Simon test. Holmes's good friend Walter Lippmann, writing in his beloved *New Republic*, had explained that the number of people intelligence tests were labeling as mentally deficient was "silly," and warned that they were being misused by "muddleheaded and prejudiced men."

Even if Holmes was inclined to accept that Carrie and Emma were "feeble minded," there was nothing in the record to support his claim in the opinion that Vivian was "feeble minded." Caroline Wilhelm had said she was "not quite a normal baby," and Estabrook had testified that she was "below the average for a child of eight months of age." Both of these assessments were quite different from a diagnosis of being "feeble minded." The mislabeling of Vivian was no small error on Holmes's part, given Taft's statement that the "strength of the facts in three generations" was "of course" the case's "strongest argument."

Holmes's description of the sterilization procedure showed a similar lack of interest in facts. He simply repeated the benign assessment contained in the Virginia statute—the very statute whose constitutionality the court had to resolve—without any skepticism. Salpingectomy was, he reported, a procedure "without serious pain or substantial danger to life." It was an excessively generous description of an operation that would require Carrie to spend an hour under the knife, and two weeks in recuperation, while hospital staff regularly changed the dressing on her incision.

Continuing to rely on the Virginia law, Holmes described the subjects of sterilization as people who "if now discharged would become a menace but if incapable of procreating might be discharged with safety and become self-supporting with benefit to themselves and to society." The first part of the description—which indicated that the feeble-minded were a "menace"—did not take into account the growing body of scientific evidence suggesting that people with mental defects did not pose a threat. The second part, particularly the claim that sterilization provided a "benefit" to its subjects, failed to consider its serious detriments, especially for someone like Carrie, who strongly wanted to have children.

Holmes also accepted the sterilization law's view of heredity. "Experience has shown that heredity plays an important part in the transmission of insanity, imbecility, &c," he wrote. It was a remarkably shallow account of one of the key points in the case: whether sterilization would actually reduce the number of mentally defective people to any significant degree. Holmes made no reference to the growing skepticism from scientists like Fernald, Goddard, and East about the eugenicists' assumptions. Whitehead had, of course, given the court no skeptical science to work with, either at trial or in his briefs. The court could, however, have introduced some of it into the discussion on its own.

Holmes similarly presented the procedural facts of the case in a way that was unduly favorable to the colony. He talked of how under the Virginia statute the inmate was given notice of the time and place of the sterilization hearing, the right to attend, and a right of appeal to the local circuit court. Holmes ignored the more problematic realities of this particular case, such as the fact that at trial Carrie's lawyer and guardian did not put on any witnesses or facts for her side.

Next, Holmes moved on to the substantive legal issues. In this part of the opinion, his rhetoric and style were striking—one critic has rightly referred to its "alarming tone." Rather than assessing the constitutional and statutory issues in the neutral, legalistic way the court generally did, Holmes delivered an urgent warning to the nation. The Virginia statute was necessary, he insisted, "to prevent our being swamped with incompetence."

Holmes presented a dark vision of what would happen if sterilization laws were struck down, and the "incompetent" were allowed to reproduce. He declared, in one of the opinion's most notable passages: "It is better for all the world, if instead of waiting to execute degenerate offspring for crime, or to let them starve for their imbecility, society can prevent those who are manifestly unfit from continuing their kind."

Holmes's lofty rhetoric far exceeded the evidence in the record. There had been no support at trial for the claim that the feebleminded were likely to have children who committed crimes so serious they would have to be "executed." In fact, criminologists like Clark University's Carl Murchison were challenging the connection between criminals and mental defect. Nor was there any evidence that the feebleminded were in danger of starving, as Holmes said—or that any of the thousands, or millions, of feebleminded the eugenicists claimed were in the population actually were starving.

Holmes's fevered words reached their apex in the opinion's best-known sentence: "Three generations of imbeciles are enough." Holmes's aphorism is one of the most notorious statements to appear in a Supreme Court opinion. It was, on the simplest level, the sort of cruel insult that has rarely, if ever, been delivered by a majority of the court—even in cases involving the most cold-blooded of criminals. More profoundly, it gave the Supreme Court's endorsement to the very essence of the eugenic argument: that defective people must be stopped from reproducing, surgically if necessary, because otherwise their defects will be visited on the next generation—and forever plague the world.

Holmes's bold declaration that three generations of imbeciles were enough was one of his "general propositions" that broke down on closer inspection. To begin with, there were not "three generations" of imbeciles. On the record, Vivian was "not quite a normal baby," according to Wilhelm, and "below the average" for an eight-month-old baby, according to Estabrook. Holmes made no effort to explain how those mild observations supported his claim that Vivian was an "imbecile," a serious level of mental defect—or that she was feebleminded at all.

Just as there were not "three generations," there were also no "imbeciles." The colony had recorded Carrie as having a mental age of nine and classified her as a "Middle grade Moron." "Moron" was the highest of the three levels of mental defect, above "imbecile" and "idiot." These categories were precise and official. The U.S. Department of Commerce included them in its official publication *Feeble-Minded and Epileptics in State Institutions,* stating expressly that anyone with a mental age between seven and twelve was a "moron," while "imbeciles" had a mental age between three and seven. Holmes, however, casually downgraded Carrie from "moron" to "imbecile."

Carrie was not the only Buck woman Holmes downgraded. Emma had also tested as a moron, not an imbecile, at the colony. With Vivian, that made three Buck women described as more defective than the record supported. It might be said that Holmes was using "imbecile" for literary effect, simply because it sounded better than "moron." In doing so, however, he handed the eugenics movement a false, but powerful, rallying cry.

The third part of Holmes's aphorism—"is enough"—was also untrue. With that phrasing, Holmes was asserting that mental defect was a directly inherited trait, and that sterilizing Carrie would bring it to a halt; however, this was not so. Feeblemindedness could not be defined with any precision, and it was not genetically determined in this way. There was also considerable doubt over whether even a large program of sterilization could appreciably affect the nation's gene pool. Scientists had begun to turn decidedly against the eugenicists on all of these issues. But Holmes simply assumed that if Carrie was sterilized the line of imbecility could be stopped in this, the third generation.

The most striking thing about Holmes's "haughty epigram," as it has been called, was not the factual errors but the disdain that dripped from it. Carrie was a living, breathing young woman who came to the highest court in the land hoping to vindicate her constitutional rights, and to stop the state from taking away her ability to have children. But to Holmes and the seven justices who signed on to his opinion, she was nothing more than one "imbecile" in a line of imbeciles, of whom, the court declared with exasperation, the nation had already had "enough."

A mean-spirited ethos permeated the whole opinion. Holmes's language was every bit as harsh as the epithets hurled by the eugenics movement. He called the people being considered for sterilization "defectives" and "unfit," and their potential offspring "inadequate" and "degenerate."

Holmes knew his language was crueler than some of the other justices were comfortable with. In a letter to Harold Laski, Holmes said he was "amused (between ourselves) at some of the rhetorical changes suggested" by his colleagues in his case about "the sterilizing of imbeciles." He had, he said, "purposely used short and rather brutal words for an antithesis, polysyllables that made them mad." Holmes had no patience with the justices who wanted to speak more kindly—or less insultingly—about people like Carrie and Emma. A "man must be allowed his own style," Holmes insisted.

Holmes's legal analysis was just as disconcerting as his rhetoric. He began by quickly disposing of the due process challenge, following Taft's guidance. He highlighted the "very careful" protections that Strode, influenced by Laughlin's model statute, had written into the law. Laughlin's and Strode's intuition that these safeguards would insulate the law from constitutional attack was correct. "There can be no doubt that so far as procedure is concerned the rights of the patient are most carefully considered," Holmes wrote.

In reaching this conclusion, Holmes overlooked a great deal. The Virginia law guaranteed inmates like Carrie a right to be present at their sterilization hearings, but when Carrie attended, no one made any effort to ensure that she understood what was at stake—and it seems clear she did not. The statute also guaranteed inmates the right to appeal their sterilization orders to the circuit court, but Carrie's appeal had been a hollow formality. The law required her guardian to "defend" her "rights and interests." At the trial, however, her guardian and her lawyer had not put on a case of any kind, which appeared to fall short of the guardian's statutory duty. To say her rights were "most carefully considered" was a vast overstatement.

Holmes was equally dismissive of the equal protection challenge. He made clear he was no fan of equal protection claims generally, calling them "the usual last resort of constitutional arguments." Holmes's dismissive reference seemed to reflect his view that "almost any law" could be seen "as discriminating against someone." It was an unduly negative assessment. In fact, the court frequently struck down laws on equal protection grounds. From 1920 to 1927, it did so fourteen times, making it seem like far more than a "last resort." Holmes joined the majority in many of these cases. Less than two months earlier, he had written the opinion for a unanimous court in a case in which the plaintiffs prevailed on a Fourteenth Amendment equal protection claim.

After denigrating equal protection claims as a whole, Holmes quickly dismissed the specific one lodged against the Virginia sterilization law. Unlike a number of state court jurists, he was not troubled that it applied only to inmates of state hospitals, and not to members of the general public. Holmes invoked Strode's and Dr. Priddy's defense: once inmates were sterilized they could be released, making room for new inmates. That meant even people not currently institutionalized might eventually be sterilized—which, in Holmes's view, meant that all Virginians were being treated equally.

It was not a convincing analysis. There was, in fact, no program or infrastructure in place for identifying members of the general public who were feebleminded and having them institutionalized. A feebleminded inmate at the colony would have a high likelihood of being sterilized. A feebleminded person at liberty living somewhere in the state of Virginia would have little chance. Saying the two groups were being treated equally "was really a matter of form over substance."

The central legal issue, however, was not due process or equal protection—it was whether the state had the power to carry out eugenic sterilization. With his devotion to judicial deference, Holmes could easily have played judicial spectator. He could simply have said legislatures have the right to combat feeblemindedness and he was not concerned—as he said of rent control laws—whether their "means were the wisest."

Strode had made a plea for just this sort of judicial restraint in his brief to the court. He had urged the justices to remember that "a large discretion is vested in the legislature to determine what the interests of the public require." This argument should have resonated especially strongly with Holmes, given his willingness to enforce even foolish laws because if his "fellow citizens want to go to Hell I will help them." Declining to second-guess Virginia's legislature would have been faithful to his oft-professed philosophy. But that was not what Holmes did. He instead launched into a legal analysis of the law and the sterilization order.

Holmes began by explaining why he believed Virginia had the

power to enact the sterilization law. Because government was allowed to "call upon the best citizens for their lives," he argued: "It would be strange if it could not call upon those who already sap the strength of the State for these lesser sacrifices . . . in order to prevent our being swamped with incompetence." It was a variation on Holmes's old "greater power includes the lesser" logic, which he had used in 1892 to explain why New Bedford had the right to fire a police officer for political speech. Here, Holmes was saying that if the state had the power to draft people into the army and send them to their deaths, it clearly had the right to take the lesser step of sterilizing them.

The logic behind Holmes's "call upon the best citizens for their lives" argument was flawed. The military draft only required citizens to serve, not give their lives, and the great majority of those drafted survived. If the state passed a law requiring its "best citizens" to literally give their lives—and put them to death—it is unlikely it would survive a constitutional challenge. Nor was it true, as Holmes said, that sterilization was a "lesser sacrifice." Many people Carrie's age volunteered for the military—as Holmes himself had—but far fewer voluntarily submitted to sterilization.

Holmes's reasoning was not only unpersuasive—it was dangerous. One critic has called his argument "surely one of the most 'totalitarian' statements in the history of the Court." It is hard, after all, to imagine what government action could not be justified on the logic that if the state can "call upon the best citizens for their lives," it can certainly also do this. Holmes's constitutional analysis was a gift to tyrants, arguably offering the court's imprimatur to anything from suppressing free speech to torture.

Until this point—almost a full four paragraphs into an opinion that was only five paragraphs long—Holmes had not cited any legal precedents. He was "famously skeptical about conventional legal reasoning," and his opinion demonstrated it. In the end, however, Holmes did cite one case—that old standby, *Jacobson v. Massachusetts*, in which the court upheld Cambridge's compulsory vaccination law—but he did not trouble himself to explain the analogy in any detail. He simply wrote that the "principle that sustains compulsory vaccination is broad enough to cover cutting the Fallopian tubes."

The analogy to *Jacobson* was hardly one Holmes thought up on his own. The eugenicists had been making the comparison between forced sterilization and compulsory vaccination for years, to anyone who would listen. Laughlin had cited *Jacobson* in his 1922 treatise *Eugenical Sterilization in the United States,* arguing that vaccination and sterilization were "parallel cases," in that each was a "surgical treatment" that was "done supposedly for the public good." The Virginia Supreme Court of Appeals had relied heavily on *Jacobson,* and Strode cited it extensively in his briefs to both the Virginia Supreme Court of Appeals and the Supreme Court.

The comparison was a poor one, and Holmes should have known this as well as anyone, because he had been in the *Jacobson* majority twenty-two years earlier. The burden imposed by a forced sterilization law, being permanently prevented from having children, was far greater than that of a compulsory vaccination law, which required only an inoculation. The Massachusetts law, however, did not even impose that burden. Anyone could refuse to be vaccinated and simply pay a fine of five dollars. Holmes's claim that the *Jacobson* ruling required that the Virginia law be upheld was not only unpersuasive but disingenuous.

Of course, Holmes could have led the Supreme Court in a completely different direction. Rather than view the case as one of due process, or equal protection, or public health, he could have focused on the real tension at its center: the conflict between "the power of the State to legislate" and "the right of the individual to liberty of person." In his brief opinion Holmes had a lot to say about why the state should have the power to engage in a program of eugenic sterilization. He said nothing at all about what right of liberty Carrie might have had in the situation.

There was, however, a great deal he could have said. Modern rights to privacy, to bodily integrity, and to have children were not well established in the 1920s, which is why the state courts that struck down eugenic sterilization laws generally did so on the grounds that their procedural protections were lacking or they applied unequally to different classes of people. But when the court heard Carrie's case, it was actively at work creating just the sort of right that could have protected her: an expanded right of liberty.

The court was beginning to recognize that the Fourteenth Amendment due process clause protected basic aspects of life from government intrusion. In *Meyer v. Nebraska* and *Pierce v. Society of Sisters,* which had been decided four and two years earlier, respectively, the court started to define which aspects of life the right of liberty covered. In both cases, the court expressly stated that family and parenthood were protected from the intrusions of the state. The *Meyer* court said the ability to "establish a home and bring up children" was one of the liberties "essential to the orderly pursuit of happiness by free men."

If Holmes had considered Carrie's right to liberty he might have concluded, as one critic put it, that there are "some things which decent government simply should not do"—things that included forced sterilization. Taft suggested that there might be something inherently indecent about sterilization when he alluded, in his note to Holmes, to "the shock that many feel over such a remedy." If Holmes had considered Carrie's rights under *Meyer* and *Pierce,* he still could have come out in favor of sterilization—both of those cases called for balancing liberty interests against the interests of the state in imposing a regulation. Taking the right of liberty into account would, however, have forced Holmes to include Carrie, and her right to have children, in an opinion from which she was almost entirely absent.

In the end, it seems clear that Holmes did not arrive at his decision through reason. His famous statement in *The Common Law* that "the life of the law has not been logic—it has been experience" suggested the large role he believed feeling and intuition played in deciding cases. So it was in *Buck v. Bell.* More than any doctrines of police power or due process, Holmes was driven by his fear of a world "swamped" by tides of the "manifestly unfit."

In sounding the alarm, Holmes was expressing his deepest values, ones impressed on him from an early age. He had been raised to believe he and his peers were part of a hereditary aristocracy. He had learned from his father that they were part of a special caste whose refined physiognomy set them apart, and whose elevated intellect was "congenital and hereditary." Eugenics was a movement of people who believed themselves to be inherently superior, and in Holmes it found a fitting judicial standard-bearer. Holmes believed in the cause deeply: as he wrote to a friend two days after his opinion was released, "sooner or later one gets a chance to say what one thinks."

Holmes, who had spent much of his career as a judicial spectator, leapt to life as an enthusiastic advocate for the eugenic cause. He had been a skeptic about all of the other progressive reforms of his day, including child labor bans and minimum wage and maximum hours laws. He was not skeptical about eugenics, however, and he was eager to do what he could to help the movement. *Buck v. Bell* was "one decision that I wrote," he later told a friend, that "gave me pleasure."

Holmes, of course, did not have the power to decide the case alone—he needed a majority of the justices to sign on to his opinion. He won the support, in the end, of seven of his fellow justices. There may have been more doubts about the Virginia law than was apparent in the final vote—Taft had suggested as much with his note to Holmes saying that "some of the brethren are troubled about the case." Yet in the end only one of those troubled justices was moved to dissent.

It was no great surprise that some of the justices signed Holmes's opinion. As chairman of the board of the Life Extension Institute, Taft had already lent his name to promoting eugenic ideas. The bigoted and mean-spirited McReynolds, who would not sit next to Brandeis, might have been expected to support eugenics—and the same could be said for Van Devanter, who reportedly would join McReynolds in asking the president not to "afflict the Court with another Jew." Sutherland's and Stone's exposure in college to intellectual mentors with strong social Darwinist beliefs could explain their votes.

Perhaps most notable was the decision of Brandeis, a man who had built a career by standing up for the underdog, to join the majority. It is a vote that has never been adequately explained, by Brandeis himself or by his biographers. Brandeis may have been attracted to eugenics in the way many progressives of the era were—seeing it as a movement dedicated to using scientific advances and government policy to create a better world. He might also have been one of the "troubled" justices Taft referred to, yielding in the end to persuasion from his old friend Holmes, and Taft's efforts in "massing the court." Brandeis later admitted that to maintain unity on the court, and to placate the consensus-seeking Taft, he sometimes voted for opinions with which he did not agree.

Whatever the explanation for the votes of individual justices, the court as a whole did not acquit itself well. Not a single justice questioned the underlying record in the case, with its spurious intelligence testing and dubious scientific assumptions. None was prepared to say the Constitution guaranteed individual rights that the Virginia law infringed on. None had the inherent sense of justice to say what more enlightened minds understood, even at that time—that, in the words of Governor Samuel Pennypacker of Pennsylvania, involuntary sterilization was fundamentally wrong because it inflicted "cruelty upon a helpless class in the community, which the State has undertaken to protect."

The sole dissent came from Butler. This was a possibility Taft had foreshadowed in the note he wrote to Holmes indicating that some of the justices were troubled by the case, "especially Butler." Butler was not someone the court generally looked to for leadership on difficult questions. He was, however, the only Catholic on the court, as well as one of its most conservative members, and he had a different perspective on the case from the rest of the court.

Just how his perspective differed is lost to history. Butler did not write a dissenting opinion, and he never explained his vote. Legal scholars have focused on his religious faith as a likely factor. He was an observant Catholic, and he had been appointed to what was coming to be regarded as the "Catholic seat" on the court with support from members of the church hierarchy. If Butler's Catholicism did lead him to object to Virginia's sterilization law, he would hardly have been alone. In state legislatures across the country, Catholics were the single most outspoken group in opposition to eugenic sterilization laws, and their influence was often decisive.

Butler did not expressly invoke his Catholic faith in his work on the court, but there are suggestions it may have helped to guide his decisions. One time it might have been a factor was in the 1934 case *Hansen v. Haff*, in which the court had to decide whether a Danish immigrant should be deported for having an affair with a married man. The government argued that the woman could be deported under a law that called for excluding prostitutes or anyone entering the country for prostitution or "any other immoral purpose." The court ruled that the law was aimed at people engaged in actual prostitution and did not apply. Butler was the only dissenter, arguing that the woman had acted like the "concubine of a married man" and should therefore have been deported.

Butler was no doubt aware, as a committed Catholic, of the deep reservations the church had about interference with human procreation. When *Buck v. Bell* was decided, that concern was still largely focused on birth control, but in 1930 Pope Pius XI would formally oppose eugenic sterilization in his encyclical *Casti connubii* (On Christian Marriage). The pope condemned people who were "over solicitous for the cause of eugenics" and those who "wish to legislate to deprive" others of the ability to reproduce "by medical action despite their unwillingness."

Catholics were beginning to speak out against eugenics even before the encyclical. John Ryan, a leading American Catholic theologian, noted in a 1916 essay that one of the arguments being made for birth control was that it could be used to reduce the birth rate of people who were considered to be unfit. Ryan insisted that these arguments about the "welfare of the race" were morally troubling. The church, he said, "always looks upon the spiritual and moral side of individuals and institutions as much more important than their physical aspects or consequences."

Catholics had another reason to oppose eugenic sterilization: many Protestant eugenicists thought Catholics were the kind of people who should not be reproducing. Francis Galton himself had argued that Catholics had diminished the "good stock" of Europe since the Middle Ages because their monasteries "drained off the cream" of society, who then did not reproduce. In the United States, the debate over the 1924 immigration law had shown that many eugenicists believed Catholics posed a threat to the national germplasm—and that more Protestant northern European stock was needed.

Butler's dissent could also have been prompted by more secular beliefs. Butler had been born on the frontier, and was by nature skeptical of government, an instinct that found its way into his decisions. He had dissented, also on his own, in a challenge brought by a man whose alcohol had been seized because of Prohibition, even though he had obtained the alcohol before it was illegal. Eight of the court's justices found nothing wrong with the state taking the alcohol once it became illegal, but Butler disagreed, calling the seizure "oppressive" and arguing that it violated due process. In reviewing Virginia's eugenic sterilization law, Butler may have bridled at the government's deciding who should be allowed to reproduce and sterilizing the rest—for him, perhaps, another example of government oppression.

Whatever his motivation, Butler was the one member of the nation's highest court who was not willing to endorse eugenic sterilization, or to say that the state should be allowed to take away Carrie's ability to have children. Because he did not write an opinion, one scholar has called his stand a "silent protest." The "silent" is a source of frustration for those who would like to understand his reasoning, but in the end it is the "protest" that matters most.

When the *Buck v. Bell* ruling came down, the *New York Times* reported it on page 19, alongside a story on Harvard's decision to build a new dining hall. The front page was filled with stories the editors considered more significant, including one on a 227-year-old tree being cut down in New Haven, Connecticut, to allow for street widening and another on the opening of "what is expected to be one of London's most brilliant social seasons of recent years."

The *Times* story reported the facts much as Holmes had in his opinion. It described Carrie as a "feeble-minded white woman," Emma as "also feeble-minded," and Vivian as "an illegitimate feeble-minded child." The story quoted liberally from Holmes, including his "It is better for all the world" declaration. The *Times* did not raise any concerns about the court's decision or eugenic sterilization, or quote any critics.

Time magazine ran a short item on the decision. "Eugenicists cheered, sentimentalists were vexed," it reported, "when Mr. Associate Justice Oliver Wendell Holmes said: 'Three generations of imbeciles are enough.'" The *Literary Digest*, a magazine with a circulation of over one million, ran a favorable article under the headline "To Halt the Imbecile's Perilous Line"—and accompanied it with a handsome photograph of Holmes.

Newspapers across the nation weighed in, most in support. "The decision of the Supreme Court is to be hailed by all thoughtful persons," Alabama's *Birmingham Age-Herald* insisted. "Other states can be expected to follow suit, with the result that a great menace, growing rapidly so long as reproduction was possible, will now be confined, and as time goes on reduced to a minimum, by scientific means."

Carrie's hometown paper, the *Charlottesville Daily Progress,* greeted the Supreme Court's ruling enthusiastically. "Over the protests of many who held up their hands in holy horror at the thought of merely discussing such a thing publicly, much less actually practicing it with the sanction of the state," the paper editorialized, Virginia was now "in the front rank of the states which are committed to a progressive program of welfare legislation." The paper insisted Virginia was "fortunate in having had this eminently sane and beneficial law, safely run the gamut of judicial review and permanently enrolled upon its statute books."

Medical and legal publications largely greeted the decision with approval. The *American Journal of Public Health* declared that "that great jurist" Holmes had written an opinion that "opens future possibilities of vast importance in the field of eugenics and public health." Robert E. Cushman, a Cornell University law professor, praised the ruling as "trenchant" in his annual Supreme Court review and described the Virginia law as "reasonable social protection."

There were also "vexed" responses, as *Time* reported. Some of the journalistic critics understood the science better than the court had. The problem, the *Hartford Times* said, was that information about "the transmitting of characteristics" was "so slight and the variety of opinion so great" that letting the state "decide arbitrarily who shall be allowed to have children" seemed "dangerous." The Jesuit magazine *America* protested the ruling in an editorial titled "Unjustified Sterilization." It objected "based on the fact that every man, even a lunatic, is an image of God, not a mere animal."

Some of the critics reached out directly to the participants. In Lynchburg, a postcard from New York arrived for Dr. Bell. "May God protect Miss Carrie Buck," it said, with the words "from feebleminded justice" crossed out and replaced by "from injustice." Holmes also heard from the public, including one letter writer who called him a monster and told him to expect the judgment of an outraged God. Holmes was unmoved by these attacks from the rabble. He wrote to his friend Harold Laski about the unnamed critic: "Cranks as usual do not fail."

Ten

Carrie Buck

T he long journey to eugenic sterilization in Virginia was now
over. The eugenicists had their statute, and it had finally
been upheld—as Aubrey Strode had hoped—by the highest
court in the land. The colony now had an unquestionable legal right
to sterilize Carrie Buck, and it chose a date for her salpingectomy:
October 19, 1927.

The first legal sterilization in Virginia began promptly on that
Wednesday morning. Carrie, who was now twenty-one years old, was
taken to the infirmary in the colony's Halsey-Jennings Building at
9:30 a.m. The surgeon who would be performing the operation was
no stranger to the patient: it was Dr. John Bell, who had conducted
Carrie's physical examination on her arrival at the colony, and had
given his name to the Supreme Court case.

Carrie was anesthetized, and the operation began. Dr. Bell, working with another surgeon, removed an inch from each of Carrie's fallopian tubes. Her tubes were then ligated, or brought together, and the
ends cauterized using carbolic acid followed by alcohol. The surgeons

then sutured her abdominal wound. An hour after it began, the procedure was over.

When the anesthesia wore off, Carrie remained under the infirmary's care. The medical staff dressed her incision every few days, and she was fed a typical hospital diet: toast, eggs, oatmeal, hash, and similar items. After two weeks, Carrie was permitted to be up and about. Shortly after that, she was well enough to leave the colony on parole.

The colony's parole system allowed selected inmates to be released into larger society, generally to work as domestic helpers for families. Dr. Priddy had always said that one of the advantages of being sterilized for Carrie was that the colony would then be able to release her into the larger world. The freedom inmates were given under the parole system was far greater than they had at the colony, but it was provisional. Parolees remained under the institution's supervision. They had to return annually for a physical examination, and they could be recalled to the colony if they got into trouble of any kind.

On November 12, 1927, Dr. Bell sent Carrie to live with the Coleman family, who owned a lumber company in Belspring, a small town southwest of Lynchburg. At first, the placement seemed to be working out. The family wrote to Dr. Bell to say Carrie was "getting on all right" and was "feeling fine." The Colemans offered to pay Carrie's way back to the colony so she could see her mother at Christmas. After the holiday, however, things went downhill. The family wrote to the colony to report that they had caught Carrie using a dishpan as a chamber pot. They asked that Carrie be taken back, and on January 11 she returned to the colony.

Dr. Bell turned next to the Dobbses—who should have been his first choice. At the trial in the Amherst County Circuit Court, Dr. Priddy had said that if Carrie was sterilized, one of the benefits to her was that she would be able to leave the colony—and, specifically, move back in with the Dobbses. "I understand," he said in his sworn testimony, "that they want her back." Strode repeated this assertion in his brief to the Supreme Court. It was a poignant promise, because if

Carrie moved in with the Dobbses it would reunite her with the only child she would ever have.

On January 12, 1928, Dr. Bell wrote to Alice Dobbs to ask if Carrie could return to work in her home. He explained that Carrie had been sterilized under the state law, and he included a personal endorsement. "She is quite well behaved and a good worker, as you know, if a reasonable amount of control is exercised over her," Dr. Bell wrote. "Thinking that you might like to have her back with you," he said, "I am writing to advise that I will be glad to place her on parole."

Dobbs did not want Carrie back. In a letter of February 13, 1928, she declined Dr. Bell's offer. Dobbs said she thought "a great deal of Carrie," but things were too busy in the house to take her in. She put the blame on her husband, who was "now in his seventieth year." He had said "he can't take care of" Carrie, Dobbs reported.

It is unlikely Dobbs was really concerned about the burden Carrie would impose on her household. Having her do housework and help with Vivian would lighten the load. Nor was there reason to worry Carrie would misbehave—if she did, Dr. Bell could revoke her parole at any time. There were, however, other possible concerns. One was that if Carrie were reunited with her only child she might try to reassert her parental rights, and Dobbs did not want to give Vivian up. Another possible worry was that if Carrie returned to Charlottesville, she might tell people how she became pregnant, putting the Dobbses' nephew, and the family's reputation, at risk.

If Dobbs had been concerned only about strain on her household, she could have helped find Carrie another placement in Charlottesville that would have allowed her to see Vivian regularly. Instead, she made a spirited argument that Carrie should not be released at all. "Can't you still keep her at the colony?" Dobbs implored Dr. Bell. "If you would I sure would appreciate it so she would have a place to call home and not be from one place to another."

Dobbs went even further. She argued to Dr. Bell that Carrie should be kept at the colony permanently. "I thought when the Red Cross sent her their [*sic*]," she wrote, "it would be a home for her so long as she lived." When Dr. Priddy testified under oath that the Dobbses would take Carrie back, and when Strode repeated the claim to the Supreme Court, they were either mistaken or lying. The truth was, the Dobbses would never let Carrie return—and they wanted her locked up for life.

Carrie was not the only Buck woman sterilized at the colony. Her half sister, Doris, was admitted as an inmate on June 18, 1926, while Carrie's case was heading to the Supreme Court. Doris, who had been living in a private home in Charlottesville, had come to the attention of the welfare authorities after Arthur Estabrook examined her as part of his fieldwork on the Buck family. After the authorities began to get reports that Doris was acting wildly and "meeting men," they had her declared feebleminded and committed to the colony.

When Doris was examined, she was recorded as being 5 feet 1½ inches tall and 96 pounds. She was also designated a "High-grade imbecile." That ranking was lower than Carrie's or Emma's, who were both designated "morons," and it made her eligible for eugenic sterilization under the law. At least one person who knew Doris before she was sent away said she was not feebleminded though she apparently had a temper, perhaps due in part to her difficult family situation.

A few weeks after Carrie was sterilized, the colony board voted to establish a larger eugenic sterilization program. When it did, Doris was in the first group chosen for it. On January 23, 1928, Doris, who was just sixteen, was brought to the Halsey-Jennings Building, the same place where her half sister had been operated on months earlier. Doris was told the procedure she was undergoing was being done for medical reasons. She was not informed it would prevent her from having children.

After the refusal from the Dobbses, Dr. Bell continued trying to find a placement for Carrie. He received a letter, sent on February 18, from Mr. A. T. Newberry of Bland, Virginia. Newberry was writing to say that he needed help with keeping up a busy household that included his wife, his mother, and his two sons. He was, he said, "really anxious to get a good girl from your institution."

Dr. Bell responded that if Newberry provided transportation money, he would send "a girl by the name of Carrie Buck, who has been in the institution for years." Dr. Bell again provided a personal recommendation, calling Carrie "strong and healthy and capable of doing good work." He vouched that, in spite of her problems with the Colemans, Carrie was "good tempered and easy to handle." Dr. Bell told Newberry he should pay Carrie a salary of about $5 a month, and that he should have someone meet her when she arrived at the train station.

On February 25 Carrie set off by train for Bland, a small town near the West Virginia border, about 150 miles from Lynchburg. Newberry had agreed to meet her at the station in nearby Wytheville, but he had trouble with his car and arrived late. When he finally got there, Carrie was waiting for him patiently.

Carrie made a good first impression on the Newberry family. After spending an afternoon with Carrie, Mrs. Newberry wrote to Dr. Bell to ask why she had been sent to the colony. "We would like to know what to look for and guard against," she said. In particular, Mrs. Newberry wanted to know if Carrie was epileptic and likely to have seizures. She apologized if her questions seemed "too insensitive," but said she did "want to know about her." Dr. Bell wrote back to say Carrie was not epileptic and had been "committed here on account of being feebleminded." It was, perhaps, revealing about Carrie's actual mental abilities that Mrs. Newberry, after spending some time with her, could not tell on her own that Carrie was a "moron."

Carrie's first few months in Bland went well. In May Mrs. Newberry wrote to tell Dr. Bell that Carrie was "getting on nicely" and that "we like her very much." Carrie worked well with her and her husband, she said, though she was sometimes stubborn when Mr. Newberry's mother tried to tell her what to do. That was "the only fault we find so far," Mrs. Newberry said, and she was sure Carrie would "do better."

Carrie was enjoying her freedom. She tried to get Dr. Bell to grant her a formal discharge from the colony, and Mrs. Newberry reported that Carrie talked often about her hopes of being permanently released. If that happened, it would be the first time in her adult life that she would be in charge of her own destiny, not needing the colony's approval to take a new job or move. It would also free her of the threat that always hung over her: if her employers were unhappy with her, she might be returned to live at the colony.

But Dr. Bell was not ready to let Carrie go. He wrote to her in August denying the request. "I do not think it advisable to discharge you," he said, "as you have no home of your own, and are not capable of looking after your own affairs at the present time." Dr. Bell insisted he was acting in Carrie's interest, so she would have a home to return to if she needed it. He told her to wait at least another year.

While Carrie was away from the colony, she made efforts to keep in touch with her family. Over the summer she wrote to a colony staff member about her unsuccessful efforts to contact Doris. Carrie also said she had received a letter from her mother, who had asked her for some things, and she wanted to know if it would be all right for her to send them. Emma, Carrie, and Doris tried repeatedly over the years to correspond and to see each other, though the challenges they faced were considerable.

In December 1928 Carrie's situation in the Newberry household took a turn for the worse. She wrote Dr. Bell to tell him she was "getting along very well." She had "a real nice home," she said, "and you don't know how much I appreciate it." There was a problem, however, and she expected Mrs. Newberry would soon write him about "some trouble I have had." Carrie said she hoped Dr. Bell would not "put it against me and have me to come back" to the colony. He had promised her a discharge "in a years [sic] time," she noted, "but I guess the trouble I had will throw me back in getting it but I hope not."

Carrie was correct—Mrs. Newberry did write to Dr. Bell. She had never seen "a better girl to work" than Carrie, who was "as obedient with Mr. Newberry and myself as can be," Mrs. Newberry reported, "and tries so hard to please us with her work and we like her very much." But there was a problem. Carrie was "beginning her adultery again," Mrs. Newberry told Dr. Bell. "I say again for I believe she is an old hand at the business," she wrote.

Mrs. Newberry insisted that she had done what she could to put Carrie on a moral path. She tried to "impress upon Carrie the importance of living a clean pure life," she said. And Carrie promised to "conduct herself right, or try as best she can" because she "hates the idea of going back to Lynchburg." If Carrie "lives right we will give her a home as long as she wants it," Mrs. Newberry said. But if not, she would not be able to stay, because "we cannot have this conduct in our house."

Dr. Bell's reply was not encouraging. Carrie's "sexual delinquency is probably a thing that will have to be contended with for many years," he wrote, "unless she should find herself a suitable husband and . . . settle down." He asked Mrs. Newberry to keep in mind that Carrie had "a sister who was also delinquent" and that "they come from a long line of mental defectives and delinquents." The Newberrys were no doubt doing their best, he wrote, "and I hope that she appreciates it."

Just after that flurry of letters—perhaps because he was not interested in continuing to supervise Carrie's activities in such detail—Dr. Bell finally granted Carrie's request: on January 1, 1929, she was formally discharged from the colony. In Carrie's first days as a free woman, her life remained much the same. She continued to live with the Newberrys, who still kept Dr. Bell informed about her activities.

There was one change—or at least the suggestion of one. In a letter to Dr. Bell, Mr. Newberry added in a postscript that he did not "know for sure yet whether" Carrie "will marry or not." In case she did, he asked Dr. Bell to "please keep a good girl in reserve for me as I will want one." It was the first time the Newberrys had made such a reference, and it seemed they might have had a reason for doing so.

Back at the colony, Doris was now eligible for parole. Having been sterilized, she could be released into the world with no danger that she would become pregnant and give birth to feebleminded offspring. She was placed with families, much as Carrie had been, and ran into the same difficulty—being chastised for her interest in meeting men. After steadily lobbying Dr. Bell, on December 5, 1930, Doris was formally discharged from the colony. She told Dr. Bell that she was going to be married.

Although her daughters were now free, Emma remained at the colony. Carrie looked for opportunities to spend time with her mother. On December 19, 1930, she wrote to Dr. Bell to ask if she could come back to celebrate the holidays with Emma. Dr. Bell agreed, and said that if she called the colony from the train station someone would meet her there. Carrie spent Christmas with her mother, who had not been feeling well. On December 27 Mrs. Newberry sent $7 to the colony to pay for Carrie's transportation back to Bland.

In Dr. Bell's years of corresponding with Carrie about work placements, travel, parole, and discharge, one thing stands out: he did not write to her, or make plans for her, as if she was a "Middle grade Moron" with a mental age of nine, as the colony insisted she was. It is hard to imagine that Dr. Bell would send Carrie letters full of instructions and logistics, and tell her to take long train rides on her own and call when she got to the station, if he truly believed he was dealing with someone with the mental capacity of a nine-year-old.

Carrie's own letters also belied the colony's claims about her intelligence and mental age. They were, on the whole, well written, in neat handwriting. There were occasional grammatical errors—but no more than appeared in the letters that her employers were sending to the colony at the same time. She expressed complicated ideas, like her warning to Dr. Bell in her December 1928 letter of a negative report that was likely to come from the Newberrys, and her effort to lobby him not to further delay her furlough as a result. In other letters, she expressed concern for her mother and sister, and arranged to visit Emma and send her gifts. Carrie's letters revealed her to be precisely what she was: an undereducated woman of perfectly normal intelligence.

The wedding that Mr. Newberry appeared to be hinting at finally occurred on May 14, 1932. Carrie, who was now twenty-five, married

William D. Eagle, a sixty-three-year-old widower. A Lutheran minister performed the ceremony at the Newberry home in Bland, and the couple celebrated with a trip over the border to West Virginia.

Carrie's new husband, who had four daughters and two sons from a prior marriage, was a jack-of-many-trades. He listed his occupation as carpenter on their marriage license, but he had also been a justice of the peace and a deputy sheriff. In a May 17 letter to Dr. Bell, Carrie—now Mrs. W. D. Eagle in her correspondence—explained that she and her husband had been "going" together for three years. He was a "good man," she wrote, and three days into the marriage she was "getting along alright so far." As usual, Carrie inquired after her mother and asked Dr. Bell to tell her "I will send her some things when I can."

Carrie settled into a quiet domestic life. The Eagles joined the Methodist Church and attended services and Sunday school. Carrie and her husband grew much of their own food, planting onions, cabbages, tomatoes, lettuce, and pepper seed. Carrie canned what they did not eat, so they would have food for the winter, and to send to her mother at the colony.

About seven weeks after Carrie's wedding, on July 3, her daughter, Vivian, died from a stomach infection following the measles. Vivian, who had been living with the Dobbs family, was eight years old. Carrie was never able to live with her only child, or to spend much time with her. She did tell a colony superintendent she had been able to see "Babie," as she called Vivian. Her daughter was, Carrie said, "so very sweet."

In March 1933 the colony received a letter from one of the nation's leading eugenicists asking about Vivian. Paul Popenoe of the Human Betterment Foundation in Pasadena, California, was seeking photos of Carrie, Emma, and Vivian. Carrie's case was a "milestone" for eugenics, Popenoe said, and he thought it should be properly documented. Dr. Bell could take a photograph of Emma, who was still at the colony, but he asked Carrie for a photo of herself and Vivian. Carrie sent a photographic negative of herself and her husband, asking that he return it. She told Dr. Bell that she did not have a photograph of Vivian. Neither she nor Dr. Bell was aware that Vivian had died the previous summer.

Dr. Bell began to look for a photograph of Vivian. He contacted the Charlottesville chapter of the Red Cross, which had been responsible for taking both Emma and Carrie to the colony, and asked if it could help in the search. Margaret Faris, who worked for the Red Cross, agreed to try. The Red Cross visited Alice Dobbs and learned that she had a photo of Vivian, but they were unable to obtain it. Dobbs emphatically refused to lend it, Faris told Dr. Bell. Dobbs urged the Red Cross to write to Dr. Bell "to discontinue your investigation as the child was . . . considered a member of her own family."

A month earlier, the Red Cross had learned more about Carrie's daughter. It had interviewed Dobbs to find out how Vivian, whom it had placed with the Dobbs family, was doing. Dobbs told the Red Cross workers that Vivian had died the previous summer—and she set the record straight about her intelligence. Nearly nine years after a Red Cross social worker had labeled Vivian "not quite a normal baby," Dobbs told the Red Cross something very different: that she had completed the second grade and "was very bright."

Dobbs's assessment of Vivian's mental ability was supported by objective evidence—school records. Vivian Alice Elaine Dobbs, as the family named her, attended Venable Public Elementary School in Charlottesville. The Harvard biologist Stephen Jay Gould examined Vivian's school records and found that she received strong grades in "deportment" and did reasonably well in her academic subjects. Vivian was left back one term for failing math and spelling, and made the honor roll another term. In Gould's view, she had "performed adequately, although not brilliantly." He concluded that Vivian was a "quite average student" and "perfectly normal."

Carrie was living a simple life in Bland. In a letter to Dr. Bell on August 19, 1933—the depths of the Great Depression—she reported that her husband "works regularly," but money was still tight. "We live out in the country," she wrote. "We have a pig and a nice garden."

Now that Carrie had settled into a home of her own, she wanted to get her mother out of the colony. She asked Dr. Bell if Emma could come to stay with her. Carrie promised she would see to it that her mother was "well taken care of" and had "plenty to eat." Carrie was also in touch with Doris. She said she had recently received a letter from her half sister, who reported that her husband had left her. "I am sorry about that," Carrie wrote, adding that she "was hoping she would do well."

Dr. Bell responded two days later, saying that if Carrie wanted to take her mother in "and you can support her and take care of her, and it is agreeable to your husband, it will be all right with me." He cautioned Carrie to "think it over well, however, before you take any steps in the matter." In September Dr. Bell took a leave of absence due to ill health, and soon after he resigned. When he did, Carrie's close connection to the leadership of the colony ended, and her letters became more infrequent. Emma was never released into Carrie's care.

Carrie and her husband soldiered on as the Great Depression raged. With the economy battered, employment was scarce in small southern towns like Bland. Mr. and Mrs. Eagle took whatever jobs they could find, including working as caretakers of the local high school in the late 1930s and early 1940s. A neighbor who knew Carrie during these years remembered her as a quiet woman who gave every appearance of being "mentally sound."

World War II began, and Carrie continued her life of quiet domesticity. In October 1940 she wrote to Dr. G. B. Arnold, who was now superintendent of the colony, to ask after Emma. Carrie had not heard from her mother in some time, and wanted to see how she was doing and to send some supplies. Dr. Arnold responded that Emma was "still well and healthy," if getting a bit more frail. "She remains happy most of the time," he said.

When William Eagle died, Carrie left Bland, moving across the state to Front Royal. Her new home was near large orchards, where she could get seasonal work picking apples. Now that Carrie was on her own, it was a struggle for her to support herself. She did housekeeping for families in the area and washed dishes in a local restaurant, along with the agricultural labor. The work was physically demanding, and Carrie's health suffered. Her weight fell to just one hundred pounds at one point.

One of Carrie's jobs was caring for the parents of a friend. The woman recalled that Carrie kept house and looked after the elderly couple well, and that she was a "nice, kind person." She also remembered something else: Carrie "knew what she was doing, there was nothing wrong with that woman's mind."

On April 15, 1944, Emma died of bronchial pneumonia at the age of seventy-one. Her life had been a hard one, and she spent the last twenty-four years of it as an inmate of the colony. Having heard Emma was in decline, Carrie and her half brother, Roy, went to see her, but by the time they arrived their mother had been dead for two weeks and her funeral had already been held. "The son and daughter were a bit upset," Emma's record stated. "However, they were most considerate and accepted the explanation."

With Emma's death, Carrie no longer had reason to remain in contact with the colony. After a few years, the institution lost touch with its most famous former inmate. When a Detroit professor who was researching eugenic sterilization asked about Carrie in 1942, Dr. D. L. Harrell Jr., who was then superintendent, was unable to help. The colony had received "no official reports" of late, he said, but "it is the general impression here that she made a satisfactory adjustment to society."

Carrie's life in Front Royal was uneventful. On April 25, 1965, she married again. Charles Albert Detamore was a sixty-one-year-old orchard worker with whom she shared a geographical connection: both were originally from Albemarle County.

Five years later, with her health starting to fail, Carrie moved back to Charlottesville with her husband. The couple lived in a dimly lit single-room home on a dirt road. Carrie remained in contact with Doris, and the two women saw each other from time to time. Carrie was living in obscurity, however, unknown to the larger world as the woman at the center of the Supreme Court's eugenics case.

Dr. K. Ray Nelson, the director of the Lynchburg Training Center—as the colony had been renamed—had been trying to find Carrie for years. In 1979 he learned of Doris's location when she wrote to ask for her date of birth, so she could apply for Social Security. He went to visit Doris in Front Royal, where she was living with her husband of thirty-nine years, Matthew Figgins. Dr. Nelson brought along copies of her colony records.

When Dr. Nelson met with Doris, he read from her file, and informed her that she was sixty-seven—old enough to collect Social Security. He also told her the date that the colony had sterilized her. When he looked up, he could see that Doris and her husband were crying. Doris told Dr. Nelson that she had tried for years to get pregnant, and never realized it was impossible. When she was operated on at the colony, she said, she was told she was getting an appendectomy.

Doris and her husband were crying because, she said, they "wanted babies bad" and had always thought her inability to get pregnant was their fault. Years earlier they had visited a doctor to learn more, and Doris had explained that the scar on her abdomen was from an appendectomy, something she now realized was not true. When she learned from Dr. Nelson that the state had intentionally sterilized her, she told a reporter later, it "just hurt real bad."

Dr. Nelson had been looking for Carrie since he assumed his position at the Lynchburg Training Center in 1973. He learned from Doris that she was living in Albemarle County. Dr. Nelson located Carrie and brought the two women back to the colony on July 4, 1980. They found Emma's grave marker in the "Briar Patch" and, with tears in their eyes, left flowers. Next they visited the building where both Carrie and Doris had been sterilized. Carrie's legs were weak, and she could not make it upstairs, but Doris returned to the room where her sterilization had taken place more than a half century earlier.

After Carrie's visit to the colony, a local newspaper wrote about her—and, for the first time, she began to tell her own story. In an interview with the *Lynchburg Daily Advance,* she revealed that her pregnancy had been the result of being raped by Mrs. Dobbs's nephew. When the colony operated on her, she said, it was never explained to her that she was losing the ability to have children.

Carrie's account revealed two more important falsehoods in the colony's case against her. Carrie had never been an "immoral" woman— even as that term was understood in the 1920s. She had been a rape victim. The colony had also failed to tell the truth about the procedural protections it claimed to have extended to Carrie. For all of the guardians and lawyers and hearings and notice, Carrie had never been told the most critical fact: that the colony was trying to operate on her to prevent her from having children.

Carrie's final years were difficult. While living in their modest home in the countryside outside of Charlottesville, Carrie and her husband, Charlie, were found to be suffering from malnutrition and exposure. They were taken first to the University of Virginia Hospital and then to the District Home in Waynesboro, a facility for the indigent elderly.

Carrie was deeply devoted to Charlie, a District Home social worker later recalled. With no children or grandchildren to care for, she doted on her husband, often using her allotment at the canteen to buy snacks and cigarettes for him. Some of the staff thought Carrie cared for Charlie too much, and put his interests too far above her own.

Carrie was an active member of the District Home community. She participated in its social activities, including reading groups, and enjoyed theater and music. The home's social worker remembered Carrie as an "alert and pleasant lady," and she recalled one more thing: like many others who knew Carrie, the social worker said she was not mentally deficient, and certainly no imbecile.

Carrie died in January 1983, about six months after Doris.

Carrie's body was taken back to her hometown of Charlottesville, where she was buried in the Dobbs family plot, near the graves of her daughter, Vivian, and John and Alice Dobbs, who had taken her in as a young girl—and then cast her out.

In the end, three main themes ran through Carrie's life. One was hard work. When Carrie was taken in by the Dobbses, she was less a foster child than a housekeeper, and before long she was also being hired out to the neighbors. Because the Dobbses ended her education after the fifth grade, Carrie's employment options were limited. She spent a lifetime doing poorly paid manual labor: cleaning homes, washing dishes, harvesting crops. She was, by all accounts, a good and dedicated worker.

A second theme was deep devotion to family, despite a lifetime of obstacles. She was close to her mother, Emma, caring for her both when they lived together in the colony and when they lived far from each other. For years, Carrie wrote to the colony asking after Emma, sending her things, and trying to arrange times to see her. She was also close to her half sister, Doris, despite the difficult lives they both led. Carrie was a devoted wife to two husbands. She also managed to see her daughter, even though the state took her baby away and gave her to another family—and that family insisted on keeping Carrie at a distance.

The final theme running through Carrie's life was precisely what the Supreme Court had refused to see: a quiet intelligence. Carrie's lively mind is preserved for posterity in the many letters she sent to the colony. Neatly written and well composed, they reveal a thinking, caring woman with a love for life.

Carrie's friends and employers all appear to have considered her smart, and there is no record of anyone questioning her intelligence once the campaign to sterilize her was over. A friend from the retirement home where Carrie lived late in life recalled that she was devoted to something Oliver Wendell Holmes had no interest in: reading newspapers. "Carrie watched for that paper—she lived to get that paper," the friend recalled.

An academic who visited Carrie in her later years found that she was reading the newspaper daily and "joining a more literate friend to assist at regular bouts with the crossword puzzles." The professor thought that Carrie was "not a sophisticated woman, and lacked social graces," but he was also convinced that "she was neither mentally ill nor retarded."

Carrie never got over what the state of Virginia did to her. When reporters tracked her down five decades after the fateful procedure, she told them she was sad about it—once she found out what it was. "I didn't want a big family," she said, but she had wanted to have "a couple of children." Sadness was not the only feeling she was left with. "Oh yeah, I was angry," she said. "They done me wrong. They done us all wrong."

Conclusion

Oliver Wendell Holmes's opinion in *Buck v. Bell*, with its bold declaration that "three generations of imbeciles are enough," gave the eugenic sterilization movement "a constitutional blessing and an epigrammatic battle cry." Harry Laughlin announced that the ruling marked the end of eugenic sterilization's "experimental period." Now he said, "eugenical sterilization will be looked upon by the American people as a reasonable and conservative matter." Laughlin had long advocated an expansive national program of sterilization— and now he believed his dream was on the verge of becoming a reality.

Buck v. Bell breathed new life into the sterilization movement. In the years leading up to it, the eugenicists had encountered substantial opposition in courts and statehouses across the country. Now supporters of sterilization laws were emboldened, and their opponents were suddenly on the defensive.

In 1928, a new governor took office in Mississippi, and he declared in his inaugural address that his state had spent an enormous amount "to advance our civilization, to educate and uplift our people yet our feeble-minded, epileptic, insane, paupers and criminals can reproduce without restriction, thus continuing to corrupt our society and increase tax burdens on our people." That same year, the Mississippi legislature adopted a sweeping eugenical sterilization law, with little opposition. William Faulkner, who began work in 1928 on *The Sound and the Fury*, immortalized his state's newfound eugenic fervor in the novel, in which Benjy Compson, the "idiot" of the family, is castrated.

The sterilization movement gained greater force in 1929, when nine states enacted laws, three of them—Arizona, West Virginia, and Maine—for the first time. The momentum continued over the next several years. In 1931 ten state legislatures considered sterilization bills, and in five states they became law. By that year twenty-eight of the nation's forty-eight states had laws authorizing eugenic sterilization.

Even with the new enthusiasm, there continued to be opposition. The main obstacle to sterilization laws remained the Catholic Church and its members. In states where the church "could mobilize sufficiently," one study found, eugenic sterilization bills "often against the odds, failed." In New Jersey, reform groups, including the League of Women Voters, pushed for a eugenic sterilization law to replace the one that had been struck down by the New Jersey Supreme Court. New Jersey, however, was about 26 percent Catholic—one of the highest percentages of any state—and the church and its supporters played a major role in stopping the sterilization bill.

One leading eugenicist complained bitterly that when sterilization bills were being considered throughout the country "the Catholics descend upon the capitol in numbers—priests, nuns and laity—and attack the bill as 'against the will of God' and 'an attack on the American home.'" This opposition was effective even in states with relatively few Catholics. In Colorado, which was about 12 percent Catholic, church leaders and laity helped to defeat four consecutive eugenic sterilization bills. In Ohio, which was less than 15 percent Catholic, several bills "crashed . . . against the rocks of Roman Catholic opposition."

Not all of the opposition came from Catholics. The Supreme Court's decision had not done away with the discomfort a considerable number of people of all sorts, state legislators included, felt about sterilization. In the wake of the ruling, Kentucky's state legislature voted down a eugenic sterilization bill. One lawmaker helped to rally opposition to the bill by arguing that if it had been enacted in an earlier generation, "there would not be so many fools [in the legislature] now."

Despite this resistance, in the years after the Supreme Court's decision, the number of eugenic sterilizations increased sharply, due both to new laws and to an increased willingness to use those that were already in place. In 1925 there were just 322 sterilizations of institutionalized people nationwide. In the two-year period from 1928 through 1929, there were 2,362—more than triple the annual rate from before the court's ruling.

There was also a significant change in the gender of the people being sterilized. At the end of 1927, men made up about 53 percent of all of the legal sterilizations that had been performed in the United States. Over the next five years, 67 percent of the institutionalized people who were sterilized were female. Many of the women, institutional records show, were admitted for the express purpose of being sterilized and then released. The "clearing house" model Laughlin, Dr. Priddy, and Dr. DeJarnette proposed was increasingly becoming a reality.

Not surprisingly, there was also a pronounced class bias to who was sterilized. Poor women like Carrie and Doris Buck were the most common victims of the eugenic sterilization boom. The procedures were performed so often on poor white southerners that they acquired a nickname: "Mississippi appendectomies."

Virginia was one of the main drivers of the increase in sterilizations. Before the Supreme Court's ruling, there had been no eugenic sterilizations in Virginia—or at least no legally sanctioned ones. Ten years after the court's ruling, there were more than one thousand. The people who were sterilized, like Carrie and Doris, were often not told what was being done to them. Many tried to have children and did not understand why they were unable to conceive.

Virginia's sterilizations occurred in all five state hospitals, but almost half of them occurred at the colony. The sterilization program reached its peak in the 1930s and 1940s, when the colony was likely performing the most sterilizations of any hospital in the country. "It was as routine as taking out tonsils," according to one newspaper account. "Men on Tuesdays, women on Thursday[s]."

The impact of the Supreme Court's ruling was felt beyond the United States. Over the next few years, European countries began to adopt eugenic sterilization laws along the American model. Denmark enacted "voluntary" sterilization in 1929, and forced sterilization of "mental defectives" in 1934. Sweden and Norway also enacted sterilization laws in 1934, followed by Finland in 1935, Estonia in 1936, and Iceland in 1938. An American medical researcher who traveled to Europe to study eugenic developments noted that the United States had "pioneered" eugenic sterilization for the rest of the world.

Nazi Germany adopted its Law for the Prevention of Hereditarily Diseased Offspring in the summer of 1933. The Nazis also established an elaborate system of Hereditary Health Courts—the *Erbgesundheitsgerichte*—to decide who should be sterilized. Laughlin, who was proud of his influence on German eugenics, published an article in the *Eugenical News* by a leading Nazi attesting that "Germany learned from the United States" when it drafted its own sterilization laws.

The influence of American eugenics reportedly reached the highest levels of the Nazi regime. Otto Wagener, a high-ranking economic adviser to Adolf Hitler, quoted Hitler as saying: "I have studied with great interest the laws of several American states concerning prevention of reproduction by people whose progeny would, in all probability, be of no value or be injurious to the racial stock."

The German eugenic sterilization program operated on a scale that eclipsed its American model. The law authorized sterilization for many of the reasons in Laughlin's model law, including feeblemindedness, alcoholism, and epilepsy. The Nazis also used sterilization against Jews and people of partial Jewish background, Roma, the children of German women and black French soldiers, and other disfavored racial and religious groups. When the Final Solution was adopted, provisions were made for Germans with mixed Aryan and Jewish blood to be sterilized as an alternative to extermination. The hereditary courts issued 375,000 sterilization orders, but some estimates of the number of people sterilized by the Nazis are far higher.

At the Nuremberg trials, where the victorious Allies prosecuted Nazi leaders for war crimes, the charges included mass sterilization. Otto Hofmann, the head of the SS Race and Settlement Office, one of the Nazis charged with mass sterilization, defended himself in part by referring to the American states that had adopted eugenic sterilization laws—and the *Buck v. Bell* decision. One of Hofmann's submissions included a quote from Holmes's opinion, which was mangled by being translated into German and back into English:

> In a judgment of the [United States] Supreme Court . . . it says, among other things: "It is better for everybody if society, instead of waiting until it has to execute degenerate offspring or leave them to starve because of feeble-mindedness, can prevent obviously inferior individuals from propagating their kind."

The classic 1961 movie *Judgment at Nuremberg* captures in dramatic fashion how the Nazi defendants used the case. At a key moment in the trial, a defense lawyer asks the witness if he is aware that "sexual sterilization was not invented by National Socialism," but had "advocates among leading citizens in many other countries." He then reads an excerpt from *Buck v. Bell*, ending with "three generations of imbeciles are enough." The Nazi lawyer then states triumphantly that the words were those of "that great American jurist, Supreme Court Justice Oliver Wendell Holmes."

For Aubrey Strode, *Buck v. Bell* was the capstone to a distinguished legal career. Few lawyers ever appear before the Supreme Court, much less win a case that helps to set social policy for the nation.

Strode's victory was all the greater because he had been involved with the issue from the beginning. He had sponsored the legislation that created the colony, drafted the eugenic sterilization law, advised the hospital board on a strategy for winning in the courts, and then litigated all the way to the highest court in the land. Strode was lauded for his role in the case and received little criticism. He did not live long enough to see popular opinion turn against sterilization.

For all of his hard work—and his permanent place in eugenics history—there is little evidence Strode was a great believer in eugenic sterilization. Toward the end of his life, Strode was asked to create a written account of how Virginia's sterilization law came about. His retelling of the events underscored how unenthusiastic he appeared to be at critical junctures. It could even be read as the story of someone who was swept up in a cause with which he did not entirely agree and worked from the inside to minimize the damage.

Strode's account began in 1921, when he was counsel for the colony, and Dr. Priddy approached him about drafting a eugenic sterilization bill. Strode had been a member of the legislature himself when many states were enacting such laws, but he had never been moved to introduce a bill on his own. Indeed, when a eugenic sterilization bill was introduced by Dr. Charles Carrington, there is no evidence Strode supported it. On the day it came up for a vote, he was present and voted on other bills, but he apparently did not vote on eugenic sterilization.

Rather than accept the assignment to draft a sterilization bill, as many lawyers might have under the circumstances, Strode instead investigated how these laws had fared in the rest of the country. He then told the State Hospital Board, Dr. Priddy's bosses, that in every case he could find where such a law had been challenged, it had been defeated. Strode succeeded in persuading his client not to pursue the law.

In his account, Strode recalled that Dr. Priddy approached him again two years later, telling him that the hospital board and the governor still wanted a eugenic sterilization law. This time, Strode did draft a bill, though one that was far narrower in several important respects than the model statute he was given as a guide. When Strode's bill became law, the board asked him, he recalled, whether "it might safely proceed under the Act." Many states were carrying out sterilizations under even more expansive laws, with fewer procedural protections. but Strode once again put on the brakes.

Strode persuaded the State Hospital Board not to begin sterilizing anyone until the law was tested in the courts, all the way up to the Supreme Court, if it got that far. If he had not given that advice, the hospitals might have sterilized hundreds, even thousands, of people before any sort of legal challenge was mounted. Strode's advice delayed sterilizations in Virginia by three years, and created a significant possibility that none would occur at all.

After his victory in the Supreme Court, Strode had a new opportunity to show enthusiasm for the eugenic sterilization cause. He could have become one of the public faces of the movement and spoken out in support of sterilization. Instead, he seemed content to let the matter drop. Shortly after the ruling, the *Virginia Law Review*—for which he had already written one article about eugenic sterilization—invited him to write about his Supreme Court triumph. It was an honor many lawyers would have been quick to accept, and many eugenics advocates would have seen the invitation as an opportunity to lay out the next steps in the battle. Strode informed the editor in chief, however, that he doubted that "this matter would justify" an article or that he could "find the time in the near future" to write one.

Unlike most of the other major participants in *Buck v. Bell*, Strode almost never spoke publicly about sterilization once the case ended. Dr. John Bell, whose name had replaced Dr. Priddy's in the Supreme Court case and who performed Carrie's sterilization, lectured widely on eugenic sterilization. He spoke to the Medical Society of Virginia on the importance of the procedure in protecting the commonwealth from the tide of "degenerates and defectives" that was threatening to engulf it. Addressing a national audience at the American Psychiatric Association, Dr. Bell called eugenic sterilization a key spoke of the "wheel of social progress."

Like Dr. Priddy before him, Dr. Bell used the colony annual reports as a platform to promote eugenic sterilization. The program was, he insisted, working well. In the 1932 report, he said nearly all of the inmates who were sterilized had been returned to their families, relieving the state of "the immense financial burden incident to the care of them and the long line of defective descendants that would naturally have followed." In the following year's report, Dr. Bell wrote: "Now is the time to apply the pruning knife with vigor and without fear or favor."

Dr. Bell's career as an evangelist for eugenic sterilization was short-lived. On September 11, 1933, he took a leave of absence due to poor health and moved to Asheville, North Carolina. Shortly thereafter, he resigned. On December 9, 1934, he died of heart failure at the age of fifty-one, after serving as colony superintendent for just under ten years.

While Dr. Bell carried the sterilization banner to the end of his life, Strode largely remained silent. In 1934 he ended a three-decade career as a trial lawyer to become a judge on Lynchburg's corporation court, as the municipal court was then known. In all of his years as a lawyer and judge after the ruling in *Buck v. Bell,* only one instance has come to light of Strode speaking publicly about eugenic sterilization, and, not surprisingly perhaps, it was anything but a call to arms.

Strode's reference to sterilization came nearly a decade after his Supreme Court victory, in a 1936 address to the Virginia Social Science Association. In "The Utility and Futility of Punishment for Crime in Virginia," Strode had more to say about the role of environment than heredity in producing criminals. In discussing convict labor laws, he observed that while the state took advantage of prisoners' labor, their children were often condemned to grow up in poverty. If those children ended up "in the struggle for existence" driven to steal, he said, people mistakenly then argued "that their children are criminal because their father was a criminal." Strode disagreed with this "hereditarian" analysis, focusing instead on the environmental factors that would have led the children astray. He went on to advocate a long list of progressive measures that could be used to reduce crime, including full employment programs and doing away with slums. Strode included on his list "carefully guarded measures for the sterilization of" the "unfit," but it was the last factor he raised—and it was undercut by everything he had said up until then. At best, the speech offered a very ambivalent and weak endorsement of the *Buck v. Bell* advocacy that had made him famous.

If Strode had been trying to quietly moderate the drive for sterilization in Virginia, it did not hurt his standing with the state's eugenicists, who remained grateful for his work. At a 1939 celebration of Dr. DeJarnette's fiftieth anniversary at Western State Hospital, the guest of honor had warm words for Dr. Priddy—and for his former lawyer. "I knew him as a boy and I thought he was the handsomest young man I had ever seen," Dr. DeJarnette recalled of Strode. He was a "wonderful lawyer," who had written a "law for sterilization of the unfit that has stood the test of the Courts."

Strode's health declined in the 1940s, when he suffered several strokes. He remained on the bench until a friend in the legislature could rewrite the state law to give full pensions to judges who retired because of physical disabilities. On May 17, 1946, four years into his retirement, Strode died at Kenmore. A brief *New York Times* obituary said he was "known for his interest in social legislation," a description that would doubtless have pleased him. But there was no avoiding the reason the *Times* was reporting his death, the achievement he would forever be remembered for: Strode had, the obituary said, drafted "the Virginia Sterilization Act, which became a model for other states."

After the ruling in *Buck v. Bell*, Harry Laughlin had no shortage of new projects, including writing an analysis of the court's decision. Laughlin's study was published in 1930 under the title *The Legal Status of Eugenical Sterilization: History and Analysis of Litigation Under the Virginia Sterilization Statute, Which Led to a Decision of the Supreme*

Court of the United States Upholding the Statute. In his introduction, Chief Justice Harry Olson of the Municipal Court of Chicago said Laughlin "is entitled to the thanks of the American people" for his success in promoting eugenic sterilization.

Laughlin ended his study by presenting the path forward for sterilization. He included more model sterilization laws, along with an appeal for his own work. The "next task," Laughlin said, was "building up a body of knowledge and of legal practice for evaluating evidence of hereditary degeneracy." Among the organizations doing this work, he noted, was the Eugenics Record Office.

Laughlin continued his interest in immigration. After his success with the exclusionary Immigration Act of 1924, he turned to a new tactic: deportation. It was, he believed, the only way to undo the damage of decades of immigration from the wrong countries. On February 21, 1928, Laughlin testified on the eugenic aspects of deportation to the House Committee on Immigration and Naturalization. Deportation was, he said, the "last line of defense against contamination of American family stocks by alien hereditary degeneracy."

Laughlin helped Madison Grant with his follow-up to *The Passing of the Great Race,* the book Hitler reportedly called "my Bible." Grant was finishing up *The Conquest of a Continent,* a book of which a *New York Times* reviewer would write: "Substitute Aryan for Nordic, and a good deal of Mr. Grant's argument would lend itself without much difficulty to the support of some recent pronouncements in Germany." Laughlin gave Grant editorial suggestions on the manuscript, and when it came out he helped promote it. He wrote to the publisher to urge "wide and continuous distribution." Laughlin suggested it be sent to high school and college American history departments across the country and in Canada.

In 1937, Laughlin made his last great effort for his friend. He embarked on his unsuccessful lobbying campaign to persuade Yale to award him an honorary degree. In his energetic letter writing to the degree committee, Laughlin described Grant as an "exemplar of American ideals"—and so he was for Laughlin. Decades later, a leading historian of the American eugenics movement would offer up another description of Grant: America's "most influential racist."

Laughlin's dreams for the American eugenics movement continued to grow. His attention was increasingly turning from the states, which had been the drivers of eugenic policies, to the federal government. He wanted Congress to create an official Bureau of Eugenics, which would administer its own federal eugenics statute, and in 1929 he drew up a blueprint for it. Laughlin also tried, without success, to persuade the U.S. Census Bureau to use the 1930 census to collect eugenics data on the American population. His aim was to turn the census into "a permanent and complete pedigree record of the American people as individuals"—information that could be used for future eugenic purposes.

While Laughlin's ambitions for the movement were growing, the tide was turning against eugenics. In the early years scientists had generally kept silent, but they were becoming more openly critical. In the fall of 1927, Raymond Pearl, a Johns Hopkins biologist, became the most prominent scientist to come out strongly against eugenics. Because Pearl had once been an active eugenicist, even addressing the First International Eugenics Congress in London, his stand carried particular weight. In an article in H. L. Mencken's *American Mercury* magazine, titled "The Biology of Superiority," Pearl lambasted eugenicists for the deficiency of their science. The eugenics literature, he insisted, had "largely become a mingled mess of ill-grounded and uncritical sociology, economics, anthropology, and politics, full of emotional appeals to class and race prejudices, solemnly put forth as science, and unfortunately accepted as such by the general public."

While criticism was growing, the eugenics movement was also weakening from within. With the Crash of 1929 and the Great Depression, the nation suddenly had new and more important things to worry about than defective germplasm. In 1931, after the Democrats won a majority in Congress, Albert Johnson was replaced as chairman of the House Committee on Immigration and Naturalization by Samuel Dickstein, a New York Democrat who was a Jewish immigrant from Russia. Laughlin's career as a congressional Expert Eugenics Agent was over.

Laughlin's position at the Eugenics Record Office was also increasingly precarious. John Merriam, the president of the Carnegie Institution, was uncomfortable with how politicized the office had become under Laughlin, and he raised his concerns with Charles Davenport. Merriam also reprimanded Laughlin for using the office's stationery to lobby Congress. The Carnegie Institution had long been hearing from critics who objected to the Eugenics Record Office's scientific methods, and Merriam decided to appoint a committee to review its work. The committee concluded that the office's records were deficient and its research protocols unduly subjective.

As the Nazis rose to power in Germany, Laughlin was a strong supporter of their eugenics programs. He corresponded regularly with leading Nazi scientists, including one who praised Hitler for being the first politician to recognize that "the central mission of all politics is race hygiene." Laughlin ran regular reports in the *Eugenical News* on the Nazis' progress, and he published his own work in the Society for Racial Hygiene's journal, *Archiv für Rassen- und Gesellschafts-Biologie.*

Laughlin was an admirer of Germany's infamous Sterilization Act of 1933. The law called for forced sterilization of anyone, institutionalized or not, who suffered from a wide array of purported defects. Feeblemindedness, drug and alcohol addiction, blindness, and physical deformity were all grounds for sterilization. Laughlin published the new law as the lead article in the September–October 1933 issue of *Eugenical News,* and he shared the special pride he felt in it. "To one versed in the history of eugenical sterilization in America," he wrote, "the text of the German statute reads almost like the 'American model sterilization law.'"

Laughlin followed developments in Germany closely. An inveterate newspaper clipper, he collected articles on German eugenic and race policies, including one from the August 16, 1933, *New York Times* with the headline: "Hindenburg Asked to Save Reich Jews: 500,000 Are Facing 'Certain Extermination,' American Congress Declares."

None of the grim news out of Germany caused Laughlin to temper his enthusiasm. In December 1934—after laws were enacted expelling Jews from the civil service, and removing many Jewish children from school—the *Eugenical News* published an essay on the Germany's Sterilization Act of 1933 that appeared to endorse the broader Nazi agenda. "In the new Germany," it said, "laws are made for the benefit of posterity, regardless of the approval or disapproval of present generations."

Laughlin's lack of outrage over Nazi racial policies had a simple explanation: his own views were not so different. In a November 19, 1932, letter to Madison Grant, Laughlin indicated that he would like to make the United States *judenrein*—"cleansed of Jews," in Nazi terminology—if it were possible. In a passage he carefully marked "not for publication," Laughlin wrote: "Whether we like it or not, a Jew must be assimilated or deported. The deportation of four million Jews would be many more times more difficult than the repatriation of three times as many Negroes." All they could do, Laughlin said, was work to keep the nation's Jewish population from growing any larger.

Preventing more Jews from coming to the United States was Laughlin's response to the gathering storm in Europe. With the disturbing reports coming out of Germany—and the threat, as the *New York Times* headline noted, of "certain extermination"—there were growing calls to loosen, at least temporarily, the immigration quotas Laughlin himself had helped put in place. The New York Chamber of Commerce commissioned Laughlin to investigate the subject, and in May 1934 he authored a report recommending that no special efforts be made to admit Jews fleeing Nazi Germany. In his report, which received prominent press coverage, Laughlin insisted the nation should adhere to a policy of admitting immigrants because they are "desirable human seed-stock of future American citizens" and "not because of persecution."

Laughlin's political stands and Nazi sympathies attracted criticism, some of it directed to his funders at the Carnegie Institution. Hyman Achinstein, a Brooklyn resident who said he had known Andrew Carnegie well, wrote to object to Laughlin's report urging no exceptional admissions for Jews fleeing Nazi Germany and to say it was a "disgrace" that the Carnegie Institution kept him on staff. If Carnegie were to "arise of his restful abode and see for himself what spirit pervades his institutions," Achinstein said, "he would say Halt."

Charles Davenport consistently stood by Laughlin when his critics attacked, but in 1934 Davenport retired, leaving Laughlin vulnerable. John Merriam appointed a new visiting committee the following year to review Laughlin and the Eugenics Record Office. Its members were less favorable than the first committee toward eugenics, and less likely to support Laughlin.

The new committee's report, which was released in June 1935, was a broad indictment of the Eugenics Record Office for engaging in worthless research and undertaking inappropriate political crusades. The chairman of the committee attacked Laughlin personally for having "a messiah attitude toward eugenics" that was "out of place" in a "scientific institution." The committee called for the office to cease its politics and propaganda and focus on "pure research."

Laughlin resented the inference, and he refused to rein in his politically charged activities. In August 1935 he and Clarence Campbell, an associate from the Eugenics Record Office, served as vice presidents of the International Congress for Population Science in Berlin—a conference that has been singled out for being "the apex of international support of Nazi race policies." Laughlin did not attend, but contributed a paper on eugenic sterilization in the United States. Campbell gave his own remarks praising Nazi racial policies. At the end of the conference, Campbell gave a toast "To that great leader, Adolf Hitler!"

In May 1936 Laughlin was informed that he was to be recognized the following month with an honorary doctorate of medicine from the University of Heidelberg in recognition of his work on the "science of racial cleansing." The university was marking its 550th year, and it had decided to celebrate not on the actual anniversary in October, but on June 30, the two-year anniversary of Germany's "blood purge" of Jewish university faculty. With German universities entirely under Nazi control, the award was effectively an honor from the Third Reich it-self, and one of the anniversaries it was marking was an odious one.

Laughlin was delighted by the recognition, and not put off by the Nazis' actions, including, the previous September, adopting the in-famous Nuremberg laws, which made marriage or sexual relations between Jews and non-Jewish Germans illegal and stripped Jews and other "non-Aryans" of German citizenship. Laughlin did not attend in person, but he wrote to the university to express his "deep gratitude" for "this high honor." Laughlin particularly appreciated it, he said, because it came "from a nation which for many centuries nurtured the human seed-stock which later founded my own country and thus gave basic character to our present lives and institutions."

Laughlin continued the political activism and propaganda that the Carnegie visiting committee had directed him to stop. In 1937 he and a wealthy friend, Wickliffe Draper, founded the Pioneer Fund. One of the organization's main purposes, it declared at its founding, was to aid in the education of children of parents who were "deemed to have such qualities and traits of character as to make such parents of unusual value as citizens." The Pioneer Fund charter gave priority to "children who are deemed to be descended predominantly from white persons who settled in the original thirteen states prior to the adoption of the Constitution of the United States and/or from related stocks."

Another factor working against Laughlin, besides the decline of eugenics and mounting criticism of him and the Eugenics Record Of-fice, was his health. The man who had lobbied for laws that described epileptics as "defective" and authorized their sterilization was showing increased symptoms of his own epilepsy. Laughlin was having seizures in public, and in 1937 had one while driving in downtown Cold Spring Harbor. He would have driven directly into the ocean if he had not crashed into a retainer wall. The Carnegie Institution's board of direc-tors expressed concerns about Laughlin's health, and Merriam ordered him to get a full medical checkup.

At the end of 1938, Merriam retired as president of the Carnegie Institution and was replaced by Vannevar Bush. A respected scientist and inventor, Bush was even more opposed to Laughlin's work than Merriam had been. Four days after he took office on January 1, 1939, Bush told Laughlin there would be a new review of his work. In June Bush asked for Laughlin's resignation, based on concerns about his research and his health. Laughlin resisted at first, but he agreed when the Carnegie Institution offered him a lifetime pension.

In December, which was to be his final month, Laughlin had a change of heart. He wanted to stay, and he had Senator Robert Reynolds of North Carolina—the leading Nazi sympathizer in Congress—lobby members of the Carnegie board. Bush, however, stood his ground, and Laughlin agreed to leave. On December 31, the Eugenics Record Office was effectively shut down. At Bush's direction, it was renamed the Genetics Record Office, and its budget was slashed.

The *Eugenical News* was also freed from Laughlin's influence. In new editorial hands—and once the United States formally entered the war against Germany—the publication abandoned the Nazi sympathies it had exhibited during the Laughlin era. In June 1943, after recounting German atrocities, it declared: "These almost unbelievable facts bring to our hearts a rush of pity for those victims of sadism, brutality and planned race extinction." The *Eugenical News* was no longer the propaganda organ for Nazi racial policies it once was.

Because American eugenics was effectively over as anything but a fringe cause, Laughlin's career was at an end. His work lived on in limited form: sterilization laws remained on the books, and sterilizations were still being performed. There would be no new legislative victories, however, no federal eugenics agency, and no more cooperative work with Nazi eugenicists. An internal memo prepared to help Carnegie Institution staff answer questions about Laughlin's departure noted tersely that the Eugenics Record Office was no longer in a "position to furnish information regarding genealogy, marriage advice, nor to assist students in preparation of themes on eugenics."

The transition memo also advised that Laughlin's personal mail should be forwarded to his new home: 201 West Normal Avenue, Kirksville, Missouri. In his retirement, Laughlin returned to his early roots, living quietly in the small town where he had first absorbed his mother's fiery reform spirit—and where, as a college student, he had written a term paper predicting that "eventually the world will be inhabited by an enlightened race, Caucasian in blood, Christian in religion and free in government."

Laughlin no longer concerned himself with germplasm, biological immigration policy, eugenic sterilization, or guarding the nation against refugees fleeing Nazi Germany. He devoted his final days to leisurely, small-town pursuits, including building a new house and gardening. On January 26, 1943—a little more than a year after his country formally declared war on the German regime he admired so much—Laughlin died, at the age of sixty-two.

Holmes was eighty-six years old when he delivered the Supreme Court's decision in *Buck v. Bell*. He no longer had the fire of youth that led him into battle with the Harvard Regiment, or the burning ambition that caused William James to describe him as gouging "a deep self-beneficial groove through life." Holmes was still, however, a man of strong principles and committed to acting on them. After the ruling, he told his friend Harold Laski of the satisfaction he took from the case. "I wrote and delivered a decision upholding the constitutionality of a state law for sterilizing imbeciles the other day," he wrote, "and felt that I was getting near to the first principle of real reform."

Holmes would live nearly another eight years, and remain on the court for almost five. He did not return to eugenic sterilization in his judicial work or legal writings. Holmes's final years on the court were filled with other matters, both great and inconsequential, and the quiet process of winding down a legendary career in the law.

In August 1927 Holmes was asked to enter the controversy over Nicola Sacco and Bartolomeo Vanzetti, the Boston anarchists who had been convicted of murder and sentenced to death. Their supporters contended that they were victims of ethnic and political prejudice.

Sacco and Vanzetti's lawyers showed up at Holmes's summer home asking him to block their clients' execution, but he refused, insisting it was not a matter for the federal courts. Many leading progressives championed the men's innocence, including old friends like Felix Frankfurter, but Holmes was unmoved. Privately, he scorned all the fuss, saying the case had simply given "the reds a chance to howl."

Holmes wrote several major opinions in his final years. When Taft wrote for the majority in *Olmstead v. United States* upholding the conviction of a bootlegger based on phone calls recorded with a warrantless wiretap, Holmes delivered a famous dissent that liberals cheered. "I think it a less evil that some criminals should escape," he said, "than that the Government should play an ignoble part." As he entered his late eighties, Holmes remained devoted to his duties, but he showed signs of decline—falling asleep at work and expressing frustration at his own "muddle-headed" thinking at oral arguments. It was a great blow when Fanny died suddenly in April 1929, after taking a bad fall and breaking a hip.

The following month, Holmes dissented in another important civil liberties case. Rosika Schwimmer, a Hungarian pacifist, was barred from immigrating because she would not take an oath to defend the United States. The majority in *United States v. Schwimmer* upheld the decision, and Holmes wrote a dissent with another of his famous aphorisms: "the principle of free thought" is "not free thought for those who agree with us but freedom for the thought that we hate."

In March 1931 Holmes turned ninety. It was increasingly clear to some of his colleagues that he could no longer adequately perform his duties, and the chief justice approached him in January 1932 and asked him to retire. Holmes did not resist or delay in writing a formal note to the president. He was stepping down with "deep regret," he said, but "the time has come and I bow to the inevitable."

In retirement, Holmes read and greeted visitors—most notably, on his ninety-second birthday, Franklin Roosevelt, who had just been sworn in as president. With his work on the court behind him, Holmes withdrew from the world, even when Felix Frankfurter tried to interest him in events of the day. "It's all very remote to me," he told his old friend. "I'm dead," he said. "I'm like a ghost on the battlefield with bullets flying through me." Holmes died of pneumonia on March 6, 1935, two days shy of his ninety-fourth birthday. The *New York Times* reported his death on its front page, with a large photograph. The headline hailed Holmes as the Supreme Court's "Chief Liberal," and the obituary did not mention *Buck v. Bell*.

Fifteen years after *Buck v. Bell*, the Supreme Court revisited eugenic sterilization. In *Skinner v. Oklahoma*, the court considered a challenge to Oklahoma's Habitual Criminal Sterilization Act, which provided for sterilization of people convicted of at least two felonies involving moral turpitude. A prisoner facing sterilization claimed, among other things, that the law was not within Oklahoma's police power "in view of the state of scientific authorities respecting inheritability of criminal traits."

The case arrived at the Supreme Court in 1942, at a time when at least some of the horrors occurring in Germany were known, and when the nation was fighting a world war to defeat Nazism. The inmate's claim gave the court a chance to overrule *Buck v. Bell* and declare that the American Constitution did not allow the state to engage in this sort of bodily mutilation, or to deprive people of the right to have children for committing two nonviolent crimes. The Supreme Court, however, declined to issue a sweeping ruling.

The court struck down Oklahoma's sterilization statute on narrow grounds. William O. Douglas, writing for the majority, said the law violated the equal protection clause of the Fourteenth Amendment because it did not draw a proper line between crimes of moral turpitude and other crimes. The court noted that the law included theft but not embezzlement, so a stranger who stole $20 from a store would be guilty of a crime of moral turpitude, but a clerk who worked at the same store and embezzled $20 would not. These "conspicuously artificial lines" violated equal protection, the court said. The seven justices who signed only the majority opinion raised no larger objections to the sterilization itself.

Neither did the two justices who wrote separate concurring opinions. Chief Justice Harlan Fiske Stone argued that the law violated due process because the inmate being sterilized was not given a proper hearing. Robert H. Jackson thought the law violated both equal protection and due process. Jackson, who would soon take a leave from the court to prosecute Nazis at the Nuremberg trials, came the closest to challenging the state's right to engage in eugenic sterilization. He stated that there were "limits to the extent to which a legislatively represented majority may conduct biological experiments at the expense of the dignity and personality and natural powers of a minority." Rather than think about what those limits might be, however, Jackson said he would "reserve judgment."

The decision in *Skinner v. Oklahoma* was not intended to overturn or even limit *Buck v. Bell*. Douglas, the author of the majority opinion, confirmed the limited nature of the ruling in an interview decades later. "I thought that this kind of legislation was permissible and constitutional," he said, "but that it had to be surrounded by very careful procedural safeguards lest it be used oppressively or arbitrarily."

In fact, *Buck v. Bell* remains good law, and courts have continued to cite it into the twenty-first century. In 2001 Margaret Vaughn, a young woman who had been labeled mildly mentally retarded, sued Columbia County, Missouri, for trying to force her to be sterilized. In *Vaughn v. Ruoff*, the U.S. Court of Appeals for the Eighth Circuit explained that "involuntary sterilization is not always unconstitutional." The state had to have a good reason for the sterilization, the court said, and there had to be appropriate "procedural protections." As authority for the correctness of its constitutional analysis, the Eighth Circuit cited *Buck v. Bell*.

Neither the Supreme Court's ruling in *Skinner* nor the revelations of eugenic sterilization abuses in Nazi Germany brought an end to sterilization in America. In the post-*Skinner*, post–World War II years, the number of sterilizations rose. In 1944, a year and a half after the court struck down Oklahoma's sterilization law, there were 1,183 sterilizations nationally, and the number increased over the next two years, to 1,476 in 1946. By 1950 there were 1,526. After *Buck v. Bell* was decided, Virginia carried out eugenic sterilization on a mass scale, and that continued through the 1940s and 1950s. As late as 1958, Virginia state hospitals were still sterilizing more than one hundred inmates a year.

It was only in the 1960s, when popular attitudes toward marginalized groups, including the developmentally disabled, changed, that sterilization began to lose favor. From 1965 to 1979, at least fifteen states repealed laws, and in 1973 Alabama's sterilization statute was ruled unconstitutional. In Virginia, sterilization began to decline, but it took a long time to disappear entirely. In 1974 the legislature repealed the 1924 law, but other statutory provisions allowing for sterilization of people with hereditary mental defects remained on the books until 1979. The colony performed two sterilizations in 1978, and two more in 1979, the last year it had the legal authority to do so. Nationally, Oregon was among the last holdouts. It ordered its final forced sterilization in 1981 and abolished its Board of Eugenics—renamed the Board of Social Protection—in 1983.

By the end of the twentieth century, legal eugenic sterilization had come to an end, but the number of Americans who had been involuntarily sterilized between 1907 and 1983 was staggering: between sixty and seventy thousand. That number included at least 7,450 people in Virginia, which made the state—and, in particular, the Colony for Epileptics and Feeble-Minded—one of the nation's busiest centers for eugenic sterilization. Virginia was not, however, the most active state: that title went to California, which sterilized about twenty thousand people. California's nation-leading numbers were due in large part to a statute that did not give inmates an adequate mechanism for challenging sterilization orders—as well as the willingness of the state's hospitals to sterilize people for a wide array of minor "defects."

The names of most of the sixty to seventy thousand victims are lost to history. Unlike Carrie and Doris, many never even got the grim satisfaction of being told what their government had done to them. For the subjects, sterilization took a profound personal toll. "I see people with babies and I think how much I would have loved to have a young one," a sixty-two-year-old woman sterilized in North Carolina told a reporter. "It should have been my choice whether I wanted to have a baby or not," she said. "You just feel like you were held back, like you never had any say in your life."

The pendulum has swung strongly against eugenic sterilization, but the question remains: will it swing back? The philosophy of Dr. Priddy and Laughlin lives on, and periodically it comes to the fore. In 2013 the Center for Investigative Reporting discovered that California had been coercing female prisoners to get salpingectomies as recently as 2010. A year later, the first vice chairman of the Arizona Republican Party, a former state senator, was forced to resign after he publicly called for the sterilization of women on public assistance. And in the spring of 2015, the Associated Press reported that Nashville prosecutors were making sterilization part of plea negotiations with female defendants.

If eugenic sterilization becomes a national movement again, it could, like the last time, be driven by advances in genetics. The Human Genome Project, a massive international research effort, is aiming to map every human gene, and it is already providing vast new amounts of data and insights about hereditary traits. Scientists have raised concerns. One study in the *American Journal of Human Genetics* cautioned that "there is a significant risk that there will be an increased sentiment for instituting eugenic measures in the United States." The official website of the federal government's National Human Genome Research Institute notes that the eugenic implications of the Human Genome Project must be "carefully studied."

There have been major advances in recent years in "DNA editing." Scientists have begun to talk of an era of "designer" babies, whose DNA will be edited to remove genes associated with diseases and other disfavored traits—and perhaps edited to add more desirable traits. This technology could raise an array of eugenics issues, from whether parents should be allowed to modify the embryos of their future children to whether the government should be allowed to require it.

The intellectual origins of eugenics trace back to the Darwinian revolution of nineteenth-century England. In *On the Origin of Species* and *The Descent of Man,* Darwin explained the role competition and natural selection played in the animal world and in human progress. Francis Galton, Darwin's half cousin, fashioned these ideas into a theory that called on society to help human progress along by giving "the more suitable races or strains of blood" a better chance of prevailing.

It was an idea that had strong appeal in America, particularly during the 1920s, when the middle and upper classes felt threatened by mass immigration, urbanization, and other forces that were profoundly disrupting the social order. Like many movements, eugenics attracted different people for different reasons. Progressives saw in it a way for government to use science to reform society. Conservatives saw in it a confirmation of their view that there were inherent differences among people, and that not everyone could be lifted up simply by improving their economic situation or environment.

Eugenics offered Dr. Albert Priddy, as he saw it, a way of achieving his life's mission: improving the mental health of Virginians. Like many doctors nationwide, he believed eugenic sterilization provided an elegant, scientific way of ending feeblemindedness. He also used it as a tool to elevate his profession of superintendent. Rather than waste time and resources trying to cure patients who showed few signs of improvement, he would use sterilization to turn the colony into a "clearing house" that could drive a major improvement in the state's germplasm—with the goal of eradicating inherited mental defects.

For Harry Laughlin, who was driven by a combination of missionary zeal and deep-seated bigotry, eugenics was a secular religion, and he was one of its greatest evangelists. Laughlin believed the nation was threatened by defective germplasm, and he saw traces of it everywhere: in the feebleminded, in Jewish and Italian immigrants, and in many other varieties of "deficient" people, including epileptics—a group to which he himself belonged. Laughlin sought to use sterilization and other eugenic tools to extirpate the "lowest one-tenth" and redeem a fallen nation.

For Aubrey Strode, the dutiful lawyer and moderate reformer, eugenics was not a passion, or even a deeply held belief, but primarily a subject to which to apply his formidable legal skills. At various junctures, he passed on the opportunity to promote a program of eugenic sterilization, slowed down its adoption, and narrowed its scope. Of course, Strode could have refused to have anything to do with eugenic sterilization, or he could have actively opposed it, if he believed it was morally wrong. Instead, in his slow and deliberate way, he secured the biggest legal victory for eugenics in American history.

Eugenics held a special appeal for people at the top of society's hierarchies, like Oliver Wendell Holmes Jr., who were convinced they belonged there. Born into Boston's elite—its Brahmin class, to use his father's term—Holmes believed his elevated status was part of the natural order. As he saw it, people who were not winning the great struggle of life—whether they were gas stokers striking in England, or black people in Alabama trying to vote—deserved to lose. It followed easily on this philosophy that society's weakest members should be prevented from creating more of their own kind.

These were the intellectual currents that Carrie Buck stumbled into when she had the misfortune to be born into a poor family, to be taken in by a heartless foster family, to be raped, and to be falsely labeled feebleminded. She was committed to the Colony for Epileptics and Feeble-Minded, and attracted the attention of Dr. Priddy, at just the wrong time. Carrie was not allowed to be an actor in her own story—no one had any interest in telling her what was at stake in the historic legal conflict. In the only words she was recorded as saying in the proceedings over her sterilization, Carrie told Strode and the

Amherst County Circuit Court that she would leave her fate "up to my people." Carrie never understood—and no one ever explained to her—that there was no one on her side.

In an era when so much of America was caught up in social Darwinism, and channeling ideas about survival of the fittest into a cruel biological ideology, few paused to contemplate what Charles Darwin himself had said on the subject. In *The Descent of Man,* he conceded there might well be practical advantages to abandoning "the weak and helpless." But doing so, he insisted, also brought with it "an overwhelming present evil." We must allow the weak to "surviv[e] and propagat[e] their kind," Darwin insisted. Doing anything less, he said, would mean abandoning not only the weak and the helpless but "the noblest part of our nature."

Acknowledgments

Book writing holds many pleasures, and surprises both negative and positive. In writing this one, an unfortunate surprise came early on when a helpful librarian at the University of Virginia informed me that I was welcome to use the Aubrey Strode papers—but that I should know in advance that there were 158 boxes of them, and they were not organized in any way. A happier surprise came when I was looking for the original *Buck v. Bell* files in the Amherst County Courthouse. When the clerk's search turned up nothing in the courthouse's neatly organized 1924 file drawers, she asked if this was a "famous case." When I said it was, she called out to a colleague to get out "that box under your desk"—and I was handed a cardboard box overflowing with history.

Although writing can be a solitary endeavor, no one completes a nonfiction book without an enormous amount of help—including from those who came before. Anyone working on *Buck v. Bell* follows in the formidable footsteps of Paul Lombardo, who wrote his doctoral dissertation on Strode, and essential books and law review articles on the case, and on eugenics more broadly. Professor Lombardo's work was a constant source of inspiration and guidance. I also benefited from excellent scholarship on the case by J. David Smith and K. Ray Nelson, Harry Bruinius, Victoria Nourse, and Walter Berns; on eugenics by Daniel Kevles, Gregory Michael Dorr, Steven Noll, Philip R. Reilly, Edwin Black, Randall Hansen, Desmond King, Edward J. Larson, and Stephen Jay Gould; on Harry Laughlin by Garland

E. Allen and Frances Hassencahl; and on Oliver Wendell Holmes by G. Edward White, Liva Baker, Sheldon Novick, Yosal Rogat, Albert Alschuler, and Mary Dudziak.

In the author's daunting task of trying to understand long-ago events, librarians are the unsung heroes. The keepers of the Aubrey Strode Papers at the Albert and Shirley Small Special Collections Library, University of Virginia were patient and kind. The librarians at Truman State University's Pickler Memorial Library were incredibly helpful—including on sites to see in and around Kirksville, Missouri. I am also indebted to the Library of Virginia, which holds the papers of the Virginia Colony for Epileptics and Feeble-Minded; the University at Albany library, where the Arthur Estabrook papers reside; the American Philosophical Society library in Philadelphia, which has the Charles Davenport papers; the New York Public Library, whose vast and well-deployed resources were invaluable; the Amherst County Clerk's Office; and the Virginia State Law Library—with a special thanks to Ben Almoite.

In turning thoughts and ideas into a book, editors and publishers are an author's greatest allies. I do not know what good deeds I did in a past life to deserve the legendary Ann Godoff as both my editor and my publisher. Penguin has been brilliant and wonderfully supportive on every aspect of this book. When Ann sent me the cover design her team came up with for me to weigh in on, she wrote with typical panache that she was "mad about" it. Well, I am mad about her. Much gratitude to my amazing copy editor, Maureen Clark, who made everything better and saved me from so many troubles, and to the excellent Casey Rasch, Bruce Giffords, William Heyward, and Juliana Kiyan. Those good deeds in a past life also got me the best literary agent there is, Kris Dahl of ICM, to whom I am unendingly grateful.

Friends have been a source of enormous pleasure and immeasurable support as I worked on this book. Liz Taylor has been my partner in literary crime since, so many years ago, she was transferred to Chicago and called to tell me that there was no major biography of Mayor Richard J. Daley—a gap we worked together to fill. Paul Engelmayer has been a wonderful friend since our college newspaper days. I was fortunate that such a remarkable thinker and writer, who also happens to be a federal judge, took the time to read the whole manuscript and provide insightful comments.

Great and brilliant friends were willing to listen, again and again, to my half-formed thoughts about eugenic theory, due process and the police power, and the folkways of Boston Brahmins—and to drag me away from it all with dinners around New York City; excursions to Woods Hole, Fire Island, North Salem, East Hampton, Park Slope, and Montgomery, Alabama; and, of course, the incomparable annual Engelmayer fishing trip—all settings where it was mercifully difficult to work on footnotes. Much appreciation and love to Michael Abramowitz, Caroline Arnold, Elisabeth Benjamin, Noah Benjamin-Pollak, Kathy Bishop, Tony Blinken, Lavea Brachman, Amy Chua, Carolyn Curiel, Claudia Dowling, Michael Dubno, Loren Eng, Laura Franco, Patti Galluzzi, Amy Goodman, Jason Grumet, Amy Gutman, Laura Haight, Eileen Hershenov, Matthew Klein, Mark Kirch, Aisha Labi, Maria Laurino, Barbara Maddux, Emily Mandelstam, Peter Mandelstam, Carol Owens, P. J. Posner, David Propp, Jim Rosenthal, Jed Rubenfeld, Dorothy Samuels, Amy Schwartz, David Shipley, Tina Smith, Shan Sullivan, Mindy Tarlow, Olivia Turner, Peter Vigeland, Eric Washburn, and Maya Wiley.

Family was an unending source of support and inspiration—my wonderful father, Stuart Cohen; brothers Harlan and Noam; sister-in-law Aviva Michaelov; and those magical new arrivals, Kika and Nuli, who light up any room they enter.

While I was working on this book, the world lost three people who cared deeply about the issues it raises. Charles M. Young was an enormously gifted writer, a kind soul, and a good friend. Elaine Rivera was an irreplaceable friend and journalistic colleague, and a relentless champion of the Carrie Bucks of the world. Finally, my incomparable mother, Judge Beverly Sher Cohen, was able to read the whole manuscript but not to see it published. The sense of justice that drew me to this book's subject I owe entirely to her.

Notes

INTRODUCTION

1   **"The eugenics movement":** "Virginia Governor Apologizes for Eugenics Law," *USA Today,* May 2, 2002.

2   **"Three generations of imbeciles are enough":** *Buck v. Bell,* 274 U.S. 200, 207 (1927).

2   **"sap the strength":** *Id.* at 207.

2   **the "defective human":** Angela Franks, *Margaret Sanger's Eugenic Legacy: The Control of Female Fertility* (Jefferson, NC: McFarland, 2005), 38.

2   **Alexander Graham Bell became chairman:** "Frontispiece: Alexander Graham Bell as Chairman of the Board of Scientific Directors of the Eugenics Record Office," *Eugenical News,* August 1929.

3   **"forbidden to leave offspring behind them":** Theodore Roosevelt, "Twisted Eugenics," *Outlook,* Jan. 3, 1914, 30–34, 32; Philip R. Reilly, *The Surgical Solution: A History of Involuntary Sterilization in the United States* (Baltimore: Johns Hopkins University Press, 1991), 43.

3   **Prominent scientists formed organizations:** Kenneth Ludmerer, *Genetics and American Society: A Historical Appraisal* (Baltimore: Johns Hopkins University Press, 1972), 92.

3   **Others were more severe:** Nicole H. Rafter, ed., *The Origins of Criminology: A Reader* (New York: Routledge, 2009), 237; Nell Irvin Painter, *The History of White People* (New York: W. W. Norton, 2011), 259.

3   **hereditary improvement:** Daniel Siemens, "The 'True Worship of Life': Changing Notions of Happiness, Morality, and Religion in the United States, 1890–1940," in *Fractured Modernity: America Confronts Modern Times, 1890s to 1940s,* ed. Thomas Welskopp and Alan Lessoff (Munich: Oldenbourg, 2012), 52; Eugene F. Provenzo and John P. Renaud, eds., *Encyclopedia of the Social and Cultural Foundations of Education* (Thousand Oaks, CA: SAGE, 2009), 330; Albert Edward Wiggam, *The Decalogue of Science* (Rockville, MD: Wildside Press, 2012).

3   **Clergymen competed:** "Eugenics Is Theme in Sermon Contest," *Pittsburgh Press,* Feb. 24, 1930.

3   **The "inspiring, the wonderful":** Daniel J. Kevles, *In the Name of Eugenics: Genetics and the Uses of Human Heredity* (Cambridge, MA: Harvard University Press, 1985), 67.

3   **Hollywood released a feature-length horror movie:** Martin Pernick, *The Black Stork: Eugenics and the Death of "Defective" Babies in American Medicine and Motion Pictures Since 1915* (New York: Oxford University Press, 1996), 6.

3   **New York's American Museum of Natural History:** Edwin Black, *War Against the Weak* (New York: Four Walls Eight Windows, 2003), 236.

3   **The congress opened:** Henry Fairfield Osborn, "The Second International Congress of Eugenics: Address of Welcome," *Science* 54 (Oct. 7, 1921): 313.

4   **At the Sesquicentennial Exposition:** Kevles, *In the Name of Eugenics,* 62.

4   **Eugenics was taught:** Siemens, "The 'True Worship of Life,'" 50; Kevles, *In the Name of Eugenics,* 69; *Encyclopedia of the Social and Cultural Foundations of Education,* 330.

4   **Prominent professors were outspoken:** Kerry Soper, "Classical Bodies Versus the Criminal Carnival: Eugenics Ideology in 1930s Popular Art," in *Popular Eugenics: National Efficiency and*

American Mass Culture in the 1930s, ed. Susan Currell and Christina Cogdell (Athens: Ohio University Press, 2006), 278.

4   **"Love or Eugenics":** Kevles, *In the Name of Eugenics,* 58.

4   **The driving force:** Siemens, "The 'True Worship of Life,'" 50.

5   **The eugenicists claimed:** Stephen Jay Gould, *The Mismeasure of Man,* rev. ed. (New York: W. W. Norton, 2006), 195–96.

5   **"Thank God we have":** Ellison DuRant Smith, "Shut the Door," in *A History of the U.S. Political System: Ideas, Interests, and Institutions,* ed. Richard A. Harris and Daniel J. Tichenor (Santa Barbara, CA: ABC-CLIO, 2010), 3:181.

5   **Within six years:** Reilly, *Surgical Solution,* 39.

6   **Fears of "the rising tide of feeblemindedness":** Lewis Terman, "Feeble-Minded Children in the Public Schools of California: The Menace of Feeble-Mindedness," *School and Society* 5 (Feb. 10, 1917): 161–65.

6   **A leading psychologist:** Henry Herbert Goddard, *The Kallikak Family: A Study in the Heredity of Feeble-Mindedness* (New York: Macmillan, 1919), 589.

6   **The eugenicists insisted:** H. H. Laughlin, "Calculations on the Working Out of a Proposed Program of Sterilization," *Official Proceedings of the National Conference on Race Betterment* (Battle Creek, MI: Race Betterment Foundation, 1914), 1:489; Paul A. Lombardo, *Three Generations, No Imbeciles: Eugenics, the Supreme Court, and* Buck v. Bell (Baltimore: Johns Hopkins University Press, 2008), 48.

8   **"Race Suicide for Social Parasites":** William Belfield, "Race Suicide for Social Parasites," *JAMA* 50 (1908): 55; Reilly, *Surgical Solution,* 34.

8   **He was the most prominent advocate:** Harry Laughlin, *Eugenical Sterilization in the United States* (Chicago: Psychopathic Library of the Municipal Court of Chicago, 1922), 489; Lombardo, *Three Generations,* 48.

8   **It was Laughlin:** Laughlin, "Calculation on the Working Out," 489; Lombardo, *Three Generations,* 48.

8   **Scientific American editorialized:** Reilly, *Surgical Solution,* 42.

8   **Some of the nation's leading lawyers:** Mark A. Largent, *Breeding Contempt: The History of Coerced Sterilization in the United States* (New Brunswick, NJ: Rutgers University Press, 2011), 64–65.

9   **The Municipal Court of Chicago:** Reilly, *Surgical Solution,* 63; Laughlin, *Eugenical Sterilization,* v.

9   **Holmes had long been:** Oliver Wendell Holmes, "Ideals and Doubts," *Illinois Law Review* 1 (1915): 10; William Leuchtenburg, *The Supreme Court Reborn: The Constitutional Revolution in the Age of Roosevelt* (New York: Oxford University Press, 1995), 18.

9   **Before the Civil War:** *Scott v. Sandford,* 60 U.S. 393, 403 (1857).

9   **In the Jim Crow era:** *Plessy v. Ferguson,* 163 U.S. 537 (1896).

10   **During World War II:** *Korematsu v. United States,* 323 U.S. 214 (1944).

10   **And midway through the modern gay rights era:** *Bowers v. Hardwick,* 478 U.S. 186, 194 (1986).

10   **a prominent law school dean:** Erwin Chemerinsky, *The Case Against the Supreme Court* (New York: Viking, 2014), 4.

10   **In its aftermath:** Leuchtenburg, *Supreme Court Reborn,* 15.

11   **And at the Nuremberg trials:** Jonathan Peter Spiro, *Defending the Master Race: Conservation, Eugenics, and the Legacy of Madison Grant* (Lebanon, NH: University Press of New England, 2009), 238.

11   **The second edition of American Constitutional Law:** Laurence Tribe, *American Constitutional Law,* 2nd ed. (Mineola, NY: Foundation Press, 1988), 1339.

11   **A recent 953-page biography of Brandeis:** Melvin Urofsky, *Louis D. Brandeis: A Life* (New York: Pantheon, 2009), 874.

11   **Board of Eugenics:** Julie Sullivan, "State of Oregon Will Admit Sterilization Past," *Oregonian,* Nov. 15, 2002; Nadine Attewell, *Better Britons: Reproduction, Nation, and the Afterlife of Empire* (Toronto: University of Toronto Press, 2014), 4.

11   **nearly 150 female prisoners in California:** "Following Reports of Forced Sterilization of Female Prison Inmates, California Passes Ban," *Washington Post,* Sept. 26, 2014.

11   **"the Century of Biology":** Craig Venter and Daniel Cohen, "The Century of Biology," *New Perspectives Quarterly* 21, no. 4 (Nov. 1, 2004): 77.

12   **In a later case:** *Skinner v. Oklahoma,* 316 U.S. 535 (1942).

12   In the twenty-first century: *Vaughn v. Ruoff*, 253 F.3d 1124 (8th Cir. 2001).

12   The Code of Hammurabi: Jackson Spielvogel, *Western Civilization*, vol. 1, *To 1715* (Stamford, CT: Cengage Learning, 2008), 10–11; Hammurabi, *The Code of Hammurabi* (Rockville, MD: Wildside Press, 2009), 7.

13   In the Massachusetts Bay Colony: Donald Black, *The Behavior of Law* (New York: Academic Press, 1976), 21.

13   The legal theorist Donald Black: Ibid.

CHAPTER ONE: CARRIE BUCK

15   She would later recall: J. David Smith and K. Ray Nelson, *The Sterilization of Carrie Buck: Was She Feebleminded or Society's Pawn?* (Far Hills, NJ: New Horizon Press, 1989), 1.

15   an "act of kindness": Petition in the Matter of the Commitment of Carrie E. Buck, an Epileptic and Feebleminded Person, in the Court of the Honorable Charles D. Shackelford, Justice of the Peace and Judge of the Juvenile & Domestic Relations Court for the City of Charlottesville, Virginia, *Buck v. Bell* file, Clerk's Office, Amherst County Courthouse, Amherst, VA

15   it was time for her to leave: Harry Bruinius, *Better for All the World: The Secret History of Forced Sterilization and America's Quest for Racial Purity* (New York: Alfred A. Knopf, 2006), 41, 51–52.

16   John Dobbs made an appointment: "Carrie Buck Trial Transcript, 51–100" (2009), *Buck v. Bell Documents*, Paper 32, http://readingroom.law.gsu.edu/buckvbell/32, 57, 61; Homer Richey to Dr. Albert Priddy, Mar. 10, 1924, Carrie Buck file, Library of Virginia.

16   At their meeting: "Carrie Buck Trial Transcript, 51–100," 57.

16   She had never met Carrie: Ibid., 62.

16   Mrs. Dobbs told Duke: Ibid.

16   Instead, they petitioned: Petition in the Matter of the Commitment of Carrie E. Buck, 121.

16   The term "feebleminded": Victoria Nourse, *"Buck v. Bell:* A Constitutional Tragedy from a Lost Work," *Pepperdine Law Review* 105-6 (2011): 39.

17   The Dobbses' petition: Petition in the Matter of the Commitment of Carrie E. Buck; Paul A. Lombardo, "Eugenic Sterilization in Virginia: Aubrey Strode and the Case of *Buck v. Bell*" (Ph.D. diss., University of Virginia, 1982), 121.

17   Carrie Elizabeth Buck was born: Paul A. Lombardo, *Three Generations, No Imbeciles: Eugenics, the Supreme Court, and* Buck v. Bell (Baltimore: Johns Hopkins University Press, 2008), 103.

17   Charlottesville was the seat of Albemarle County: Jean L. Cooper, *A Guide to Historic Charlottesville & Albemarle County, Virginia* (Charleston, SC: History Press, 2007), 22–24; Lombardo, *Three Generations*, 103.

17   The English who arrived: K. Edward Lay, *The Architecture of Jefferson Country: Charlottesville and Albemarle County* (Charlottesville: University of Virginia Press, 2000), 26; Cooper, *Guide to Historic Albemarle County*, 26–28; Federal Writers' Project, *Virginia: A Guide to the Old Dominion* (Washington, DC: U.S. History Publishers, 1952), 204; Smith and Nelson, *Sterilization of Carrie Buck*, 54.

17   one gratified settler: Federal Writers' Project, *Virginia*, 44.

18   Thomas Jefferson: Lay, *Architecture of Jefferson Country*, 11.

18   They and James Monroe: Gerald Lee Gutek, *Plantations and Outdoor Museums in America's Historic South* (Columbia: University of South Carolina Press, 1996), 305, 309, 350.

18   "the proudest achievement": Garry Wills, *Mr. Jefferson's University* (Washington, DC: National Geographic Society, 2002), 7.

18   When Jefferson was a student: Ibid., 25.

18   Jefferson resolved to infuse: Natalie Bober, *Thomas Jefferson: Draftsman of a Nation* (Charlottesville: University of Virginia Press, 2008), 290.

18   It was now primarily: Gregory Michael Dorr, *Segregation's Science: Eugenics and Society in Virginia* (Charlottesville: University of Virginia Press, 2008), 48–49; "Edwin A. Alderman," in *Dictionary of North Carolina Biography*, ed. William S. Powell (Chapel Hill: University of North Carolina Press, 1979); Federal Writers' Project, *Virginia*, 205.

19   "southern poor white caste": Wayne Flynt, *Dixie's Forgotten People* (Bloomington: Indiana University Press, 2009), 38.

19   In the post–Civil War South: Ibid., 62.

19   Carrie's paternal grandfather: Harry Bruinius, *Better for All the World: The Secret History of Forced Sterilization and America's Quest for Racial Purity* (New York: Alfred A. Knopf, 2006), 26; "History and Clinical Notes," June 4, 1924, box 11, Carrie Buck file, Library of Virginia.

19   Carrie Buck's mother: Bruinius, *Better for All the World*, 6; Lombardo, *Three Generations*, 105.

19   **Her father, Richard Harlowe:** Lombardo, *Three Generations,* 105–6; Bruinius, *Better for All the World,* 26–27; "History and Clinical Notes," June 4, 1924.

19   **Records at the Colony:** "History and Clinical Notes," June 4, 1924; Petition in the Matter of the Commitment of Carrie E. Buck; Lombardo, *Three Generations,*105–6.

19   **Whatever the reason:** Smith and Nelson, *Sterilization of Carrie Buck,* 1–2; "History and Clinical Notes," June 4, 1924.

20   **a single woman:** Edward L. Ayers, *Southern Crossing: A History of the American South, 1877–1906* (New York: Oxford University Press, 1995), 44.

20   **The people who would:** Bruinius, *Better for All the World,* 28; Lombardo, *Three Generations,* 105–6; Courtney Beale, "Brothels Shaped Charlottesville's History," *Charlottesville Tomorrow,* June 1, 2012.

20   **Anne Harris, a nurse:** "Carrie Buck Trial Transcript, 51–100," 43.

20   **Emma and her baby:** Ibid.

20   **In the absence of a husband:** Bruinius, *Better for All the World,* 26–27; Lombardo, *Three Generations,* 105–6.

20   **Harris recalled:** "Carrie Buck Trial Transcript, 51–100," 43.

20   **There was growing sentiment:** Anthony Platt, *The Child Savers: The Invention of Delinquency* (Chicago: University of Chicago Press, 1977), 3; Marilyn Irvin Holt, "Adoption Reform, Orphan Trains, and Child-Saving, 1851–" in *Children and Youth in Adoption, Orphanages, and Foster Care: A Historical Handbook and Guide,* ed. Lori Askeland (Westport, CT: Greenwood, 2006); Tim Hacsi, "From Indenture to Family Foster Care," in *A History of Child Welfare,* ed. Eve P. Smith and Lisa A. Merkel-Holguin (New York: Child Welfare League of America 1996), 164.

20   **Reformers had pushed:** Hacsi, "From Indenture to Family Foster Care," 165.

20   **When the municipal court:** Bruinius, *Better for All the World,* 40–41; Edwin Black, *War Against the Weak* (New York: Four Walls Eight Windows, 2003), 109.

21   **Carrie called her foster parents:** Smith and Nelson, *Sterilization of Carrie Buck,* 2.

21   **Carrie's school records:** Ibid.; Lombardo, *Three Generations,* 105.

21   **Her last teacher:** Smith and Nelson, *Sterilization of Carrie Buck,* 3; "Carrie Buck Trial Transcript, 51–100," 46; Black, *War Against the Weak,* 109.

21   **In some southern states:** William J. Cooper Jr. and Thomas E. Terill, *The American South: A History* (Lanham, MD: Rowman and Littlefield, 2009), 616.

21   **John Spargo:** John Spargo, *The Bitter Cry of the Children* (1906; repr., New York: Macmillan, 1915), 147–48; Richard Hofstadter, *The Progressive Movement, 1900–1915* (Englewood Cliffs, NJ: Prentice-Hall, 1963), 39.

21   **Parents "should be left alone":** Ayers, *Southern Crossing,* 176.

21   **She was also now available:** Smith and Nelson, *Sterilization of Carrie Buck,* 3; Lombardo, *Three Generations* 103; Bruinius, *Better for All the World,* 51.

22   **Carrie's day-to-day existence:** Smith and Nelson, *Sterilization of Carrie Buck,* 2–3.

22   **Emma was taken:** Bruinius, *Better for All the World,* 40; Black, *War Against the Weak,* 108; Smith and Nelson, *Sterilization of Carrie Buck,* 7.

22   **Emma could have been accused:** Smith and Nelson, *Sterilization of Carrie Buck,* 8–9.

22   **Emma's life history:** Ibid., 10–12.

22   **After hearing all the evidence:** Ibid., 12; Bruinius, *Better for All the World,* 40.

22   **The court directed:** Smith and Nelson, *Sterilization of Carrie Buck,* 15; Bruinius, *Better for All the World,* 41.

22   **On her arrival:** Bruinius, *Better for All the World,* 41.

23   **She was found to be suffering:** Lombardo, *Three Generations,* 105–6; Black, *War Against the Weak,* 108.

23   **The examiner observed:** Lombardo, *Three Generations,* 106.

23   **The records included a list:** Smith and Nelson, *Sterilization of Carrie Buck,* 15.

23   **intelligence test:** Bruinius, *Better for All the World,* 41–42.

23   **On the basis:** Lombardo, *Three Generations,* 106.

23   **The Commission of Feeblemindedness:** *Buck v. Priddy,* Argument and Submission and Order, Nov. 18, 1924, "Carrie Buck Trial Transcript, 1–50" (2009), *Buck v. Bell Documents,* Paper 31; Lombardo, *Three Generations,* 104.

23   **Though it should not have been relevant:** Petition in the Matter of the Commitment of Carrie E. Buck.

24 **The Dobbses said Carrie:** Smith and Nelson, *Sterilization of Carrie Buck* 3; Black, *War Against the Weak,* 109.

24 **Years later:** John Bell to Mrs. Allen T. Newberry, Feb. 22, 1928, Carrie Buck file, Library of Virginia.

24 **During the visit:** Lombardo, *Three Generations,* 140–41.

24 **"I didn't run around":** Smith and Nelson, *Sterilization of Carrie Buck,* 3–5.

24 **Carrie said that after Clarence:** Lombardo, *Three Generations,* 140; interview of Paul Lombardo, DNA Learning Center, http://www.dnalc.org/view/15234-The-rape-of-Carrie-Buck -Paul-Lombardo.html.

25 **These problems:** Smith and Nelson, *Sterilization of Carrie Buck,* 5; Lombardo, *Three Generations,* 141.

25 *The Survey:* Steven Noll, *Feeble-Minded in Our Midst* (Chapel Hill: University of North Carolina Press, 1995), 1, 5.

25 **In 1904, 17.3 feebleminded people:** Ibid., 4, 25–26.

25 **The medical establishment:** Leuchtenburg, *The Supreme Court Reborn,* 7.

26 **Hastings Hart:** Noll, *Feeble-Minded in Our Midst,* 15–16.

26 **Henry Goddard:** Melissa A. Bray and Thomas J. Kehle, eds., *The Oxford Handbook of School Psychology* (Oxford: Oxford University Press, 2011), 27.

26 **Because of these concerns:** Noll, *Feeble-Minded in Our Midst,* 16.

26 **She was in her seventh month:** Findings and Adjudication of the Commission, Special Board of Directors of State Colony for Epileptics and Feeble-Minded, Jan. 23, 1924, "Carrie Buck Trial Transcript, 1–50" (2009), *Buck v. Bell Documents,* Paper 31, http://readingroom.law.gsu.edu/ buckvbell/31, 18-19; "Carrie Buck Adjudged 'Feeble-minded or Epileptic,'" Jan. 23, 1924, http://www.encyclopediavirginia.org/Carrie_Buck_Adjudged_Feeble-minded_or_Epileptic _January_23_1924.

26 **Dr. J. C. Coulter:** Lombardo, *Three Generations,* 104.

27 **Emma, who was by now:** Warrant, J. T. Dobbs, Special Constable of the City of Charlottesville, Jan. 23, 1924, "Carrie Buck Trial Transcript, 1–50" (2009), *Buck v. Bell Documents,* Paper 31, http://readingroom.law.gsu.edu/buckvbell/31, 21.

27 **In brief written findings:** Findings and Adjudication of the Commission, "Carrie Buck Trial Transcript, 1–50."

27 **Judge Shackelford then ordered** "Order of Commitment, Special Board of Directors of State Colony for Epileptics and Feeble-Minded," Jan. 23, 1924, "Carrie Buck Trial Transcript, 1–50" (2009), *Buck v. Bell Documents,* Paper 31, http://readingroom.law.gsu.edu/buckvbell/31.

27 **Mrs. Dobbs wanted:** Caroline Wilhelm to Albert Priddy, Mar. 11, 1924, Carrie Buck file, Library of Virginia; Lombardo, *Three Generations,* 104; "Carrie Buck Trial Transcript, 51–100," 59.

27 **It was long past time:** Richey to Priddy, Mar. 10, 1924.

27 **Caroline Wilhelm:** Bruinius, *Better for All the World,* 52; Smith and Nelson, *Sterilization of Carrie Buck,* 105; "Carrie Buck Trial Transcript, 51–100," 57.

27 **Carrie was due to give birth:** Wilhelm to Priddy, Mar. 11, 1924; Lombardo, *Three Generations,* 104.

28 **The superintendent, Dr. Albert Priddy:** Albert Priddy to Caroline Wilhelm, Mar. 14, 1924, Carrie Buck file, Library of Virginia.

28 **On March 28:** Lombardo, *Three Generations,* 104.

28 **She wrote Dr. Priddy:** Caroline Wilhelm to Albert Priddy, May 5, 1924, Carrie Buck file, Library of Virginia.

28 **They emphasized, however:** Ibid.; Lombardo, *Three Generations,* 104–5.

28 **Dr. Priddy did not care:** Albert Priddy to Caroline Wilhelm, May 7, 1924, Carrie Buck file, Library of Virginia; Bruinius, *Better for all the World,* 53.

28 **On June 4:** Caroline Wilhelm to Albert Priddy, May 25, 1924, box 11, Central Virginia Training Center Papers, Library of Virginia; Albert Priddy to Caroline Wilhelm, May 27, 1924, box 11, Central Virginia Training Center Papers, Library of Virginia; Bruinius, *Better for all the World,* 53.

28 **Wilhelm escorted Carrie:** Caroline Wilhelm to Dr. Priddy, May 30, 1924, box 11, Central Virginia Training Center Papers, Library of Virginia.

29 **Lynchburg, which was then:** Clifton W. Potter and Dorothy Bundy Turner Potter, *Lynchburg: A City Set on Seven Hills* (Mount Pleasant, SC: Arcadia, 2004), 124–26.

29 **After disembarking at Union Station:** Caroline Wilhelm to Albert Priddy, May 30, 1924,

box 11, Central Virginia Training Center Papers, Library of Virginia; Lombardo, *Three Generations*, 104–5.

29 **Despite its somber mission:** *State Colony for Epileptics and Feeble-Minded: Second Biennial Report*, 15-16, box 7, Central Virginia Training Center Papers; Smith and Nelson, *Sterilization of Carrie Buck*, 39–41.

29 **The rustic surroundings:** Smith and Nelson, *Sterilization of Carrie Buck*, 40.

29 **Out in the country:** Noll, *Feeble-Minded in Our Midst*, 25–26.

29 **Inmates were able:** Dorr, *Segregation's Science*, 120.

29 **When states throughout the South:** Edward J. Larson, *Sex, Race, and Science: Eugenics in the Deep South* (Baltimore: Johns Hopkins University Press, 1995), 94–95.

29 **The "History and Clinical Notes" drawn up:** "History and Clinical Notes," June 4, 1924.

30 **The next day, Dr. John Bell:** "Physical Examination of a Patient on Admission to the State Colony," June 5, 1924, Carrie Buck file, Library of Virginia.

30 **Carrie's admissions records:** "History and Clinical Notes," June 4, 1924.

30 **In evaluating Carrie's intellect:** Ibid.

30 **Based on it:** Ibid.; Smith and Nelson, *Sterilization of Carrie Buck*, 44.

30 **It had been invented:** Stephen J. Gould, *The Mismeasure of Man* (New York: W. W. Norton, 1981), 149.

30 **Binet and another psychologist:** George Domino and Maria L. Domino, *Psychological Testing: An Introduction* (Cambridge: Cambridge University Press, 2006), 100.

30 **"One might almost say":** Gould, *Mismeasure of Man*, 149.

31 **They established a scale:** Anna Cianciolo and Robert J. Sternberg, *Intelligence: A Brief History* (New York: John Wiley and Sons, 2008), 34; Domino and Domino, *Psychological Testing*, 101; Daniel J. Kevles, *In the Name of Eugenics: Genetics and the Uses of Human Heredity* (Cambridge, MA: Harvard University Press, 1985), 77.

31 **"to identify in order to help and improve":** Gould, *Mismeasure of Man*, 152.

31 **"They have neither sympathy":** Ibid., 183.

31 **The man who launched:** Kevles, *In the Name of Eugenics*, 77.

31 **"The tests":** John Carson, *The Measure of Merit: Talents, Intelligence, and Inequality in the French and American Republics, 1750–1940* (Princeton, NJ: Princeton University Press, 2007) 178.

31 **"hierarchical, unidimensional vision of intelligence":** Ibid., 179.

31 **"Each human being":** Leila Zenderland, *Measuring Minds: Henry Herbert Goddard and the Origins of American Intelligence Testing* (Cambridge: Cambridge University Press, 1998), 301.

32 **Goddard redefined the field:** Michael L. Wehmeyer, ed., *The Oxford Handbook of Positive Psychology and Disability* (Oxford: Oxford University Press, 2013), 5.

32 **At the bottom of Goddard's pyramid:** William Estabrook Chancellor, "The Measurement of Human Ability," *Journal of Education* 77, no. 16 (April 17, 1913): 425–26; Kevles, *In the Name of Eugenics*, 78; Henry Herbert Goddard, *The Kallikak Family: A Study in the Heredity of Feeble-Mindedness* (New York: Macmillan, 1919), 101–2; Wehmeyer, *Oxford Handbook of Positive Psychology and Disability*, 5.

32 **"Morons are often":** Henry Herbert Goddard, *Feeble-Mindedness: Its Causes and Consequences* (New York: Macmillan, 1926), 4.

32 **Intellectual deficiencies, he insisted:** Goddard, *The Kallikak Family*, 53; Gould, *Mismeasure of Man*, 159.

32 **Terman added new questions:** Nicholas Mackintosh, *IQ and Human Intelligence* (Oxford: Oxford University Press, 2011), 16.

32 **Terman also introduced:** Mackintosh, *IQ and Human Intelligence*, 16.

32 **The Binet-Simon was presented:** Stephen Jay Gould, "A Nation of Morons," *New Scientist* (May 6 1982): 349.

33 **According to the "Record Sheet":** "Record Sheet for the Standard Revision of the Binet Simon Tests," Carrie Buck and Doris Buck Figgins Sterilization, ca. 1920s–1980s file, Central Virginia Training Center Papers.

33 **Cyril Burt:** Cyril Burt, *Mental and Scholastic Tests* (London: P. S. King and Son, 1922), 175, 198–99; Kevles, *In the Name of Eugenics*, 337–38.

33 **"Intelligence," an article in *Mental Hygiene*:** Maurice B. Hexter and Abraham Myerson, "13.77 Versus 12.05: A Study in Probable Error; A Critical Review of Brigham's *American Intelligence*," *Mental Hygiene* 8 (1924), quoted in James Trent, *Who Shall Say Who Is a Useful Person?* (Dearborn, MI: Alpha Academic Press, 2001), 42.

33 **"Not a single one of these persons":** Noll, *Feeble-Minded in Our Midst*, 31–32.

33 **Goddard administered the Binet-Simon:** Stephen Jay Gould, *The Mismeasure of Man* (New York: W. W. Norton, 1981), 165–66.

34 **"We cannot escape":** Ibid., 166–67.

34 **Yerkes worked with Terman:** Ibid., 194–95.

34 **Yerkes found:** Victoria Nourse, *In Reckless Hands: Skinner v. Oklahoma and the Near Triumph of American Eugenics* (New York: W. W. Norton, 2008), 25.

34 **Yerkes's results:** Ibid., 25.

34 **"a nation of morons":** Gould, "A Nation of Morons," 349.

34 **Carrie was assigned:** Smith and Nelson, *Sterilization of Carrie Buck*, 40.

35 **Carrie was reunited:** Ibid., 41.

35 **Carrie also kept in touch:** Ibid.; Lombardo, *Three Generations* 106.

CHAPTER TWO: ALBERT PRIDDY

37 **Albert Sidney Priddy was born:** Transactions of the Forty-Third Annual Session of the Medical Society of Virginia (Richmond, VA: The Richmond Press, 1913), 393.

37 **The Civil War had ended:** "Draft Resolutions to Honor A. S. Priddy," enclosed with letter of Aubrey Strode to S. L. Ferguson, May 5, 1925, box 90, Aubrey Strode Papers, Albert and Shirley Small Special Collections Library, University of Virginia (hereafter cited as Strode Papers); Cheryl A. Veselik, *Superintendents and Directors of Southwestern Virginia Mental Health Institute* (Marion, VA: Southwestern Virginia Mental Health Institute, 2012).

37 **The Priddys soon moved:** "Tribute to Albert Sidney Priddy," in "16th Annual Report of the State Colony for Epileptics and Feeble-Minded, 1924–1925," box 17, Central Virginia Training Center Papers, Library of Virginia.

37 **Young Albert began:** "Charlotte County, Virginia: Historical Notes of Town of Keysville," http://genealogytrails.com/vir/charlotte/hist_keysville_historicalnotes.html; "Tribute to Albert Sidney Priddy"; J. David Smith and K. Ray Nelson, *The Sterilization of Carrie Buck: Was She Feebleminded or Society's Pawn?* (Far Hills, NJ: New Horizon Press, 1989).

37 **He graduated in 1886:** "Charlotte County, Virginia: Historical Notes of Town of Keysville."

37 **Dr. Priddy integrated the latest procedures:** "Tribute to Albert Sidney Priddy."

38 **He was elected:** "Draft Resolutions to Honor A. S. Priddy"; "Tribute to Albert Sidney Priddy"; Veselik, *Superintendents and Directors*, 4.

38 **He helped draft a law:** "Draft Resolutions to Honor A. S. Priddy"; Veselik, *Superintendents and Directors*, 4; Thomas Johnson Michie et al., *Virginia Reports: Jefferson–33 Grattan, 1730–1880* (Charlottesville, VA: Michie, 1901), 102.

38 **The progressives had faith:** John Q. LaFond and Mary L. Durham, *Back to the Asylum: The Future of Mental Health Law and Policy in the United States* (New York: Oxford University Press, 1992), 5.

38 **As a legislator:** Veselik, *Superintendents and Directors*, 4.

38 **Dr. Priddy closed up:** Ibid.

38 **Francis Fauquier:** Harry Groom, *Fauquier During the Proprietorship* (Baltimore: Genealogical Publishing Company, 2009); "Francis Fauquier," *Encyclopedia Virginia*, http://www.encyclopediavirginia.org/Fauquier_Francis_bap_1703-1768; Julian C. Houseman, "Department History: 1766 to 1968," in Board of the Department of Mental Hygiene and Hospitals of the Commonwealth of Virginia, special edition, *Mental Health in Virginia* 18, no. 2 (Winter 1968): 5, box 7, Central Virginia Training Center Papers.

39 **It was the first hospital:** Gregory Michael Dorr, *Segregation's Science: Eugenics and Society in Virginia* (Charlottesville: University of Virginia Press, 2008), 120; Houseman, "Department History: 1766 to 1968," 5.

39 **The hospital in Williamsburg:** Dorr, *Segregation's Science*, 120.

39 **Central State Hospital for Negroes:** Ibid., 120–21; Houseman, "Department History: 1766 to 1968," 7.

39 **Epilepsy was little understood:** Thomas Stephen Szasz, *Cruel Compassion: Psychiatric Control of Society's Unwanted* (Syracuse, NY: Syracuse University Press, 1998), 49.

39 **Across the nation:** Ibid., 47–51.

39 **Without specialized facilities:** W. I. Prichard, "History—Lynchburg Training School and Hospital," *Mental Health in Virginia*, 11 (Summer 1960): 41.

39 **Colonies, with their "vocations":** Szasz, *Cruel Compassion*, 50.

39 **"the myth of the dangerous epileptic":** Ibid., 49.

39 **There was a long tradition:** Ibid., 56.

NOTES

40 **There was interest:** Houseman, "Department History: 1766 to 1968," 23.

40 **A wealthy resident of Amherst County:** Ibid.; *Report of the Attorney General to the Governor of Virginia* (Richmond, VA: Division of Purchase and Printing, 1910), 26; Prichard, "History—Lynchburg Training School and Hospital," 40.

40 **The legislature passed a bill:** Houseman, "Department History: 1766 to 1968," 23; *Western State Hospital v. General Board*, 112 Va. 230, 232 (Supreme Court of Appeals of Virginia, 1911); Prichard, "History—Lynchburg Training School and Hospital," 41; *First Report of Virginia State Epileptic Colony at Lynchburg, Virginia, from February 20, 1906 to September 30, 1909*, in *Annual Reports of Officers, Boards, and Institutions of the Commonwealth of Virginia for the Year Ending September 30, 1909* (Richmond: Davis Bottom, Superintendent of Public Printing, 1909), 67.

40 **The State Hospital Board:** Prichard, "History—Lynchburg Training School and Hospital," 42.

40 **The donated land:** *Western State Hospital*, 112 Va. 230, 232; *First Report of Virginia State Epileptic Colony at Lynchburg, Virginia*, 69.

40 **The State Hospital Board and the legislature:** *Id.* at 235; Houseman, "Department History: 1766 to 1968," 23; *State Colony for Epileptics and Feeble-Minded Second Biennial Report, 1922–1923*, 1–5.

41 **On April 8, 1910:** Prichard, "History—Lynchburg Training School and Hospital," 42, 46.

41 **As a medical doctor:** Ibid., 46; "Tribute to Albert Sidney Priddy"; Veselik, *Superintendents and Directors*, 4.

41 **He had to build:** Prichard, "History—Lynchburg Training School and Hospital," 42, 46.

41 **There was considerable room:** *State Colony for Epileptics and Feeble-Minded: Second Biennial Report*, 5, 16–17; Bruce Roberts and Elizabeth Kedash, *Plantation Homes of the James River* (Chapel Hill: University of North Carolina Press, 1990), 1.

41 **In the colony's early days:** Prichard, "History—Lynchburg Training School and Hospital," 46.

41 **The first epileptic patients:** Ibid., 42.

41 **The first wave:** Ibid.

42 **Before arriving at the colony:** Paul A. Lombardo, *Three Generations, No Imbeciles: Eugenics, the Supreme Court, and* Buck v. Bell (Baltimore: Johns Hopkins University Press, 2008), 14.

42 **The colony was necessarily "custodial":** W. I. Prichard, "History—Lynchburg Training School and Hospital, Pt. II" *Mental Health in Virginia* 11 (Autumn 1960), 29.

42 **If the colony could not offer cures:** Ibid., 41.

42 **For the more spiritually inclined:** *State Colony for Epileptics and Feeble-Minded: Second Biennial Report*, 11–15.

42 **In keeping with the colony model:** Ibid., 16–17.

42 **He took satisfaction:** Ibid., 9.

43 **If relatives insisted:** Ibid., 5.

43 **After initially admitting:** Lombardo, *Three Generations*, 15.

43 **A few years earlier** "Chap. 48 of Acts 1906—An Act to Establish an Epileptic Colony on Land of the Western State Hospital, in Amherst County," in *Pollard's Code Biennial, 1908* (Richmond, VA: E. Waddey, 1908), 434.

43 **In a 1914 annual report:** Steven Noll, *Feeble-Minded in Our Midst* (Chapel Hill: University of North Carolina Press, 1995), 115.

43 **The women "morons":** A. S. Priddy, *Biennial Report of the State Epileptic Colony* (Lynchburg, VA: State Epileptic Colony, 1923), cited in Smith and Nelson, *Sterilization of Carrine Buck*, 32.

43 **Several new buildings:** Prichard, "History—Lynchburg Training School and Hospital," 44.

43 **In recognition of its wider mission:** Commonwealth of Virginia Department of Mental Health/Mental Retardation, *Central Virginia Training Center*, box 7, Central Virginia Training Center Papers; Prichard, "History—Lynchburg Training School and Hospital," 46.

44 **By 1925 more than two-thirds:** Prichard, "History—Lynchburg Training School and Hospital, Pt. II," 28.

44 **He insisted on housing:** Ibid.

44 **"Pitiful appeals in behalf":** *State Colony for Epileptics and Feeble-Minded: Second Biennial Report*, 11.

44 **Unlike Virginia:** David J. Rothman, *The Discovery of the Asylum* (Piscataway, NJ: Transaction, 1971), 130.

44 **States began to establish:** Alfred A. Baumeister, "Mental Retardation: Confusing Sentiment with Science," in *What Is Mental Retardation?: Ideas for an Evolving Disability in the 21st Century*, ed. Harvey N. Switzky and Stephen Greenspan (Washington, DC: American Association on

Mental Retardation, 2006), 101; David Wright, *Downs: The History of a Disability* (Oxford: Oxford University Press, 2011), 69.

44 **This "cult of asylum":** John M. Herrick and Paul H. Stuart, eds., *Encyclopedia of Social Welfare History in North America* (Thousand Oaks, CA: Sage Publications, 2005), 234; Rothman, *Discovery of the Asylum*, 130.

44 **It was a sign:** Baumeister," Mental Retardation," 101; Wright, *Downs*, 69–70.

44 **These institutions:** Donna R. Kemp, *Mental Health in America: A Reference Handbook* (Santa Barbara, CA: ABC-CLIO, 2007), 5.

45 **"The power of population":** Thomas Malthus, *An Essay on the Principle of Population* (London: J. Johnson, in St. Paul's Church-Yard, 1803), 350; Elof Axel Carlson, *The Unfit: A History of a Bad Idea* (Cold Spring Harbor, NY: Cold Spring Harbor Laboratory Press, 2001), 102–3.

45 **"survival of the fittest":** Herbert Spencer, *The Principles of Biology* vol. 2 (Edinburgh: Williams and Norgate, 1867) 53; Frederick Burkhardt et al., eds., *The Correspondence of Charles Darwin* (Cambridge: Cambridge University Press, 2004), 14:230.

45 **"[L]ife has reached":** Herbert Spencer, *Social Statics; Or the Conditions Essential to Human Happiness Specified, and the First of them Developed* (New York: D. Appleton and Co., 1892), 303; Eric Foner, introduction to *Social Darwinism in American Thought*, by Richard Hofstadter (Boston: Beacon Press, 1992), xiv; Herbert Spencer, *The Coming Slavery and Other Essays* (New York: The Humboldt Publishing Company, 1888), 2.

45 **Spencer believed this violent sorting out:** Spencer, *Social Statics*, 415–16; Foner, introduction to *Social Darwinism*, xiv; Herbert Spencer, *Political Writings*, ed. John Offer (Cambridge: Cambridge University Press), 127.

46 **process of natural selection:** Foner, introduction to *Social Darwinism in American Thought*, xiv; Jonathan Hodge and Gregory Radick, introduction to *The Cambridge Companion to Darwin*, ed. Jonathan Hodge and Gregory Radick (Cambridge: Cambridge University Press, 2009), 5.

46 **Galton concluded:** Francis Galton, *Hereditary Genius: An Inquiry into Its Laws and Consequences* (London: Macmillan, 1999), 1.

46 **"the subject in a statistical manner":** Ibid., vi.

46 **Derived from the Greek:** Francis Galton, *Inquiries into Human Faculty and Its Development* (New York: Macmillan, 1883), 24–25n.

46 **Galton called on humanity:** Ibid.

46 **"what Nature does blindly":** Edward J. Larson, *Sex, Race, and Science: Eugenics in the Deep South* (Baltimore: Johns Hopkins University Press, 1995), 19.

46 **Having invented eugenics:** Karl Pearson, *The Life, Letters and Labours of Francis Galton*, vol. 3, pt. 1 (Cambridge: Cambridge University Press, 1930), 221.

46 **Galton was convinced that eugenics:** Ibid., 274.

47 **In his writings, Galton described:** Ibid., 351.

47 **Galton saw a value:** Kathy Wilson Peacock, *Biotechnology and Genetic Engineering* (New York: Infobase Publishing, 2010) 37.

47 **"some other less drastic yet adequate measure":** Richard Lynn, *Eugenics: A Reassessment* (Westport, Conn.: Praeger, 2001) 12; Galton, *Inquiries into Human Faculty*, 27; Pearson, *Life, Letters and Labours of Francis Galton*, 3:349.

47 **"our democracy will ultimately refuse consent":** Lynn, *Eugenics: A Reassessment*, 12.

47 **Jane Hume Clapperton:** Angelique Richardson, *Love and Eugenics in the Late Nineteenth Century: Rational Reproduction and the New Woman* (Oxford: Oxford University Press, 2003), 67.

47 **Many eugenicists and Tory politicians:** Arthur Allen, *Vaccine: The Controversial Story of Medicine's Greatest Lifesaver* (New York: W. W. Norton, 2007), 56.

48 **Anyone who had ever:** Charles Darwin, *The Descent of Man, and Selection in Relation to Sex* (New York: D. Appleton, 1872), 162.

48 **"the helpless":** Ibid.

48 **Darwin believed:** Ibid.

48 **The new thinking:** Don E. Fehrenbacher, *The Slaveholding Republic: An Account of the United States Government's Relations to Slavery* (Oxford: Oxford University Press, 2001), 15–37; Dorr, *Segregation's Science*, 26–33.

48 **"every serious thinker felt obligated":** Foner, introduction to *Social Darwinism*, xiv.

49 **The book that set this field:** Joseph F. Spillane and David Wolcott, *A History of Modern American Criminal Justice* (Los Angeles: Sage Publications, 2013), 52; *The Jukes: A Study in Crime, Pauperism, Disease, and Heredity;, also Further Studies of Criminals* (New York: G.P. Putnam's Sons, 1877).

49 **He looked back:** Carlson, *The Unfit*, 168–72; Larson, *Sex, Race, and Science*, 19; Francis T. Cul-

len and Pamela Wilcox, eds., *Encyclopedia of Criminological Theory* (Thousand Oaks, CA: SAGE, 2010), 1:274–77.

49   **Dugdale concluded:** Carlson, *The Unfit*, 168–72; James W. Trent, *Inventing the Feebleminded: A History of Mental Retardation in the United States* (Berkeley: University of California Press, 1994), 70–71.

49   **To the eugenicists:** Carlson, *The Unfit*, 168–72.

49   **When the book was republished:** Ibid.; Anthony Platt, *The Child Savers: The Invention of Delinquency* (Chicago: University of Chicago Press, 1977), 26.

50   **Oscar McCulloch, a minister:** Nathaniel Deutsch, *Inventing America's "Worst" Family: Eugenics, Islam, and the Fall and Rise of the Tribe of Ishmael* (Berkeley: University of California Press, 2008), 26–28; *Encyclopedia of Criminological Theory* 1:276.

50   **In *The Tribe of Ishmael*:** Deutsch, *Inventing America's "Worst" Family*, 49–51.

50   **In his analysis:** Oscar McCulloch, *The Tribe of Ishmael: A Study in Social Degradation* (Indianapolis: Charity Organization Society, 1891).

50   **He described the harsh conditions:** Brent Ruswick, *Almost Worthy: The Poor, Paupers, and the Science of Charity in America, 1877–1917* (Bloomington: Indiana University Press, 2012), 46–47.

50   **More than environment:** McCulloch, *Tribe of Ishmael*, 3, 8.

50   **His theories revolutionized:** Carlson, *The Unfit*, 130–37.

50   **Before Mendel:** Rita Mary King, *Biology Made Simple* (New York: Broadway Books, 2003), 42.

51   **Mendel's work provided:** Daniel J. Kevles, *In the Name of Eugenics: Genetics and the Uses of Human Heredity* (Cambridge, MA: Harvard University Press, 1985), 42.

51   **Eugenics argued:** Garland E. Allen, "The Eugenics Record Office at Cold Spring Harbor, 1910–1940: An Essay in Institutional History," *Osiris* 2 (1986): 226.

51   **The eugenicists argued:** Carol Isaacson Barash, *Just Genes: The Ethics of Genetic Technologies* (New York: Praeger, 2008), 4.

51   **In the eugenicists' view:** Michael Willrich, "The Two Percent Solution: Eugenic Jurisprudence and the Socialization of American Law, 1900–1930," *Law and History Review* (Spring 1998), 64.

51   **The eugenicists' plan:** Kevles, *In the Name of Eugenics*, 145–46.

51   **Thomas Hunt Morgan:** Diane Paul and Hamish Spencer, "Did Eugenics Rest on an Elementary Mistake?," 105

52   **Supporters of my eugenics had little interest:** Barash, *Just Genes*, 4.

52   **Bleecker Van Wagenen:** Stefan Kuhl, *For the Betterment of the Race: The Rise and Fall of the International Movement for Eugenics and Racial Hygiene* (New York: Palgrave Macmillan, 2013), 21; Harry Bruinius, *Better for All the World: The Secret History of Forced Sterilization and America's Quest for Racial Purity* (New York: Alfred A. Knopf, 2006), 171.

52   **Some of the most urgent warnings:** Wehmeyer, *Oxford Handbook of Positive Psychology and Disability*, 5.

52   **In 1912 Goddard published:** Henry Herbert Goddard, *The Kallikak Family: A Study in the Heredity of Feeble-Mindedness* (New York: Macmillan, 1912).

52   **In *The Kallikak Family*:** Kevles, *In the Name of Eugenics*, 78; Goddard, *Kallikak Family*, 16.

52   **Kallikak produced two lines:** Goddard, *Kallikak Family*, viii, 18, 50.

53   **The line from Kallikak's wife:** Ibid., 18–19, 30; Philip R. Reilly, *The Surgical Solution: A History of Involuntary Sterilization in the United States* (Baltimore: Johns Hopkins University Press, 1991), 21.

53   **Goddard presented the Kallikaks:** Goddard, *Kallikak Family*, 104, 116.

53   **What was at stake:** Henry Herbert Goddard, *Feeble-Mindedness: Its Causes and Consequences* (New York: Macmillan, 1914), 4–9, 17, 588–90.

53   **In his 1917 essay:** Lewis Terman, "Feeble-Minded Children in the Public Schools of California: The Menace of Feeble-Mindedness," *School and Society* 5 (Feb. 10, 1917): 161-65.

54   **Samuel J. Holmes:** Samuel J. Holmes, *The Trend of the Race: A Study of Present Tendencies in the Biological Development of Civilized Mankind* (New York: Harcourt, Brace, 1921), 131, 382, 383.

54   **A study prepared:** Lewis M. Terman, "Feeble Minded Children in the Schools," in *Report of the 1915 Legislature Committee on Mental Deficiency and the Proposed Institution for the Care of Feebleminded and Epileptic Persons*, ed. Fred C. Nelles (Whittier, CA: Whittier State School Department of Printing, 1917), xiv.

54   **The same year:** Board of Charities and Corrections, *Mental Defectives in Virginia* (Richmond: Davis Bottom, Superintendent, Public Printing, 1915), 16.

NOTES

54 *Scientific American* **warned:** Robert DeC. Ward, "Our Immigration Laws from the Viewpoint of National Eugenics," *Scientific American,* May 4, 1912, 287.

54 **An article the following year:** John M. Connolly, "The Foundation Law of the Science of Heredity," *Life and Health: The National Health Magazine* 28, no.5, 198 (May 1913), 235.

54 **"The Village of a Thousand Souls":** Ben Harris, "Arnold Gesell's Progressive Vision: Child Hygiene, Socialism and Eugenics," *History of Psychology* 14, no. 3, 311 (2011) 311–12; Ron Seely, "'The Village of a Thousand Souls,' Sheds Light on Eugenics," *Winona Daily News,* August 28, 2011.

55 **As rural residents fled:** Richard Hofstadter, *The Age of Reform* (Knopf Doubleday, 2011), 7.

55 **At the same time:** John Higham, *Strangers in the Land: Patterns of American Nativism 1860–1925* (New Brunswick, NJ: Rutgers University Press, 2002), 147.

55 **Native-born, white, middle-class, Protestant Americans:** Hofstadter, *Age of Reform,* 144.

55 **These reform campaigns:** John Ehrenreich, *The Altruistic Imagination: A History of Social Work and Social Policy in the United States* (Ithaca, NY: Cornell University Press, 1985), 28.

55 **"the diseased, the deficient":** Hofstadter, *Social Darwinism,* 162.

55 **The eugenicists matched:** Hofstadter, *Age of Reform,* 5.

55 **Both the leaders:** Kevles, *In the Name of Eugenics,* 64.

56 **Hofstadter observed:** Hofstadter, *Age of Reform,* 148.

56 **So it was with eugenics:** Kevles, *In the Name of Eugenics,* 64; Marcus Graser, "A 'Jeffersonian Skepticism of Urban Democracy'? The Educated Middle Class and the Problem of Political Power in Chicago, 1880–1940," in *Who Ran the Cities? City Elites and Urban Power Structures in Europe and North America, 1750–1940,* ed. Ralf Roth and Robert Beachy (Burlington, VT: Ashgate, 2007), 215.

56 **"practical deterrent":** Mark A. Largent, *Breeding Contempt: The History of Coerced Sterilization in the United States* (New Brunswick, NJ: Rutgers University Press, 2011), 64–65.

56 **"We prolong the lives":** G. Hudson Makuen, "Some Measures for the Prevention of Crime, Pauperism, and Mental Deficiency," *American Academy of Medicine* (August 1900): 1–2.

56 **The Very Reverend Walter Taylor Sumner:** Christine Rosen, *Preaching Eugenics: Religious Leaders and the American Eugenics Movement* (New York: Oxford University Press, 2004), 53.

56 **Other religious leaders:** Amy Laura Hall, *Conceiving Parenthood: American Protestantism and the Spirit of Reproduction* (Grand Rapids, MI: Wm. B. Eerdmans, 2008), 254.

56 **Women were active:** Kevles, *In the Name of Eugenics,* 64.

57 **Many influential feminists:** Wilma Pearl Mankiller et al., eds., *The Reader's Companion to U.S. Women's History* (New York: Houghton Mifflin Harcourt, 1999), 178; Angela Franks, *Margaret Sanger's Eugenic Legacy: The Control of Female Fertility* (Jefferson, NC: McFarland, 2005), 10–17.

57 **Sanger lectured:** Jonathan Peter Spiro, *Defending the Master Race: Conservation, Eugenics, and the Legacy of Madison Grant* (Lebanon, NH: University Press of New England, 2009), 235. At least one Sanger biographer contends that the speech may have been inaccurately reported, or at the least has been misinterpreted; see Ellen Chesler, *Woman of Valor: Margaret Sanger and the Birth Control Movement in America* (New York: Simon and Schuster, 2007), 614n21.

57 **Edward J. Larson:** Larson, *Sex, Race, and Science,* 75.

57 **Eugenics found support:** Mary Beth Norton, Carol Sheriff, David W. Blight, and Howard Chudacoff, *A People and a Nation: A History of the United States,* vol. 2, *Since 1865* (Stamford, CT: Cengage Learning, 2011), 583; Cynthia Davis, *Charlotte Perkins Gilman: A Biography* (Palo Alto, CA: Stanford University Press, 2010), 302.

57 **Theodore Roosevelt:** Theodore Roosevelt, "Twisted Eugenics," *Outlook,* Jan. 3, 1914, 30–34, 32; Reilly, *Surgical Solution,* 43. American radicals were not great believers in eugenics, in part because of its anti-immigrant orientation. Kevles, *In the Name of Eugenics* 106.

58 *Hereditary Genius:* Galton, *Hereditary Genius,* 338–39, 342; Richard S. Levy, ed., *Anti-Semitism: A Historical Encyclopedia of Prejudice and Persecution* (Santa Barbara, CA: ABC-CLIO, 2005), 1:212.

58 **Paul Popenoe:** Paul Popenoe, *Applied Eugenics* (New York: Macmillan, 1920), 284; Kevles, *In the Name of Eugenics,* 65.

58 **Their primary interest:** Larson, *Sex, Race, and Science,* 2, 93; Randall Hansen and Desmond King, *Sterilized by the State: Eugenics, Race, and the Population Scare in Twentieth-Century North America* (Cambridge: Cambridge University Press, 2013), 15.

58 **One Louisiana doctor:** Larson, *Sex, Race, and Science,* 2.

58 **It defined every person:** Wilbur Miller, ed., *The Social History of Crime and Punishment in America: An Encyclopedia* (Thousand Oaks, CA: SAGE, 2012), 2221.

59 **"We stand at a crisis":** Madison Grant, *The Passing of the Great Race* (1916; repr., New York: Charles Scribner's Sons, 1922), 228; John P. Jackson Jr. and Nadine Weidman, *Race, Racism, and Science: Social Impact and Interaction* (Santa Barbara, CA: ABC-CLIO, 2004) 111; Lothrop Stoddard, *The Rising Tide of Color Against White World-Supremacy* (1920; repr., New York: Charles Scribner's Sons, 1921), 229, 299.

59 **"Whoever will take":** Jerome Karabel, *The Chosen: The Hidden History of Admission and Exclusion at Harvard, Yale, and Princeton* (New York: Houghton Mifflin Harcourt, 2006), 84.

59 **The reference is to *The Rising Tide of Color*:** Alberto Lena, "Deceitful Traces of Power: An Analysis of the Decadence of Tom Buchanan in *The Great Gatsby*," in *Scott Fitzgerald's "The Great Gatsby,"* ed. Harold Bloom (New York: Infobase, 2010), 49.

60 **A 1915 *Atlantic Monthly*:** S. J. Holmes, "Some Misconceptions of Eugenics," *Atlantic Monthly*, Feb. 1915, 222–27.

60 **In the early days:** Higham, *Strangers in the Land*, 150–51.

60 **"Courses in Eugenics":** "Courses in Eugenics Increase in Colleges of This Country," *New York Times*, Nov. 20, 1927.

60 ***New Orleans Times-Picayune*:** Larson, *Sex, Race, and Science*, 109–10.

60 **Harry F. Ward:** Rosen, *Preaching Eugenics*, 136.

60 **"The Refiner's Fire":** Hall, *Conceiving Parenthood*, 260; Rosen, *Preaching Eugenics*, 124.

60 **Many years later:** Jeremy Bergen, *Ecclesial Repentance: The Churches Confront Their Sinful Pasts* (New York: T&T Clark International, 2011), 108–9.

61 **"As the Eugenics Movement":** "Repentance for Support of Eugenics," http://www.umc.org/what-we-believe/repentance-for-support-of-eugenics.

61 **There were high-profile eugenics conferences:** Robert Rydell, *World of Fairs: The Century-of-Progress Expositions* (Chicago: University of Chicago Press, 1993), 43; Joseph Soares, *The Power of Privilege: Yale and America's Elite Colleges* (Stanford, CA: Stanford University Press, 2007), 21.

61 **The Museum of Natural History:** Rydell, *World of Fairs*, 44–47.

61 **The Kansas Free Fair:** Alison Bashford and Philippa Levine, eds., *The Oxford Handbook of the History of Eugenics* (New York: Oxford University Press, 2010), 514; *Encyclopedia of Anthropology*, H. James Birx, ed. (Thousand Oaks, CA: Sage Publications, 2006), 1046.

61 **A volunteer:** Rydell, *World of Fairs*, 49–50.

61 **"All the newspapers":** Edward Caudill, *Darwinian Myths: The Legends and Misuses of a Theory* (Knoxville: University of Tennessee Press, 1997), 101–3; Kevles, *In the Name of Eugenics*, 62.

62 **In the film:** Edward J. Larson, "Biology and the Emergence of the Anglo-American Eugenics Movement," in *Biology and Ideology from Descartes to Dawkins*, ed. Denis R. Alexander and Ronald L. Numbers (Chicago: University of Chicago Press, 2010), 186; Meghan Schrader, "The Sound of Disability: Music, the Obsessive Avenger, and Eugenics in America," in *Anxiety Muted: American Film Music in a Suburban Age*, ed. Stanley C. Pelkey II and Anthony Bushard (New York: Oxford University Press, 2015), 165.

62 **Early eugenicists in the United States:** Mary L. Dudziak, "Oliver Wendell Holmes as a Eugenic Reformer: Rhetoric in the Writing of Constitutional Law," *Iowa Law Review* 71 (1986): 846 93n.

62 **In 1855 Gideon Lincecum:** Lois Wood Burkhalter, *Gideon Lincecum, 1793–1864: A Biography* (Austin: University of Texas Press, 2010), 93–94; Largent, *Breeding Contempt*, 11; Larson, *Sex, Race, and Science*, 27.

62 **"Did you never see [a] eunuch?":** Burkhalter, *Gideon Lincecum*, 93–98.

63 **Dr. W. R. Edgar:** "Asexualization of Criminals and Degenerates," *Michigan Law Journal* 6, no. 12 (Dec. 1897): 289–92.

63 **Dr. F. Hoyt Pilcher:** Trent, *Inventing the Feebleminded*, 193; Stephen Murphy, *Voices of Pineland: Eugenics, Social Reform, and the Legacy of "Feeblemindedness" in Maine* (Charlotte, NC: Information Age Publishing, 2011), 26.

63 **Dr. Pilcher's methods:** Ian Robert Dowbiggin, *Keeping America Sane: Psychiatry and Eugenics in the United States, 1880–1940* (Ithaca, NY: Cornell University Press, 1997), 76; Largent, *Breeding Contempt*, 22–23.

63 **public opposition:** Susan Baglieri and Arthur Shapiro, *Disability Studies and the Inclusive Classroom* (New York: Routledge, 2012), 73.

63 **The penalty:** Connecticut State Board of Charities, *Biennial Report of the State Board of Charities of Connecticut* (1905), 130.

63   **Other states soon followed:** Larson, *Sex, Race, and Science*, 22; Reilly, *Surgical Solution*, 26; Dowbiggin, *Keeping America Sane*, 76.

63   **"No cheap device":** Larson, *Sex, Race, and Science*, 23.

63   **In *The Kallikak Family*:** Goddard, *Kallikak Family*, 101–5.

64   **Dr. Walter E. Fernald:** Walter E. Fernald, "Some of the Limitations of the Plan for Segregation of the Feeble-Minded," *Ungraded* (May 1918): 171.

64   **"Determine the fact":** Larson, *Sex, Race, and Science*, 25.

64   **If "feeble-minded children":** Goddard, *Kallikak Family*, 106.

65   **"Surgical Treatment of Habitual Criminals":** Hanson and King, *Sterilized by the State*, 74; Kenneth Ludmerer, *Genetics and American Society: A Historical Appraisal* (Baltimore: Johns Hopkins University Press, 1972), 91.

65   **"Vasectomy as a Means":** Largent, *Breeding Contempt*, 29–30; Paul A. Lombardo, "Eugenic Sterilization in Virginia: Aubrey Strode and the Case of *Buck v. Bell*" (Ph.D. diss., University of Virginia, 1982), 19.

65   **Dr. Sharp called for sterilizations:** Reilly, *Surgical Solution*, 32.

65   **salpingectomy:** Reilly, *Surgical Solution*, 34.

65   **Of the eighty-nine operations:** Reilly, *Surgical Solution*, 34, 98.

66   **Carl Degler:** Larson, *Sex, Race, and Science*, 32.

66   **One leading eugenics group:** Ibid.

66   **"Race Suicide for Social Parasites":** Reilly, *Surgical Solution*, 34–35; William Belfield, "Race Suicide for Social Parasites," *JAMA* 50 (1908): 55.

66   **One survey found:** Reilly, *Surgical Solution*, 35.

67   **The leaders and medical staff:** Nicole Hahn Rafter, *Creating Born Criminals* (Champaign-Urbana: University of Illinois Press, 1997), 56.

67   **Dr. S. D. Risley:** Reilly, *Surgical Solution*, 32–33.

67   **American Breeders' Association's Committee on Eugenics:** Largent, *Breeding Contempt*, 51; Edward McNall Burns, *David Starr Jordan: Prophet of Freedom* (Palo Alto, CA: Stanford University Press, 1953), 1.

67   **Isabel Barrows:** Rafter, *Creating Born Criminals*, 56.

67   **Josephine Shaw Lowell:** Jill Fields, *An Intimate Affair: Women, Lingerie, and Sexuality* (Berkeley: University of California Press, 2007), 137; Nell Irvin Painter, *The History of White People* (New York: W. W. Norton, 2010), 259.

67   **many Catholics believed sterilization violated:** Hansen and King, *Sterilized by the State*, 137; Rosen, *Preaching Eugenics*, 20.

67   **In many states:** Hansen and King, *Sterilized by the State*, 131–33.

68   **"God created these poor unfortunates":** Ibid., 133–34.

68   **Oregon had an Anti-Sterilization League:** Harry Laughlin, *Eugenical Sterilization in the United States* (Chicago: Psychopathic Library of the Municipal Court of Chicago, 1922), 43; Largent, *Breeding Contempt*, 96.

68   **Many opponents agreed:** *Davis v. Berry*, 216 F. 413 (S.D. Iowa 1914).

68   **New Jersey's eugenic sterilization:** Reilly, *Surgical Solution*, 52–54.

68   **In 1897 the Michigan legislature:** Hansen and King, *Sterilized by the State*, 84.

69   **Dr. Barr had been an outspoken supporter:** Largent, *Breeding Contempt*, 36; Baglieri and Shapiro, *Disability Studies*, 73.

69   **The Act for the Prevention of Idiocy:** Black, *War Against the Weak*, 66.

69   **Pennsylvania's legislature passed the bill:** Ibid.; Kevles, *In the Name of Eugenics*, 109; Lombardo, *Three Generations*, 22.

69   **Pennypacker used his veto message:** *Vetoes by the Governor, of Bills Passed by the Legislature, Session of 1905* (n.p.: Wm. Stanley Ray, 1905), 27; Black, *War Against the Weak*, 66; Kevles, *In the Name of Eugenics*, 109.

69   **With his veto:** Samuel Whitaker Pennypacker, *The Autobiography of a Pennsylvanian* (Philadelphia: John Winston Company, 1918), 382.

69   **"Gentlemen, Gentlemen!":** Largent, *Breeding Contempt*, 70.

70   **"confirmed criminals, idiots":** Reilly, *Surgical Solution*, 31–33; Laughlin, *Eugenical Sterilization*, 15.

70   **To help make the case:** Hansen and King, *Sterilized by the State*, 78.

70   **In 1907 Indiana became the first state:** Largent, *Breeding Contempt*, 30; Reilly, *Surgical Solution*, 32–35.

70   **In 1909 California enacted:** Reilly, *Surgical Solution*, 32–35.

70   **Dr. F. W. Hatch:** Reilly, *Surgical Solution*, 36; Lombardo, *Three Generations*, 26.

70   **People eligible for the procedure:** Hansen and King, *Sterilized by the State*, 80; Nancy Ordover, *American Eugenics: Race, Queer Anatomy, and the Science of Nationalism* (Minneapolis: University of Minnesota Press, 2003), 79.

70   **Bethenia Owens-Adair:** Reilly, *Surgical Solution*, 39; *Notable American Women 1607–1950: A Biographical Dictionary*, ed. Edward T. James (Cambridge, MA: Harvard University Press, 1971), 1:659; Peter Boag, *Same-Sex Affairs: Constructing and Controlling Homosexuality in the Pacific Northwest* (Berkeley: University of California Press, 2003), 207.

70   **Eight years later:** Hansen and King, *Sterilized by the State*, 91.

70   **At that point, twelve states:** Reilly, *Surgical Solution*, 39.

71   **Some were especially broad:** Laughlin, *Eugenical Sterilization*, 21.

71   **Kansas's law:** Ibid., 21.

71   **H. L. Mencken:** H. L. Mencken, "The Sahara of the Bozart," in *The American Scene: A Reader*, ed. Huntington Cairns (New York: Alfred A. Knopf, 1977), 157–58; Dorr, *Segregation's Science*, 107–9.

71   **In the 1910s and 1920s:** Larson, *Sex, Race, and Science*, 41.

71   **The strongest support:** Dorr, *Segregation's Science*, 11; Hansen and King, *Sterilized by the State*, 77.

71   **"anxious for their region":** Wayne Flynt, review of *Sex, Race, and Science: Eugenics in the Deep South*, by Edward J. Larson, *Florida Historical Quarterly* (Fall 1995): 226.

72   **"an epicenter of eugenical thought":** Gregory Michael Dorr, "Assuring America's Place in the Sun: Ivey Foreman Lewis and the Teaching of Eugenics at the University of Virginia, 1915–1953," *Journal of Southern History* (May 2000): 276.

72   **Forced sterilization:** Dorr, *Segregation's Science*, 63.

72   **Ivey Foreman Lewis:** Dorr, "Assuring America's Place in the Sun," 258; Dorr, *Segregation's Science*, 72.

72   **"In the 20th century":** Dorr, "Assuring America's Place in the Sun," 277–78.

72   **The idea of the melting pot:** Ibid., 272.

72   **Robert Bennett Bean:** Dorr, *Segregation's Science*, 77–79.

73   **Lemuel Smith:** Dorr, "Assuring America's Place in the Sun," 276n62.

73   **Harvey Ernest Jordan:** Lombardo, *Three Generations*, 211.

73   **a national leader in racist eugenics:** Robert Bennett Bean, "Some Racial Peculiarities of the Negro Brain," *American Journal of Anatomy* 5, no. 4 (1906): 353–432.

73   **The legislature created the board:** Lombardo, "Eugenic Sterilization in Virginia," 87–88; Hansen and King, *Sterilized by the State*, 105.

73   **"The child of normal parents":** Lombardo, "Eugenic Sterilization in Virginia," 88, 89–90.

73   **He advocated a law:** Ibid., 93–94.

74   **A. Einer:** Dorr, *Segregation's Science*, 112, 249n8.

74   **Dr. H. W. Dew of Lynchburg:** Ibid., 111, 114.

74   **"We must have a sterilization law":** Lombardo, "Eugenic Sterilization in Virginia," 107.

74   **Dr. Charles Carrington:** *Charles Richmond Henderson, Preventive Agencies and Methods* (New York: Charities Publication Committee, 1910), 61; Dorr, *Segregation's Science*, 115–16.

74   **Dr. Carrington described:** Dorr, *Segregation's Science*, 115–16.

75   **Dr. Bernard Barrow:** Bernard Barrow, "Vasectomy for the Defective Negro with His Consent," *Virginia Medical Semi-Monthly* (Aug. 26, 1910): 226–28; Dorr, *Segregation's Science*, 116.

75   **"to prevent procreation":** Lombardo, "Eugenic Sterilization in Virginia," 104–5.

75   **Dr. Carrington's bill failed:** Ibid., 105–7.

75   **Dr. Priddy, the superintendent:** J. S. DeJarnette, "Sterilization Law of Virginia" (typed manuscript), Records of Western State Hospital, box 88, Library of Virginia.

75   **That distinction belonged:** Ibid.

75   **Dr. DeJarnette came from:** "Joseph Spencer DeJarnette," *Encyclopedia Virginia*, available at http://www.encyclopediavirginia.org/DeJarnette_Joseph_Spencer_1866-1957#start_entry.

76   **Dr. DeJarnette graduated:** Ibid.; Jeffrey W. McClurken, *Take Care of the Living: Reconstructing Confederate Veteran Families in Virginia* (Charlottesville: University of Virginia Press, 2009), 155.

76   **He then joined:** "Joseph Spencer DeJarnette," *Encyclopedia Virginia*; Lombardo, *Three Generations*, 121.

76   **He urged the state legislature:** DeJarnette, "Sterilization Law of Virginia"; Lombardo, "Aubrey Strode," 110–11.

76   **Dr. DeJarnette was the first:** DeJarnette, "Sterilization Law of Virginia."

76   **"In the treatment of all diseases":** Dorr, *Segregation's Science*, 123.

77 **He lectured to medical associations:** Lombardo, "Aubrey Strode," 112, 115.

77 **Dr. DeJarnette even composed:** Dorr, *Segregation's Science,* 124.

77 **"Oh, you wise men":** J. S. DeJarnette, "Mendel's Law," Records of Western State Hospital, box 88, Library of Virginia.

CHAPTER THREE: ALBERT PRIDDY

78 **In his first annual report:** Paul A. Lombardo, "Eugenic Sterilization in Virginia: Aubrey Strode and the Case of *Buck v. Bell*" (Ph.D. diss., University of Virginia, 1982), 115.

78 **He warned of an impending rapid increase:** Commonwealth of Virginia Department of Mental Health/Mental Retardation, Central Virginia Training Center, box 7, Central Virginia Training Center Papers, Library of Virginia; 2nd Annual Report, Virginia State Epileptic Colony, 1911, box 17, Central Virginia Training Center Papers; J. S. DeJarnette, "Sterilization Law of Virginia" (typed manuscript), Records of Western State Hospital, box 88, Library of Virginia; Lombardo, "Eugenic Sterilization in Virginia", 116.

79 **In his 1915 annual report:** Gregory Michael Dorr, *Segregation's Science: Eugenics and Society in Virginia* (Charlottesville: University of Virginia Press, 2008), 124–25.

79 **In a 1916 letter:** Albert Priddy to Horace Gillespie, Jan. 21, 1916, box 4, Central Virginia Training Center Papers.

79 **Without a "great increase":** Albert Priddy to Harry Laughlin, Oct. 14, 1924, box 11, Central Virginia Training Center Papers.

79 **Dr. Priddy argued:** Ibid.

79 **Dr. William F. Drewry:** Dorr, *Segregation's Science,* 122.

80 **the colony had performed:** Lombardo, "Eugenic Sterilization in Virginia," 118; Dorr, *Segregation's Science,* 125.

80 **They had missed:** Reilly, *Surgical Solution,* 46.

80 **Dr. DeJarnette and Dr. Priddy approached:** Dorr, *Segregation's Science,* 122.

80 **Strode's bill:** Ibid.

80 **Dr. Priddy was quick:** Lombardo, "Eugenic Sterilization in Virginia," 117.

81 **His reading was:** DeJarnette, "Sterilization Law of Virginia."

81 **In his next annual report:** *Eighth Annual Report of the Board of Directors and Superintendent of the Virginia State Epileptic Colony and the Fourth Annual Report of the Virginia Colony for Feeble-Minded,* (1917), 15.

81 **"We have continued":** Dorr, *Segregation's Science,* 125.

81 **Dr. Priddy described most of the women:** Lombardo, *Three Generations,* 61.

81 **It was only a matter of time:** Steven Noll, "The Sterilization of Willie Mallory," in *"Bad" Mothers: The Politics of Blame in Twentieth-Century America,* ed. Molly Ladd-Taylor and Lauri Umansky (New York: New York University Press, 1998), 41–45; "Willie Mallory Complaint" (2009), *Buck v. Bell Documents,* Paper 80, http://readingroom.law.gsu.edu/buckvbell/80.

81 **Willie had come:** Lombardo, "Eugenic Sterilization in Virginia," 120; Noll, "Sterilization of Willie Mallory," 45.

81 **The Mallorys had experienced:** Noll, "Sterilization of Willie Mallory," 44–48; Lombardo, "Eugenic Sterilization in Virginia," 121–23.

82 **Willie's arrest:** Noll, "Sterilization of Willie Mallory," 45, Lombardo, *Three Generations,* 65–66.

82 **The Commission of Feeblemindedness ordered:** Lombardo, "Eugenic Sterilization in Virginia," 121; Lombardo, *Three Generations,* 66; Noll, "The Sterilization of Willie Mallory," 49.

82 **Willie escaped:** "Sterilization of Willie Mallory," 45.

82 **About six months:** Lombardo, "Eugenic Sterilization in Virginia," 123–24.

82 **Neither could return:** Noll, "Sterilization of Willie Mallory," 50.

82 **she sued him:** "Willie Mallory Complaint"; A. S. Priddy Summons, http://readingroom.law.gsu.edu/buckvbell/80.

82 **Specifically, she charged:** "Willie Mallory Complaint."

82 **She also filed:** Noll, "Sterilization of Willie Mallory," 44–46.

82 **From his examination:** Ibid., 52.

82 **He insisted:** Lombardo, "Eugenic Sterilization in Virgina," 126.

82 **Dr. Priddy also claimed:** Grounds for Defense, *Mallory v. Priddy,* in the Circuit Court for the City of Richmond, http://readingroom.law.gsu.edu/buckvbell/16/.

83 **"I want to know":** Lombardo, "Eugenic Sterilization in Virginia," 127–28.

83 **He responded with a letter:** Ibid., 128–29; Noll, "Sterilization of Willie Mallory," 50–51.

83 *Schloendorff v. Society of New York Hospital: Schloendorff v. Society of New York Hospital,* 211 N.Y.

125 (1914); Lombardo, *Three Generations*, 75; Ruth R. Faden and Tom L. Beauchamp, *A History and Theory of Informed Consent* (Oxford: Oxford University Press, 1986), 123.

83   **Despite the rise of informed consent:** Lombardo, "Eugenic Sterilization in Virginia," 129.

83   **The jury, which delivered its verdict:** Ibid., 129–33; Lombardo, *Three Generations*, 76.

83   **The judge warned Dr. Priddy:** Noll, "Sterilization of Willie Mallory," 41; W. I. Prichard, "History—Lynchburg Training School and Hospital," *Mental Health in Virginia* 11 (Summer 1960), 46.

83   **The Mallory case:** Lombardo, *Three Generations*, 76.

84   **In 1919, North Carolina and Alabama:** Randall Hansen and Desmond King, *Sterilized by the State: Eugenics, Race, and the Population Scare in Twentieth-Century North America* (Cambridge: Cambridge University Press, 2013), 76–77.

84   **When the bill was introduced:** J. S. DeJarnette, "Eugenic Sterilization in Virginia," reprinted from *Virginia Medical Monthly* (1931), Records of Western State Hospital, box 88, Library of Virginia; Lombardo, "Eugenic Sterilization in Virginia," 132.

84   **"They might get all of us":** Lombardo, "Eugenic Sterilization in Virginia," 132.

84   **One required inmates:** Ibid., 143–44.

84   **Strode's second bill:** Ibid.

85   **Dr. Priddy told Strode:** Ibid.

85   **It had been rejected:** Ibid.

85   **After his discouraging:** Ibid.; Lombardo, "Eugenic Sterilization in Virginia," 154–55.

86   **"It is to be hoped":** *State Colony for Epileptics and Feeble-Minded: Second Biennial Report, 1922–1923,* box 7, Central Virginia Training Center Papers.

86   **In October 1923:** "Tribute to Albert Sidney Priddy," in "16th Annual Report of the State Colony for Epileptics and Feeble-Minded, 1924–1925," box 17, Central Virginia Training Center Papers.

86   **"carried" their "troubles":** DeJarnette, "Sterilization Law of Virginia."

86   **The board believed:** Strode to Dr. Don Preston Peters, July 19, 1939, box 29, Aubrey Strode Papers, Albert and Shirley Small Special Collections Library, University of Virginia (hereafter cited as Strode Papers).

86   **This time, Strode agreed:** Aubrey Strode, "Sterilization of Defectives," Nov. 1924 (typed unpublished manuscript), box 55, Strode Papers.

86   **Laughlin's book included:** Harry Laughlin, *Eugenical Sterilization in the United States* (Chicago: Psychopathic Library of the Municipal Court of Chicago, 1922), 445.

86   **Strode made a "diligent effort":** Strode, "Sterilization of Defectives."

87   **Strode included three of the categories:** Virginia Sterilization Act of March 20, 1924, 1924 Va. Acts 569; Laughlin, *Eugenical Sterilization*, 445–47; Dorr, *Segregation's Science*, 128.

87   **When Virginia's law was challenged:** Virginia Sterilization Act; Brief for Plaintiff in Error, *Buck v. Bell*, U.S. Supreme Court, Oct. Term, 1926, 19; Stephen A. Siegel, "Justice Holmes, *Buck v. Bell*, and the History of Equal Protection," *Minnesota Law Review* 90 (2005): 128.

88   **Like Laughlin's model:** Laughlin, *Eugenical Sterilization*, 447–50; Virginia Sterilization Act.

88   **Eugenic sterilization laws had been struck down:** *Smith v. Board of Examiners*, 88 A. 963 (N.J., 1913) In re Thomson, 169 N.Y.S. 638 (Sup. Ct. 1918), aff'd *Osborn v. Thomson*, 171 N.Y.S. 1094 (App. Div. 1918); *Haynes v. Lapeer Circuit Judge*, 201 Mich. 138, 166 N.W. 938 (1918); "Notes and Abstracts," *Journal of the American Institute of Criminal Law and Criminology* (Feb. 1919): 596–97; Harry Bruinius, *Better for All the World: The Secret History of Forced Sterilization and America's Quest for Racial Purity* (New York: Alfred A. Knopf, 2006), 219.

88   **In his treatise:** Laughlin, *Eugenical Sterilization*, 440.

88   **Despite this emphatic warning:** Virginia Sterilization Act.

89   **He was, however, apparently absent:** Lombardo, "Eugenic Sterilization in Virginia," 106 and 106n14.

90   **Strode gave his bill:** Strode to Peters, July 19, 1939; Lombardo, "Eugenic Sterilization in Virginia," 166.

90   **Dr. Priddy and Dr. DeJarnette:** Lombardo, "Eugenic Sterilization in Virginia," 165.

90   **Strode's bill became law:** Ibid., 166–67.

90   **"This proves Abraham Lincoln's theory":** Strode, "Sterilization of Defectives"; DeJarnette, "Eugenic Sterilization in Virginia."

90   **The State Hospital Board accepted Strode's advice:** Aubrey Strode to Harry Laughlin, Sept. 30, 1924, box 3, folder 8, Arthur Estabrook Papers, M. E. Grenander Department of Special Collections and Archives, University at Albany, State University of New York; Lombardo, *Three Generations*, 102.

90 **Dr. Priddy became the architect:** Strode to Peters, July 19, 1939.
91 **He began by obtaining:** Lombardo, *Three Generations,* 101.
91 **Dr. Priddy and Strode:** Lombardo, "Eugenic Sterilization in Virginia," 96.
91 **The law applied:** Virginia Sterilization Act.
91 **Based on the statutory criteria:** "Carrie Buck Trial Transcript, 51–100" (2009), *Buck v. Bell Documents,* Paper 32, http://readingroom.law.gsu.edu/buckvbell/32, 88–89.
91 **Dr. Priddy had hundreds:** Ibid.
91 **It did not take him long:** Ibid., 88–89.
92 **Dr. Priddy also had:** Ibid., 89, 90–91.
92 **That would be costly:** Ibid., 89.
92 **On July 21, 1924:** "Order of July 21, 1924," *Buck v. Bell* file, Clerk's Office, Amherst County Courthouse, Amherst, VA; "Petition to the Special Board of Directors of State Colony for Epileptics and Feeble-Minded," in "Carrie Buck Trial Transcript, 1–50" (2009), *Buck v. Bell Documents,* Paper 31, http://readingroom.law.gsu.edu/buckvbell/31, 8–10.
92 **Shelton was authorized:** "Order of July 21, 1924"; Bruinius, *Better for All the World,* 59.
93 **The law required:** Lombardo, *Three Generations,* 289.
93 **On July 24, Dr. Priddy petitioned:** Notice of Filing of Petition, Before the Special Board of Directors of State Colony for Epileptics and Feeble-Minded, in "Carrie Buck Trial Transcript, 1–50" (2009), *Buck v. Bell Documents,* Paper 31, http://readingroom.law.gsu.edu/buckvbell/31, 11.
93 **Tracking the language:** "Petition to the Special Board of Directors of State Colony for Epileptics and Feeble-Minded."
93 **It was in Carrie's:** Petition to Sterilize Carrie Buck, *Buck v. Bell* case file, Clerk's Office, Amherst County Courthouse, Amherst, VA; J. David Smith and K. Ray Nelson, *The Sterilization of Carrie Buck: Was She Feebleminded or Society's Pawn?* (Far Hills, NJ: New Horizon Press, 1989), 41.
94 **Carrie was present:** "Statement of Evidence Before Board of Directors, *Priddy v. Buck*" in "Carrie Buck Trial Transcript, 1–50," 24
94 **During his tenure:** "Carrie Buck Trial Transcript, 1–50" (2009), *Buck v. Bell Documents,* Paper 31, http://readingroom.law.gsu.edu/buckvbell/31, 24–25.
94 **What was it about:** Ibid., 25.
94 **In the "History and Clinical Notes":** "History and Clinical Notes," June 4, 1924, box 11, Carrie Buck file, Library of Virginia.
94 **Nor did he tell:** Ibid., 60.
95 **He testified:** "Carrie Buck Trial Transcript, 1–50," 25.
95 **The depositions of John and Alice Dobbs:** Inquisition, Jan. 23, 1924, in "Carrie Buck Trial Transcript, 1–50," 15.
95 **In his "History and Clinical Notes":** "History and Clinical Notes," June 4, 1924.
95 **At the time of Carrie's commitment hearing:** Inquisition, Jan. 23, 1924, in "Carrie Buck Trial Transcript, 1–50," 15.
95 **Dr. Priddy then delivered:** "Carrie Buck Trial Transcript, 1–50," 25–26.
96 **He made no attempt:** Ibid., 26–27.
96 **Dr. Priddy was able to respond:** Ibid., 26.
96 **Shelton asked:** Ibid.
96 **Carrie's sterilization hearing:** Ibid., 27.
96 **Despite Carrie's apparent confusion: Ibid.**
97 **Nonetheless, the official record:** "Continued Notes," box 11, Central Virginia Training Center Papers.
97 **"by the laws of heredity":** Order of the Board of Special Directors, in "Carrie Buck Trial Transcript, 1–50," 27–29, http://readingroom.law.gsu.edu/cgi/viewcontent.cgi?article=1030&context=buckvbell.
97 **But Shelton did appeal:** "Continued Notes," Notice of Appeal and Praecipe for Transcript of Record, October 3, 1924, Circuit Court of Amherst County, http://readingroom.law.gsu.edu/cgi/viewcontent.cgi?article=1030&context=buckvbell.
97 **Carrie's "guardian at our request":** Priddy to Laughlin, Oct. 14, 1924.
97 **The appeal claimed:** Notice of Appeal and Praecipe for Transcript of Record, October 3, 1924, in "Carrie Buck Trial Transcript, 1–50," 5.
98 **While the appeal was pending:** An Act to Provide for the Sexual Sterilization of Inmates of State Institutions in Certain Cases, Virginia Acts of Assembly, chap. 394 (1924).
98 **Whitehead had extraordinarily close:** Lombardo, *Three Generations,* 107.
98 **The two men:** Ibid., 74, 216.

98 **He served on the colony's board:** Lombardo, *Three Generations*, 74, 148; Bruinius, *Better for All the World*, 61; Steven Noll, *Feeble-Minded in Our Midst* (Chapel Hill: University of North Carolina Press, 1995), 65.

98 **In April the colony had recognized:** Bruinius, *Better for All the World*, 61; *State Colony for Epileptics and Feeble-Minded: Second Biennial Report*, 7; Paul Lombardo, "Three Generations, No Imbeciles: New Light on *Buck v. Bell*," *New York University Law Review* 60 (April 1985): 55 147n.

98 **Whitehead had moved:** Lombardo, *Three Generations*, 74.

98 **Whitehead had supported:** Ibid.

99 **Further complicating the relationships:** Priddy to I. P. Whitehead, Dec. 12, 1924, box 11, Central Virginia Training Center Papers.

99 **His representation of Carrie:** Lombardo, *Three Generations*, 154.

99 **The Amherst County Circuit Court:** "Carrie Buck Trial Transcript, 1–50," 42.

100 **The eugenicists had won:** *State v. Feilen*, 70 Wash. 65, 126 P. 75 (1912); Reilly, *Surgical Solution*, 51; Laughlin, *Eugenical Sterilization*, 196.

100 **In 1913 the New Jersey Supreme Court:** "Notes and Abstracts," 596–97.

100 **The court ruled:** Mark A. Largent, *Breeding Contempt: The History of Coerced Sterilization in the United States* (New Brunswick, NJ: Rutgers University Press, 2011), 86.

100 **another ruling against sterilization:** *Davis v. Berry*, 216 F. 413, 416–17 (S.D. Iowa 1914); Laughlin, *Eugenical Sterilization*, 186–90.

100 **Those rulings were relevant:** "Notes and Abstracts," 596–97; Bruinius, *Better for All the World*, 219.

101 **The court ruled that the 1907:** Hansen and King, *Sterilized by the State*, 78; *Williams v. Smith*, *190* Ind. 526, 131 N.E. 2d (1921).

101 **In all, from 1913 to 1921:** Siegel, "Justice Holmes," 106, 121–22; William Leuchtenburg, *The Supreme Court Reborn: The Constitutional Revolution in the Age of Roosevelt* (New York: Oxford University Press, 1995), 6.

101 **not everyone was caught up in the eugenic mania:** Laughlin, *Eugenical Sterilization*, 35, 40, 46, 48; Leuchtenburg, *The Supreme Court Reborn*, 6.

101 **Nebraska's governor insisted:** Laughlin, *Eugenical Sterilization*, 48.

102 **In a letter to Dr. Priddy:** Aubrey Strode to Albert Priddy, Oct. 7, 1924, box 11, Central Virginia Training Center Papers.

CHAPTER FOUR: HARRY LAUGHLIN

103 **The states that followed:** Randall Hansen and Desmond King, *Sterilized by the State: Eugenics, Race, and the Population Scare in Twentieth-Century North America* (Cambridge: Cambridge University Press, 2013), 77.

103 **This large national movement:** Garland E. Allen, "The Eugenics Record Office at Cold Spring Harbor, 1910–1940: An Essay in Institutional History," *Osiris* 2 (1986), 226, 238.

104 **Harry Hamilton Laughlin:** Francis Marion Green, *Hiram College and Western Reserve Eclectic Institute: Fifty Years of History 1850–1900* (Cleveland: O. S. Hubbell, 1901), 261; Harry Bruinius, *Better for All the World: The Secret History of Forced Sterilization and America's Quest for Racial Purity* (New York: Alfred A. Knopf, 2006), 174–80; newspaper obituary of Deborah Laughlin (no title, undated, no publication), box E-1-1:10, Harry H. Laughlin Papers, Pickler Memorial Library, Truman State University, Kirksville, MO (hereafter cited as Laughlin Papers).

104 **George Laughlin:** *History of Portage County, Ohio* (Chicago: Warner, Beers, 1885), 747.

105 **they settled in Hiram:** Green, *Hiram College*, 260–61; Jan Onofrio, *Iowa Biographical Dictionary* (St. Clair Shores, Mich.: Somerset Publishers, Inc. 2000), 1:464.

105 **The family finally settled:** Bruinius, *Better for All the World*, 180; newspaper clipping, box E-1-1:10, Laughlin Papers; "Biography of Harry H. Laughlin," Special Collections University Archives, Pickler Memorial Library, Truman State University, https://library.truman.edu/manuscripts/laughlinbio.asp; Frances Janet Hassencahl, "Harry H. Laughlin, 'Expert Eugenics Agent' for the House Committee on Immigration and Naturalization, 1921 to 1931" (Ph.D. diss., Case Western Reserve University, 1970), 43.

105 **Laughlin's parents had met:** Bruinius, *Better for All the World*, 176.

105 **Deborah Ross Laughlin:** Hassencahl, "Expert Eugenics Agent," 45–46; *History of Portage County, Ohio*, 747.

105 **When she was not busy:** Hassencahl, "Expert Eugenics Agent," 45–46.

105 **A compelling public speaker:** Obituary of Deborah Laughlin, *Kirksville Daily Express*, Sept. 20, 1918, box E-1-1:7, Laughlin Papers; Hassencahl, "Expert Eugenics Agent," 45–46; Bruinius, *Better for All the World*, 177–78.

105 **She was especially drawn:** "Woman's Christian Temperance Union," *Encyclopedia of American Religion and Politics*, ed. Paul Dupe and Laura Olson (New York: Facts on File, 2003), 487.

105 **Deborah Laughlin led antidrinking "pray-ins":** Hassencahl, "Expert Eugenics Agent," 46; Bruinius, *Better for All the World*, 178.

105 **His mother's ancestry:** Hassencahl, "Expert Eugenics Agent," 43, 46; *History of Portage County, Ohio*, 747.

105 **His father's family:** Green, *Hiram College*, 261.

106 **In "Cosmopolitanism in America," a paper:** Harry Laughlin, "Cosmopolitanism in America" (1899), 15, box E-1-1, Laughlin Papers.

106 **That intellectual moralism:** Allen, "Eugenics Record Office," 236.

106 **"eventually the world will be inhabited":** Laughlin, "Cosmopolitanism in America," 15.

106 **after graduating from college:** "Biography of Harry H. Laughlin," https://library.truman.edu/manuscripts/laughlinbio.asp.

106 **In 1902 he married:** Bruinius, *Better for All the World*, 186.

106 **Laughlin came home:** "Biographical Sketches," box E-1-1:7, Laughlin Papers; Daniel J. Kevles, *In the Name of Eugenics: Genetics and the Uses of Human Heredity* (Cambridge, MA: Harvard University Press, 1985), 102; *Catalogue of Princeton University, 1918–19* (Princeton, NJ: Princeton University Press, 1918), 358–59.

106 **A profile:** "Biographical Sketches," box E-1-1:7, Laughlin Papers.

106 **Davenport, the director:** Harry Laughlin to Charles Davenport, Feb. 25, 1907, Laughlin folder 1, Charles Benedict Davenport Papers, American Philosophical Society, Philadelphia (hereafter cited as Davenport Papers); Davenport to Laughlin, March 1, 1907, Laughlin folder 1, Davenport papers.

107 **He arranged to meet:** Allen, "Eugenics Record Office," 237; Hassencahl, "Expert Eugenics Agent," 54; Philip R. Reilly, *The Surgical Solution: A History of Involuntary Sterilization in the United States* (Baltimore: Johns Hopkins University Press, 1991), 58.

107 **Laughlin persuaded Davenport:** Allen, "Eugenics Record Office," 237.

107 **"Your visit here":** Laughlin to Davenport, Jan. 30, 1909, Laughlin folder 1, Davenport Papers; Davenport to Laughlin, Dec. 10, 1908, ibid.; Laughlin to Davenport, Dec. 15, 1908, ibid.

107 **The next year:** Allen, "Eugenics Record Office," 237.

107 **"the most profitable six weeks":** Laughlin to Davenport, Mar. 30, 1908, Laughlin folder 1, Davenport Papers.

107 **a mentor:** Hassencahl, "Expert Eugenics Agent," 53; Allen, "Eugenics Record Office," 237–38.

107 **Charles Benedict Davenport:** Stamford Historical Society, "Portrait of a Family: Stamford Through the Legacy of the Davenports, Amzi Benedict Davenport, 1817–1894," http://www.stamfordhistory.org/dav_amzi.htm; Amzi Benedict Davenport, *A Supplement to the History and Genealogy of the Davenport Family, in England and America, from A.D. 1086 to 1850 and Continued to 1876* (Stamford: private printing, 1876), 331.

107 **The Davenports traced:** Bruinius *Better for all the World*, 108–9.

107 **Reverend Davenport, who cofounded:** Ibid., 15; Francis J. Bremer, *Building a New Jerusalem* (New Haven, CT: Yale University Press, 2012), 3.

108 **The book—the title page:** Stamford Historical Society, "Portrait of a Family"; *A History and Genealogy of the Davenport Family in England and America, from A.D. 1086 to 1850* (New York: S.W. Benedict, 1851); Amzi Benedict Davenport, *A Supplement to the History and Genealogy of the Davenport Family;* Edwin Black, *War Against the Weak* (New York: Four Walls Eight Windows, 2003), 32–33; Reilly, *Surgical Solution*, 18.

108 **Charles Davenport attended Harvard:** Kevles, *In the Name of Eugenics*, 45; *Harvard University Directory* (Cambridge, MA: Harvard University Press, 1914), 202; Joshua Chamberlain, ed. *Universities and Their Sons: History, Influence and Characteristics of American Universities* (Boston: R. Herndon 1900), 15.

108 **He began to look:** Allen, "Eugenics Record Office," 228.

108 **Davenport secured annual funding:** Ibid., 230.

108 **In 1904 he founded:** Kevles, *In the Name of Eugenics*, 45; Allen, "Eugenics Record Office," 229–30.

108 He wrote a paper: Allen, "Eugenics Record Office," 230–31, 232.
108 Davenport had traveled to England: Carolyn Fluehr-Lobban, *Race and Racism: An Introduction* (Lanham, MD: AltaMira Press, 2006), 118.
109 It sought to bring together: Allen, "Eugenics Record Office," 232.
109 The Breeders' Association's members: Allen, "Eugenics Record Office," 232.
109 "Science is taking hold": Mark A. Largent, *Breeding Contempt: The History of Coerced Sterilization in the United States* (New Brunswick, NJ: Rutgers University Press, 2011), 50.
109 It formed a Committee on Eugenics: Ibid., 51.
109 The committee chairman: Hassencahl, "Expert Eugenics Agent," 55–61; Allen, "Eugenics Record Office," 232.
109 Davenport served as secretary: Hassencahl, "Expert Eugenics Agent," 55–61; Allen, "Eugenics Record Office," 232; James W. Trent Jr., *Inventing the Feeble Mind: A History of Mental Retardation in the United States* (Berkeley: University of California Press, 1994), 171.
109 At a Breeders' Association meeting: American Breeders' Association, *Report of the Meeting Held at Omaha, Nebraska, Dec. 8, 9 and 10, 1909* (Washington, DC: American Breeders' Association, 1911), 93, quoted in Hassencahl, "Expert Eugenics Agent," 31.
109 Davenport persuaded the Breeders' Association: Largent, *Breeding Contempt*, 52–55.
109 Davenport published his first major book: Charles Benedict Davenport, *Eugenics: The Science of Human Improvement by Better Breeding* (New York: Henry Holt, 1910).
109 In *Eugenics*: Davenport, *Eugenics*, 31, 34; Paul A. Lombardo, *Three Generations, No Imbeciles: Eugenics, the Supreme Court, and* Buck v. Bell (Baltimore: Johns Hopkins University Press, 2008), 31.
110 "Vastly more effective": Davenport, *Eugenics*, 35.
110 Davenport had a connection: Kevles, *In the Name of Eugenics*, 54.
110 "What is the matter": William Leuchtenburg, *The Supreme Court Reborn: The Constitutional Revolution in the Age of Roosevelt* (New York: Oxford University Press, 1995), 5.
110 In his diary: Largent, *Breeding Contempt*, 56.
110 Harriman became the main patron: Allen, "Eugenics Record Office," 227, 234–35.
110 Over the next five years: Hassencahl, "Expert Eugenics Agent," 68.
110 Bell, who was the son: Melvia Nomeland and Ronald Nomeland, *The Deaf Community in America: History in the Making* (Jefferson, NC: McFarland, 2012), 47.
111 In a paper presented: Alexander Graham Bell, "Upon the Formation of a Deaf Variety of the Human Race" (Washington, DC: Government Printing Office, 1884), 41.
111 Irving Fisher: "Harriman Philanthropy to Have a Board of Scientific Directors," *New York Times*, Mar. 31, 1913; Allen, "Eugenics Record Office," 238.
111 In 1909 he wrote: Irving Fisher, *A Report on National Vitality: Its Wastes and Conservation* (Washington, DC: Government Printing Office, 1909), 52.
111 Davenport also persuaded: "Social Problems Have a Proven Basis of Heredity," *New York Times*, Jan. 12, 1913.
111 Rockefeller, who was troubled: Theresa Richardson and Donald Fisher, eds. *The Development of the Social Sciences in the United States and Canada: The Role of Philanthropy* (Stamford, CT: Ablex, 1999), 103.
111 An organization affiliated with the bureau: Garland Allen, "The Role of Experts in Scientific Controversy," in *Scientific Controversies: Case Studies in the Resolution and Closure of Disputes in Science and Technology*, ed. H. Tristram Engelhardt Jr. and Arthur Caplan (Cambridge: Cambridge University Press, 1987), 183–85.
111 Davenport wrote to Galton: Fluehr-Lobban, *Race and Racism*, 118.
111 He had been impressed: Allen, "Eugenics Record Office," 236, 237.
112 Davenport offered: Ibid., 226.
112 "As rapidly as we can": Laughlin to Davenport, Sept. 2, 1910, Laughlin folder 2, Davenport Papers.
112 Davenport responded a few days later: Davenport to Laughlin, Sept. 6, 1910, Laughlin folder 2, Davenport Papers.
112 They moved into the large house: Allen, "Eugenics Record Office," 238.
112 "center for research in human genetics": Mark Haller, *Eugenics: Hereditarian Attitudes in American Thought* (New Brunswick, NJ: Rutgers University Press, 1963), 64; Ruth Engs, *The Progressive Era's Health Reform Movement: A Historical Dictionary* (Westport, CT: Praeger, 2003), 117.

NOTES

112 **It was assigned reading:** Ann Gibson Winfield, *Eugenics and Education in America: Institutionalized Racism and the Implications of History, Ideology, and Memory* (New York: Peter Lang, 2007), 69.

112 **He argued that:** Charles Davenport, *Heredity in Relation to Eugenics* (New York: Henry Holt, 1911), 80–92.

112 **"When both parents are shiftless":** Ibid., 82.

113 **America's earliest immigrants:** Ibid., 212.

113 **Jews had positive attributes:** Ibid., 216.

113 **Davenport began by noting that Italians:** Ibid., 217–18.

113 **Davenport credited the Irish:** Ibid., 213–14, 218–19.

113 **The "great influx of blood":** Ibid., 219.

114 **It was this national stock of germplasm:** Ibid., 221.

114 **Decades before the Nazis:** Hassencahl, "Expert Eugenics Agent," 30; Sheila Faith Weiss, *Race Hygiene and National Efficiency: The Eugenics of Wilhelm Schallmayer* (Berkeley: University of California Press, 1987), 197n9; Lombardo, *Three Generations*, 199.

114 **In 1907 the Gesellschaft für Rassenhygiene:** Stefan Kuhl, *The Nazi Connection: Eugenics, American Racism, and German National Socialism* (New York: Oxford University Press, 1994), 13.

114 **The German Society for Racial Hygiene circulated a flyer:** Ibid., 15–16.

115 **Under Laughlin's leadership:** Allen, "Eugenics Record Office," 238.

115 **The trainees attended classes:** Luis A. Cordon, *Freud's World: An Encyclopedia of His Life and Times* (Santa Barbara, CA: ABC-CLIO, 2012), 109.

115 **Jane Addams:** David Rothman, *Conscience and Convenience: The Asylum and Its Alternatives in Progressive America* (Hawthorne, NY: Aldine de Gruyter, 2002), 47.

115 **Eugenics Record Office trainees:** Allen, "Eugenics Record Office," 243.

115 **The researchers were also taught practical skills:** Cordon, *Freud's World.* 108–9.

115 **The trainees:** Allen, "Eugenics Record Office," 241; Hassencahl, "Expert Eugenics Agent," 69; Reilly, *Surgical Solution*, 58; Cordon, *Freud's World.* 108–9.

115 **They were also sent to Ellis Island:** Cordon, *Freud's World*, 109.

115 **The data:** Reilly, *Surgical Solution*, 58.

116 **As part of its "clearinghouse" function:** Lombardo, *Three Generations*, 35.

116 **An admiring profile:** "Social Problems Have Proven Basis of Heredity," *New York Times*, Jan. 12, 1913.

116 **In a report released:** Cordon, *Freud's World*, 108.

116 **Pansy Laughlin wrote:** Bruinius, *Better for All the World*, 196. In at least one version of the play, the peddler is not Felix Rosenfeld but Jim Weeks, a "happy-go-lucky peddler"; see http://www.dnalc.org/view/10497--Acquired-or-inherited-A-eugenical-comedy-in-four-acts-play-written-by-P-Laughlin-F-Danielson-and-H-Laughlin.html.

117 **He also investigated:** Hassencahl, "Expert Eugenics Agent," 69; Allen, "Eugenics Record Office," 239.

117 **Committee to Study and to Report on the Best Practical Means:** Kenneth Ludmerer, *Genetics and American Society: A Historical Appraisal* (Baltimore: Johns Hopkins University Press, 1972), 92.

117 **Laughlin was named secretary:** Ian Robert Dowbiggin, *Keeping America Sane: Psychiatry and Eugenics in the United States and Canada, 1880–1940* (Ithaca, NY: Cornell University Press, 1997), 78.

117 **First National Conference on Race Betterment:** Black, *War Against the Weak,* 88; Bruinius, *Better for all the World*, 209.

117 **Kellogg promoted:** Black, *War Against the Weak*, 88.

117 **"all serious-minded men and women":** J. H. Kellogg, "Needed—A New Human Race," *Michigan Public Health* 2, no. 4 (February 1913): 104–5.

118 **Attendance at the first session:** Report of the Secretary, *Official Proceedings of the National Conference on Race Betterment* (Battle Creek, MI: Race Betterment Foundation, 1914), 1:594–95; Reilly, *Surgical Solution*, 43.

118 **There were exhibits:** Official Proceedings of the National Conference on Race Betterment, 1:597, 600–602, 606.

118 **In Laughlin's presentation:** H. H. Laughlin, "Calculations on the Working Out of a Proposed Program of Sterilization," in ibid., 1:478.

118 **The "lowest ten percent":** Ibid., 1:480, 485, 486.

118   **To rid the nation:** Ibid., 1:489–90; Lombardo, *Three Generations*, 48.

119   **Current sterilization regimens:** Laughlin, "Calculations on the Working Out," 1:490.

119   **"The shorter the periods":** Ibid., 1:487.

119   **He argued that the increased expenditures:** Ibid., 1:488, 491.

119   **Laughlin's American Breeders' Association report:** *Eugenics Record Office Bulletin No. 10*: Harry H. Laughlin, "The Scope of the Committee's Work," in *Report of the Committee to Study and to Report on the Best Practical Means of Cutting Off the Defective Germ-Plasm in the American Population* (Cold Spring Harbor, NY: Eugenics Record Office, 1914); Lombardo, *Three Generations*, 49.

119   **The report was the most thorough argument:** Laughlin, "The Scope of the Committee's Work," 16; Mary L. Dudziak, "Oliver Wendell Holmes as a Eugenic Reformer: Rhetoric in the Writing of Constitutional Law," *Iowa Law Review* 71 (1986): 846.

119   **ten defective classes:** Laughlin, "The Scope of the Committee's Work," 16–57.

120   **"There must be selection":** Ibid., 57.

120   **The report put the rate:** Ibid., 46, 60.

120   **Sterilization was also an option:** Ibid., 46–47.

120   **the report was far more skeptical:** Laughlin, "Calculations on the Working Out," 489; Lombardo, *Three Generations*, 48.

120   **The report included a second part:** Harry H. Laughlin, "The Legal, Legislative and Administrative Aspects of Sterilization," in *Report of the Committee to Study and to Report on the Best Practical Means of Cutting Off the Defective Germ-Plasm in the American Population*, vol. II, 115–17.

121   **It recommended sterilization:** Ibid., 117, 125.

121   **"If America is to escape the doom":** Laughlin, "The Scope of the Committee's Work," 59.

121   **With the research he was now conducting:** "Biographical Sketches," box E-1-1:7, Laughlin Papers; Kevles, *In the Name of Eugenics*, 102.

122   **At Davenport's suggestion:** Hassencahl, "Expert Eugenics Agent," 62.

122   **Laughlin moved through the doctoral program:** *Catalogue of Princeton University, 1918–19* (Princeton, NJ: Princeton University, 1918), 358–59.

122   **He studied with Edwin G. Conklin:** Bert Bender, *Evolution and "the Sex Problem": American Narratives During the Eclipse of Darwinism* (Kent, OH: Kent State University Press, 2004), 225; Hassencahl, "Expert Eugenics Agent," 62–63.

122   **Laughlin focused on science:** Hassencahl, "Expert Eugenics Agent," 62; *Catalogue of Princeton University, 1918–19*, 358–59.

122   **The Eugenics Record Office launched a new journal:** Kevles, *In the Name of Eugenics*, 56.

122   **The *Eugenical News*:** Black, *War Against the Weak*, 98.

122   **It published research:** Allen, "Eugenics Record Office," 246.

122   **In keeping with the views:** Black, *War Against the Weak*, 298; Stefan Kuhl, "The Cooperation of German Racial Hygienists and American Eugenicists Before and After 1933," in *The Holocaust and History: The Known, the Unknown, the Disputed, and the Reexamined*, ed. Michael Berenbaum and Abraham Peck (Bloomington: Indiana University Press, 1998), 137–38.

122   **He conducted his research:** Hassencahl, "Expert Eugenics Agent," 63.

122   **He finally succeeded:** Black, *War Against the Weak*, 159.

122   **Laughlin used his access:** Bureau of the Census, *Statistical Directory of State Institutions for the Defective, Dependent, and Delinquent Classes* (Washington, DC: Government Printing Office, 1919), 5.

122   **His work was slowed:** Ibid.; Black, *War Against the Weak*, 160.

122   **Laughlin would go on:** *Biological Aspects of Immigration: Hearings Before the Committee on Immigration and Naturalization*, 66th Cong., 2nd sess., Apr. 16 and 17, 1920, statement of Harry H. Laughlin (Washington, DC: Government Printing Office, 1921), 16–17.

123   **Madison Grant:** Jonathan Peter Spiro, *Defending the Master Race: Conservation, Eugenics, and the Legacy of Madison Grant* (Lebanon, NH: University Press of New England, 2009), xii, 35.

123   **He was a cofounder:** Winfield, *Eugenics and Education in America*, 74; Ludmerer, *Genetics and American Society*, 53.

123   **The two men even agreed on the percentage:** Madison Grant to Charles Davenport, July 6, 1914, Madison Grant folder 1 BD, Davenport Papers.

123   **Grant was particularly focused:** Ibid.

123 **He was contemptuous:** Ibid.

123 **Grant was also fixated on Polish Jews:** Spiro, *Defending the Master Race*, 152.

123 **"native American aristocracy":** Madison Grant, *The Passing of the Great Race; or, The Racial Basis of European History* (New York: Charles Scribner's Sons, 1918), 5.

124 **divided the people of Europe:** Ibid., 19–20, 27; Kevles, *In the Name of Eugenics*, 75.

124 **Grant extolled the Nordic race:** Grant, *Passing of the Great Race*, 27.

124 **"Races must be kept apart":** Ibid., 222.

124 **Grant's proposed responses:** Ibid., 50–51.

124 **The book would later be discovered:** Timothy Ryback, *Hitler's Private Library* (New York: Alfred A. Knopf, 2008), 110; Spiro, *Defending the Master Race*, 357.

124 **Laughlin had already been the subject:** Reilly, *Surgical Solution*, 68.

125 **In his private correspondence with Grant:** Harry Laughlin to Madison Grant, Nov. 19, 1932, folder C-2-1:8, Laughlin Papers.

125 **Laughlin and Grant collaborated:** Hassencahl, "Expert Eugenics Agent," 196–97.

125 **He reviewed:** Allen, "Eugenics Record Office," 246n51.

125 **"The wide and continuous":** Harry Laughlin to R. V. Coleman, Nov. 25, 1935, folder C-2-1:8, Laughlin Papers.

126 **Laughlin was effusive:** See Harry Laughlin to Edward B. Greene, Mar. 16, 1937, folder C-2-1:8, Laughlin Papers; Allen, "Eugenics Record Office," 246.

126 **In 1900 the foreign-born:** Paul S. Boyer and Melvyn Dubofsky, eds., *The Oxford Companion to United States History* (New York: Oxford University Press, 2001), 362.

126 **immigration had continued:** Black, *War Against the Weak*, 186.

126 **Since 1896 Protestants had ceased:** Kristofer Allerfeldt, *Race, Radicalism, Religion, and Restriction: Immigration in the Pacific Northwest, 1890-1924* (Westport, CT: Praeger, 2003), 34.

126 **Grant expressed these resentments:** Grant, *Passing of the Great Race*, 81.

127 **immigration opponents had more specific concerns:** Steven G. Koven and Frank Gotzke, *American Immigration Policy: Confronting the Nation's Challenges* (New York: Springer, 2010), 30; Boyer and Dubofsky, *Oxford Companion to United States History*, 361–63.

127 **immigrants were of inferior genetic stock:** Carlson, *The Unfit*, 257.

127 **literacy test for immigrants:** Koven and Gotzke, *American Immigration Policy*, 130; Spiro, *Defending the Race*, 198.

127 **The Immigration Restriction League:** Hassencahl, "Expert Eugenics Agent," 165.

127 **immigrants were bringing genetic defects:** Reilly, *Surgical Solution*, 24.

127 **"The same arguments":** Leila Zenderland, *Measuring Minds: Henry Herbert Goddard and the Origins of American Intelligence Testing* (Cambridge: Cambridge University Press, 1998), 264.

127 **Hall helped to form:** Hassencahl, "Expert Eugenics Agent," 165.

128 ***Dearborn Independent*:** Christine Rosen, *Preaching Eugenics: Religious Leaders and the American Eugenics Movement* (New York: Oxford University Press, 2004), 106.

128 **Ku Klux Klan:** Maldwyn Allen Jones, *American Immigration* (Chicago: University of Chicago Press, 1992), 236; Wyn Craig Wade, *The Fiery Cross: The Ku Klux Klan in America* (New York: Oxford University Press, 1998), 179; Kathleen Arnold, ed., *Anti-Immigration in the United States: An Historical Encyclopedia* (Santa Barbara, CA: ABC-CLIO, 2011), 311.

128 **Franz Boas:** Carlson, *The Unfit*, 257; Jeanne Petit, *The Men and Women We Want: Gender, Race, and the Progressive Era Literacy Test Debate* (Rochester, NY: University of Rochester Press, 2010), 77.

128 **Madison Grant attacked Boas:** Winfield, *Eugenics and Education*, 74.

128 **Albert Johnson:** Thomas Gossett, *Race: The History of an Idea in America* (New York: Oxford University Press, 1997), 405–6.

128 **The main reason:** Albert Johnson to W. F. Newel, Mar. 24, 1929, quoted in Hassencahl, "Expert Eugenics Agent," 205.

129 **The blond, blue-eyed Johnson:** Hassencahl, "Expert Eugenics Agent," 205.

129 **an admirer of *The Passing of the Great Race*:** Gossett, *Race*, 406.

129 **Grant introduced Johnson to Laughlin:** Spiro, *Defending the Master Race*, 204.

129 **On April 16 and 17:** *Biological Aspects of Immigration: Hearings Before the Committee on Immigration and Naturalization*, statement of Harry H. Laughlin, 3.

129 **Federal immigration policy:** Ibid.

129 **prospective immigrants:** Ibid.

130 **non–northern European immigrants were a problem:** Ibid., 17–18.
130 **Johnson was so pleased:** Letterhead, "House of Representatives Committee on Immigration and Naturalization (Sixty-Seventh Congress), Albert Johnson (Wash.), Chairman, Harry H. Laughlin, Expert Eugenics Agent," box E-1-1:4, Laughlin Papers.
130 **"the great American watchdog":** Spiro, *Defending the Master Race*, 204.
130 **Emergency Immigration Restriction Act of 1921:** Patrick J. Hayes, ed., *The Making of Modern Immigration: An Encyclopedia of People and Ideas* (Santa Barbara, CA: ABC-CLIO, 2012), 186; Michael LeMay and Elliott Robert Barkan, eds., *U.S. Immigration and Naturalization Laws and Issues: A Documentary History* (Westport, CT: Greenwood Press, 1999) 133.
131 **The number of immigrants from Europe:** Koven and Gotzke, *American Immigration Policy*, 132.
131 **In November 1922:** *An Analysis of America's Modern Melting Pot, Hearings Before the Committee on Immigration and Naturalization,* 67th Cong., 3rd sess., Nov. 21, 1922, statement of Harry H. Laughlin (Washington, DC: Government Printing Office, 1923) 725–831.
131 **Covering the committee room walls:** Spiro, *Defending the Master Race*, 215; Kevles, *In the Name of Eugenics*, 103.
131 **"Making all logical allowances":** *Analysis of America's Modern Melting Pot,* statement of Harry H. Laughlin, 755, quoted in Ludmerer, *Genetics and American Society*, 101.
131 **"one of the most valuable documents":** Ludmerer, *Genetics and American Society*, 103.
132 **Russian immigrants in America:** Kevles, *In the Name of Eugenics*, 103.
132 **In March 1924 Laughlin testified:** *Europe as an Emigrant-Exporting Continent and the United States as an Immigrant-Receiving Nation: Hearings Before the Committee on Immigration and Naturalization,* 68th Cong., 1st sess., March 8, 1924, statement of Harry H. Laughlin (Washington, DC: Government Printing Office, 1924), 1146 (chart).
132 **"Immigration is an insidious invasion":** Ibid., 1305.
132 **serious problems with Laughlin's data:** Stephen Jay Gould, "A Nation of Morons," *New Scientist* (May 6, 1982): 351.
132 **Herbert Spencer Jennings:** Herbert S. Jennings, "Undesirable Aliens," *Survey* 51 (1923): 311, cited in Ludmerer, *Genetics and American Society*, 123.
133 **Joseph Gillman:** Gillman, "Statistics and the Immigration Problem," *American Journal of Sociology* 30, no. 1 (July 1924): 38.
133 **The "primary reason":** Kevles, *In the Name of Eugenics*, 97.
133 **"the arrest of a negro in New York":** Edward J. Larson, *Sex, Race, and Science: Eugenics in the Deep South* (Baltimore: Johns Hopkins University Press, 1995), 103; "The Passing of Tom Heflin," *Life*, May 7, 1951, 40.
133 **"infected with the germ":** Spiro, *Defending the Master Race*, 224.
133 **Adolph Sabath:** Representative Sabath speaking against H.R. 7995, 68th Cong., 1st sess., April 5, 1924, *Congressional Record* 65, 5662, quoted in Hassencahl, "Expert Eugenics Agent," 223.
134 **A new edition:** Ludmerer, *Genetics and American Society*, 103.
134 **In 1921 *Good Housekeeping* published:** Calvin Coolidge, "Whose Country Is This?," *Good Housekeeping*, Feb. 1921, 13–14, 106–9.
134 **"Biological laws tell us":** John J. Miller, *The Unmaking of Americans: How Multiculturalism Has Undermined America's Assimilation Ethic* (New York: The Free Press, 1998), 79.
134 ***Saturday Evening Post:*** "Saturday Evening Post," in *The Great Depression in America: A Cultural Encyclopedia,* ed. William H. Young and Nancy K. Young (Westport, CT: Greenwood Press, 2007), 2:452.
134 **"If America doesn't keep out":** Otis L. Graham, *Unguarded Gates: A History of America's Immigration Crisis* (Lanham, MD: Rowman and Littlefield, 2006), 51.
134 **The new formula:** Gulie Ne'eman Arad, *America, Its Jews, and the Rise of Nazism* (Bloomington: Indiana University Press, 2000), 64.
135 **"America's Second Declaration of Independence":** Donna Gabaccia, *Foreign Relations: American Immigration in Global Perspective* (Princeton, NJ: Princeton University Press, 2012), 142.
135 **Madison Grant hailed:** Spiro, *Defending the Master Race*, 233.
135 **"simply excluding certain races":** Adolf Hitler, *Mein Kampf,* trans. Ralph Manheim (1925; repr., Boston: Houghton Mifflin, 1971), 440; Paul Lombardo, "'The American Breed': Nazi Eugenics and the Origins of the Pioneer Fund," *Albany Law Review* 65 (2002): 756.
135 **Southern and eastern Europeans:** Koven and Gotzke, *American Immigration Policy*, 133.
135 **Jewish immigration fell:** Howard M. Sachar, *A History of Jews in the Modern World* (New York: Random House, 2007), 384.

135 The "biological" immigration policies: Ibid.; Gould, "A Nation of Morons," 352.
135 Among the many victims: Patricia Cohen, "In Old Files, Fading Hopes of Anne Frank's Family," *New York Times*, Feb. 15, 2007.

CHAPTER FIVE: HARRY LAUGHLIN
136 In 1914, in his address: H. H. Laughlin, "Calculations on the Working Out of a Proposed Program of Sterilization," *Official Proceedings of the National Conference on Race Betterment* (Battle Creek, MI: Race Betterment Foundation, 1914), 1:478, 489; Paul A. Lombardo, *Three Generations, No Imbeciles: Eugenics, the Supreme Court, and* Buck v. Bell (Baltimore: Johns Hopkins University Press, 2008), 48.
136 That same year, with the report: Harry H. Laughlin, *Report of the Committee to Study and to Report on the Best Practical Means of Cutting Off the Defective Germ-Plasm in the American Population* (Cold Spring Harbor, NY: Eugenics Record Office, 1914).
137 The exhibits at the congress: Harry Laughlin, *The Second International Exhibition of Eugenics* (Baltimore: Williams & Wilkins, 1923), 1, 17, 110–11.
137 502-page treatise: Harry H. Laughlin, *Eugenical Sterilization in the United States* (Chicago: Psychopathic Laboratory of the Municipal Court of Chicago, 1922), ix–xxii.
137 The committee initially supported sterilization: Frances Janet Hassencahl, "Harry H. Laughlin: 'Expert Eugenics Agent' for the House Committee on Immigration and Naturalization, 1921 to 1931" (Ph.D. diss., Case Western Reserve University, 1970), 152–54.
138 The Carnegie Institution: Laughlin, *Eugenical Sterilization*, ix–xxii.
138 The bureau conceded: Philip R. Reilly, *The Surgical Solution: A History of Involuntary Sterilization in the United States* (Baltimore: Johns Hopkins University Press, 1991), 63.
138 Laughlin eventually turned: Ibid.; Laughlin, *Eugenical Sterilization*, i, v–vi.
138 As the prospective funders anticipated: Laughlin, *Eugenical Sterilization.*, v, vi.
138 In the book itself: Laughlin, *Report of the Committee to Study and to Report on the Best Practical Means of Cutting Off the Defective Germ-Plasm in the American Population.*
138 He did not believe: Harry H. Laughlin, "The Legal, Legislative and Administrative Aspects of Sterilization," in *Report of the Committee to Study and to Report on the Best Practical Means of Cutting Off the Defective Germ-Plasm in the American Population*, 125.
139 Writing now on his own: Laughlin, *Eugenical Sterilization*, 446.
139 "socially inadequate classes": Ibid., 446–47; Laughlin, "Legal, Legislative and Administrative Aspects of Sterilization," 125.
139 He had his first reported seizure: Hassencahl, "Expert Eugenics Agent," 66; Nathaniel Comfort, *The Science of Human Perfection: How Genes Became the Heart of American Medicine* (New Haven, CT: Yale University Press, 2012), 97; Jonathan Peter Spiro, *Defending the Master Race: Conservation, Eugenics, and the Legacy of Madison Grant* (Lebanon, NH: University Press of New England, 2009), 351.
139 When Laughlin's first seizure struck: Hassencahl, "Expert Eugenics Agent," 65–66; Comfort, *Science of Human Perfection*, 97; Spiro, *Defending the Master Race*, 351.
140 The year before: William Leuchtenburg, *The Supreme Court Reborn: The Constitutional Revolution in the Age of Roosevelt* (New York: Oxford University Press, 1995), 6.
140 Laughlin argued: Laughlin, *Eugenical Sterilization*, 438.
140 To bolster this argument: Ibid., 322, 324–36.
141 To insulate against: Ibid., 447, 449–50.
141 Laughlin strongly advised the states: Ibid., 446.
141 *Eugenical Sterilization in the United States*: Leon F. Whitney, *The Case for Sterilization* (New York: Frederick Stokes, 1934), 126–28.
141 Its charter members included: Reilly, *Surgical Solution*, 66.
142 to observe his favorite racial groups: Hassencahl, "Expert Eugenics Agent," 191; Harry Laughlin to Hon. Harry Olson, Chief Justice of the Municipal Court of Chicago, Oct. 12, 1923, box D-2-3:6, Harry H. Laughlin Papers, Pickler Memorial Library, Truman State University, Kirksville, MO (hereafter cited as Laughlin Papers).
142 "The strenuous struggle for existence": Laughlin to Olson, Oct. 12, 1923.
142 In January 1924: Reilly, *Surgical Solution*, 66; Harry Laughlin, "Eugenics in America," an address delivered at Burlington House, London, Jan. 29, 1924, reprinted in *Eugenics Review* 17 (April 1925), 28–35; Nathaniel Deutsch, *Inventing America's "Worst" Family: Eugenics, Islam, and the Fall and Rise of the Tribe of Ishmael* (Berkeley: University of California Press, 2009), 218.
142 In his remarks: Laughlin, "Eugenics in America," 28–31.

142 The United States and the "white British colonies": Ibid., 35.

142 "a zealot for passing laws": Kenneth Ludmerer, *Genetics and American Society: A Historical Appraisal* (Baltimore: Johns Hopkins University Press, 1972), 92.

142 "the procreation of feeble-minded": Laughlin, *Eugenical Sterilization*, 99.

143 He would soon boast: "Annual Report of H. H. Laughlin for the Year Ending June 30, 1925," in Laughlin folder 15, Charles Benedict Davenport Papers, American Philosophical Society, Philadelphia (hereafter cited as Davenport Papers); Laughlin, *Eugenical Sterilization*, 99.

143 As well as things were going: Stephen A. Siegel, "Justice Holmes, *Buck v. Bell*, and the History of Equal Protection," *Minnesota Law Review* 90 (2005): 120–21; Lombardo, *Three Generations*, 316.

143 There had been a deluge: Leuchtenburg, *Supreme Court Reborn*, 6; Siegel, "Justice Holmes," 106, 121–22.

143 On September 30, 1924: Aubrey Strode to Harry Laughlin, Sept. 30, 1924, box 3, folder 8, Arthur Estabrook Papers, M. E. Grenander Department of Special Collections and Archives, University at Albany, State University of New York (hereafter cited as Estabrook Papers).

144 His client was "unwilling to proceed": Ibid.

144 The law's defenders: Ibid.

144 Strode gave Laughlin a brief synopsis: Ibid.

144 Laughlin wrote back to Strode: Harry Laughlin to Aubrey Strode, Oct. 3, 1924, box 11, Central Virginia Training Center Papers, Library of Virginia.

145 The nation's highest court: Ibid.

145 He agreed with Dr. Priddy: Ibid.

145 It would be enough: Strode to Laughlin, Sept. 30, 1924.

145 Laughlin agreed to do that: Aubrey Strode to Albert Priddy, Oct. 29, 1924, box 11, Central Virginia Training Center Papers.

145 To begin the scientific study: Laughlin to Strode, Oct. 3, 1924; "Memorandum Outlining the Data Needed for a Family History or Pedigree Analysis of the Subject of the Test Case Under the Virginia Eugenic Sterilization Statute," Carrie Buck and Doris Buck Figgins Sterilization, ca. 1920s–1980s file, Central Virginia Training Center Papers; Lombardo, *Three Generations*, 108–9, 319n26.

145 Laughlin sent a memorandum: Laughlin to Strode, Oct. 3, 1924; "Memorandum Outlining the Data Needed"; Lombardo, *Three Generations*, 108–9, 319n26.

145 He asked Strode for information: "Memorandum Outlining the Data Needed."

146 Laughlin sent two tools: Laughlin to Strode, Oct. 3, 1924; "Memorandum Outlining the Data Needed."

146 Strode wrote to Dr. Priddy: Strode to Albert Priddy, Oct. 7, 1924, box 11, Central Virginia Training Center Papers; "Memorandum Outlining the Data Needed."

146 Dr. Priddy reminded Laughlin: Albert Priddy to Harry Laughlin, Oct. 14, 1924, box 11, Central Virginia Training Center Papers.

146 At a meeting: Ibid.

146 It was a conception: Ibid.

147 He asked Wilhelm: Albert Priddy to Caroline Wilhelm, Sept. 18, 1924, box 11, Central Virginia Training Center Papers.

147 the supervisor informed Dr. Priddy: Mary Duke to Albert Priddy, Sept. 22, 1924, unnamed folder, Carrie Buck and Doris Buck Figgins Sterilization, ca. 1920s–1980s file, Central Virginia Training Center Papers.

147 "I have had the Red Cross": Albert Priddy to Aubrey Strode, Oct. 14, 1924, box 11, Central Virginia Training Center Papers.

147 Dr. Priddy wrote to Laughlin: Priddy to Laughlin, Oct. 14, 1924,.

147 "all of the Bucks and Harlows": Ibid.

147 That "line of baneful heredity": Ibid.

147 The picture of Carrie's immediate family: Ibid.

148 Dr. Priddy offered more specific information: Ibid.

148 In a formal legal document: "Interrogatories of Harry H. Laughlin," in "Carrie Buck Trial Transcript, 1–50" (2009), *Buck v. Bell Documents*, Paper 31, 31–41, http://readingroom.law.gsu.edu/buckvbell/31.

149 "short analysis": Ibid., 29, 32.

149   Laughlin's description of Carrie: Ibid., 32, 33.

149   Laughlin described Emma: Ibid., 32.

149   "These people belong to the shiftless": Ibid. 32–33.

150   Laughlin's most dubious assertions: Ibid.

150   Laughlin's statement was similar: "Carrie Buck Trial Transcript, 1–50," 25.

150   It was a useful inaccuracy: Laughlin to Strode, Oct. 3, 1924.

150   In the "Analysis of Facts" section: "Interrogatories of Harry H. Laughlin," 34.

151   Laughlin also purported: Ibid.

151   There was, in fact, nothing: Ibid.

151   Laughlin then addressed a critical question: Ibid., 34–35.

151   "give in brief outline": Ibid., 30.

152   salpingectomy and vasectomy: Ibid., 39, 40.

152   "give any other information": Ibid., 30, 41.

152   It was agreed from the beginning: Strode to Laughlin, Sept. 30, 1924; Strode to Priddy, Oct. 29, 1924.

152   Strode was enthusiastic: Strode to Priddy, Oct. 29, 1924.

153   Estabrook joined the Eugenics Record Office: Deutsch, *Inventing America's "Worst" Family*, 102; Lombardo, *Three Generations*, 36.

153   "highly inbred rural community": Arthur H. Estabrook and Charles B. Davenport, *The Nam Family: A Study in Cacogenics* (Cold Spring Harbor, NY: Eugenics Record Office, 1912), 1, 66–75.

153   The "Nam" of the title: Deutsch, *Inventing America's "Worst" Family*, 104.

153   In keeping with their positions: Nancy Gallagher, *Breeding Better Vermonters: The Eugenics Project in the Green Mountain State* (Lebanon, NH: University Press of New England, 1999), 37.

153   They insisted that the role of heredity: Estabrook and Davenport, *Nam Family*, 66.

153   The book's subtitle: Stuart Hayashi, *Hunting Down Social Darwinism: Will This Canard Go Extinct?* (Lanham, MD: Lexington Books, 2015), 98.

153   a rural New York community: Estabrook and Davenport, *Nam Family*, 1–2; Deutsch, *Inventing America's "Worst" Family*, 104.

154   "No State can afford": Estabrook and Davenport, *Nam Family*, 84.

154   Estabrook and Davenport considered the possibility: Ibid.

154   There was one solution: Ibid.

154   "Asexualization," as they called it: Ibid.

155   "It has been persistently carried on": Arthur H. Estabrook, *The Jukes in 1915* (Washington, DC: Carnegie Institution of Washington, 1916), 1; Francis T. Cullen and Pamela Wilcox, eds., *Encyclopedia of Criminological Theory*, (Thousand Oaks, CA: SAGE, 2010), 1:276; "Carrie Buck Trial Transcript, 51–100" (2009), 77, *Buck v. Bell Documents*, Paper 32, http://readingroom.law .gsu.edu/buckvbell/32; Lombardo, *Three Generations*, 4.

155   In a typical entry, Estabrook described: Estabrook, *The Jukes in 1915*, 4.

155   In one eugenic analysis: Ibid., 59–60.

155   the Jukes were still defective: Ibid., 85.

155   "No matter": Ibid.

156   But if the six hundred living feebleminded and epileptic Jukes: Ibid.

156   McCulloch had focused: Oscar McCulloch, *The Tribe of Ishmael: A Study in Social Degradation* (Indianapolis: Charity Organization Society, 1891).

156   In his follow-up: Deutsch, *Inventing America's "Worst" Family*, 109.

156   As he had with the Nams: Arthur Estabrook, "The Tribe of Ishmael," *Eugenics, Genetics and the Family* 1, no. 6 (1922): 404, http://www.dnalc.org/view/11453—The-Tribe-of-Ishmael-by -Arthur-H-Estabrook-in-Eugenics-Genetics-and-the-Family-vol-1-6-.html.

156   "considered the work to be highly problematic": Deutsch, *Inventing America's "Worst" Family*, 126–27.

156   Estabrook studied a mixed-race: Arthur Estabrook and Ivan McDougle , *Mongrel Virginians: The Win Tribe* (Baltimore: Williams & Wilkens, 1926); review of *Mongrel Virginians: A Study in Triple Race Mixture*, by Arthur H. Estabrook and Ivan McDougle, *Journal of Negro History* 11, no. 2 (Apr. 1926): 416.

157   *Mongrel Virginians*: Nikki L. M. Brown and Barry Stentiford, eds., *The Jim Crow Encyclopedia* (Westport, CT: Greenwood, 2008), 1:275; Abraham Myerson, review of *Mongrel Virginians: The*

Win Tribe, by Arthur H. Estabrook and Ivan McDougle, *The Annals of the American Academy,* n.d., 165.

156 **The community's ancestors:** Myerson, review of *Mongrel Virginians, Annals of the American Academy,* 165; Wayne Winkler, *Walking Toward the Sunset: The Melungeons of Appalachia* (Macon, GA: Mercer University Press, 2005), 125.

157 **"among the American eugenicists":** Brown and Stentiford, *Jim Crow Encyclopedia,* 275.

157 **"Ichabod Ross":** Abraham Myerson, review of *Mongrel Virginians: The Win Tribe,* by Arthur H. Estabrook and Ivan McDougle, *Mental Hygiene,* n.d., 640, box 3, folder 4, Estabrook Papers.

157 **Another was said:** Ibid., 640–41.

157 **The authors invoked:** Estabrook and McDougle, *Mongrel Virginians,* 201; Winkler, *Walking Toward the Sunset,* 126.

157 **Abraham Myerson:** Myerson, review of *Mongrel Virginians, Annals of the American Academy,* 165–66.

157 **The authors began the fieldwork:** Winkler, *Walking Toward the Sunset,* 125.

157 **While they were researching the book:** Walter Wadlington, "The Loving Case: Virginia's Anti-Miscegenation Statute in Historical Perspective," in *Mixed Race America and the Law: A Reader,* ed. Kevin R. Johnson (New York: New York University Press, 2003), 53–54, 97.

157 **"What Happens When White":** Williams and Wilkins Company, "What Happens When White, Indian, and Negro Blood Intermingles?" box 3, folder 4, Estabrook Papers.

158 **"the result of this race admixture":** Review of *Mongrel Virginians, Journal of Negro History,* 417.

158 **"While many of the better white families":** Ibid., 418.

158 **Strode appealed to Laughlin:** Strode to Laughlin, Nov. 5, 1924; Lombardo, *Three Generations,* 111.

158 **"Superintendent Priddy Lynchburg":** Telegram of Jessie Estabrook to Arthur Estabrook, Oct. 23, 1924, box 3, folder 8, Estabrook Papers.

158 **Strode asked his new expert:** Aubrey Strode to Arthur Estabrook, Nov. 6, 1924, box 3, folder 8, Estabrook Papers.

159 **"I am a days":** Arthur Estabrook to Aubrey Strode, Nov. 8, 1924, box 3, folder 8, Estabrook Papers.

159 **"We wish to present":** Strode to Estabrook, Nov. 6, 1924.

CHAPTER SIX: AUBREY STRODE

160 **"scarcely any political question":** Alexis de Tocqueville, *Democracy in America* (New York: Barnes & Noble Books, 2003), 254.

161 **he drafted such a weak statute:** Gregory Michael Dorr, *Segregation's Science: Eugenics and Society in Virginia* (Charlottesville: University of Virginia Press, 2008), 122.

161 **He was the scion:** "Biography," handwritten notes in a folder titled "Ca. 20,000 items, papers of Judge Aubrey Ellis Strode," Aubrey Strode Papers, Albert and Shirley Small Special Collections Library, University of Virginia (hereafter cited as Strode Papers); Harry Bruinius, *Better for All the World: The Secret History of Forced Sterilization and America's Quest for Racial Purity* (New York: Alfred A. Knopf, 2006), 31.

161 **The Strodes traced their lineage:** "The Strode Record—Historical Facts, Etc.," box 107, Strode Papers; "Memorandum of the Ellis Family," box 107, Strode Papers.

162 **Kenmore:** Sherese Gore, "Amherst County's Kenmore Farm Added to List of Virginia Landmarks," *Lynchburg News & Advance,* Dec. 27, 1914; 1957 Historic Home Tour, Amherst County Historical Society, http://www.amherstcountymuseum.org/tour1957.html#kenmore.

162 **It was "one of the most charming":** William Shands Meacham to Mrs. Aubrey Strode, May 17, 1944, box 57, Strode Papers.

162 **His father, Henry Aubrey Strode:** Jerome V. Reel, *The High Seminary: 1: A History of the Clemson Agricultural College of South Carolina, 1889–1964* (Clemson, SC: Clemson University Digital Press, 2011) 1:77; Strode letter (no addressee), Aug. 19, 1907, box 24, Strode Papers; *Historical Catalogue, University of Mississippi, 1849–1909,* http://archive.org/stream/historicalcatalo00univ/historicalcatalo00univ_djvu.txt, 19.

162 **Strode's maternal grandfather:** Mark Hughes, *The New Civil War Handbook: Facts and Photos for Readers of All Ages* (New York: Savas Beatie, 2009), 33.

162 **He would later say:** Strode letter (no addressee), Aug. 19, 1907.

162 **Strode's father, Henry, attended:** *Historical Catalogue, University of Mississippi, 1849–1909,* 19.

162 **In 1872 Henry Strode married:** *Historical Catalogue, University of Mississippi, 1849–1909*, 19; Paul A. Lombardo, "Eugenic Sterilization in Virginia: Aubrey Strode and the Case of *Buck v. Bell*" (Ph.D. diss., University of Virginia, 1982), 37.

162 **The Kenmore School:** J. Damiel Pezzoni, *Amherst County Historic Resources Survey Report* (Amherst, VA: County of Amherst, 2010), 47.

163 **respected training ground:** Ibid.

163 **He graduated in 1887:** Lombardo, "Eugenic Sterilization in Virginia," 38

163 **After the Civil War:** John D. Wright, *The Routledge Encyclopedia of Civil War Era Biographies* (New York: Routledge, 2013), 346; Lombardo, "Eugenic Sterilization in Virginia," 38.

163 **Henry Strode closed:** Lombardo, "Eugenic Sterilization in Virginia," 38.

163 **he moved to South Carolina:** *Historical Catalogue, University of Mississippi, 1849–1909*, 19.

163 **His presidency ended abruptly:** Ibid.

163 **He left college:** Lombardo, "Eugenic Sterilization in Virginia," 38.

163 **Aubrey studied political economy:** Ibid., 38–39; *University of Virginia Catalogue, 1895–96* (Charlottesville: University of Virginia, 1896), 66.

163 **Aubrey, who was twenty-two:** Lombardo, "Eugenic Sterilization in Virginia," 38–39.

163 **The 1897–98 catalog:** *Kenmore High School, Amherst, Va., Catalogue for 1897–98* (Lynchburg, VA: J. P. Bell, Book and Job Printers, 1898), box 35, Strode Papers.

164 **The school promised:** Pezzoni, *Amherst County*, 47.

164 **"Mr. Strode has been familiarized":** *Kenmore High School, Amherst, Va., Catalogue for 1897–98.*

164 **Sprague Correspondence School of Law:** Lombardo, "Eugenic Sterilization in Virginia," 39; "Study Law at Home" (advertisement), *Law Student's Helper*, Feb. 10, 1911, 208.

164 **But given his early interest in education:** Lombardo, "Eugenic Sterilization in Virginia," 39.

164 **Strode had to commit his parents:** *Historical Catalogue, University of Mississippi, 1849–1909*, 19; Lombardo, "Eugenic Sterilization in Virginia," 39–40, 64–65; letters of condolence to Aubrey Strode, box 5, Strode Papers.

164 **He set up a law office:** Henry Little to Aubrey Strode, Jan. 15, 1899, box 6, Strode Papers; Lombardo, "Eugenic Sterilization in Virginia," 39–40.

164 **Strode's legal career:** Lombardo, "Eugenic Sterilization in Virginia," 40–41.

164 **In 1903 he married:** Ibid., 42; receipt from W. D. Diuguid Funeral Directing and Embalming, July 1923, for Mrs. Rebekah Davies Brown Strode, box 88, Strode Papers; "Biography," handwritten notes in a folder titled "Ca. 20,000 items, papers of Judge Aubrey Ellis Strode," Strode Papers.

165 **Strode continued to help:** Lombardo, "Eugenic Sterilization in Virginia," 41.

165 **"Miss Alice Burke":** Aubrey Strode to William King Junior, Feb. 21, 1907, box 65, Strode Papers.

165 **In 1903 Strode participated:** Lombardo, "Eugenic Sterilization in Virginia," 42–44; "Judge Cowhides a Minister," *Los Angeles Herald*, July 6, 1902; William Asbury Christian, *Richmond: Her Past and Present* (Richmond, VA: L. H. Jenkins, 1912), 487–88.

165 **Campbell inflicted "painful injuries":** Lombardo, "Eugenic Sterilization in Virginia," 42–44; "Judge Cowhides a Minister"; Christian, *Richmond*, 487–88.

166 **The victory helped:** Christian, *Richmond*, 487–88; Lombardo, "Eugenic Sterilization in Virginia," 42–46.

166 **He gave his first political speech:** Lombardo, "Eugenic Sterilization in Virginia," 40–41, 46–47.

166 **In 1905 Strode announced:** Aubrey Strode Campaign Leaflet 1 (1905), box 21, Strode Papers.

166 **He printed up campaign leaflets:** Ibid.

166 **Strode billed himself:** Aubrey Strode to W. E. Allen, May 1, 1916, box 31, Strode Papers; Lombardo, "Eugenic Sterilization in Virginia," 48–49.

166 **"Rotation in Office":** Aubrey Strode Campaign Leaflet 2–3 (1905), box 21, Strode Papers.

166 **"We are reaping in illiteracy":** Aubrey Strode Campaign Leaflet 4–5 (1905), box 21, Strode Papers; Lombardo, "Eugenic Sterilization in Virginia," 53.

167 **Strode also called for improving Virginia's roads:** Aubrey Strode Campaign Leaflet (1905) 2–3.

167 **Strode also supported election reform:** Aubrey Strode Campaign Leaflet 2–3 (1907), box 48, Strode Papers.

167 **When a black man:** Aubrey Strode to Charles Clark, May 3, 1926, box 20, Strode Papers; Kristina DuRocher, *Raising Racists: The Socialization of White Children in the Jim Crow South* (Lexington: University of Kentucky Press, 2011), 21.

167 the "grandfather clause": Nicholas J. Swartz and Liliokanio Peaslee, *Virginia Government: Institutions and Policy* (Washington, DC: CQ Press, 2013), 16–17.
168 In his campaign leaflets: Aubrey Strode Campaign Leaflet (1905), 3.
168 When blacks went to the polls: Lombardo, "Eugenic Sterilization in Virginia," 50–51.
168 With the electorate essentially all white: Aubrey Strode Campaign Leaflet (1905), 3.
168 Strode won the primary: Lombardo, "Eugenic Sterilization in Virginia," 55–56.
168 Progressives across the country: Rothman, *Conscience and Convenience*, 294.
168 for more personal reasons: Lombardo, "Eugenic Sterilization in Virginia," 63–64.
169 According to the bill: "Chap. 48 of Acts 1906—An Act to Establish an Epileptic Colony on Land of the Western State Hospital, in Amherst County," *Pollard's Code Biennial, 1908* (Richmond, VA: E. Waddey, 1908), 434; *First Report of Virginia State Epileptic Colony at Lynchburg, Virginia*, 1.
169 bring about improved treatments: "Chap. 48 of Act of 1906," 434.
169 Strode's bill passed: Lombardo, "Eugenic Sterilization in Virginia," 76; *First Report of Virginia State Epileptic Colony at Lynchburg, Virginia*, 1.
169 A colony for epileptics: Lombardo, "Eugenic Sterilization in Virginia," 75–76.
169 The most likely site: Ibid., 74; Julian C. Houseman, "Department History: 1766 to 1968," in Board of the Department of Mental Hygiene and Hospitals of the Commonwealth of Virginia, special edition, *Mental Health in Virginia* 18, no. 2 (Winter 1968): 23, box 7, Central Virginia Training Center Papers, Library of Virginia; *Report of the Attorney General to the Governor of Virginia* (Richmond, VA: Division of Purchase and Printing, 1910), 26; W. I. Prichard, "History—Lynchburg Training School and Hospital," *Mental Health in Virginia* 11 (Summer 1960): 40.
169 When the Murkland land parcel: Lombardo, "Eugenic Sterilization in Virginia," 77–79.
170 On April 22: Richard Hamm, *Murder, Honor, and Law: Four Virginia Homicides from Reconstruction to the Great Depression* (Charlottesville: University of Virginia Press, 2003), 97.
170 Estes, who was the son: Newspaper clipping, *New York American*, June 2, 1907, box 25, Strode Papers; Hamm, *Murder, Honor, and Law*, 97, 103–4.
170 Estes dropped Elizabeth off: Hamm, *Murder, Honor, and Law*, 97, 104, 108.
170 Loving said no power: Ibid., 106; newspaper clipping, *New York American*, June 2, 1907.
170 The Martin Organization: "Thomas Staples Martin," *Encyclopedia Virginia*, available at http://www.encyclopediavirginia.org/Martin_Thomas_Staples_1847-1919.
170 Loving and Strode were part: Hamm, *Murder, Honor, and Law*, 112–13.
170 "As might be supposed": "Strode Deserves Thanks," *Union Star*, April 7, 1916, box 26, Strode Papers.
170 Strode was joined by lawyers: Hamm, *Murder, Honor, and Law*, 126; newspaper clipping, *New York American*, June 2, 1907.
171 the "unwritten law": Hamm, *Murder, Honor, and Law*, 100; Lombardo, "Eugenic Sterilization in Virginia," 58.
171 Early news reports: Hamm, *Murder, Honor, and Law*, 108.
171 As the trial approached: Ibid., 117, 121.
171 Popular opinion: Ibid., 132–33.
172 "I do not undervalue life": Ibid., 136.
172 "Mr. Strode spoke": Newspaper clipping, *New York American*, undated, box 25, Strode Papers.
172 After deliberating: Hamm, *Murder, Honor, and Law*, 137.
172 One news report: Ibid., 147.
172 In 1907 Strode ran for reelection: Strode Senate Re-election Pamphlet, Democratic Primary, August 24, 1907, box 48, Strode Papers; "Elections. Status of Contesting Candidate at a Void Election," Sec. 145a, Va. Code 1904, in *Virginia Law Register*, vol. 11, no. 2 (June 1905), 147.
172 In his campaign literature: Strode Senate Re-election Pamphlet, Democratic Primary, August 24, 1907.
173 In a letter: Strode letter (no addressee), Aug. 19, 1907.
173 He left the legislature: Lombardo, "Eugenic Sterilization in Virginia," 96.
173 Henry D. Flood: Aubrey Strode to J. M. Miles, May 16, 1916, box 26, Strode Papers.
173 his old state senate seat: Lombardo, "Eugenic Sterilization in Virginia," 96.
173 On August 3 he won: Aubrey Strode to J. B. Woodson, May 5, 1915, box 26, Strode Papers.
173 received "a good deal": Strode to Allen, May 1, 1916.
173 That June: *Guinn and Beal v. United States*, 238 U.S. 347 (1915).
173 Given the "rapid education": Aubrey Strode to W. N. Ruffin, Feb. 15, 1916, box 31, Strode Papers.

174 **single bathroom for black men and women:** Aubrey Strode to Capt. R.W.B. Hart, Jan. 30, 1940, box 29, Strode Papers.

174 **restriction on black doctors:** Aubrey Strode to Dr. Belle Boon Beard, April 10, 1940, box 29, Strode Papers.

174 **"We have here in the South":** Ibid.

174 **"it would be impossible":** Aubrey Strode to S. R. Church, Feb. 17, 1916, box 31, Strode Papers.

175 **In 1910 Strode introduced a bill:** Ibid.; Samuel C. Shepherd Jr., *Avenues of Faith: Shaping the Urban Religious Culture of Richmond, Virginia, 1900–1929* (Tuscaloosa: University of Alabama, 2001), 191.

175 **There was substantial opposition:** "Open Letters from Alumni," *University of Virginia Alumni News*, Jan. 21, 1914, 109–12.

175 **"We have seen":** Campaign leaflet, Aubrey Strode for State Senate, Aug. 3, 1915, box 26, Strode Papers.

175 **After he was elected:** Strode to Church, Feb. 17, 1916.

175 **They succeeded in getting:** Anne Hobson Freeman, "Mary Munford's Fight for a College for Women Co-ordinate with the University of Virginia," *Virginia Magazine of History and Biography*, Oct. 1970, 481, 483.

175 **the legislature voted:** Shepherd, *Avenues of Faith*, 192–93.

175 **It would take many years:** Freeman, "Mary Munford's Fight," 490.

175 **When Strode returned:** Lombardo, "Eugenic Sterilization in Virginia," 95.

175 **He continued to serve:** Albert Priddy to Aubrey Strode, Feb. 2, 1916, box 31, Strode Papers.

175 **When Dr. Priddy wanted to buy:** Aubrey Strode to Albert Priddy, Feb. 11, 1920, box 147, Strode Papers.

175 **When Dr. Priddy had trouble:** Albert Priddy to Aubrey Strode, May 1, 1922, box 147, Strode Papers.

176 **When Dr. Priddy wanted advice:** Aubrey Strode to Albert Priddy, Sept. 2, 1921, box 147, Strode Papers.

176 **He sponsored bills:** Lombardo, "Eugenic Sterilization in Virginia," 99–100; Priddy to Strode, Feb. 2, 1916.

176 **In May 1918, in the waning months:** Lombardo, "Eugenic Sterilization in Virginia," 139–40.

176 **He secured the appointment:** Ibid.

176 **Strode began his service:** Ibid., 141.

176 **Strode drew up two bills:** Ibid., 143–44; Aubrey Strode to Dr. Don Preston Peters, July 19, 1939, box 29, Strode Papers.

176 **In 1922, Strode** "Rep. Henry Flood Dies in Washington," *Ellensburg Daily Record*, Dec. 9, 1921.

177 **The Democratic Party scheduled:** Aubrey Strode to W. C. Barker, Feb. 29, 1922, box 83, Strode Papers; Aubrey Strode to C. E. Jones, Dec. 13, 1921, box 83, Strode Papers; Lombardo, "Eugenic Sterilization in Virginia," 146–47.

177 **Dr. Priddy and Irving Whitehead:** Aubrey Strode to Irving Whitehead, Dec. 20, 1921, box 83, Strode Papers; Aubrey Strode to Irving Whitehead, Jan. 17, 1922, box 83, Strode Papers; Aubrey Strode to Albert Priddy, Jan. 5, 1922, box 83, Strode Papers; Lombardo, "Eugenic Sterilization in Virginia," 147–48.

177 **Strode was left:** Lombardo, "Eugenic Sterilization in Virginia," 148; receipt from W. D. Diuguid Funeral Directing and Embalming, July 1923.

177 **Louisa Dexter Hubbard:** Lombardo, "Eugenic Sterilization in Virginia," 149–50.

177 **After Rebekah's death:** Ibid.

177 **"I am widowed and she is single":** Aubrey Strode to Clerk of the Circuit Court of Bedford County, Bedford, Va., Dec. 22, 1923, box 84, Strode Papers.

177 **Strode delivered:** Strode to Peters, July 19, 1939; Lombardo, "Eugenic Sterilization in Virginia," 166.

CHAPTER SEVEN: AUBREY STRODE

179 **Laughlin had stated:** "Interrogatories of Harry H. Laughlin," in "Carrie Buck Trial Transcript, 1–50" (2009), 34–35, 40–41, *Buck v. Bell Documents*, Paper 31, http://readingroom.law.gsu.edu/buckvbell/31.

180 **He visited the colony:** Paul A. Lombardo, *Three Generations, No Imbeciles: Eugenics, the Supreme Court, and* Buck v. Bell (Baltimore: Johns Hopkins University Press, 2008), 111.

180 **and traveled across:** "Carrie Buck Trial Transcript, 51–100" (2009), 81, *Buck v. Bell Documents*, Paper 31, http://readingroom.law.gsu.edu/buckvbell/31.

180 **He had concluded:** Ibid., 81, 83.
180 **Estabrook would also provide:** Ibid., 25.; Aubrey Strode to Harry Laughlin, Sept. 30, 1924, box 3, folder 8, Arthur Estabrook Papers, M. E. Grenander Department of Special Collections and Archives, University at Albany, State University of New York (hereafter cited as Estabrook Papers); "Interrogatories of Harry H. Laughlin," 33
180 **Wilhelm had instructed Dr. Priddy:** Caroline Wilhelm to Albert Priddy, Oct. 15, 1924, box 11, Central Virginia Training Center Papers, Library of Virginia.
180 **Laughlin was still citing her:** "Interrogatories of Harry H. Laughlin," 31.
181 **reached the conclusion:** "Carrie Buck Trial Transcript, 51–100," 82–83.
181 **In a letter to Dr. Priddy:** Aubrey Strode to Albert Priddy, Oct. 29, 1924, box 11, Central Virginia Training Center Papers.
181 **he sent out word:** Court summons, unnamed folder, Carrie Buck and Doris Buck Figgins Sterilization, ca. 1920s–1980s file, Central Virginia Training Center Papers; Strode to Priddy, Oct. 29, 1924.
182 *Requiem for a Nun:* William Faulkner, *Requiem for a Nun* (New York: Vintage, 1994), 32; Paul T. Hellmann, *Historical Gazetteer of the United States* (New York: Routledge, 2006), 1133.
182 **In Amherst County:** Harry Bruinius, *Better for All the World: The Secret History of Forced Sterilization and America's Quest for Racial Purity* (New York: Alfred A. Knopf, 2006), 63.
182 **Its most prominent ornamentation:** Lombardo, *Three Generations,* 112.
182 **"You will Do well":** R. A. Brock, *History of Virginia from Settlement of Jamestown to Close of the Civil War* (Richmond, VA: H. H. Hardesty, 1888), 54–55; David Koplow, *Smallpox: The Fight to Eradicate a Global Scourge* (Berkeley: University of California Press, 2003), 62.
182 **Strode started the testimony:** Bruinius, *Better for all the World,* 63.
182 **Harris was a district nurse:** "Carrie Buck Trial Transcript, 1–50," 42–43.
182 **"absolutely irresponsible":** Ibid., 43–44.
183 **"Well, I don't know anything":** Ibid., 44.
183 **"mentally normal children":** Ibid.
183 **Carrie's sister, Doris:** Ibid., 45.
184 **"She told me":** Ibid., 46.
184 **Eula Wood:** "Carrie Buck Trial Transcript, 51–100," 48–49.
184 **Whitehead chose not to cross-examine:** Ibid., 49.
184 **Virginia Beard:** Ibid., 49–50.
185 **Whitehead did a better job:** Ibid., 50.
185 **Hopkins said he did not know:** Ibid., 52–53.
185 **Caroline Wilhelm:** Ibid., 57.
185 **In her testimony:** Ibid.; Lombardo, *Three Generations,* 116.
185 **Wilhelm followed the colony's script:** "Carrie Buck Trial Transcript, 51–100," 57–58.
186 **On October 15:** Wilhelm to Priddy, Oct. 15, 1924.
186 **"not quite a normal baby":** "Carrie Buck Trial Transcript, 51–100," 58–59.
186 **The only explanation:** Ibid.
186 **"Mrs. Dobb[s's] daughter's baby":** Ibid., 59.
186 **Whitehead's cross-examination:** Ibid., 60–61.
187 **"Your idea":** Ibid., 61.
187 **Strode's next witness:** Ibid., 57; Homer Richey to Albert Priddy, Mar. 10, 1924, box 11, Central Virginia Training Center Papers.
187 **Duke described:** "Carrie Buck Trial Transcript, 51–100," 61–62.
187 **Duke recounted:** Ibid.
187 **extremely limited contact:** Ibid., 62; Lombardo, *Three Generations,* 119.
188 **He estimated:** "Carrie Buck Trial Transcript, 51–100," 63.
188 **Dr. DeJarnette testified:** Ibid., 64.
188 **"differential fecundity":** Ibid., 67.
188 **feeblemindedness was hereditary:** Ibid., 65.
188 **discourse on Mendel's hereditary theory:** Ibid., 66.
189 **The Virginia law:** An Act to Provide for the Sexual Sterilization of Inmates of State Institutions in Certain Cases, Virginia Acts of Assembly, chap. 394 (1924); "Carrie Buck Trial Transcript, 51–100," 69.
189 **if a patient in a state hospital:** "Carrie Buck Trial Transcript, 51–100," 69.
189 **The overall "standard":** Ibid.
189 **Strode asked if he had heard:** Ibid., 70.

189   On cross-examination: Ibid., 71–75.
189   most unusual line of questioning: Ibid., 72–73.
190   "fire-ship": Francis Grose, *The Vulgar Tongue: Buckish Slang and Pickpocket Eloquence* (Chichester, West Sussex, UK: Summersdale Publishers, 2004) 121; "Carrie Buck Trial Transcript, 51–100," 73.
190   The "man contracting syphilis": "Carrie Buck Trial Transcript, 51–100," 73–74.
190   Arthur Estabrook: Ibid., 75.
190   Estabrook described the work: Ibid., 76–77.
191   Strode asked Estabrook: Ibid., 77–78.
191   After a forty-five-minute lunch break: Ibid., 81.
191   Estabrook began his analysis: Ibid., 81–82.
192   Given Emma's parents: Ibid., 82.
192   Estabrook responded: Ibid.
192   If that was all: Ibid.
192   "I gave the child": Ibid., 83.
193   Whitehead once again did little: Ibid., 84–87.
193   Estabrook had designated: Ibid., 81–82.
194   Estabrook diagnosed other relatives: Abraham Myerson, review of *Mongrel Virginians: The Win Tribe,* by Arthur H. Estabrook and Ivan McDougle, *The Annals of the American Academy,* n.d., 165.
194   Dr. Priddy began by reciting: "Carrie Buck Trial Transcript, 51–100," 88.
194   Dr. Priddy responded that: Ibid., 88–89.
194   That would cost: Ibid., 89.
194   Strode asked what: Ibid. 90–91.
195   "Every human being": Ibid., 91–92
195   And they understood: Ibid.
195   Between 1916 and the winter of 1917: Ibid., 92, 93.
195   He told the story of one boy: Ibid., 93.
196   "this girl here": Ibid., 96.
196   "I understand," he said: Ibid., 97.
196   Unfortunately, it was not: Alice Dobbs to John Bell, Feb. 13, 1928, unnamed folder, Carrie Buck and Doris Buck Figgins Sterilization, ca. 1920s–1980s file, Central Virginia Training Center Papers.
196   When he was done: "Carrie Buck Trial Transcript, 51–100," 97; Lombardo, *Three Generations,* 135.
197   Most of all, Whitehead: Harry Laughlin, *The Legal Status of Eugenical Sterilization: History and Analysis of Litigation Under the Virginia Sterilization Statute, Which Led to a Decision of the Supreme Court of the United States Upholding the Statute* (Chicago: Chicago Municipal Court, 1930), 20.
197   she had never been told: J. David Smith and K. Ray Nelson, *The Sterilization of Carrie Buck: Was She Feebleminded or Society's Pawn?* (Far Hills, NJ: New Horizon Press, 1989), 218.
198   J. E. Wallace Wallin: Steven Noll, *Feeble-Minded in Our Midst* (Chapel Hill: University of North Carolina Press, 1995), 31–32.
198   Wallin wondered how: Carl Degler, *In Search of Human Nature: The Decline and Revival of Darwinism in American Social Thought* (Oxford: Oxford University Press, 1991), 141.
198   He could have evaluated: "Record Sheet for the Standard Revision of the Binet Simon Tests," Carrie Buck and Doris Buck Figgins Sterilization, ca. 1920s–1980s file, Central Virginia Training Center Papers.
198   There were scientists: Walter Berns, *"Buck v. Bell:* Due Process of Law?," *Western Political Quarterly* 6, no. 4 (Dec. 1953): 767.
198   He understood that: Diane Paul and Hamish Spencer, "Did Eugenics Rest on an Elementary Mistake?," in *Thinking About Evolution: Historical, Philosophical, and Political Perspectives,* ed. Rama S. Singh et al. (New York: Cambridge University Press, 2001), 105; Lombardo, *Three Generations,* 143.
198   Davenport had testified: Lombardo, *Three Generations,* 143.
199   In his 1914: Harry H. Laughlin, "The Scope of the Committee's Work," in *Report of the Committee to Study and to Report on the Best Practical Means of Cutting Off the Defective Germ-Plasm in the American Population* (Cold Spring Harbor, NY: Eugenics Record Office, 1914), 46–47.
199   One of the pieces of expert writing: "Carrie Buck Trial Transcript, 1–50," 30, 37.
199   Most of the genes: Paul and Spencer, "Did Eugenics Rest on an Elementary Mistake?," 112; Lombardo, *Three Generations,* 146.

199 **The reality was:** Carol Isaacson Barash, *Just Genes: The Ethics of Genetic Technologies* (New York: Praeger, 2008), 5.

199 **Carl Murchison:** Degler, *In Search of Human Nature*, 140.

200 **"I am willing to say":** Ibid., 143; *American Association for the Study of the Feeble-Minded: Proceedings and Addresses of the Forty-Second Annual Session Held at Buffalo, New York, May 31 and June 1, 1918* (American Association for the Study of the Feeble-Minded, 1918), 130.

200 **If *Buck v. Priddy* was appealed:** Graham Hughes, "Common Law Systems," in *Fundamentals of American Law*, ed. Alan Morrison (New York: Oxford University Press, 1996), 22.

200 **He added that:** Albert Priddy to Caroline Wilhelm, Nov. 26, 1924, Carrie Buck and Doris Buck Figgins Sterilization, ca. 1920s–1980s file, Central Virginia Training Center Papers, unnamed file.

200 **On December 11, he wrote:** Aubrey Strode to Arthur Estabrook, Dec. 11, 1924, box 3, Estabrook Papers.

200 **Over the summer:** Aubrey Strode to Charles Nash, Aug. 6, 1924, box 154, Aubrey Strode Papers, Albert and Shirley Small Special Collections Library, University of Virginia (hereafter cited as Strode Papers).

200 **Strode ended up:** Charles Nash to Aubrey Strode, Oct. 1, 1924, box 154, Strode Papers.

201 **In late November:** Aubrey Strode to Charles Nash, Nov. 29, 1924, box 154, Strode Papers.

201 **He told the law review:** Ibid.

201 **In a November 2 letter:** Albert Priddy to Aubrey Strode, Nov. 2, 1924, box 11, Central Virginia Training Center Papers.

201 **Dr. Priddy said he would:** Albert Priddy to Irving Whitehead, Dec. 12, 1924, box 11, Central Virginia Training Center Papers.

201 **On January 13, 1925:** Bruinius, *Better for All the World*, 69; "Buck v. Bell," *Encyclopedia Virginia*, http://www.encyclopediavirginia.org/buck_v_bell_1927.

201 **Dr. Priddy "took a profound":** Lombardo, "Eugenic Sterilization in Virginia," 208–9.

202 **a history of the colony:** W. I. Prichard, "History—Lynchburg Training School and Hospital," *Mental Health in Virginia* 11 (Summer 1960): 46.

202 **The court stayed:** Laughlin, *Legal Status of Eugenical Sterilization*, 20–21; Aubrey Strode to John Bell, Feb. 12, 1925, box 11, Central Virginia Training Center Papers.

202 **Strode wrote to:** Strode to Bell, Feb. 12, 1925.

202 **"It is agreeable":** John Bell to Aubrey Strode, Feb. 13, 1925, box 11, Central Virginia Training Center Papers; J. S. DeJarnette, "Eugenic Sterilization in Virginia," reprinted from *Virginia Medical Monthly* (1931), box 88, Records of Western State Hospital, Library of Virginia.

202 **New court papers:** Final Order, Buck v. Bell file, Clerk's Office, Amherst County Courthouse, Amherst, VA.

202 **Dr. Bell had practiced medicine:** "Physical Examination of a Patient on Admission to the State Colony," J. H. Bell, June 5, 1924, Carrie Buck and Doris Buck Figgins Sterilization, ca. 1920s–1980s file, Central Virginia Training Center Papers; Lombardo, *Three Generations*, 150

203 **As Dr. Bell saw it:** Dr. John Bell, "The Protoplasmic Blight," delivered to the Clinic on Mental Diseases at the Meeting of the Medical Society of Virginia, Charlottesville, VA, Oct. 22, 1929, box 88, Western State Hospital Papers.

203 **On June 1, 1925:** Petition for Appeal, *Buck v. Bell*, No. 1700, Supreme Court of Appeals of Virginia, State Law Library of Virginia.

203 **three constitutional objections:** Ibid., 2–3.

203 **two classes of "defective" people:** Ibid., 4–8.

204 **a 1913 ruling:** Ibid.; *Smith v. Board of Examiners*, 88 A. 963, 966 (N.J., 1913).

204 **cases in two other states:** In re Thomson, 169 N.Y.S. 638 (Sup. Ct. 1918), aff'd *Osborn v. Thomson*, 171 N.Y.S. 1094 (App. Div. 1918); *Haynes v. Lapeer Circuit Judge*, 201 Mich. 138, 166 N.W. 938 (1918); *State Bd. of Eugenics v. Cline*, No. 15,442 (Or. Cir. Ct. Dec. 13, 1921).

204 **the Iowa and Nevada laws:** Petition for Appeal, *Buck v. Bell*, No. 1700, Supreme Court of Appeals of Virginia, 1-8; Siegel, "Justice Holmes, *Buck v, Bell*, and the History of Equal Protection," 113–14.

204 **One of his main due process objections:** Reply Brief for Appellant, *Buck v. Bell*, Supreme Court of Appeals of Virginia, 3–4, "Whitehead Virginia Supreme Court Brief" (2009), *Buck v. Bell Documents*, Paper 38, http://readingroom.law.gsu.edu/buckvbell/38.

204 **Strode's legal brief:** Brief for Appellee, *Buck v, Bell*, 143 Va. 310 (1925), 2, 4, 8–12.

205 **Strode compared compulsory sterilization:** *Id.* at 27–29.

205 **eugenic sterilization was a "parallel case":** *Id.* at 19–21.

205 **since it was not punitive:** Ibid., 21.
206 **"all the requirements of due process":** Lombardo, *Three Generations*, 152.
206 **despite the warning:** *Smith v. Board of Examiners*, 88 A. 963, 966 (N.J. 1913); In re Thomson, 169 N.Y.S. 638 (Sup. Ct. 1918), aff'd *Osborn v. Thomson*, 171 N.Y.S. 1094 (App. Div. 1918); *Haynes v. Lapeer Circuit Judge*, 201 Mich. 138, 166 N.W. 938 (1918); *State Bd. of Eugenics v. Cline*, No. 15,442 (Or. Cir. Ct. Dec. 13, 1921); Harry Laughlin, *Eugenical Sterilization in the United States* (Chicago: Psychopathic Library of the Municipal Court of Chicago, 1922), 440.
206 **"part of a general plan":** Albert Priddy to Harry Laughlin, Oct. 14, 1924, box 11, Central Virginia Training Center Papers; Laughlin, H. H. Laughlin, "Calculations on the Working out of a Proposed Program of Sterilization," *Official proceedings of the National Conference on Race Betterment* (Battle Creek, MI: Race Betterment Foundation, 1914), 1:490; Brief for Appellee, *Buck v. Bell*, 143 Va. 310 (1925), 32–33.
206 **"Poor the Commonwealth":** Brief for Appellee, *Buck v. Bell*, 143 Va. 310 (1925), 31–32.
206 **"We are not permitted":** *Id.* at 48.
207 **It rejected all:** *Buck v. Bell*, 143 Va. 310 (1925), reprinted in Laughlin, *Legal Status of Eugenical Sterilization*, 30.
207 **Because Whitehead had:** *Id.* at 31.
207 **It also asserted:** *Id.* at 31, 34.
207 **The court's reasoning:** *Id.* at 31; "Carrie Buck Trial Transcript, 51–100," 92.
208 **In Carrie's case:** *Buck v. Bell*, 143 Va. 310 (1925), in Laughlin, *Legal Status of Eugenical Sterilization*, 31, 34.
208 **The court also rejected:** *Id.* at 35.
208 **The court said:** *Id.* at 35.
208 **The Virginia ruling:** *Smith v. Wayne Probate Judge*, 231 Mich. 409, 425, 204 N.W. 140 (1925); Mary L. Dudziak, "Oliver Wendell Holmes as a Eugenic Reformer: Rhetoric in the Writing of Constitutional Law," *Iowa Law Review* 71 (1986): 855; Hansen and King, *Sterilized by the State*, 86.
208 **Strode and Whitehead attended:** Lombardo, *Three Generations*, 154.
210 **"I notice from the paper":** Noll, *Feeble-Minded in Our Midst*, 73.
211 **On Strode's advice:** Aubrey Strode to Dr. Don Preston Peters, July 19, 1939, box 29, Strode Papers.
211 **Robert Shelton filed:** Writ of Error, Supreme Court of Appeals of Virginia, Jan. 26, 1926, "Carrie Buck Trial Transcript, 101–116" (2009), *Buck v. Bell Documents*, Paper 33, http://reading room.law.gsu.edu/buckvbell/33.
211 **"supple tool of power":** Merlo J. Pusey, *Charles Evans Hughes* (New York: Macmillan, 1951), 2:287, cited in Yosal Rogat, "The Judge as Spectator," *University of Chicago Law Review* 31 (1964): 249–50.

CHAPTER EIGHT: OLIVER WENDELL HOLMES
212 **The praise that has been showered:** Charles E. Wyzanski Jr., "The Democracy of Justice Oliver Wendell Holmes," *Vanderbilt Law Review* 7 (1954): 311, 323.
212 **Felix Frankfurter:** Felix Frankfurter, "Twenty Years of Mr. Justice Holmes' Constitutional Opinions," *Harvard Law Review* 36 (June 1923): 909, 919.
212 **Holmes had a gift:** Oliver Wendell Holmes Jr., *The Common Law* (Boston: Little, Brown, 1881), 1.
212 **He also had a rare ability:** *Schenck v. United States*, 249 U.S. 47 (1919), 52.
213 **To that august lineage:** G. Edward White, *Justice Oliver Wendell Holmes Law and the Inner Self* (New York: Oxford University Press, 1993), 3.
213 **Holmes was not:** *Schenck*, 249 U.S. at 302.
213 **On the occasion:** *Time*, Mar. 15, 1926.
213 **On his ninetieth:** Liva Baker, *The Justice from Beacon Hill: The Life and Times of Oliver Wendell Holmes* (New York: HarperCollins, 1991), 3.
213 **After his death:** Ibid., 8.
213 **later made into a Hollywood movie:** Norman Rosenberg, "The Supreme Court and Popular Culture," in *The United States Supreme Court: The Pursuit of Justice*, ed. Christopher L. Tomlins (New York: Houghton Mifflin, 2005), 415.
213 **a bestselling biography:** Catherine Drinker Bowen, *Yankee from Olympus* (New York: Bantam, 1944).
214 **One critic has:** Irving Bernstein, "The Conservative Justice Holmes," *New England Quarterly* 23

(1950): 435; William Leuchtenburg, *The Supreme Court Reborn: The Constitutional Revolution in the Age of Roosevelt* (New York: Oxford University Press, 1995), 369n54.

214 **H. L. Mencken:** H. L. Mencken, "The Great Holmes Mystery," *American Mercury*, May 1932, 123.

214 **The Yale law professor:** Grant Gilmore, *The Ages of American Law* (New Haven, CT: Yale University Press, 2014), 44; Baker, *Justice from Beacon Hill*, 10–11.

214 **only the nation's fifth largest city:** G. Edward White, "The Rise and Fall of Justice Holmes," *University of Chicago Law Review* 39 (1971): 51; White, *Justice Oliver Wendell Holmes*, 7; U.S. Bureau of the Census, "Population of the 100 Largest Urban Places," available at https://www.census.gov/population/www/documentation/twps0027/tab07.txt.

214 **Margaret Fuller:** Tiffany Wayne, *Encyclopedia of Transcendentalism* (New York: Facts-on-File, 2006), 101; Meg McGavran Murray, *Margaret Fuller, Wandering Pilgrim* (Athens: University of Georgia, 2012), xviii; William Hutchison, *Religious Pluralism in America: The Contentious History of a Founding Ideal* (New Haven: Yale University Press, 2003), 118.

215 **"an aristocracy":** Oliver Wendell Holmes Sr., *The Works of Oliver Wendell Holmes: Elsie Venner* (Boston: Houghton Mifflin, 1891), 5:3.

215 **"They lived in":** Baker, *Justice from Beacon Hill*, 22–23.

215 **a famous Boston poem:** Chaim Rosenberg, *The Life and Times of Francis Cabot Lowell, 1775–1817* (Lanham, MD: Lexington Books, 2011), 27.

215 **On her first visit:** Betty Farrell, *Elite Families: Class and Power in Nineteenth-Century Boston* (Albany, NY: SUNY Press, 1993), 21.

215 **Holmes's father contributed:** Charlene Mires, *Capital of the World: The Race to Host the United Nations* (New York: New York University Press, 2013), 91.

215 **Their Puritan ancestors':** Roger Williams, *On Religious Liberty: Selections from the Works of Roger Williams*, ed. Roger Davis (Cambridge, MA: Harvard University Press, 2009), 13; Darlene Stille, *Anne Hutchinson: Puritan Protester* (Minneapolis, MN: Compass Point Books, 2006), 12.

216 **In the mid-1800s:** Baker, *Justice from Beacon Hill*, 57.

216 **The Boston Athenæum:** Peter S. Field, *The Crisis of the Standing Order: Clerical Intellectuals and Cultural Authority in Massachusetts, 1780–1833* (Amherst: University of Massachusetts Press, 1998), 108.

216 **The Holmes family:** Baker, *Justice from Beacon Hill*, 15; Oliver Wendell Holmes Jr., autobiographical statement, July 2, 1861, reprinted in Frederick C. Fiechter Jr., "The Preparation of an American Aristocrat," *New England Quarterly* 6 (1933): 3, 4–5, cited in White, *Justice Oliver Wendell Holmes*, 7.

216 **He was a direct descendant of:** Bowen, *Yankee from Olympus*, 135; Kathrynn Seidler Engberg, *The Right to Write: The Literary Politics of Anne Bradstreet and Phillis Wheatley* (Lanham, MD: University Press of America, 2010), 3.

216 **His paternal grandfather:** Bowen, *Yankee from Olympus*, 1–2.

216 **Holmes's maternal grandfather:** Mark DeWolfe Howe, *Justice Oliver Wendell Holmes: The Shaping Years 1841–1870* (Cambridge, MA: Harvard University Press, 1957), 29; White, *Justice Oliver Wendell Holmes*, 17.

216 **Dubbed "the Greatest Brahmin":** Charles S. Bryan, "'The Greatest Brahmin': Overview of a Life," in *Oliver Wendell Holmes: Physician and Man of Letters*, ed. Scott H. Podolsky and Charles S. Bryan (Sagamore Beach, MA: Science History Publications, 2009), 3.

216 **As a physician:** Sheldon Novick, *Honorable Justice: The Life of Oliver Wendell Holmes* (Boston: Little, Brown, 1989), 18–19; Bowen, *Yankee from Olympus*, 81.

216 **The paper he wrote:** Alvin Powell, "How Oliver Wendell Holmes Helped Conquer the 'Black Death of Childbed,'" *Harvard Gazette*, Sept. 18, 1997; Bowen, *Yankee from Olympus*, 80–81.

216 **Dr. Holmes, who was:** Ronald D. Miller, ed., *Miller's Anesthesia* (Philadelphia: Churchill Livingstone, 2010), 12; Harvard Medical School, "Past Deans of the Faculty of Medicine," https://hms.harvard.edu/about-hms/facts-figures/past-deans-faculty-medicine.

217 **Dr. Holmes's poem:** Baker, *Justice from Beacon Hill*, 33–34; White, *Oliver Wendell Holmes*, 7.

217 **As an adult, Dr. Holmes:** David McCullough, *Brave Companions: Portraits in History* (New York: Simon & Schuster, 1992), 29.

217 **In 1857 he joined:** Novick, *Honorable Justice*, 19.

217 **It is said:** Christopher Redmond, *Sherlock Holmes Handbook* (Toronto: Dundurn, 2009), 68.

217 **the day after his son's birth:** Howe, *Shaping Years*, 1.

217 **The relationship between:** White, *Justice Oliver Wendell Holmes*, 11.

217 **Adding to Holmes's difficulty:** Brad Snyder, "The House That Built Holmes," *Law and History Review* 30 (2012): 669.
217 **William James:** Howe, *Shaping Years*, 18.
217 **Holmes had a warmer:** White, *Justice Oliver Wendell Holmes*, 16.
217 **He started out:** Howe, *Shaping Years*, 2.
217 **Then he attended:** White, *Justice Oliver Wendell Holmes*, 20, 23–24, 33; Howe, *Shaping Years*, 5.
218 **In the summers:** Novick, *Honorable Justice*, 11; Bowen, *Yankee from Olympus*, 95.
218 **Holmes followed:** Howe, *Shaping Years*, 6–7, 35.
218 **Harvard had been the choice:** Baker, *Justice from Beacon Hill*, 72; Bowen, *Yankee from Olympus*, 106.
218 **a great-great-uncle had been Harvard treasurer:** Bowen, *Yankee from Olympus*, 85.
218 **"Any other education":** Henry Adams, *The Education of Henry Adams: An Autobiography* (Boston: Houghton Mifflin, 1918), 54.
218 **The instruction he received was uninspired:** Ibid., 55; Howe, *Shaping Years*, 36; White, *Justice Oliver Wendell Holmes*, 26.
218 **Holmes was, for his part:** Howe, *Shaping Years*, 39, 45.
218 **As with almost everything:** White, *Justice Oliver Wendell Holmes*, 27; "Harvard College Societies," *Harvard Magazine* (May 1864), 268–70.
218 **As President Abraham Lincoln:** James M. McPherson, *Battle Cry of Freedom: The Civil War Era* (New York: Oxford University Press, 1988), 273.
219 **"The heather is on fire":** George Ticknor, *Life, Letters and Journals of George Ticknor* (London: Sampson, Low, Marston, Searle & Rivington, 1876), 2:433–34; McPherson, *Battle Cry of Freedom*, 274.
219 **He left college before:** Howe, *Shaping Years*, 68.
219 **He had been elected class poet:** Baker, *Justice from Beacon Hill*, 100; Howe, *Shaping Years*, 76.
219 **Holmes joined:** Baker, *Justice from Beacon Hill*, 107, 110.
219 **first lieutenant:** Howe, *Shaping Years*, 86; Novick, *Honorable Justice*, 39.
219 **On a stop:** Richard Miller, *Harvard's Civil War: A History of the Twentieth Massachusetts Voluntary Infantry* (Lebanon, NH: University Press of New England, 2005), 46; Novick, *Honorable Justice*, 39.
219 **The regiment was assigned:** White, *Justice Oliver Wendell Holmes*, 51.
219 **On October 20:** Ibid., 52; Novick, *Honorable Justice*, 44–45.
219 **The Union men:** Novick, *Honorable Justice*, 44–45.
219 **Holmes was shot:** Howe, *Shaping Years*, 102.
219 **Writing to his mother:** Ibid., 99 (citing letter from Oliver Wendell Holmes Jr. to Mrs. Oliver Wendell Holmes Sr., Oct. 23, 1861), 108–11.
220 **In March 1862:** White, *Justice Oliver Wendell Holmes*, 52, 57.
220 **In the fighting at Antietam:** McPherson, *Battle Cry of Freedom*, 544; Michael Lee Lanning, *Civil War 100: The Stories Behind the Most Influential Battles, People, and Events in the War Between the States* (Naperville, IL: Sourcebooks, 2008), 10.
220 **A bullet entered:** Edmund Wilson, *Patriotic Gore: Studies in the Literature of the American Civil War* (New York: W. W. Norton, 1962), 749.
220 **When Dr. Holmes:** Howe, *Shaping Years*, 130–31; White, *Justice Oliver Wendell Holmes*, 58–59.
220 **The elder Holmes:** Oliver Wendell Holmes Sr., "My Hunt After 'The Captain,'" *Atlantic Monthly*, Dec. 1862, 738–63.
220 **Holmes returned home:** Howe, *Shaping Years*, 135.
220 **He traveled from Boston:** Novick, *Honorable Justice*, 69–70.
220 **He no longer believed:** Wilson, *Patriotic Gore*, 749.
220 **Holmes and Little Abbott:** Novick, *Honorable Justice*, 70.
220 **He took a bullet:** Barbara Berenson, *Boston and the Civil War: Hub of the Second Revolution* (Charleston, SC: History Press, 2014), 91.
220 **Holmes wrote his mother:** Howe, *Shaping Years*, 154–55.
221 **Ten of its thirteen officers:** Baker, *Justice from Beacon Hill*, 143.
221 **Several of Holmes's close friends:** Howe, *Shaping Years*, 157.
221 **When he returned:** Wilson, *Patriotic Gore*, 750.
221 **Decades later, he would recall:** Howe, *Shaping Years*, 164–65; Oliver Wendell Holmes Jr., *The Soldier's Faith*, in *The Essential Holmes: Selections from the Letters, Speeches, Judicial Opinions, and Other Writings of Oliver Wendell Holmes, Jr.*, ed. Richard Posner (Chicago: University of Chicago Press, 1992), 85.

221 **Holmes's youthful enthusiasm:** Howe, *Shaping Years,* 170–71; White, *Justice Oliver Wendell Holmes,* 65.

221 **He told his parents:** Howe, *Shaping Years,* 170, 174–75.

221 **In the most famous line:** Holmes Jr., *The Soldier's Faith,* 86, 91.

222 **His college classmate:** Wendell Phillips Garrison, "Sentimental Jingoism," *Nation,* Dec. 19, 1895, 440–41.

222 **"loathed the thick-fingered clowns":** Oliver Wendell Holmes Jr. to Amelia Holmes, Nov. 16, 1862, in *Touched with Fire* (Cambridge, MA: Harvard University Press, 1946), 70, quoted in Albert Alschuler, *Law Without Values: The Life, Work, and Legacy of Justice Holmes* (Chicago: University of Chicago Press, 2000), 233n73.

222 **The critic Edmund Wilson:** Wilson, *Patriotic Gore,* 755, 763.

222 **In a short autobiography:** Oliver Wendell Holmes Jr., autobiographical statement, July 2, 1861, cited in White, *Justice Oliver Wendell Holmes,* 7–8.

222 **probate judge of Suffolk County:** Baker, *Justice from Beacon Hill,* 164.

222 **Harvard Law School:** Howe, *Shaping Years,* 184, 188–89, 204–5; Novick, *Honorable Justice,* 96.

222 **Most students were not:** Novick, *Honorable Justice,* 96.

222 **"Just as a certain number":** "Harvard University Law School," *American Law Review* 5 (1870): 177; Howe, *Shaping Years,* 204–5.

223 **He returned to law school:** Novick, *Honorable Justice,* 100–102.

223 **The time he had put in:** Howe, *Shaping Years,* 204.

223 **Holmes dined at the home:** Ibid., 223, 225–27.

223 **He traveled on to Scotland:** Novick, *Honorable Justice,* 111–13.

223 **On his return:** Howe, *Shaping Years,* 245; Novick, *Honorable Justice,* 116.

223 **George Shattuck:** Novick, *Honorable Justice,* 114–15.

223 **James Bradley Thayer:** Howe, *Shaping Years,* 247.

223 **The firm had blue-chip clients:** Baker, *Justice from Beacon Hill,* 188–89.

223 **"a powerful battery":** William James to Henry James, July 5, 1876, quoted in White, *Justice Oliver Wendell Holmes,* 89.

223 **He was also named:** Howe, *Shaping Years,* 273.

223 **"It is noticeable":** Ibid., 274.

224 **"All the noble":** Baker, *Justice from Beacon Hill,* 197.

224 **In a letter:** Oliver Wendell Holmes Jr. to Frederick Pollock, Sept. 24, 1910, in *Holmes-Pollock Letters: The Correspondence of Mr. Justice Holmes and Sir Frederick Pollock, 1874–1932,* ed. Mark deWolfe Howe (Cambridge, MA: Harvard University Press, 1961), 1:171.

224 **Like Holmes, Fanny Dixwell:** Novick, *Honorable Justice,* 131–32; Baker, *Justice from Beacon Hill,* 219.

224 **Holmes had known Fanny:** Oliver Wendell Holmes Jr. to Mrs. Howard Kennedy, Mar. 11, 1872, quoted in White, *Justice Oliver Wendell Holmes,* 92.

224 **One member of Fanny's extended family:** Howe, *Shaping Years,* 200n.g.

224 **Holmes once said:** Oliver Wendell Holmes Jr. to Ethel Scott, Jan. 6, 1912, quoted in White, *Justice Oliver Wendell Holmes,* 105.

224 **Holmes's journal entry:** Michael Hoffheimer, *Justice Holmes and the Natural Law Legal Philosophy* (New York: Routledge, 2013), 78.

225 **Fanny, who suffered from rheumatic fever:** Novick, *Honorable Justice,* 133, 147, 433n49.

225 **He offered up another:** Oliver Wendell Holmes Jr. to Lewis Einstein, Aug. 31, 1928, quoted in White, *Justice Oliver Wendell Holmes,* 105–6.

225 **She dismissed Lady Belper:** Novick, *Honorable Justice,* 143–44.

225 **an article titled "The Gas-Stokers' Strike":** Oliver Wendell Holmes Jr., "The Gas-Stokers' Strike," *American Law Review* 7 (1873): 582, in *Essential Holmes,* 120.

225 **Legislation, "like every other device":** Ibid., 122.

226 **His claim that:** Herbert Spencer, *Social Statics; Or the Conditions Essential to Human Happiness Specified, and the First of Them Developed* (New York: D. Appleton and Co., 1892), 303; Eric Foner, introduction to *Social Darwinism in American Thought,* by Richard Hofstadter (Boston: Beacon Press, 1992).

226 **With this argument:** Baker, *Justice from Beacon Hill,* 214.

226 **His Boston Brahmin upbringing:** Andrea Greenwood and Mark W. Harris, *An Introduction to the Unitarian and Universalist Traditions* (Cambridge; Cambridge University Press, 2011), 60.

226 **After all, the friend:** Jennifer Viegas, *William James: American Philosopher, Psychologist, and Theologian* (New York: Rosen Publishing Group, 2006), 6.

227 **Holmes's social networks mobilized on his behalf:** White, *Justice Oliver Wendell Holmes,* 110–11; Novick, *Honorable Justice,* 154; Baker, *Justice from Beacon Hill,* 241–42.

227 **The Lowell Institute:** Mark W. Harris, *Elite: Uncovering Classism in Unitarian Universalist History* (Boston: Unitarian Universalist Association of Congregations, 2011), 37–38; Harriette Knight Smith, *The History of the Lowell Institute* (Boston: Lamson, Wolffe and Company, 1898), 11.

227 **Over twelve nights:** Novick, *Honorable Justice,* 158; White, *Justice Oliver Wendell Holmes,* 148.

227 **It was likely:** Novick, *Honorable Justice,* 157–59.

227 **He insisted the law:** *Southern Pacific Co. v. Jensen,* 224 U.S. 205, 222 (1917) (Holmes, J., dissenting); Fred Rodell, "Justice Holmes and His Hecklers," *Yale Law Journal* 60 (1951): 620, 624; H. L. Pohlman, *Oliver Wendell Holmes: Free Speech and the Living Constitution* (New York: New York University Press, 1991), 22.

228 **Law "cannot be dealt with":** Holmes Jr., *Common Law,* 1.

228 **With the success:** Yosal Rogat, "The Judge as Spectator," *University of Chicago Law Review* 31 (1964) 213, 214; Alschuler, *Law Without Values,* 84.

228 **In a few years:** Oliver Wendell Holmes Jr., "The Profession of the Law: Conclusion of a Lecture Delivered to Undergraduates of Harvard University on February 17, 1886," in *Speeches by Oliver Wendell Holmes* (Boston: Little, Brown, 1900), 22.

228 **After being approached:** Novick, *Honorable Justice,* 166.

228 **"Academic life is but half life":** Oliver Wendell Holmes Jr. to Felix Frankfurter, July 15, 1913, quoted in White, *Justice Oliver Wendell Holmes,* 206.

228 **At the urging:** Novick, *Honorable Justice,* 168–69.

229 **James Bradley Thayer:** White, *Justice Oliver Wendell Holmes,* 204.

229 **In *Commonwealth v. Perry*:** *Commonwealth v. Perry,* 155 Mass. 117 (1891).

229 **In his view:** Baker, *Justice from Beacon Hill,* 298–99.

229 **Holmes's *Perry* dissent:** Oliver Wendell Holmes Jr., *The Mind and Faith of Justice Holmes: His Speeches, Essays, Letters, and Judicial Opinions,* ed. Max Lerner (New Brunswick, NJ: Transaction, 1989), 92.

229 **"I know nothing about the matter":** Holmes Jr., *Mind and Faith of Justice Holmes,* 95.

229 **In a major case:** *McAuliffe v. Mayor of New Bedford,* 155 Mass. 216 (1892).

230 **If the city's power to fire:** Michael Herz, "Justice Byron White and the Argument That the Greater Includes the Lesser," *Brigham Young University Law Review* (1994): 227, 239.

230 **"I have known":** Oliver Wendell Holmes Jr. to Frederick Pollock, Apr. 2, 1894, in *Holmes-Pollock Letters,* 1:50.

230 **Fanny, who had suffered:** Novick, *Honorable Justice,* 201.

230 **Holmes argued for:** Oliver Wendell Holmes Jr., *The Path of the Law and the Common Law* (New York: Kaplan Publishing, 2009), 5, 11, 15.

230 **Holmes was named chief justice:** Ibid., 253.

230 **Holmes described the caseload:** Ibid., 292.

231 **"As we don't shut up bores":** Oliver Wendell Holmes Jr. to Frederick Pollock, March 17, 1898 in *Holmes-Pollock Letters,* 1:81–82.

231 **Holmes had long dreamed:** Baker, *Justice from Beacon Hill,* 196.

231 **The court already had:** White, *Justice Oliver Wendell Holmes,* 253; Baker, *Justice from Beacon Hill,* 339.

231 **That was good news:** Novick, *Honorable Justice,* 233; Baker, *Justice from Beacon Hill,* 339.

231 **Hemenway was in fact:** White, *Justice Oliver Wendell Holmes,* 299.

231 **Lodge had also attended:** Baker, *Justice from Beacon Hill,* 341–42.

232 **"the favorite residential resort":** Porter Sargent, *A Handbook of New England* (Boston: Porter E. Sargent, 1917), 654.

232 **Holmes and Lodge:** Baker, *Justice from Beacon Hill,* 39; "A Fresh Look at Lodge," *Life,* Sept. 14, 1953, 175, 177.

232 **Roosevelt was said:** White, *Justice Oliver Wendell Holmes,* 81–82, 299.

232 **Roosevelt was not himself a Brahmin:** Gerald Gawalt, *My Dear President: Letters Between President and Their Wives* (New York: Black Dog & Leventhal, 2006), 33.

232 **Holmes, Lodge, and Roosevelt:** Rosenberg, *The Life and Times of Francis Cabot Lowell,* 60.

232 **On August 11:** Novick, *Honorable Justice,* 235–36.

232 **In an editorial:** Oliver Wendell Holmes Jr. to Frederick Pollock, Aug. 13, 1902, in *Holmes-Pollock Letters,* 1:103–4.

232 *Boston Evening Transcript*: White, *Justice Oliver Wendell Holmes,* 306.

232 **"incompetence and inadequacy":** Holmes Jr. to Pollock, Aug. 13, 1902.

232 **He did not need to worry:** Novick, *Honorable Justice*, 242.

232 **"the president's choice of me":** Oliver Wendell Holmes Jr. to Lady Georgina Pollock, Sept. 6, 1902, in *Holmes–Pollock Letters*, 1:105.

233 **Holmes put his Boston life:** Holmes Jr. to Pollock, Aug. 13, 1902.

233 **On December 8:** White, *Justice Oliver Wendell Holmes*, 311; Kenneth Jost, *The Supreme Court A-Z* (New York: Routledge, 2013), 212.

233 **He heard oral arguments:** Novick, *Honorable Justice*, 243–45.

233 **They were regularly invited:** Ibid., 259–60.

233 **In the 1903 case:** *Giles v. Harris*, 189 U.S. 475 (1903).

233 **He charged that:** Charles S. Bullock III and Mark J. Rozell, eds., *The Oxford Handbook of Southern Politics* (Oxford: Oxford University Press, 2012), 451–52.

234 **Blacks were subjected:** *Giles*, 189 U.S. at 483; Gloria J. Browne-Marshall, *Race, Law, and American Society: 1607 to Present* (New York: Routledge, 2013), 184.

234 **The convention delegates:** *Giles v. Teasley*, 193 U.S. 146, 148 (1904).

234 **The convention president:** *Hunter v. Underwood*, 471 U.S. 222, 229 (1985), quoting statement of John B. Knox, president of the Alabama Constitutional Convention of 1901.

234 **Giles argued that the voting rules:.** *Giles*, 189 U.S. at 482.

234 **"a fraud upon the Constitution":** *Id.* at 486–87.

234 **"the great mass":** *Id.* at 488.

234 **"decisive turning point":** Richard Pildes, "Democracy, Anti-Democracy, and the Canon," *Constitutional Commentary* 17 (2000): 259, 296.

234 **There was nothing:** *Giles*, 189 U.S. at 504 (Harlan, J., dissenting).

235 **Holmes's view that "political rights":** The Supreme Court abandoned Holmes's doctrine that "political rights" were not enforceable in the courts in 1962, in *Baker v. Carr*, 369 U.S. 186 (1962); see Pildes, "Democracy, Anti-Democracy, and the Canon," 298.

235 **It was the gas stokers' strike:** Holmes Jr., "The Gas-Stokers' Strike," 122.

235 **Joseph Lochner, a baker:** *Lochner v. New York*, 198 U.S. 45 (1905); Bernard Schwartz, *A History of the Supreme Court* (Oxford: Oxford University Press, 1993), 193.

235 **Rufus Peckham:** *Lochner*, 198 U.S. at 53.

235 **"The 14th Amendment":** *Id.* at 68

235 **Charles Beard:** David Bernstein, *Rehabilitating Lochner: Defending Individual Rights Against Progressive Reform* (Chicago: University of Chicago Press, 2011), 45.

236 **His sympathy lay with legislatures:** Felix Frankfurter, *Mr. Justice Holmes and the Supreme Court* (Cambridge, MA: Harvard University Press, 1938), 24, cited in Rogat, "Judge as Spectator," 245.

236 **"The only limit I can see":** Oliver Wendell Holmes Jr. to Harold J. Laski, in Mark de Wolfe Howe, *Holmes–Laski Letters* (New York: Atheneum, 1963) 1:84.

236 **John Marshall Harlan:** *Lochner*, 198 U.S. 70 (Harlan, J., dissenting).

236 **In 1911, in *Bailey v. Alabama*:** *Bailey v. Alabama*, 219 U.S. 219 (1911).

236 **"iron manacles . . . riveted upon their legs":** *Jamison v. Wimbish*, 130 F. 351, 355–56 (S.D. Ga. 1904).

236 **The Supreme Court agreed:** *Bailey*, 219 U.S. at 245.

237 **"Breach of a legal contract":** *Id.* at 246 (Holmes, J., dissenting).

237 **In *Berea College v. Kentucky*:** *Berea College v. Kentucky*, 211 U.S. 45, 58 (1908).

237 **"it is difficult to perceive":** *Id.* at 68, 69.

237 **In *United States v. Ju Toy*:** *United States v. Ju Toy*, 198 U.S. 253 (1905).

237 **"Fanny has got":** Oliver Wendell Holmes Jr. to Ethel Scott, June 5, 1911, Oliver Wendell Holmes Papers, Harvard Law School (hereafter cited as OWH Papers), quoted in Novick, *Honorable Justice*, 303.

238 **He complained frankly:** Oliver Wendell Holmes to Clara Stevens, March 6, 1909, OWH Papers, quoted in Snyder, "House That Built Holmes," 661, 667.

238 **"I should like":** Oliver Wendell Holmes Jr. to Patrick Sheehan, Dec. 15, 1912, in Oliver Wendell Holmes Jr., *The Fundamental Holmes: A Free Speech Chronicle and Reader*, ed. Ronald K. L. Collins (Cambridge: Cambridge University Press, 2010), 263.

238 **There was, as it happened:** Snyder, "House That Built Holmes," 669–70.

238 **Many of them lived in:** Ronald Steel, *Walter Lippmann and the American Century* (Boston: Little, Brown, 1980), 120–21; Snyder, "House That Built Holmes," 670.

238 **The group's influence:** Snyder, "House That Built Holmes," 663.

238 **At the center of the group:** Ibid., 674; Steel, *Walter Lippmann,* 121.

238 **On March 8, 1916:** Novick, *Honorable Justice,* 317.

238 **When Holmes dissented:** *Hammer v. Dagenhart,* 247 U.S. 251 (1918); *Adkins v. Children's Hospital,* 261 U.S. 525 (1923); Snyder, "House That Built Holmes," 679-80.

239 **Holmes berated the pacifists:** Oliver Wendell Holmes Jr. to John Wigmore, Nov. 1915, OWH Papers, quoted in Novick, *Honorable Justice,* 469n11; Alschuler, *Law Without Values,* 27.

239 **hereditary elite:** Holmes Sr., *Elsie Venner,* 3–4.

240 **"If genius and talent are inherited":** Oliver Wendell Holmes Sr., "Crime and Automatism," *Atlantic Monthly,* Apr. 1875, 466, 475; Lombardo, *Three Generations,* 9.

240 **"must tend in the long run":** Holmes Jr., "The Gas-Stokers' Strike," 122.

240 **"If the typical criminal":** Holmes Jr., *Path of the Law and the Common Law,* 19.

240 **"a future in which science":** Holmes Jr., *The Soldier's Faith,* 88.

241 **"I think it probable":** Holmes Jr., *Mind and Faith of Justice Holmes,* 387, 391.

241 **In 1914 he bought a copy:** Thomas Robert Malthus, *An Essay on Population* (New York: E. P. Dutton, 1914); Baker, *Justice from Beacon Hill,* 601.

241 **"Malthus pleased me immensely":** Oliver Wendell Holmes Jr. to Frederick Pollock, Aug. 30, 1914, in *Holmes-Pollock Letters,* 1:219.

241 **"devout Malthusian":** Oliver Wendell Holmes Jr. to Harold J. Laski, June 14, 1922, in *Holmes-Laski Letters,* 658.

241 **"I look at men":** Oliver Wendell Holmes Jr. to Harold J. Laski, July 23, 1925, in *Essential Holmes,* 140.

241 **"wholesale social regeneration":** Oliver Wendell Holmes Jr., "Ideals and Doubts," *Illinois Law Review* 10 (1915): 1, cited in Leuchtenburg, *Supreme Court Reborn,* 18.

241 **"complaint against war":** Frederick Pollock to Oliver Wendell Holmes Jr., April 11, 1920, in *Holmes-Pollock Letters,* 2:39.

241 **Holmes agreed:** Oliver Wendell Holmes Jr. to Frederick Pollock, April 25, 1920, in *Holmes-Pollock Letters,* 2:40–41.

242 **"intelligent socialism":** Oliver Wendell Holmes Jr. to Felix Frankfurter, Sept. 3, 1921, in *Holmes and Frankfurter: Their Correspondence, 1912–1934,* ed. Robert Mennell and Christine Compston (Hanover, NH: University Press of New England, 1996), 125.

242 **Holmes wrote favorably:** White, *Justice Oliver Wendell Holmes,* 572n135.

242 **Many prominent people:** Alschuler, *Law Without Values,* 29; Kevles, *In the Name of Eugenics,* 106.

242 **But as one legal scholar:** Alschuler, *Law Without Values,* 29.

242 **Holmes's support for eugenics:** Ibid., 29–30.

243 **"deeply cynical":** Herbert Hovenkamp, *The Opening of American Law: Neoclassical Legal Thought, 1870–1970* (Oxford: Oxford University Press, 2015), 4.

243 **In March 1919:** *Schenck v. United States,* 249 U.S. 47 (1919); Terry Eastland, ed., *Freedom of Expression in the Supreme Court: The Defining Cases* (Lanham, MD: Rowman & Littlefield, 2000), 1.

243 **Schenck had mailed:** *Schenck,* 249 U.S. at 49–51.

243 **protect "falsely shouting fire":** *Id.* at 52.

243 **But Holmes considered:** Yosal Rogat and James M. O'Fallon, "Mr. Justice Holmes: A Dissenting Opinion—The Speech Cases," *Stanford Law Review* 36 (1984): 1349, 1376.

243 **In *Frohwerk v. United States*:** *Frohwerk v. United States,* 249 U.S. 204 (1919) at 206–10.

244 **In *Debs v. United States*:** *Debs v. United States,* 249 U.S. 211 (1919) at 212–13.

244 **As in the *Frohwerk* case:;** Edgar J. McManus and Tara Helfman, *Liberty and Union: A Constitutional History of the United States* (New York: Routledge, 2014), 328

244 **"I am beginning to get":** Oliver Wendell Holmes Jr. to Frederick Pollock, April 5, 1919, in *Holmes-Pollock Letters,* 2:7; Martin Hickman, "Mr. Justice Holmes: A Reappraisal," *Western Political Quarterly* (Mar. 1952): 76.

244 **Holmes's anti-speech rulings:** *McAuliffe,* 155 Mass. 216.

244 **The court heard:** *Abrams v. United States,* 250 U.S. 616 (1919) at 630.

244 **A few years later:** *Gitlow v. New York,* 268 U.S. 652 (1925).

245 **"Freedom of Speech in War Time":** Snyder, "House That Built Holmes," 680–81.

245 **Another theory:** Rogat and O'Fallon, "Dissenting Opinion," 1378; see generally: Thomas Healy, *The Great Dissent: How Oliver Wendell Holmes Changed His Mind—and Changed the History of Free Speech in America* (New York: Metropolitan Books, 2013).

245 **The *New Republic* paid tribute:** Snyder, "House That Built Holmes," 684, 685.

NOTES

245 **"little basketful":** Novick, *Honorable Justice*, 337.
246 **"we have no concern":** *Block v. Hirsh*, 256 U.S. 135, 158 (1921).
246 **Warren G. Harding:** Peter Renstrom, *The Taft Court: Justices, Rulings, and Legacy* (Santa Barbara, CA: ABC-CLIO, 2003), 39.
246 **Taft, who had been:** "Taft Gained Peaks in Unusual Career," *New York Times*, March 9, 1930.
246 **Holmes and Taft liked each other:** Novick, *Honorable Justice*, 346.
246 **In April 1923:** *Adkins v. Children's Hospital*, 261 U.S. 525 (1923) at 562, 571.
246 **A parochial school teacher:** *Meyer v. Nebraska*, 262 U.S. 390 (1923).
247 **"to acquire useful knowledge":** *Id.* at 399.
247 **"We all agree":** *Bartels v. Iowa*, 262 U.S. 404, 412 (1923), containing dissent for *Meyer v. Nebraska*.
247 **"to direct the upbringing":** *Pierce v. Society of Sisters*, 268 U.S. 510, 594 (1925).
247 **His appearance that year:** *Time*, Mar. 15, 1926.
248 **"in every high court":** Snyder, "House That Built Holmes," 705–6.
248 **"the tender, wise and beautiful being":** Baker, *Justice from Beacon Hill*, 590.
248 **important blow for defendants' rights:** *Silverthorne Lumber Co. v. United States*, 251 U.S. 385 (1920).
248 **he would notably dissent:** *Olmstead v. United States*, 277 U.S. 438 (1928).
249 **"We accept the judgment":** Oliver Wendell Holmes Jr. to Harold Laski, Oct. 23, 1926, in *Holmes-Laski Letters*, 2:887–88; Richard Posner, *Reflections on Judging* (Cambridge, MA: Harvard University Press, 2013), 169.
249 **Holmes's approach to judging:** Rogat, "Judge as Spectator," 213, 230.
249 **"I have little doubt":** Oliver Wendell Holmes Jr. to Harold Laski, Mar. 4, 1920, in *Holmes-Laski Letters*, 1:194; David Burton, ed., *Progressive Masks: Letters of Oliver Wendell Holmes, Jr., and Franklin Ford* (East Brunswick, NJ: Associated University Presses, 1982), 44.
249 **"he didn't care a straw":** Merlo J. Pusey, *Charles Evans Hughes* (New York: Macmillan, 1951), 2:287, 289, cited in White, "Rise and Fall of Justice Holmes," 70.
249 **One critic observed:** Hickman, "Reappraisal," 67 (quoting Harold B. McKinnon, "The Secret of Mr. Justice Holmes," *American Bar Association Journal* 36 (1950): 261, 344.

CHAPTER NINE: OLIVER WENDELL HOLMES
252 **Judges in New Jersey:** William Leuchtenburg, *The Supreme Court Reborn: The Constitutional Revolution in the Age of Roosevelt* (New York: Oxford University Press, 1995), 6; Stephen A. Siegel, "Justice Holmes, *Buck v. Bell*, and the History of Equal Protection," *Minnesota Law Review* 90 (2005): 121–22, 124.
252 **The federal court:** *Davis v. Berry*, 216 F. 413, 416–17 (S.D. Iowa 1914); Victoria Nourse, "*Buck v. Bell*: A Constitutional Tragedy from a Lost World," *Pepperdine Law Review* 39 (2011): 103.
252 **The New Jersey Supreme Court:** *Smith v. Board of Examiners*, 88 A. 963, 966 (N.J. 1913); Nourse, "Constitutional Tragedy," 103.
252 **Dr. Walter E. Fernald:** Joseph Wortis, *Mental Retardation and Developmental Disabilities* (New York: Brunner-Mazel, 1986), 109; Daniel J. Kevles, *In the Name of Eugenics: Genetics and the Uses of Human Heredity* (Cambridge, MA: Harvard University Press, 1985), 148.
252 **Henry Goddard:** Paul A. Lombardo, *Three Generations, No Imbeciles: Eugenics, the Supreme Court, and* Buck v. Bell (Baltimore: Johns Hopkins University Press, 2008), 156.
253 **gone over "to the enemy":** Kevles, *In the Name of Eugenics*, 148.
253 **Geneticists, who had initially said little:** Kenneth Ludmerer, *Genetics and American Society: A Historical Appraisal* (Baltimore: Johns Hopkins University Press, 1972), 123–25.
253 **By 1927 scientists had made great strides:** Allan Chase, *The Legacy of Malthus: The Social Costs of the New Scientific Racism* (Champaign-Urbana: University of Illinois Press, 1980), 315–17, cited in Leuchtenburg, *Supreme Court Reborn*, 21.
253 **In 1922 Walter Lippmann:** Walter Lippmann, "The Mental Age of Americans," *New Republic*, Oct. 25, 1922, 213, 215.
253 **Clarence Darrow:** Clarence Darrow, "The Eugenics Cult," *American Mercury*, June 1926, 129, 137; Robert J. Richards, *Darwin and the Emergence of Evolutionary Theories of Mind and Behavior* (Chicago: University of Chicago Press, 1987), 516; Kevles, *In the Name of Eugenics*, 120.
254 **Irving Whitehead and Aubrey Strode submitted legal briefs:** Brief for Defendant in Error, *Buck v. Bell*, U.S. Supreme Court, Oct. term, 1926, available at http://readingroom.law.gsu.edu/

cgi/viewcontent.cgi?article=1035&context=buckvbell and http://readingroom.law.gsu.edu/cgi/
viewcontent.cgi?article=1036&context=buckvbell; Brief for Plaintiff in Error, *Buck v. Bell*, U.S.
Supreme Court, Oct. term, 1926, available at http://readingroom.law.gsu.edu/cgi/viewcontent.
cgi?article=1095&context=buckvbell.

254 **Whitehead's brief:** Brief for Plaintiff in Error, *Buck v. Bell*, U.S. Supreme Court, Oct. term,
1926, 11–17; *Smith*, 88 A. 963; In re Thomson, 169 N.Y.S. 638 (Sup. Ct. 1918), aff'd *Osborn v.
Thomson*, 171 N.Y.S. 1094 (App. Div. 1918); *Haynes v. Lapeer Circuit Judge*, 201 Mich. 138, 166
N.W. 938 (1918); *State Bd. of Eugenics v. Cline*, No. 15,442 (Or. Cir. Ct. Dec. 13, 1921); Harry
Laughlin, *Eugenical Sterilization in the United States* (Chicago: Psychopathic Library of the Mu-
nicipal Court of Chicago, 1922), 440.

254 **Whitehead also argued:** Brief for Plaintiff in Error, *Buck v. Bell*, 1926, 9–11.

255 ***Munn v. Illinois*:** *Munn v. Illinois*, 94 U.S. 113, 123 (1876).

255 **In *Meyer*:** *Meyer v. Nebraska*, 262 U.S. 390, 399 (1923); *Pierce v. Society of Sisters*, 268 U.S. 510
(1925).

255 **a variety of classical sources:** Brief for Plaintiff in Error, *Buck v. Bell*, 1926, 7–8.

255 **not barbaric or outlandish:** *Davis*, 216 F. at 416–17; Nourse, "Constitutional Tragedy," 103.

256 **Brandeis submitted a brief:** Melvin Urofsky, *Louis D. Brandeis: A Life* (New York: Pantheon,
2009), 216; *Muller v. Oregon*, 208 U.S. 412 (1908).

256 **It could have quoted:** Walter Lippmann, "The Mental Age of Americans," 213; Lombardo,
Three Generations, 143; Ludmerer, *Genetics and American Society*, 123–25.

256 **"reign of doctors":** Brief for Plaintiff in Error, *Buck v. Bell*, 1926, 17–18.

256 **Strode's brief:** Ibid., 4–5.

257 **Strode quoted extensively:** Ibid., 7, 10.

257 **"police power":** Ibid., 30–34.

257 **The statute was "part of a general plan":** Brief for Defendant in Error, *Buck v. Bell*, 1926, 26,
37–38.

257 **"Poor the Commonwealth":** Ibid., 37.

258 **"The question before the Court":** Ibid., 48.

258 **"lived as a member of the household":** Ibid., 5.

258 **Strode was passing:** "Carrie Buck Trial Transcript, 51–100" (2009), 97, *Buck v. Bell Documents*,
Paper 32, http://readingroom.law.gsu.edu/buckvbell/32.

258 **William Howard Taft:** Philip Secor, *Chief Justice Profiles* (Bloomington, IN: iUniverse,
2013), 54.

258 **Taft attended Yale:** Robert Weir, ed., *Class in America: An Encyclopedia* (Westport, CT: Greenwood, 2007), 3:774.

259 **After graduating from:** Frank Freidel, *The Presidents of the United States of America* (Washington, DC: White House Historical Association, 1999), 58; Roger Newman, ed., *The Yale Biographical Dictionary of American Law* (New Haven, CT: Yale University Press, 2009), 535; Secor,
Chief Justice Profiles, 54.

259 **"plate the right side up":** Freidel, *Presidents of the United States of America*, 58.

259 **Taft was elected handily:** Ibid.

259 **"unscrupulous" and a "muckraker":** Jonathan Lurie, *William Howard Taft: The Travails of a
Progressive Conservative* (New York: Cambridge University Press, 2012).

260 **"an office which by both temperament and training":** "Taft Gained Peaks in Unusual Career,"
New York Times, Mar. 9, 1930; Lurie, *William Howard Taft*, 192–93.

260 **He traveled to England:** Alpheus Thomas Mason, *William Howard Taft: Chief Justice* (New
York: Simon and Schuster, 1965), 194, 286–87, 291.

260 **The new law:** Del Dickson, ed., *The Supreme Court in Conference (1940–1985): The Private
Discussions Behind Nearly 300 Supreme Court Decisions* (New York: Oxford University Press,
2001), 74.

260 **It was a major change:** Peter G. Renstrom, *The Taft Court: Justices, Rulings, and Legacy* (Santa
Barbara, CA: ABC-CLIO, 2003), 184.

260 **Several new appointments:** Ibid., 183.

260 **Taft wrote a strong pro-business opinion:** *Bailey v. Drexel Furniture Company*, 259 U.S. 20
(1922).

260 **Life Extension Institute:** Ruth C. Engs, *The Progressive Era's Health Reform Movement: A Historical Dictionary* (Westport, CT: Praeger, 2003), 204; Irving Fisher and Eugene Lyman Fisk,

How to Live: Rules for Healthful Living Based on Modern Science (New York: Funk & Wagnalls, 1916), iv, 293.

261 **It advocated "sterilization":** Fisher and Fisk, *How to Live*, iv, 323.

261 **Louis Brandeis:** Urofsky, *Brandeis*, 8, 38–42, 216, 220–22.

261 **In January 1916:** Ibid., 434–35.

261 **Adding to the anti-Brandeis sentiment:** Ibid., 438–40, 445.

261 **It "was a misfortune":** Oliver Wendell Holmes Jr. to Lady Castletown, June 20, 1916, in Oliver Wendell Holmes Papers, Harvard Law School (hereafter cited as OWH Papers), box 26, file 14, quoted in Sheldon Novick, *Honorable Justice: The Life of Oliver Wendell Holmes* (Boston: Little, Brown, 1989), 316.

261 **Despite the opposition:** Urofsky, *Brandeis*, 458.

261 **He generally supported civil rights plaintiffs:** Ibid., 639.

261 **Brandeis joined the majority:** *Gong Lum v. Rice*, 275 U.S. 78 (1927).

262 **Nevertheless, Stone was sympathetic:** Robert Cynkar, *"Buck v. Bell:* 'Felt Necessities' v. Fundamental Values?," *Columbia Law Review* 81 (1981): 1418, 1451, 1451n186; William Wiecek, *The Birth of the Modern Constitution: The United States Supreme Court, 1941–1953*, vol.6 of *History of the Supreme Court of the United States*, ed. John R. Shook (New York: Cambridge University Press, 2006), 48–52; *The Dictionary of Modern American Philosophers* (Bristol, England: Thoemmes, 2005), 883–84.

262 **He was also mean-spirited:** Dickson, *Supreme Court in Conference*, 75.

262 **When Brandeis spoke:** Urofsky, *Brandeis*, 479.

262 **George Sutherland:** Timothy L. Hall, *Supreme Court Justices: A Biographical Dictionary* (New York: Infobase, 2001), 280.

262 **Sutherland moved on:** Ibid.; Clare Cushman, ed., *Supreme Court Justices: Illustrated Biographies, 1789-2012* (Thousand Oaks, CA: CQ Press, 2013), 314–15.

263 **"Four Horsemen of the Apocalypse":** Hall, *Supreme Court Justices*, 279; Cushman, *Supreme Court Justices* 333.

263 **Willis Van Devanter:** Hall, *Supreme Court Justices*, 253–54; Rebecca Shoemaker, *The White Court: Justices, Rulings, and Legacy* (Santa Barbara, CA: ABC-CLIO, 2004), 76–81.

263 **When Taft joined him:** Hall, *Supreme Court Justices*, 254–55.

263 **During the New Deal:** Ibid.

263 **Edward T. Sanford:** Ibid., 287–88.

263 **In 1923 he dissented:** Melvin Urofsky, ed., *Biographical Encyclopedia of the Supreme Court: The Lives and Legal Philosophies of the Justices* (Washington, DC: CQ Press, 2006), 449; *Adkins v. Children's Hospital*, 261 U.S. 525 (1923).

263 **Bill of Rights applied to the states:** *Gitlow v. New York*, 268 U.S. 652 (1925); David Schultz, *The Encyclopedia of the Supreme Court* (New York: Infobase, 2005), 184.

263 **Pierce Butler:** Urofsky, *Supreme Court Justices*, 105.

263 **He began his career:** Ibid.; Cushman, ed., *Supreme Court Justices*, 318–20; Leuchtenburg, *Supreme Court Reborn*, 14; Hall, *Supreme Court Justices*, 284.

264 **"afflict the Court with another Jew":** Drew Pearson and Robert S. Allen, *The Nine Old Men* (Garden City, NY: Doubleday, 1937), 225.

264 **Butler was a strong believer:** Urofsky, *Supreme Court Justices*, 82.

264 **"taking in hand life":** Oliver Wendell Holmes Jr., *The Essential Holmes: Selections from the Letters, Speeches, Judicial Opinions, and Other Writings of Oliver Wendell Holmes, Jr.*, ed. Richard Posner (Chicago: University of Chicago Press, 1992), 122; Oliver Wendell Holmes Jr., *The Mind and Faith of Justice Holmes: His Speeches, Essays, Letters, and Judicial Opinions*, ed. Max Lerner (New Brunswick, NJ: Transaction, 1989), 391; Leuchtenburg, *Supreme Court Reborn*, 18.

264 **"to improve the quality":** G. Edward White, *Justice Oliver Wendell Holmes: The Law and Inner Self* (New York: Oxford University Press, 1993), 572n135.

264 **As the court's senior:** Dickson, *Supreme Court in Conference*, 9–11.

265 **Taft spoke for the court:** David Burton, *Taft, Holmes, and the 1920s Court: An Appraisal* (Cranbury, NJ: Associated University Presses, 1998), 126.

265 **Before Taft took over:** Dickson, *Supreme Court in Conference*, 73.

265 **He liked unanimous rulings:** Ibid., 74–75.

265 **Taft made it a practice:** Ibid., 74.

265 **"Some of the brethren":** White, *Justice Oliver Wendell Holmes*, 404–5.

NOTES

266 **Holmes's first book:** Albert Alschuler, *Law Without Values: The Life, Work, and Legacy of Justice Holmes* (Chicago: University of Chicago Press, 2000), 85.
266 **His *Lochner* opinion:** Alfred Knight, *The Wizards of Washington: Triumphs and Travesties of the United States Supreme Court* (Lincoln, NE: iUniverse, 2006), 10n4; Alschuler, *Law Without Values*, 62.
266 **One critic spoke for a vast consensus:** Nourse, "Constitutional Tragedy," 101.
267 **The opinion began:** *Buck v. Bell*, 274 U.S. 200, 205 (1927).
267 **He did not read newspapers:** Oliver Wendell Holmes Jr. to Frederick Pollock, Aug. 27, 1921, in *Holmes-Pollock Letters: The Correspondence of Mr. Justice Holmes and Sir Frederick Pollock, 1874–1932*, ed. Mark deWolfe Howe (Cambridge, MA: Harvard University Press, 1961), 2:77–78.
267 **"I never know any facts":** Oliver Wendell Holmes Jr. to Frederick Pollock and Lady Pollock, Sept. 24, 1904, in *Holmes-Pollock Letters*, 1:118.
267 **Holmes began by stating:** *Buck*, 274 U.S. at 205.
267 **Holmes's good friend:** Lippmann, "Mental Age of Americans," *New Republic*, Oct. 25, 1922, 213, 215.
268 **Both of these assessments:** "Carrie Buck Trial Transcript, 51–100," 58–59, 83.
268 **It was an excessively generous description:** "Continued Notes," box 11, Central Virginia Training Center Papers, Library of Virginia.
268 **"if now discharged":** *Buck*, 274 U.S. at 205–6.
268 **"Experience has shown":** *Id.* at 206.
269 **Holmes made no reference:** Kevles, *In the Name of Eugenics*, 148; Ludmerer, *Genetics and American Society*, 123–25; Lombardo, *Three Generations*, 156.
269 **The court could:** Arthur Best, *Evidence: Examples & Explanations* (New York: Aspen, 2009), 237.
269 **Holmes similarly presented:** Ibid.
269 **"alarming tone":** Catharine Pierce Wells, "Reinventing Holmes: The Hidden, Inner, Life of a Cynical, Ambitious, Detached, and Fascistic Old Judge Without Values," *Tulsa Law Review* 37 (2002): 801, 810.
269 **"to prevent our being swamped":** *Buck*, 274 U.S. at 207.
269 **"It is better for all the world":** *Id.*
269 **In fact, criminologists:** Carl Degler, *In Search of Human Nature: The Decline and Revival of Darwinism in American Social Thought* (Oxford: Oxford University Press, 1991), 140.
270 **"Three generations":** *Buck*, 274 U.S. at 207.
270 **The colony had recorded:** "History and Clinical Notes," June 4, 1924, box 11, Carrie Buck file, Library of Virginia; J. David Smith and K. Ray Nelson, *The Sterilization of Carrie Buck: Was She Feebleminded or Society's Pawn?* (Far Hills, NJ: New Horizon Press, 1989), 44.
270 **The U.S. Department of Commerce:** William Estabrook Chancellor, "The Measurement of Human Ability," *Journal of Education* 77, no. 16 (April 17, 1913): 425–26; U.S. Department of Commerce, *Feeble-minded and Epileptics in State Institutions and Epileptics*, vol. 3 (1926): 14.
270 **Emma had also tested as a moron:** Lombardo, *Three Generations*, 106.
271 **There was also considerable doubt:** Kevles, *In the Name of Eugenics*, 145–46, 148; Diane Paul and Hamish Spencer, "Did Eugenics Rest on an Elementary Mistake?," in *Thinking About Evolution: Historical, Philosophical, and Political Perspectives*, ed. Rama S. Singh et al. (New York: Cambridge University Press, 2001), 105; Carol Isaacson Barash, *Just Genes: The Ethics of Genetic Technologies* (New York: Praeger, 2008).
271 **The most striking thing:** Walter Berns, "*Buck v. Bell*: Due Process of Law?," *Western Political Quarterly* 6, no. 4 (Dec. 1953): 763.
271 **A mean-spirited ethos:** *Buck*, 274 U.S. at 205–7; Wells, "Reinventing Holmes," 810n57.
271 **Holmes said he was "amused":** Oliver Wendell Holmes Jr. to Harold Laski, April 29, 1927, in *Holmes-Laski Letters* (Cambridge: Harvard University Press, 1953), 2:938–39.
272 **"There can be no doubt":** *Buck*, 274 U.S. at 207.
272 **The Virginia law:** An Act to Provide for the Sexual Sterilization of Inmates of State Institutions in Certain Cases, Virginia Acts of Assembly, chap. 394 (1924).
272 **"the usual last resort":** *Buck*, 274 U.S. at 208.
272 **Holmes's dismissive reference:** Siegel, "Justice Holmes," 108; Erwin Chemerinsky, *Constitutional Law: Principles and Policies*, 2nd ed. (New York: Aspen Law & Business, 2002), 642.
272 **From 1920 to 1927:** Siegel, "Justice Holmes," 132.

272 **Less than two months earlier:** *Nixon v. Herndon,* 273 U.S. 536 (1927), decided March 7; Siegel, "Justice Holmes," 139–41 (appendix 1).
273 **Holmes invoked Strode's and Dr. Priddy's defense:** *Buck,* 274 U.S. at 208.
273 **Saying the two groups:** Siegel, "Justice Holmes," 130.
273 **"means were the wisest":** *Block v. Hirsh,* 256 U.S. 135, 158 (1921).
273 **"a large discretion":** Brief for Appellee, *Buck v. Bell,* 143 Va. 310 (1925) 48.
273 **to enforce even foolish laws:** Oliver Wendell Holmes Jr. to Harold Laski, March 4, 1920, in *Holmes-Laski Letters,* 1:194.
274 **"call upon the best citizens":** *Buck,* 274 U.S. at 207.
274 **"greater power includes the lesser":** *McAuliffe v. Mayor of New Bedford,* 155 Mass. 216 (1892).
274 **"surely one of the most 'totalitarian' statements":** Berns, "Due Process of Law?," 762.
274 **He was "famously skeptical":** Richard Posner, *Reflections on Judging* (Cambridge, MA: Harvard University Press, 2013), 168.
274 **Holmes did cite one case:** *Jacobson v. Massachusetts,* 197 U.S. 11 (1905).
275 **"principle that sustains":** *Buck,* 274 U.S. at 207.
275 **Laughlin had cited *Jacobson*:** Laughlin, *Eugenical Sterilization,* 339.
275 **The Virginia Supreme Court:** *Buck v. Bell,* 143 Va. 310 (1925); Brief for Plaintiff in Error, *Buck v. Bell,* 1926, 36–37; Brief for Appellee, *Buck v. Bell,* 143 Va. 310 (1925), 27–29
275 **The Massachusetts law:** *Jacobson,* 197 U.S. at 12.
275 **Rather than view the case:** Leuchtenburg, *Supreme Court Reborn,* 17–18, Berns, "Due Process of Law?," 766.
275 **Modern rights to privacy:** Nourse, "Constitutional Tragedy," 107.
276 **In *Meyer v. Nebraska*:** Laurence Tribe, "*Lawrence v. Texas:* The 'Fundamental Right' That Dare Not Speak Its Name," *Harvard Law Review* 117 (2004): 1934.
276 **In both cases:** Ibid.
276 **The *Meyer* court:** *Meyer v. Nebraska,* 262 U.S. 390, 399 (1923).
276 **"some things which decent government":** Walter Berns, "*Buck v. Bell:* Due Process of Law?" *The Western Political Quarterly* 6, no. 4, 262, 763.
276 **His famous statement:** Oliver Wendell Holmes Jr., *The Common Law* (Boston: Little, Brown, 1881), 1.
276 **More than any doctrines:** *Buck,* 274 U.S. at 207.
277 **"sooner or later":** Holmes to Laski, April 29, 1927, 2:939.
277 **He had been a skeptic:** White, *Justice Oliver Wendell Holmes,* 320.
277 ***Buck v. Bell* was "one decision":** Oliver Wendell Holmes Jr. to Lewis Einstein, May 19, 1927, in *Holmes-Einstein Letters,* ed. J. Peabody (New York: St. Martin's, 1964), 267.
278 **It is a vote:** Urofsky, *Brandeis,* 874 (*Buck v. Bell* is mentioned only in a footnote).
278 **Brandeis later admitted:** Dickson, *Supreme Court in Conference,* 75.
278 **it inflicted "cruelty upon a helpless class":** *Vetoes by the Governor, of Bills Passed by the Legislature, Session of 1905* (Wm. Stanley Ray, 1905), 27; Edwin Black, *War Against the Weak* (New York: Four Walls Eight Windows, 2003), 66.
278 **The sole dissent:** Novick, *Honorable Justice,* 352.
278 **Butler was not:** Phillip Thompson, "Silent Protest: A Catholic Justice Dissents in *Buck v. Bell,*" *Catholic Lawyer* 43 (2004): 125, 132.
278 **He was an observant Catholic:** "Religion Q & A: How Catholics Became a Majority on the U.S. Supreme Court," *Washington Post,* June 20, 2009; James Hitchcock, *The Supreme Court and Religion in American Life,* (Princeton, NJ: Princeton University Press, 2004), 2:88–89.
279 **In state legislatures:** Randall Hansen and Desmond King, *Sterilized by the State: Eugenics, Race, and the Population Scare in Twentieth-Century North America* (Cambridge: Cambridge University Press, 2013), 21.
279 **One time it might have been a factor:** *Hansen v. Haff,* 291 U.S. 559, 564 (1934).
279 **as a committed Catholic:** Thompson, "Silent Protest," 136, 137.
279 **John Ryan:** Sharon M. Leon, "'A Human Being, and Not a Mere Social Factor': Catholic Strategies for Dealing with Sterilization Statutes in the 1920s," *Church History* 73 (2004): 383, 389.
280 **Francis Galton himself:** Hansen and King, *Sterilized by the State,* 128–30.
280 **Butler had been born on the frontier:** Thompson, "Silent Protest," 137.
280 **Eight of the court's justices:** *Samuels v. McCurdy,* 267 U.S. 188, 203 (1925) (Butler, J., dissenting).
280 **"silent protest":** Thompson, "Silent Protest," 125.

280 **When the *Buck v. Bell* ruling came down:** "Upholds Operating on Feeble-Minded," *New York Times*, May 3, 1927; "For Harvard Dining Hall," *New York Times*, May 3, 1927.
280 **The front page was filled:** "Tree in New Haven 227 Years Old Cut Down; Landmark Falls Victim to Street Widening," *New York Times*, May 3, 1927; "London Season Opens with King at Opera; Four or Five Queens to Make It Brilliant," *New York Times*, May 3, 1927.
281 **The *Times* story:** "Upholds Operating on Feeble-Minded."
281 **"Eugenicists cheered":** "The Judiciary: Sterilization," *Time*, May 16, 1927.
281 **The *Literary Digest*:** "To Halt the Imbecile's Perilous Line," *Literary Digest*, May 21, 1927, 11; Lombardo, *Three Generations*, 175.
281 **"The decision of the Supreme Court":** "To Halt the Imbecile's Perilous Line," 11.
281 **"Over the protests of many":** Gregory Michael Dorr, *Segregation's Science: Eugenics and Society in Virginia* (Charlottesville: University of Virginia Press, 2008), 134–35.
282 **"that great jurist":** Lombardo, *Three Generations*, 174–75.
282 **Robert E. Cushman:** Cushman, "Constitutional Law in 1926–27," 70, 92.
282 **"the transmitting of characteristics":** "To Halt the Imbecile's Perilous Line," 11.
282 **"Unjustified Sterilization":** "Unjustified Sterilization," *America*, May 14, 1927, 102, quoted in Leon, "A Human Being and Not a Mere Social Factor," 403.
282 **"May God protect":** Lombardo, *Three Generations*, 176.
282 **"Cranks as usual do not fail":** Oliver Wendell Holmes Jr. to Harold Laski, July 23, 1927, in *Holmes-Laski Letters*, 2:964.

283 **The colony now had:** Paul A. Lombardo, *Three Generations, No Imbeciles: Eugenics, the Supreme Court, and* Buck v. Bell (Baltimore: Johns Hopkins University Press, 2008), 177–81, 185. There had been one further delay after the Supreme Court ruling. An anti-eugenics group filed a petition for rehearing with the Supreme Court, and Strode advised waiting until the rehearing was denied, which it soon was.
283 **The surgeon who would be performing:** "Continued Notes," Oct. 1927, box 11, Central Virginia Training Center Papers, Library of Virginia; "Operation Record," unnamed file, Carrie Buck and Doris Buck Figgins Sterilization, ca. 1920s–1980s file, Central Virginia Training Center Papers; J. David Smith and K. Ray Nelson, *The Sterilization of Carrie Buck: Was She Feebleminded or Society's Pawn?* (Far Hills, NJ: New Horizon Press, 1989), 179–81.
283 **Carrie was anesthetized:** "Continued Notes," Oct. 1927; "Operation Record"; Smith and Nelson, *Sterilization of Carrie Buck*, 179–81.
284 **The medical staff:** Carrie Buck Hospital Records, unnamed file, Carrie Buck and Doris Buck Figgins Sterilization, ca. 1920s–1980s file, Central Virginia Training Center Papers.
284 **After two weeks:** "Continued Notes," Oct. 1927; Paul Lombardo, "Three Generations, No Imbeciles: New Light on *Buck v. Bell*," *New York University Law Review* 60 (April 1985): 30, 60.
284 **The colony's parole system:** Lori Andrews, Maxwell Mehlman, and Mark Rothstein, *Genetics: Ethics, Law, and Policy* (New York: Thomson/West, 2006), 56.
284 **On November 12, 1927:** Lombardo, *Three Generations*, 185–86, 187; Smith and Nelson, *Sterilization of Carrie Buck*, 187–88, 189.
284 **"I understand," he said:** "Carrie Buck Trial Transcript, 51–100" (2009), 97, *Buck v. Bell Documents*, Paper 32, http://readingroom.law.gsu.edu/buckvbell/32.
284 **Strode repeated this assertion:** Brief for Defendant in Error, *Buck v. Bell*, U.S. Supreme Court, Oct. term, 1926, 5, available at http://readingroom.law.gsu.edu/cgi/viewcontent.cgi?article=1035&context=buckvbell.
285 **"She is quite well behaved":** John Bell to Alice Dobbs, Jan. 12, 1928, unnamed folder, Carrie Buck and Doris Buck Figgins Sterilization, ca. 1920s–1980s file, Central Virginia Training Center Papers.
285 **Dobbs did not want Carrie back:** Alice Dobbs to John Bell, Feb. 13, 1928, unnamed folder, Carrie Buck and Doris Buck Figgins Sterilization, ca. 1920s–1980s file, Central Virginia Training Center Papers.
285 **"Can't you still keep her":** Ibid.
285 **"I thought when the Red Cross":** Ibid.
286 **Her half sister, Doris, was admitted as an inmate:** Lombardo, *Three Generations*, 186; Records of Doris Figgins, unnamed file, Carrie Buck and Doris Buck Figgins Sterilization, ca. 1920s–1980s file, Central Virginia Training Center Papers.
286 **"High-grade imbecile":** Records of Doris Figgins.

286 **At least one person:** Lombardo, *Three Generations,* 186–87.

286 **the colony board voted:** Ibid., 185–86 and 333n2.

286 **On January 23, 1928:** Records of Doris Figgins; Smith and Nelson, *Sterilization of Carrie Buck,* 180, 216; Ben A. Franklin, "Teen-Ager's Sterilization an Issue Decades Later," *New York Times,* Mar. 7, 1980.

286 **Doris was told:** Smith and Nelson, *Sterilization of Carrie Buck,* 216–18; Lombardo, *Three Generations,* 187.

286 **A. T. Newberry:** A. T. Newberry to John Bell, Feb. 18, 1928, unnamed folder, Carrie Buck and Doris Buck Figgins Sterilization, ca. 1920s–1980s file, Central Virginia Training Center Papers.

287 **Dr. Bell responded:** John Bell to A. T. Newberry, Feb. 20, 1928, unnamed folder, Carrie Buck and Doris Buck Figgins Sterilization, ca. 1920s–1980s file, Central Virginia Training Center Papers.

287 **Dr. Bell told Newberry:** John Bell to A. T. Newberry, Feb. 22, 1928, quoted in Smith and Nelson, *Sterilization of Carrie Buck,* 191.

287 **On February 25:** Smith and Nelson, *Sterilization of Carrie Buck,* 191–92.

287 **Mrs. Newberry wrote to Dr. Bell:** Ibid., 192.

287 **Dr. Bell wrote back:** John Bell to Mrs. A. T. Newberry, Feb. 28, 1928, unnamed folder, Carrie Buck and Doris Buck Figgins Sterilization, ca. 1920s–1980s file, Central Virginia Training Center Papers.

287 **In May Mrs. Newberry wrote:** Smith and Nelson, *Sterilization of Carrie Buck,* 193.

288 **She tried to get Dr. Bell:** Ibid., 194.

288 **"I do not think it advisable":** Ibid., 195.

288 **While Carrie was away:** Ibid., 194.

288 **She wrote Dr. Bell:** Ibid., 195–96.

288 **Mrs. Newberry did write to Dr. Bell:** Mrs. A. T. Newberry to John Bell, Dec. 9, 1928, unnamed folder, Carrie Buck and Doris Buck Figgins Sterilization, ca. 1920s–1980s file, Central Virginia Training Center Papers; Smith and Nelson, *Sterilization of Carrie Buck,* 196–97.

289 **She tried to "impress upon Carrie":** Newberry to Bell, Dec. 9, 1928; Smith and Nelson, *Sterilization of Carrie Buck,* 196–97.

289 **Carrie's "sexual delinquency":** Bell to Newberry, Dec. 11, 1928; Smith and Nelson, *Sterilization of Carrie Buck,* 198.

289 **Dr. Bell finally granted Carrie's request:** Lombardo, *Three Generations,* 189.

289 **Mr. Newberry added in a postscript:** A. T. Newberry to John Bell, June 22, 1929, unnamed folder, Carrie Buck and Doris Buck Figgins Sterilization, ca. 1920s–1980s file, Central Virginia Training Center Papers; Smith and Nelson, *Sterilization of Carrie Buck,* 200.

289 **She was placed with families:** Lombardo, *Three Generations,* 189; John Bell to Carrie Buck, Dec. 22, 1930, Records of Doris Figgins, unnamed file, Carrie Buck and Doris Buck Figgins Sterilization, ca. 1920s–1980s file, Central Virginia Training Center Papers.

290 **She told Dr. Bell:** Bell to Buck, Dec. 22, 1930; Lombardo, *Three Generations,* 189.

290 **Dr. Bell agreed:** Bell to Buck, Dec. 22, 1930.

290 **On December 27:** John Bell to Mrs. A. T. Newberry, Dec. 29, 1930, box 11, Central Virginia Training Center Papers.

290 **the colony insisted she was:** "History and Clinical Notes," June 4, 1924, box 11, Carrie Buck file, Library of Virginia; Smith and Nelson, *Sterilization of Carrie Buck,* 44.

290 **May 14, 1932:** Smith and Nelson, *Sterilization of Carrie Buck,* 203.

291 **Carrie's new husband:** Ibid., 203–4.

291 **In a May 17 letter to Dr. Bell:** Mrs. W. D. Eagle to John Bell, May 17, 1932, box 11, Central Virginia Training Center Papers; Smith and Nelson, *Sterilization of Carrie Buck,* 203.

291 **Carrie settled into a quiet domestic life:** Smith and Nelson, *Sterilization of Carrie Buck,* 205.

291 **About seven weeks after Carrie's wedding:** Lombardo, *Three Generations* 190; Margaret Faris to John Bell, June 21, 1933, box 11, Central Virginia Training Center Papers.

291 **"so very sweet":** Smith and Nelson, *Sterilization of Carrie Buck,* 212; Lombardo, *Three Generations,* 190.

291 **Paul Popenoe:** Paul Popenoe to John Bell, Mar. 16, 1933, unnamed folder, Carrie Buck and Doris Buck Figgins Sterilization, ca. 1920s–1980s file, Central Virginia Training Center Papers; Lombardo, *Three Generations,* 190.

291 **Carrie sent a photographic negative:** Smith and Nelson, *Sterilization of Carrie Buck*, 210–12; Lombardo, *Three Generations*, 190.

292 **Neither she nor Dr. Bell:** Lombardo, *Three Generations*, 190.

292 **Margaret Faris:** Margaret Faris to John Bell, June 27, 1933, unnamed folder, Carrie Buck and Doris Buck Figgins Sterilization, ca. 1920s-1980s file, Central Virginia Training Center Papers.

292 **Dobbs emphatically refused:** Ibid.

292 **Nearly nine years after:** "Carrie Buck Trial Transcript, 51–100," 58–59; Faris to Bell, June 21, 1933.

292 **Stephen Jay Gould examined Vivian's school records:** Stephen Jay Gould, "Carrie Buck's Daughter," *Constitutional Commentary* 2 (1985): 331, 338.

293 **"We live out in the country":** Mrs. W. D. Eagle to John Bell, Aug. 19, 1933, box 11, Central Virginia Training Center Papers.

293 **She asked Dr. Bell:** Ibid.

293 **Dr. Bell responded:** John Bell to Mrs. W. D. Eagle, Aug. 21, 1933, unnamed file, Carrie Buck and Doris Buck Figgins Sterilization, ca. 1920s–1980s file, Central Virginia Training Center Papers.

293 **When he did:** W. I. Prichard, "History—Lynchburg Training School and Hospital, Pt. II," *Mental Health in Virginia* 11 (Autumn 1960):29.

293 **Carrie and her husband:** Smith and Nelson, *Sterilization of Carrie Buck*, 207.

293 **Dr. Arnold responded:** Ibid., 209–10.

294 **Her new home:** Ibid., 213.

294 **Carrie "knew what she was doing":** Ibid., 214.

294 **Emma died of bronchial pneumonia:** Lombardo, *Three Generations*, 216.

294 **"no official reports":** D. L. Harrell Jr. to J. E. Coogan, Oct. 26, 1942, box 11, Central Virginia Training Center Papers.

294 **Charles Albert Detamore:** Smith and Nelson, *Sterilization of Carrie Buck*, 215.

295 **The couple lived:** "Carrie Buck Detamore, 8-30-1979 1 pm," unnamed file, Carrie Buck and Doris Buck Figgins Sterilization, ca. 1920s–1980s file, Central Virginia Training Center Papers; Smith and Nelson, *Sterilization of Carrie Buck*, 215–16.

295 **Carrie was living in obscurity:** Smith and Nelson, *Sterilization of Carrie Buck*, 215.

295 **Dr. K. Ray Nelson:** Franklin, "Teen-Ager's Sterilization"; Smith and Nelson, *Sterilization of Carrie Buck*, 216.

295 **He went to visit Doris:** Franklin, "Teen-Ager's Sterilization"; Smith and Nelson, *Sterilization of Carrie Buck*, 216; William Leuchtenburg, *The Supreme Court Reborn: The Constitutional Revolution in the Age of Roosevelt* (New York: Oxford University Press, 1995), 23–24; Smith and Nelson, *Sterilization of Carrie Buck*, 216.

295 **Dr. Nelson brought:** Franklin, "Teen-Ager's Sterilization"; Smith and Nelson, *Sterilization of Carrie Buck*, 216; Lombardo, *Three Generations*, 250.

295 **When he looked up:** Smith and Nelson, *Sterilization of Carrie Buck*, 216; Lombardo, *Three Generations*, 250; Franklin, "Teen-Ager's Sterilization."

295 **Doris told Dr. Nelson:** Smith and Nelson, *Sterilization of Carrie Buck*, 216–18.

295 **"wanted babies bad":** Lombardo, *Three Generations*, 251.

295 **When she learned:** Franklin, "Teen-Ager's Sterilization."

295 **Next they visited the building:** Smith and Nelson, *Sterilization of Carrie Buck*, 218; Leuchtenburg, *Supreme Court Reborn*, 24.

295 **Carrie's legs were weak:** Smith and Nelson, *Sterilization of Carrie Buck*, 218.

296 **In an interview:** Ibid.

296 **While living in their modest home:** Ibid., 219.

296 **They were taken:** Ibid.; Lombardo, *Three Generations*, 254.

296 **Some of the staff:** Smith and Nelson, *Sterilization of Carrie Buck*, 221.

296 **an "alert and pleasant lady":** Ibid.

296 **Carrie died in January 1983:** Ibid., 219; Lombardo, *Three Generations*, 254–56.

297 **Carrie's body:** Smith and Nelson, *Sterilization of Carrie Buck*, 221–22; Lombardo, "New Light on *Buck v. Bell*," 61.

297 **She also managed:** Leuchtenburg, *Supreme Court Reborn*, 25.

297 **"Carrie watched for that paper":** Smith and Nelson, *Sterilization of Carrie Buck*, 214.

298 **An academic who visited Carrie:** Gould, "Carrie Buck's Daughter," 336.

NOTES

298 **"I didn't want a big family"**: Smith and Nelson, *Sterilization of Carrie Buck*, 218.
298 **"They done me wrong"**: Carlos Santos, "Historic Test Case: Wrong to Carrie Buck Remembered," *Richmond Times-Dispatch*, Feb. 17, 2002.

CONCLUSION
299 **"a constitutional blessing"**: *Buck v. Bell*, 274 U.S. 200, 207 (1927); William Leuchtenburg, *The Supreme Court Reborn: The Constitutional Revolution in the Age of Roosevelt* (New York: Oxford University Press, 1995), 15.
299 **"experimental period"**: Harry Laughlin, *The Legal Status of Eugenical Sterilization: History and Analysis of Litigation Under the Virginia Sterilization Statute, Which Led to a Decision of the Supreme Court of the United States Upholding the Statute* (Chicago: Chicago Municipal Court, 1930), 53.
299 **In the years:** Mary L. Dudziak, "Oliver Wendell Holmes as a Eugenic Reformer: Rhetoric in the Writing of Constitutional Law," *Iowa Law Review* 71 (1986): 836.
299 **a new governor took office in Mississippi:** Edward J. Larson, *Sex, Race, and Science: Eugenics in the Deep South* (Baltimore: Johns Hopkins University Press, 1995), 116–18.
300 **William Faulkner:** Cleanth Brooks, *William Faulkner: The Yoknapatawpha Country* (Baton Rouge: Louisiana State University Press, 1963), 4; Michael Gresset, *A Faulkner Chronology* (Oxford: University Press of Mississippi, 1985), 27.
300 **The sterilization movement gained greater force:** Philip R. Reilly, *The Surgical Solution: A History of Involuntary Sterilization in the United States* (Baltimore: Johns Hopkins University Press, 1991), 88.
300 **By that year:** Robert Cynkar, "*Buck v. Bell*: 'Felt Necessities' v. Fundamental Values?," *Columbia Law Review* 81 (1981): 1454.
300 **In states where the church "could mobilize sufficiently":** Randall Hansen and Desmond King, *Sterilized by the State: Eugenics, Race, and the Population Scare in Twentieth-Century North America* (Cambridge: Cambridge University Press, 2013), 122.
300 **In New Jersey:** Reilly, *Surgical Solution*, 88–89.
300 **New Jersey, however:** Ibid.; Hansen and King, *Sterilized by the State*, 130.
300 **One leading eugenicist:** Marouf A. Hasian Jr., *The Rhetoric of Eugenics in Anglo-American Thought* (Athens: University of Georgia Press, 1996), 109.
300 **In Colorado:** Hansen and King, *Sterilized by the State*, 128–29, 132.
301 **"there would not be so many fools":** Reilly, *Surgical Solution*, 89.
301 **the number of eugenic sterilizations increased:** Ibid., 96.
301 **The "clearing house" model:** Ibid., 98; Albert Priddy to Harry Laughlin, Oct. 14, 1924, box 11, Central Virginia Training Center Papers, Library of Virginia.
301 **"Mississippi appendectomies":** Leuchtenburg, *Supreme Court Reborn*, 16.
301 **Ten years after the court's ruling:** Reilly, *Surgical Solution*, 96.
301 **Many tried to have children:** Paul A. Lombardo, "Eugenic Sterilization in Virginia: Aubrey Strode and the Case of *Buck v. Bell*" (Ph.D. diss., University of Virginia, 1982), 254.
302 **"It was as routine":** Robert Reinhold, "Mass Sterilization Law Protested," *Lawrence Journal-World*, Feb. 24, 1980.
302 **European countries began to adopt:** Diane Paul and Hamish Spencer, "Did Eugenics Rest on an Elementary Mistake?," in *Thinking About Evolution: Historical, Philosophical, and Political Perspectives*, ed. Rama S. Singh et al. (New York: Cambridge University Press, 2001) 112.
302 **An American medical researcher:** Marie Kopp, "Eugenic Sterilization Laws in Europe," *American Journal of Obstetrics and Gynecology* (Sept. 1937), 499–504; Garland Allen, "'Culling the Herd': Eugenics and the Conservation Movement in the United States, 1900–1940" (2013) Biology Faculty Publications Paper 6, http://openscholarship.wustl.edu/bio_facpubs/6, 39n89.
302 **Nazi Germany adopted:** Paul A. Lombardo, *Three Generations, No Imbeciles: Eugenics, the Supreme Court, and Buck v. Bell* (Baltimore: Johns Hopkins University Press, 2008), 202.
302 **The Nazis also established:** Reilly, *Surgical Solution*, 107–8; Stefan Kuhl, *The Nazi Connection* (New York: Oxford University Press, 1994), 54.
302 **"Germany learned from the United States":** Lombardo, *Three Generations*, 203.
302 **Otto Wagener:** Kuhl, *Nazi Connection*, 37.
302 **The law authorized sterilization:** Reilly, *Surgical Solution*, 107.
302 **sterilization against Jews and people of partial Jewish background:** Ibid. 109; Kuhl, *Nazi*

Connection, 126n62; Hansen and King, *Sterilized by the State*, 150; Edwin Black, *War Against the Weak* (New York: Four Walls Eight Windows, 2003), 407–8.

303 **"In a judgment":** Black, *War Against the Weak*, 405–9.

303 *Judgment at Nuremberg: Judgment at Nuremberg*, dir. Stanley Kramer, perf. Spencer Tracy, Burt Lancaster, Richard Widmark, Marlene Dietrich, and Maximillian Schell, Roxlom Films, 1961; Abby Mann, *Judgment at Nuremberg* (New York: New Directions Books, 2002), 30; Leuchtenburg, *Supreme Court Reborn*, 17.

304 **Strode's account began in 1921:** Aubrey Strode to Dr. Don Preston Peters, July 19, 1939, box 29, Aubrey Strode Papers, Albert and Shirley Small Special Collections Library, University of Virginia (hereafter cited as Strode Papers); Lombardo, "Eugenic Sterilization in Virginia," 106n14.

304 **He then told the State Hospital Board:** Strode to Peters, July 19, 1939.

305 **Many states were carrying out:** Strode to Peters, July 19, 1939; Harry Laughlin, *Eugenical Sterilization in the United States* (Chicago: Psychopathic Library of the Municipal Court of Chicago, 1922), 445–52 ("Model Eugenical Sterilization Law"); Dorr, *Segregation's Science*, 128.

305 **Strode's advice delayed:** Strode to Peters, July 19, 1939.

305 **"this matter would justify":** Aubrey Strode to W. Pendleton Sandridge Jr., undated, box 92, Strode Papers.

305 **"wheel of social progress":** Lombardo, *Three Generations*, 208.

306 **"the immense financial burden":** Steven Noll, "The Sterilization of Willie Mallory," in *"Bad" Mothers: The Politics of Blame in Twentieth-Century America*, ed. Molly Ladd-Taylor and Lauri Umansky (New York: New York University Press, 1998), 42.

306 **"Now is the time":** Leuchtenburg, *Supreme Court Reborn*, 16.

306 **On September 11, 1933:** W. I. Prichard, "History—Lynchburg Training School and Hospital, Pt. II," *Mental Health in Virginia* 11 (Autumn 1960), 29.

306 **On December 9, 1934:** Lombardo, *Three Generations*, 208.

306 **Strode's reference to sterilization:** Lombardo, "Eugenic Sterilization in Virginia," 260–61. In addition to his Virginia Social Science Association address, Strode's papers contain a copy of a letter to the editor of the *Literary Digest* defending eugenic sterilization laws, ibid., 259. It is difficult to assign much weight to the letter, however, since it was never published, and it is not clear it was ever actually sent, ibid., 259n58.

307 **"I knew him as a boy":** Lombardo, *Three Generations*, 234.

307 **On May 17, 1946:** Lombardo, "Eugenic Sterilization in Virginia," 249–50.

307 **"known for his interest":** "Judge Aubrey E. Strode," *New York Times*, May 18, 1946.

307 **Laughlin's study was published:** Harry Laughlin, *The Legal Status of Eugenical Sterilization: History and Analysis of Litigation Under the Virginia Sterilization Statute, Which Led to a Decision of the Supreme Court of the United States Upholding the Statute* (Chicago: Chicago Municipal Court, 1930), 5.

308 **Laughlin ended his study:** Ibid., 62–77, 81.

308 **"last line of defense":** Harry Laughlin, "The Eugenical Aspects of Deportation," 27, box C-4-6, Harry H. Laughlin Papers, Pickler Memorial Library, Truman State University, Kirksville, MO (hereafter cited as Laughlin Papers); Desmond King, *In the Name of Liberalism: Illiberal Social Policy in the United States and Britain* (Oxford: Oxford University Press, 1999), 117.

308 **"Substitute Aryan for Nordic":** Kuhl, *Nazi Connection*, 74.

308 **He wrote to the publisher:** Harry Laughlin to R. V. Coleman, Nov. 25, 1935, box C-2-1, Laughlin Papers.

308 **In 1937, Laughlin made his last great effort:** Harry Laughlin to Edward B. Greene, Mar. 16, 1937, box C-2-1:8, Laughlin Papers; Mark Haller, *American Eugenics: Heredity and Social Thought, 1870–1930* (Madison: University of Wisconsin Press, 1959), 152.

309 **Bureau of Eugenics:** Lombardo, *Three Generations*, 196–97.

309 **Laughlin also tried:** Garland E. Allen, "The Eugenics Record Office at Cold Spring Harbor, 1910–1940: An Essay in Institutional History," *Osiris* 2 (1986): 249.

309 **"a permanent and complete pedigree record":** Nancy Ordover, *American Eugenics: Race, Queer Anatomy, and the Science of Nationalism* (Minneapolis: University of Minnesota Press, 2003), 228n67.

309 **Raymond Pearl:** Melissa Hendricks, "Raymond Pearl's 'Mingled Mess,'" *Johns Hopkins Magazine*, Apr. 2006, available at http://pages.jh.edu/~jhumag/0406web/pearl.html.

309 **"largely become a mingled mess":** Hansen and King, *Sterilized by the State,* 187; Raymond Pearl, "The Biology of Superiority," *American Mercury* (Nov. 1927), 260.

309 **Albert Johnson was replaced:** Jewish Telegraphic Agency, "Congressman Dickstein Elected Chairman of the United States House of Representatives Immigration Committee," Dec. 16, 1931.

310 **Laughlin's career:** Frances Janet Hassencahl, "Harry H. Laughlin: 'Expert Eugenics Agent' for the House Committee on Immigration and Naturalization, 1921 to 1931" (Ph.D. diss., Case Western Reserve University, 1970), 327.

310 **John Merriam:** Ibid., 329; Reilly, *Surgical Solution,* 68–69.

310 **Merriam also reprimanded Laughlin:** Reilly, *Surgical Solution,* 68–69.

310 **The committee concluded:** Hassencahl, "Expert Eugenics Agent," 331.

310 **He corresponded regularly:** Paul Lombardo, "'The American Breed': Nazi Eugenics and the Origins of the Pioneer Fund," *Albany Law Review* 65 (2002): 760.

310 **Laughlin ran regular reports:** Hassencahl, "Expert Eugenics Agent," 341–42; Allen, "Eugenics Record Office," 252–53.

310 **Sterilization Act of 1933:** Daniel J. Kevles, *In the Name of Eugenics: Genetics and the Uses of Human Heredity* (Cambridge, MA: Harvard University Press, 1985), 116.

310 **Laughlin published the new law:** Lombardo, *Three Generations,* 202, 336.

310 **"To one versed":** "Eugenical Sterilization in Germany," *Eugenical News* 18, no. 5 (Sept.–Oct. 1933): 90, cited in Hassencahl, "Expert Eugenics Agent," 340.

310 **An inveterate newspaper clipper:** "Hindenburg Asked to Save Reich Jews: 500,000 Are Facing 'Certain Extermination,' American Congress Declares," *New York Times,* Aug. 16, 1933, box E-1-4, Laughlin Papers.

311 **"In the new Germany":** Dr. C. Thomalia, "The Sterilization Law in Germany," *Eugenical News* 19, no. 6 (Nov.—Dec. 1934): 137, quoted in Walter Berns, *"Buck v. Bell:* Due Process of Law?," *Western Political Quarterly* 6, no. 4 (Dec. 1953): 772; Doris Bergen, *War and Genocide: A Concise History of the Holocaust* (Lanham, MD: Rowman and Littlefield, 2009), 58; Karl Schleunes, *The Twisted Road to Auschwitz: Nazi Policy Toward German Jews, 1933–1939* (Champaign: University of Illinois Press, 1990) 106–7.

311 **"Whether we like it or not":** Harry Laughlin to Madison Grant, Nov. 19, 1932, box C-2-1, Laughlin Papers.

311 **In his report:** "Relaxing Quotas for Exiles Fought," *New York Times,* May 4, 1934; Jonathan Peter Spiro, *Defending the Master Race: Conservation, Eugenics, and the Legacy of Madison Grant* (Lebanon, NH: University Press of New England, 2009), 369; Reilly, *Surgical Solution,* 69.

312 **If Carnegie were to "arise":** Hyman Achinstein to Director of the Dept. of Eugenics of the Carnegie Institution of Washington, DC, n.d., box C-2-1, Laughlin Papers.

312 **John Merriam appointed a new visiting committee:** Allen, "Eugenics Record Office," 251.

312 **The new committee's report:** *Report of the Advisory Committee on the Eugenics Record Office,* box C-2-1, Laughlin Papers; Hassencahl, "Expert Eugenics Agent," 332–34.

312 **"a messiah attitude":** Lombardo, *Three Generations,* 205.

312 **The committee called for the office:** *Report of the Advisory Committee on the Eugenics Record Office,* 5; Allen, "Eugenics Record Office," 252; Hassencahl, "Expert Eugenics Agent," 332–34.

312 **Congress for Population Science:** Kuhl, *Nazi Connection,* 32–33.

312 **Campbell gave his own remarks:** "U.S. Eugenist Hails Nazi Racial Policy," *New York Times,* Aug. 29, 1935; Stefan Kuhl, "The Cooperation of German Racial Hygienists and American Eugenicists Before and After 1933," in *The Holocaust and History: The Known, the Unknown, the Disputed, and the Reexamined,* ed. Michael Berenbaum and Abraham Peck (Bloomington: Indiana University Press, 2002), 139; "Praise of Nazis," *Time,* Sept. 9, 1935.

312 **In May 1936:** Carl Schneider to Harry Laughlin, May 16, 1936, box E-1-3-8, Laughlin Papers; Hassencahl, "Expert Eugenics Agent," 351; Lombardo, *Three Generations,* 211–12.

312 **The university was marking:** Hassencahl, "Expert Eugenics Agent," 351; Richard J. Evans, *The Third Reich in Power* (New York: Penguin, 2006), 16.

312 **With German universities:** Allen, "Eugenics Record Office," 253.

313 **"deep gratitude":** Harry Laughlin to Carl Schneider, May 28, 1936, box E-1-3-8, Laughlin Papers.

313 **Pioneer Fund:** Lombardo, "'American Breed,'" 798, 800; Sheila Faith Weiss, *The Nazi Symbiosis: Human Genetics and Politics in the Third Reich* (Chicago: University of Chicago Press, 2010), 275.

313 **Laughlin was having seizures:** Allen, "Eugenics Record Office," 254.

313 **Vannevar Bush:** G. Pascal Zachary, *Endless Frontier: Vannevar Bush, Engineer of the American Century* (New York: Free Press, 1997), 93.

314 **He wanted to stay:** Ibid., 90; Julian M. Pleasants, *Buncombe Bob: The Life and Times of Robert Rice Reynolds* (Chapel Hill: University of North Carolina Press, 2000), 167.

314 **renamed the Genetics Record Office:** Zachary, *Endless Frontier,* 90.

314 **"These almost unbelievable facts":** Mrs. Shepard Krech, "Maternity, the Family, and the Future," *Eugenical News* 28 (June 1943): 22, quoted in Berns, "Due Process of Law?," 773.

314 **An internal memo:** Albert Blakeslee, "Memorandum Regarding Mail Addressed to the Genetics Record Office (Formerly Eugenics Record Office)," https://www.dnalc.org/view/11599 -Albert-F-Blakeslee-memo-about-procedures-for-answering-mail-after-closure-of-the -Eugenics-Record-Office.html.

314 **Laughlin's personal mail:** Ibid.

315 **"eventually the world":** Harry Laughlin, "Cosmopolitanism in America," 15, box E-1-1, Laughlin Papers.

315 **He devoted his final days:** Hassencahl, "Expert Eugenics Agent," 356.

315 **On January 26, 1943:** Allen, "Eugenics Record Office," 254; "Harry Laughlin," Pickler Memorial Library, Truman State University, https://library.truman.edu/manuscripts/laughlinbio.asp.

315 **"a deep self-beneficial groove":** William James to Henry James, July 5, 1876, quoted in G. Edward White, *Justice Oliver Wendell Holmes: The Law and Inner Self* (New York: Oxford University Press, 1993), 89.

315 **"I wrote and delivered":** Oliver Wendell Holmes Jr. to Harold Laski, May 12, 1927, in *Holmes-Laski Letters,* (Cambridge: Harvard University Press, 1953) 2:942

316 **Sacco and Vanzetti's lawyers:** Liva Baker, *The Justice from Beacon Hill: The Life and Times of Oliver Wendell Holmes* (New York: HarperCollins, 1991), 605–11.

316 **"I think it a less evil":** *Olmstead v. United States,* 277 U.S. 438, 470 (1928); Baker, *Justice from Beacon Hill,* 617.

316 **As he entered his late eighties:** Baker, *Justice from Beacon Hill,* 618.

316 **It was a great blow:** Sheldon Novick, *Honorable Justice: The Life of Oliver Wendell Holmes* (Boston: Little, Brown, 1989), 367.

316 **"the principle of free thought":** *United States v. Schwimmer,* 279 U.S. 644, 654–55 (1929) (Holmes, J., dissenting).

316 **He was stepping down:** Novick, *Honorable Justice,* 375.

317 **"It's all very remote":** Ibid., 376.

317 **The headline hailed Holmes:** "Justice Holmes Succumbs to Pneumonia at Age of 93," *New York Times,* Mar. 6, 1935.

317 **A prisoner facing sterilization:** *Skinner v. Oklahoma,* 316 U.S. 535, 536–38 (1942).

317 **These "conspicuously artificial lines":** *Id.* at 540–42; Howard Ball, *The Supreme Court in the Intimate Lives of Americans: Birth, Sex, Marriage, Childrearing, and Death* (New York: New York University Press, 2002), 43.

318 **Chief Justice Harlan Fiske Stone:** *Skinner,* 316 U.S. at 545–46 (Stone, C. J., concurring).

318 **"limits to the extent":** *Id.* at 546–47.

318 **"I thought that this kind":** Lombardo, *Three Generations,* 232; transcript of conversations between Justice William O. Douglas and Professor Walter F. Murphy, cassette7b, http://www .princeton.edu/~mudd/finding_aids/douglas/douglas7b.html.

318 **"involuntary sterilization is not always unconstitutional":** *Vaughn v. Ruoff,* 253 F.3d 1124, 1129 (Eighth Cir. 2001).

318 **In the post-*Skinner*, post–World War II years:** Reilly, *Surgical Solution,* 135.

319 **As late as 1958:** Reilly, *Surgical Solution,* 158.

319 **From 1965 to 1979:** Lombardo, *Three Generations,* 249, 347n56.

319 **In 1974 the legislature repealed:** Ibid., 250.

319 **The colony performed two sterilizations in 1978:** Reilly, *Surgical Solution,* 158.

319 **Oregon was among the last holdouts:** Julie Sullivan, "State of Oregon Will Admit Sterilization Past," *The Oregonian,* Nov. 15, 2002; *The Oxford Handbook of Gender and Politics,* ed. Georgina Waylen, Karen Celis, Johanna Kantola, and S. Laurel Weldon (New York: Oxford University Press, 2013), 221.

319 **By the end of the twentieth century:** Leuchtenburg, *Supreme Court Reborn,* 15; Alexandra Minna Stern, *Eugenic Nation: Faults and Frontiers of Better Breeding in Modern America* (Berkeley: University of California Press, 2005), 244n15.

319 **That number included at least 7,450:** "Virginia Governor Apologizes for Eugenics Law," *USA*

Today, May 2, 2002; Stern, *Eugenic Nation,* 244n15. Gregory Michael Dorr, *Segregation's Science: Eugenics and Society in Virginia* (Charlottesville: University of Virginia Press, 2008), 135; Leuchtenburg, *Supreme Court Reborn,* 16; Reinhold, "Mass Sterilization Law Protested"; Ben A. Franklin, "Teen-Ager's Sterilization an Issue Decades Later," *New York Times,* Mar. 7, 1980.

319 **California's nation-leading numbers:** Paul Lombardo, *A Century of Eugenics in America: From the Indiana Experiment to the Human Genome Era* (Bloomington: Indiana University Press, 2011), 101; Peter Irons, "Forced Sterilizations: A Stain on California," *Los Angeles Times,* Feb. 16, 2003.

320 **"I see people with babies":** Kim Severson, "Thousands Sterilized, a State Weighs Restitution," *New York Times,* Dec. 9, 2011.

320 **coercing female prisoners:** Hunter Schwarz, "Following Reports of Forced Sterilization of Female Prison Inmates, California Passes Ban," *Washington Post,* Sept. 26, 2014.

320 **sterilization of women on public assistance:** Sean Sullivan, "Arizona GOP Official Resigns After Controversial Comments," *Washington Post,* Sept. 15, 2014.

320 **sterilization part of plea negotiations:** Sheila Burke, "Attorneys: Sterilizations Were Part of Plea Deal Talks," Associated Press, Mar. 28, 2015.

320 **"there will be an increased sentiment":** Kenneth Garver and Bettylee Garver, "The Human Genome Project and Eugenic Concerns," *American Journal of Human Genetics* 54 (1994): 148, 151.

320 **National Human Genome Research Institute:** "Issues in Genetics and Health," National Human Genome Research Institute, http://www.genome.gov/10001740.

321 **"the more suitable races":** Francis Galton, *Inquiries into Human Faculty and Its Development* (London: Macmillan, 1883), 25n.

322 **Laughlin sought to use sterilization:** H. H. Laughlin, "Calculations on the Working Out of a Proposed Program of Sterilization," in *Official Proceedings of the National Conference on Race Betterment* (Battle Creek, MI: Race Betterment Foundation, 1914).

322 **Carrie told Strode:** "Carrie Buck Trial Transcript, 1–50," (2009), 27, *Buck v. Bell Documents,* Paper 31, http://readingroom.law.gsu.edu/buckubell/31.

323 *The Descent of Man:* Charles Darwin, *Charles Darwin's Works: The Descent of Man, and Selection in Relation to Sex* (New York: D. Appleton, 1886), 134.

Index

procedures for, 62–63, 65–66, 207,
268
and societal privileging of power,
74, 301
Virginia's delay and *Buck v. Bell*, 6,
89, 90, 161, 178, 210–11, 305
sterilization, opposition to:
and castration, 62–63
and Catholic Church, 67–68,
278–80, 300
and challenges to sterilization laws,
101, 252, 300–301
and *Eugenical Sterilization in the
United States*, 137–38
and impact of *Buck v. Bell*, 300–301
and test case construction, 91
and Virginia sterilization law
campaign, 84
sterilization laws:
early attempts, 68–69
and epilepsy, 139–40
and eugenics as elitist, 66
first wave (1907–1913), 5–6, 69–71,
75, 80
Laughlin's models for, 86–87, 88,
121, 137, 139, 141, 146, 266, 272
Michigan Supreme Court decision
(1925), 208
and racism, 79–80
second wave (1921–1924), 103,
142–43
Virginia law (1916), 80–83, 84, 161,
176
Virginia law (1924), 86–90, 100,
161, 177–78, 266, 272, 304–5
See also Buck v. Bell; Virginia
sterilization law campaign
sterilization laws, challenges to, 68–
69, 143
and *Buck v. Priddy*, 100–101
and *Eugenical Sterilization in the
United States*, 140–41
and impact of *Buck v. Bell*, 300–301
Mallory case, 81–83, 84, 99

and opposition to sterilization, 101,
252, 300–301
post–*Buck v. Bell*, 317–18
Strode on, 85
and Virginia sterilization law
(1924), 87–88, 100
and Virginia Supreme Court
appeal, 203–4
sterilization movement:
apologies for, 1
and Eugenics Record Office, 103–4
Laughlin's Battle Creek address
(1914), 117, 118, 120, 136, 138,
146
middle-class professional support
for, 8–9, 66–67, 74–75
national nature of, 103
nationwide goals for, 6
in Nazi Germany, 10–11, 302–3,
310
and racism, 74–75
renewal of, 299–300, 301–2
See also "clearing house" model
Stoddard, Lothrop, 59, 72
Stone, Harlan Fiske, 262, 277, 318
Strode, Aubrey, 8, 9
account of *Buck v. Bell*, 304–5
ambivalence about eugenics of,
85, 86, 89, 160, 161, 200, 304,
306–7, 322
background of, 161–64
on Carrie Buck's post-sterilization
placement, 196, 258, 284–85,
286
and Carrie Buck's sterilization
hearing, 94–97
on "clearing house" model, 206, 257
death of, 307
and DeJarnette's testimony, 188, 189
and delay of sterilizations during
Buck v. Bell, 89, 90, 161, 178,
210–11, 305
and Estabrook's testimony, 190,
191, 192–93